W9-DHM-117

The Catalpa Bow

The Catalpa Bow

A Study of Shamanistic Practices in Japan

Carmen Blacker

Lecturer in Japanese
University of Cambridge

London   George Allen & Unwin Ltd
Ruskin House   Museum Street

First published in 1975

ISBN 0 04 398004 X

Printed in Great Britain
in 11pt. Baskerville
by The Devonshire Press Ltd., Barton Road, Torquay

For Ishibashi Hiroko
in affection and admiration

Preface and Acknowledgements

More than ten years ago my interest began to be aroused by the places in Japan which were held to be projections of the other world. In the depths of certain mountains, the legends and place-names testified to an ancient belief in paradise. In certain valleys vestiges of entrances to hell were to be discovered in the pools of hot mud which bubbled up from sulphur springs. In some of these mountains there must have existed an 'other world' even older than the Buddhist heavens and hells, for it was from these steep wooded slopes, which leapt up so precipitously from flat green rice fields, that the ancestral dead were believed to return for the annual visit to their old homes. In yet other holy hills the supernatural denizens were not the dead, but the mysterious numina known as *kami*.

From the places it was natural to turn to the people. There were still to be found in Japan, though fast disappearing, men and women who were believed capable of communicating with this other world. By means of trance, they could see the supernatural inhabitants of the other world, speak to them and hold colloquy with them, Some of them could, in a discarnate, out-of-the-body state, travel to paradise and the underworld. Others could summon the beings to come to our world and speak through their mouths. Others again, though they had lost the gift of mantic travel, nevertheless performed the other-world journey by means of a ritual ascent of the mountain and a symbolic mimesis of the adventures to be expected there. They claimed to return from their journey gifted with the powers of healing and clairvoyance that contact with the sacred often bestows. These men and women, following the custom of Japanese ethnologists, I have called shamans.

It was apparent that these specialists were the survivors of a very old stratum of Japanese religion. Some of them derived from spiritual ancestors which antedated Buddhism. Others had been absorbed by Buddhism. But it was clear that no thorough understanding of Japanese Buddhism was

9

possible without some comprehension of this older contact with the sacred world. The ancient cult was like a strong background colour which 'showed through' the rituals and practices of the various Buddhist sects. It was also like a subtle network hidden beneath the ground, but throwing up from time to time an indication of its presence—a legend, a place-name, the odd remnant of a ritual.

This book is the result of investigations into the cult and practice of these people carried out during several summers and one autumn in Japan. It is also the result of literary research. Much of the cult had already died out, even when my investigations started, and it was fortunate that the picture could be filled in by the written evidence of those who had seen and heard more than I had myself. My book will possibly irritate anthropologists, who may find it too 'merely descriptive', and lacking in analysis of the kind they find conducive to truth. I offer it nevertheless as a contribution to the study of religion in Japan, and as a memorial to an ancient cult fast vanishing as machines, organised tourism and aggressively secular thinking destroy the intuition of the other world and its spiritual inhabitants. Less and less is the temenos surrounding the sacred space able to seal off the profane forces invading from outside.

None of my investigations could have been possible or meaningful without the help of Japanese friends and teachers. My friend Ishibashi Hiroko, to whom I dedicate this book and whose poetry is full of the magic of this old half-hidden world, has given me help of a kind which is apparent in almost every chapter. My lasting gratitude goes to her for taking me to the north of Japan, to Osorezan and Iwakisan, for arranging for me to perform the *kaihōgyō* on Mt Hiei, for innumerable introductions to exactly the people who could usefully help and advise me.

Professor Hori Ichirō was never too busy, even at the height of the 'troubles' in Tokyo University, to give me advice and encouragement. I thank him now for his constant kindness, for the talks which so often made sudden order out of what had previously been a jumble of unconnected ideas, and in particular for making the necessary arrangements to enable me to join the autumn retreat on Mt

Haguro, an invaluable experience which proved con-
clusively that one seeing is better than a hundred hearings.
My grateful thanks are also due to Mr Togawa Anshō, who
was an inspiring and invaluable guide during the entire
event, explaining symbolism which would otherwise have
been incomprehensible, putting his unrivalled knowledge of
the religious practices of the Dewa Sanzan region at our
disposal, and conducting us, after the end of the retreat, on
a tour of the mummies of the Senninzawa valley. Dr
Miyake Hitoshi, who studied and participated in the event
at the same time, was also unfailingly generous in giving of
his unrivalled knowledge of Shugendō ritual.

During my stays in Kyoto Mrs Nakagawa Kyōko was of
valuable assistance in introducing me to the ascetic healers
known as *ogamiyasan* living in the district, and in guiding me
to the temple of Hōkōji in Kanazawa. My grateful thanks
are due to her. Also to Mr Suzuki Shōei of the Osaka
Museum for many kindnesses during the autumn of 1963
and in particular for taking me to the Hayama *matsuri* in
Fukushima prefecture. Also to Dr Tanaka Yoshihiro of the
Matsuri Society, whose indefatigable energy in uncovering
the lost religious life of Japan and in preserving and recording
what survives, is infectious to all who come within his orbit.
His kindness in allowing me to join the party, which included several notable folklorists from Okayama prefecture,
to observe the Gohōtobi festival at Ryōsanji and Ichinomiya
Hachiman, was unforgettable. Also to Mr Miyagi Tainen
for his particular kindness and thoughtfulness on the four
occasions when I joined the Shōgoin *yamabushi* for the
annual ascent of Mt Ōmine, and for instruction in Shugendō
doctrine and practice on many other occasions. Also to
Mrs Hiroshima Umeko for lending me the manuscript diary
of her celebrated ascetic mother, and her hospitality at the
foot of Mt Miwa. Likewise to her son for guiding me to the
summit of Mt Miwa. Buddhist priest though he was, his
careful homage to the Shinto numina whose trees and rocks
we passed on the way remains vividly in my memory. Also
to the Ajari Enami Kakushō of Mudōji on Mt Hiei for
permission to perform the *kaihōgyō* in 1961. Acknowledge-
ments should also be made to Mr Haga Hideo for his

photograph of the *namahage*, to the Tankōsha Publishing Company for the photograph on Plate 13 by Inoue Hiromichi; to the Matsuri Society for Plate 17 by Shibasaki Kōyō; to the Sansaisha Publishing Company for the photograph of Enkū's Kannon, and to Messrs Tuttle for the haniwa *miko*; to the Cambridge University Library for Plate 1.

A special expression of gratitude must go to the Oka family, whose house in Sugamo was a second home to me during most of my stays in Japan, and who received me with unfailing warmth and imaginative kindness. I thank in particular Oka Akira who accompanied me on my first climb of Mt Ontake and my first visits to Kumano and Mt Haguro, and Oka Takako whose friendship and cheerfulness sustained me in low moments. A similar special thanks must go to Mrs Osaragi Jirō for the generosity with which she and her late husband allowed me to stay in their small house in Kamakura, amongst their exquisite collections of scrolls and inkstones and large books. Both these houses in their different ways were the background against which my investigations were conducted, and perhaps in a deeper sense the 'frequented house' which is so potent a symbol on the shaman's journey.

Finally I must thank those western friends who have in so many ways given me invaluable advice and help. Joan Martin for her friendship and companionship on various journeys, including the climb of Mt Ontake in 1967, for the photograph of Zaō Gongen and for reading the manuscript; Professor Nathan Sivin for unforgettable summer seminars and for valuable comments on Taoism and the manuscript; Professor F. J. Daniels for lending me his unique collection of snake stories; Dr H. Byron Earhart for his friendship and advice during the week on Mt Haguro and on many occasions since; Mr Harold Stewart for inspiring discussions and helpful criticism on hot evenings in Kyoto; Dr D. E. Mills, Dr Stephen Morris, Dr Hilda Ellis Davidson, Dr Edith Schnapper and Dr Irmgard Schloegl for their kind and helpful comments on all or part of the manuscript; Dr Fosco Maraini for his excellent photograph of the ascetic and his fire ritual; Miss Rosina Talamonte for doing the firewalking with me at Tanukidani; the Spalding Trust for the grant which enabled me to spend the summer in Japan in 1961; and Dr Michael Loewe for more than can be specified. Finally, much of Chapter 3 has already appeared in *The Witch Figure*, edited by Venetia Newall, Routledge and Kegan Paul, 1973, to whom acknowledgement is made. It goes without saying, however, that the shortcomings in this book are no one's responsibility but my own.

NOTE: Japanese personal names are given with the surname first. The photographs are my own unless otherwise stated.

Contents

Contents

Illustrations

I
The Bridge

In the Nō play *Aoi no Ue* we are shown, limp and enigmatic in the middle of the stage, a single folded robe. It represents the prostrate form of the Princess Aoi, lying mortally sick of a malignant possession. To cure her condition two figures are summoned. The first is a woman called Teruhi, a sibyl gifted with the power of causing the spirits of both the living and the dead to manifest themselves and speak. She beats on a small drum, twangs her bow of catalpa wood, and recites the summoning spell:

> *Ten shōjō chi shōjō*
> *Naige shōjō rokkon shōjō*
> *Yoribito wa*
> *Ima zo yorikuru*
> *Nagahama no*
> *Ashige no koma ni*
> *Tazuna yurikake.*

'Pure in heaven and pure in earth. Pure within and pure without. Pure in all six roots . . . You who draw near, loosen now the reins of your grey horse as you gallop to me over the long beach.'

Compelled by the magic words and by the sound of the bow string, the spirit molesting the sick woman appears at the far end of the bridge which gives access to the stage. She wears the serene white mask of the Nō woman. Further compelled by the twanging of the catalpa bow, she begins to speak and to name herself. She is the angry apparition of the Lady Rokujō, superseded and disgraced by the woman on whom she is now revenging herself. Overcome with hatred, she crosses the bridge, creeps towards the prostrate figure and strikes it with her fan.

Though the sufferer immediately grows much worse, the sibyl is now at the end of her resources. She can summon a spirit and cause it to speak, but she cannot banish it, nor can she remove its malice. For this task a second source of

19

power is needed. This, they remember, can be be found not far away in the Saint of Yokawa, a holy man celebrated for the austerities he has performed in mountains. Reluctantly he leaves his hermitage and confronts the spirit. Her aspect is now fearfully changed. Gone is the tranquil white mask with its archaic smile. A mallet in her hand, she now reveals the face of a demon with horns, golden teeth and long black hair. Rubbing his rosary of red wooden beads, the Saint recites the Lesser Spell of Fudō Myōō:

Namaku samanda basarada.

He then invokes the Kings of the Five Directions, and intones the Middle Spell of Fudō:

Namaku samanda basarada.
Senda makaroshana
Sowataya untarata kamman.

At the sound of the holy words the phantasm shrinks, drops her mallet and retreats across the bridge to a realm where, we are given to understand, her hatred will be transformed to compassion and she will achieve the salvationary state of Buddhahood.[1]

The bridge over which the apparition has come and gone represents the tenuous joining of two divided worlds. Our familiar human world is no more than a narrow segment of the cosmos which now confronts us. Beyond it lies a further realm, altogether 'other', peopled by beings non-human, endowed with powers non-human, whose whole order of existence is ambivalent, mysterious and strange. Between these two worlds there is no ordinary continuity. Each is contained, like a walled garden, by its own order of being, and separated by a barrier which represents a rupture of level, a break in ontological plane. This barrier the ordinary man or woman is powerless to cross. They cannot at will make the passage to this other perilous plane, nor can they see, hear or in any way influence the beings who dwell there.

The spiritual beings on the other side are not so confined. To them access from one world to another is virtually free and unrestricted. Not only can they visit our world without let or hindrance, but they hold within their control a large sphere of our lives. This sphere was believed to be roughly that over which we ourselves have no control. The fertility of the rice crop, the due onset of the rains, the occurrence of storms, sickness, fire and accident, all these lay in the gift of the inhabitants of the other world beyond the barrier. Even today, although in intellectual circles in Japan an aggressive secularism tends to be the rule, the belief still persists among many sections of the community that the causes of all calamity in human life lie in the spiritual realm. Sickness, accident, drought or fire are the work either of angry ghosts or of offended numina. To discover the causes of these misfortunes we must therefore look into the other dimension where these beings live and enquire what spirit is responsible and the reason for his anger.[2]

On the goodwill of these non-human beings, therefore, depends the prosperity of the community. Treat them correctly with the right rituals and offerings, summon them correctly with the right spells, and they will leave their own world to visit ours and will exercise their superior power for the benefit of man. But once offend or neglect them and they will irrupt uninvited and furious into our world, to blast the offending community with curses.

Ordinary men and women are powerless to deal with these perilous and ambivalent forces. Certain special human beings, however, may acquire a power which enables them to transcend the barrier between the two worlds. This power bears no relation to the physical strength or mental agility with which we are ordinarily endowed. It is of a different order altogether, acquired by means which often weaken a man's bodily health and strength, and which appears from time to time in boys who are virtual halfwits. It is a special power to effect a rupture of plane, to reach over the bridge and influence the beings on the other side.

I use the word 'shaman' in the following chapters to indicate those people who have acquired this power; who in a state of dissociated trance are capable of communicating directly with spiritual beings. These people in Japan appear in two complementary forms. The first, whom I shall call the medium or the *miko*, is exemplified by the sibyl Teruhi. She can enter a state of trance in which the spiritual apparition may possess her, penetrate inside her body and use her voice to name itself and to make its utterance. She is therefore primarily a transmitter, a vessel through whom the spiritual beings, having left their world to enter ours, can make their communications to us in a comprehensible way.

The second and complementary source of power, whom I call the ascetic, is exemplified by the Saint of Yokawa. He is primarily a healer, one who is capable of banishing the malevolent spirits responsible for sickness and madness and transforming them into powers for good. To acquire the powers necessary for this feat he must accomplish a severe regime of ascetic practice, which should properly include, besides fasting, standing under a waterfall and reciting sacred texts, a journey to the other world. Whereas with the medium, therefore, it is the spiritual beings who leave their world and come to ours, with the ascetic the passage is in the opposite direction. It is he who must leave our world and make his way through the barrier to visit theirs. This journey he may accomplish in ecstatic, visionary form; his soul alone travels, his body left behind meanwhile in a state of suspended animation. Or he may accomplish the journey by means of symbolic mimesis; the other world projected by means of powerful symbolism on to the geography of our own, he can make the journey through the barrier in body as well as soul.

Corresponding with each of these figures is a particular kind of trance.[3] With the medium, infused or possessed by a spiritual being, a number of physical symptoms are commonly found. These include a violent shaking of the clasped hands, stertorous breathing or roaring, and a peculiar levitation of the body from a seated, cross-legged posture. I have seen both men and women propel themselves some six inches into the air from this position, again and again for several minutes on end. A violent medium is always considered more convincing than a docile one, the non-human character of the voice and behaviour indicating more vividly the displacement of the medium's own personality by the entry of the divinity. This kind of trance, we shall later see, can either be self-induced, or can be stimulated by a second person, usually the ascetic.

The second type of trance is entirely different. It is a deep, comatose state of suspended animation. This is the condition into which the ascetic's body must fall if his soul is to leave it in order to travel to other realms of the cosmos. His body remains behind, an empty husk, while his soul traverses barriers through which it cannot follow. We shall find that today this trance occurs only rarely. The capacity for this kind of dissociation, and for the visionary journey which goes with it, seems to have diminished in recent centuries, and today the magic journey is most commonly accomplished by symbolic action in full waking consciousness.

I have said that both the medium and the ascetic are shamans because each in their particular manner of trance acts as a bridge between one world and another. Let us at this point pause for a moment to consider what exactly are the characteristics of the shaman which differentiate him from other 'specialists in the sacred'. How does he differ from the healer or medicine man, for example, from the prophet or from the magician?

Certainly, as Eliade warns us, the word is often used with regrettable vagueness to designate almost any person possessing magic power in a 'primitive' society. More meaningful and authoritative definitions have been drawn up, however, which present the shaman in a clearer light. All base themselves on the shaman as he appears, or used to appear, in Siberia. 'Shamanism in the strict sense is pre-eminently a religious phenomenon of Siberia and Central Asia.' Siberia is the *locus classicus*, the long home of the shaman, and it is from observation of his activities among such peoples as the Tungus, the Mongols, the Samoyedes, the Eskimo and the Altaians who inhabit this vast area that the prototypal image of the shaman has been built up. The very word derives from the Tungus *saman*, which in its turn derives ultimately from the Sanscrit *śramaná* (Prakrit *samana*) through the Chinese *sha-men*. This Tungusic name was applied by the Russians to similarly gifted people among the Turks and Mongols, and later came to be adopted by historians of religion and anthropologists to persons possessing similar powers all over the world.[4] Thus shamanic persons among the North American Indians, for example, or the Australian aborigines, in Indonesia, China, Tibet or Japan, have all been so designated because to a greater or lesser extent they share the peculiar characteristics of the Siberian prototype. These can be briefly enumerated.[5]

The shaman is, first, a person who receives a supernatural gift from the spirit world. The gift is bestowed usually by a single spiritual being, who afterwards becomes his guardian and guide, sometimes even his spiritual wife. Before this critical moment in his life, the future shaman suffers for months or even years from a peculiar sickness, sometimes loosely called arctic hysteria. The symptoms range from physical pains—racking headaches, vomiting, aches in the joints and back—to more hysterical or neurasthenic behaviour of wandering off into the forest, falling asleep or fainting for long periods, or hiding from the light.

These symptoms usually disappear, however, at the critical moment of initiation. This violent interior experience often takes the form of a vision, in which a single supernatural being appears to him and commands him to abandon his former life and become a shaman. Thereafter his soul is snatched out of his body and carried off to another realm of the cosmos, either above or below the human world. There he undergoes the fearful experience of being killed and revived. He sees his own body dismembered, the flesh scraped or boiled off the bones to the point when he can contemplate his own skeleton. He then sees new flesh and new organs clothed over his bones, so that in effect he is remade, resuscitated as a new person.

From this terrifying but characteristically initiatory experience he emerges a changed character. His former oddity and sickliness give way to a new dignity and assurance of personality, strengthened by special powers conferred by the guardian spirit who calls him to his new life and which thereafter enable him to render special services to his community.

Foremost among these powers is the ability to put himself at will into altered states of consciousness in which he can communicate directly with spiritual beings. He can fall into the state of trance, for example, in which his soul separates itself from his body and travels to realms of the cosmos inaccessible to the physical body. By travelling upwards to the multiple layers of heavens, for example, he can acquire from the spiritual inhabitants there useful knowledge of hidden things. By travelling downwards to the underworld he can rescue the souls of sick people, kidnapped and taken there by spirits. From his knowledge of the topography of these other worlds, moreover, he can act as guide to the souls of the newly dead, who without his help might well lose their way along the unfamiliar road.

The shaman does not carry out this special work unaided. He is given indispensable help in his task, first by a retinue of assistant spirits and secondly by a panoply of magic clothes. The helping spirits, which often take the form of bears, wolves, eagles or crows, are given to him by his guardian at the time of his initiation. They appear at once at his behest, ready to act as messengers or guides. The magic clothes and instruments, of which the drum is the most important, embody in their shape, in the materials of which they are made, in the patterns and figures engraved upon them, symbolic links with the other world. Thus his drum, made from the wood of the World Tree, his cap of eagle and owl feathers, his cloak adorned with stuffed snakes and an immense weight of metal plaques and tubes, all resolve into means whereby his passage from one world to another is facilitated.

The shaman's work also requires a cosmos of a specific shape. For most Siberian peoples, the cosmos appears in three superimposed layers or tiers. In the middle lies the human world. Above it lie seven layers of heavens, a number to which a Babylonian origin is usually assigned. Below it lies a dark underworld, sometimes also disposed in seven levels, in the nethermost of which stands the palace of Erlik Khan, the Lord of the Underworld, and where sometimes nine underground rivers have their mouths. Joining these various cosmic levels at the very centre of the universe is a marvellous giant Tree. With its roots in the lowest underworld and its crown of branches in the highest heaven, this Tree in all its splendour is at once the axis of the cosmos and the source of ever-renewing life. Thus the shaman, as he travels either upwards to heaven or downwards to the underworld, to planes sealed off from ordinary ungifted persons, follows the 'hole' made through the universe by this Tree. His journey is therefore made at the very centre and core of the cosmos.

The trance in which the soul leaves the body is not the only condition of altered consciousness which the shaman can assume at will. He must also be capable of offering his body as a vessel for possession by spirits. Eliade, it is true, considers the faculty of possession to be secondary and derivative from the 'out of the body' consciousness. Other authorities, however, such as Dominic Schröder, accord it importance equal and complementary to the 'out of the body' trance.

Lastly, we may mention the power which Eliade considers particularly characteristic of the shaman, and closely connected with his ecstatic condition; mastery of fire. The shaman is impervious to heat and cold, to burning coals and arctic ice alike. This power he achieves by rousing within himself the interior heat known to mystics in various parts of the world, and which signifies that the heated person has passed beyond the ordinary human condition. He now participates in the sacred world.

Such is the special complex of powers by which the shaman is usually defined. He is thus a gifted person of a distinctive kind. He is at once a cosmic traveller, a healer, a master of spirits, a psychopomp, an oracular mouthpiece. These various powers, however, are combined and organised round the central faculty of trance; of so altering his consciousness at will that he can communicate directly with the inhabitants of the supernatural world.

We shall see in the following chapters that the medium and the ascetic in Japan can on this definition justifiably be called shamans. We shall find examples of initiation sickness, of the supernatural call, of the 'out of the body' trance in which the soul travels to heaven and hell. We shall find assistant spirits, magic clothes and instruments, and abundant evidence of the interior heat which produces mastery of fire. The cosmos in Japan, it is true, is somewhat differently shaped, with no evidence of the wondrous giant Tree at the centre of the world. It is true too that among the initiatory visions of the medium and the ascetic few have so far come to light which describe the dismemberment of the body, reduction to a skeleton and resuscitation with new flesh on the bones. In place of the Tree, however, we shall find an almost equally splendid Mountain; and in place of the dismemberment and remaking of the body we shall find other symbolism which equally unequivocally points to the initiatory schema of death and rebirth.

We shall find too that it is not meaningful to treat either of these figures in isolation from the other. Complementary though they may at first appear, the medium and the ascetic are closely bound together. Both, we shall find, must undergo the same ascetic practice before their particular kind of power can be acquired. Both must be present at certain rituals in order to achieve the necessary communication with spirits. Sometimes both kinds of power seem to be present, or at any rate overlapping, in the same person. During the feudal period it was common to find marriages between the two kinds of people, an ascetic husband married to a female medium. Clearly we have two mutually dependent functions, which it is convenient to treat under the same nomenclature.

The phenomena of shamanism in Japan are further complicated by the fact that they do not derive from a single homogeneous source: like the Japanese race, language and mythology, shamanism in Japan is of mixed origin. Japanese ethnologists usually relate the instances of shamanism in their country to two broad streams of culture which intermingled in prehistoric times. A northern stream, deriving from Altaic or Tungusic practices on the Asian continent and spreading throughout Korea, Hokkaido and the Ryūkyū islands, mingled with another stream deriving from a southerly source, Polynesia or Melanesia.

Hori, for example, stresses the close relationship which he believes existed between the early *miko* in Japan and similar shamanic women in Korea, among the Ainu and in the Ryūkyū islands. This ancient mantic woman, references to whom may be found scattered throughout the early chronicles, and clay representations of whom have been unearthed from the great tumuli of the fifth century, was evidently a superior and poweful figure in late prehistoric Japan. The account of Japan in the Wei chronicles includes a description of a queen, Himiko or Pimiko by name, who bears all the stigmata of the shamanic ruler. She remained unmarried, rendered service to deities which conferred upon her a special power to bewitch people, and remained secluded in her large, solemn and heavily guarded palace, only one man attending upon her and transmitting her words. The *Kojiki* too, compiled in the early eighth century, contains a description of the consort of the Emperor, later to become the Empress Jingo, who by means of a ritual became possessed by several deities, transmitting their warnings and instructions through her mouth. These ancient *miko*, whom Hori envisages as exercising influence not only in the court of late prehistoric Japan but in virtually every village community with its own tutelary deity, bears a strong resemblance to similar sacral women in other parts of north-east Asia. The Korean *son-mudang*, the Ainu *tsusu*, the Ryūkyū *yuta*, all testify to a wide area where once a feminine shamanism of a northern, Siberian type was dominant, where sacral power was believed to reside more easily and properly in women, and where in consequence women were recognised to be the natural intermediaries between the two worlds.[6]

To this northern, Siberian stream can be traced many of the names for shamans which are commonly used in Japan to this day. The word *ichiko* or *itako*, commonly used in the north-east of the main island to designate a shamanic medium, is believed to have cognate forms in the Ryūkyū *yuta*, the Kalmuck and Yakut word for shaman, *udagan*, the northern Tungus *idakon* and the Mongol *idugan*.[7]

Evidence of an entirely different and more southerly stream of cultural diffusion is to be traced, however, in certain motifs of myths, folktales and legends, in the widespread cult of possession by dead spirits, and in the remnants of a belief in a horizontal cosmology, according to which, as we shall later see, the benevolent dead return in boats at certain seasons from a marvellous land beyond the horizon of the sea.

Oka Masao, for example, sees the Japanese race in prehistoric times as composed of no less than five ethnic components, three southern and two northern, at least three of which brought with them some kind of shamanic practice. Two southern groups of people, one from Melanesia and one from south China, arriving in Japan in the course of the later Jōmon period, brought with them a matrilineal system, rice cultivation and a system of female shamans with a horizontal cosmology.

With these southern elements Oka believes were mingled two Altaic groups of people who brought with them shamanism of the Siberian type. One a north-east Asian group of Tungusic origin, the other an Altaic-speaking tribe from southern Manchuria or Korea arriving as late as the third or fourth century A.D., they brought with them a vertical cosmology according to which deities descended from a higher realm on to trees, mountains or pillars.[8]

Hori too sees shamanism in Japan as deriving from two different sources. What he terms the 'arctic hysteria type' of shamanic woman is to be found in Hokkaidō and in the Ryūkyū islands as well as among the foundresses of many of the religious cults newly arisen in the course of the last hundred years. From this is to be distinguished a 'Polynesian' type of shamanism, of which the blind mediums called *itako* in the north of the main island, to be described later, are the principal examples.[9]

We are therefore in authoritative company if we accept that by the late prehistoric period, the fifth or sixth century A.D., shortly before the coming of Buddhism, Chinese ethics and institutions and the system of writing by which they were recorded, Japanese shamanism was already a complex interminging of two broadly different streams—northern and vertical with southern and horizontal.

To this fusion must be added the further powerful influence exerted by Buddhism. It would seem that the ascetic as we know him today is primarily a Buddhist figure. No reliable evidence of his activities is to be found before the coming of Buddhism to Japan, or indeed before the eighth century. The mutual dependence in which we see the medium and the ascetic existing today is hence a relationship which developed during the centuries immediately succeeding the introduction of Buddhism, the seventh and eighth, until by the ninth century, as we shall see in a later chapter, the ascetic rises to real prominence in the wake of the widespread terror of malevolent ghosts which reigned at that time among the elegant inhabitants of the capital.

To the introduction of Buddhist and Chinese ideas must also be attributed the decline of the Shinto *miko*. In 645 occurred the Taika Reform, by which the old system of clan government in Japan was reorganised on the model of T'ang China. Under the new regime the appearance of mantic queens such as Pimiko and the Empress Jingo became impossible. Under the new system too the *miko* in the large shrines began to lose her mantic gift, and to become before long the figure she is today. Decorative in her red trousers and silver crown, she now dances, sings, assists in ritual, but no longer prophesies. The mantic power with which this ancient sibyl was endowed passed from the large shrines to the level of what Robert Redfield called the 'little tradition', the largely unrecorded, orally transmitted folk religion of the villages. The mantic gift of the ancient *miko* survived in a variety of humbler folk—in the travelling bands of women such as the Kumano *bikuni*, who like strolling minstrels walked the countryside offering their gifts of prophesy and divination, and in the blind women in the north who, without the music and dance so essentially a part of the older *miko's* shamanic performance, transmit the utterances of numina and dead spirits.

With shamanic practices surviving for so many centuries in this unrecognised, virtually hidden manner, what materials are available to the student today who wishes to record the remnants of this fast-disappearing cult and to try to reconstruct what has already vanished? Broadly two types of evidence present themselves. First, there are the living practitioners. Both the medium and the ascetic may still be encountered today. The medium, it is true, survives only sparsely and in somewhat dilapidated form in certain districts of the north-east, certain islands off the Izu peninsula and in certain village rituals where her gifts are combined with those of the ascetic. The ascetic however, is still to be found in many districts of Japan. Living alone or in enclaves, such men and women may be met in the Nara district, in the environs of Kyoto, in Shikoku and Kyūshū, along the coast of the Japan Sea, in the north-east and even occasionally in Tokyo itself. These people still employ techniques of trance and exorcism which bear the authentic stamp of an ancient origin. Wherever possible in the following chapters I have drawn on my own observations of such people made over the past ten years.

Second, the investigator has at his disposal certain kinds of written evidence. Shamanic practices may have survived chiefly on the folk level of religion, orally transmitted from one generation to another. He will find nevertheless that certain kinds of literature are an indispensable help. The collections of popular Buddhist tales, in the first place, in which Japanese literature is so rich from the tenth until the fourteenth century, contain invaluable information about the early ascetic. In works such as the *Konjaku Monogatari*, the *Uji Shūi Monogatari* and the *Nihon Ryōiki*, tales of these men may be found which tell us much about their austere disciplines and the powers which they acquired thereby.

In the Nō plays too may be found an enigmatic but illuminating aid. Many of these plays, I believe, particularly those in which a supernatural being is manifested, are in themselves concealed shamanic rituals. They contain sounds and symbols which were in former times used to call up a ghost and cause it to speak, or to cajole a divinity to descend, to dance and to deliver blessings. In these plays we may still hear the flutes and drums whose sounds were believed capable of resonance in another world, and the mantic howls and wails which were once calls to the dead and the local divinity.

In the body of recorded folk literature, myths, folktales and legends, may also be found invaluable hints. The great ethnologist Yanagita Kunio demonstrated how much, in the absence of direct descriptions, can be learnt from the motifs and types of folktales and legends. In their structure, in their symbolism, in the juxtaposition of their component elements, they convey much to us that would otherwise be lost.

Here, however, as in the Nō plays and in some of the medieval Buddhist tales, we are confronted by the language of symbols. In Japanese religion an intricate network of symbols exists, like mycelium beneath the ground. From this subtle fabric is thrown up, like scattered rings of mushrooms in a meadow, a legend here, a myth there, a place name, the name of a deity, the remnant of a rite. From these scattered appearances we must try to discover the subterranean network below, a task all the more baffling since the symbols, as is their wont, are many-faced. They are like the jewels in Indra's Net, each of which, lying at the intersections of the mesh, reflects at the same time all the other jewels. In the language of folktales one symbol melts into another, is identified with another, is substituted for another. To interpret the stories aright, therefore, we must learn the grammar of their signs.

Less baffling material, however, is also available for the study of Japanese shamanism in the shape of the works of the Japanese scholars in this field. It was only during the last forty years that Japanese ethnologists and historians of religion recognised that elements of shamanism were to be found in their own religion, and that the ancient *miko* was in fact a shamanic woman. Our debt to Yanagita Kunio, however, goes back to the beginning of the century. The extraordinary breadth of vision with which this illustrious scholar brought the rituals, iconography, nomenclature and oral literature of the folk tradition to bear on his almost religious quest for the origins of the Japanese race and culture, has left us with some thirty volumes of collected works. These books and essays are beyond question of fundamental importance to the study of shamanism in Japan.

Another pioneer of giant stature must be recognised in Origuchi Shinobu. The works of this scholar too, though occasionally branded as fanciful, are richly gifted with the intuitive insight and imagination that the task demanded. In the wake of these two pioneers have come a small but dedicated band of men devoted to the task of discovering, recording and interpreting the surviving remnants of this rich but fast-disappearing culture. In the works of Hori

御嶽
在信濃州
筑摩郡

Plate 1. Holy mountain. Mt Ontake as depicted in the *Nihon Meisan Zue* of 1850 first published in 1807.

Plate 2. Another holy mountain, Musashi Mitake. The conical tree-covered peak is typical of the ancient holy hill. The pilgrim route, an avenue flanked by cryptomeria trees planted in the seventeenth century, can be seen winding upwards towards the inner shrine near the summit.

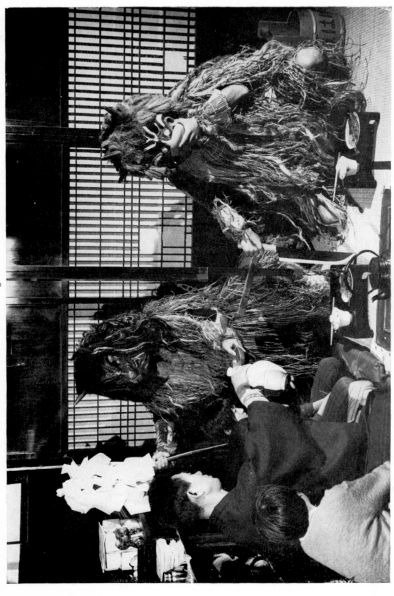

Plate 3. Namahage. These demonic figures, in red horned masks and straw raincoats, brandishing wooden swords and rattling boxes, visit houses during the New Year season in the north-east of the main island to bless the home and admonish naughty children. They are entertained with wine and fish. They are thought to be survivors of the ancient *marebito*, supernatural guests from another world across the sea.

Ichirō, Sakurai Tokutarō, Togawa Anshō, Takeda Chōshū, Ishida Eiichirō, Miyake Hitoshi and many others, the most sophisticated techniques of observation, interrogation and recording have been brought to bear on the living phenomena of Japanese shamanism.[10]

Besides these celebrated scholars, however, the student of shamanism has reason to be grateful to a lesser-known but equally dedicated band of people—the local doctor, the local schoolmaster, the incumbent of the local Buddhist temple—who have recorded rites and practices in their district which without their vigilance would certainly have been lost.

One final preliminary observation. The area in which our investigation will take place makes nonsense of that conventional distinction hitherto observed by most western writers on Japanese religion, the separation of Shinto from Buddhism. Shinto, with its liturgies, rituals and myths, has been usually treated in isolated purity, unadulterated by Buddhist elements. The Buddhist sects have likewise been described according to doctrines respectably based on scriptures with their proper place in the Buddhist canon. The large area of religious practice common to the two, in which the worshipper is scarcely aware whether the deity he is addressing is a Shinto *kami* or a bodhisattva, has been either ignored or relegated to various snail patches with pejorative labels such as superstition, syncretism or magic.

This area, however, is the very one in which most of our researches will be conducted. We shall try to show the nature of the supernatural beings, whether they appear in Shinto or Buddhist guise, with which the shaman communicates. We shall try to locate the realm where they live. We shall try to define the means whereby the shaman acquires his special powers to traverse the bridge into their world. And we shall try to demonstrate how thereby he provides the human community with an invaluable lifeline into the realm from which so many forces emanate which affect their lives, and without which they would be desperately vulnerable, wide open through ignorance and weakness to attacks by these invisible powers.

33

2
The Sacred Beings

The angry spectre which we saw make its way across the bridge on to the Nō stage is not the only type of supernatural being with which the shaman in Japan is called upon to deal. Four broad categories of spiritual entity exist whose nature and mode of activity fall within the scope of his powers. Two of these are accounted superior to man; in power, knowledge and status they transcend the human condition. These may allow themselves to be summoned by the shaman, cajoled, persuaded or petitioned, but never coerced. The other two categories are altogether different. They comprise entities whose state has fallen below that of man, who are in one way or another inferior, unregenerate, fallen or merely malevolent, and who stand in need therefore not merely of persuasion and summons, but also of forcible exorcism and restitution.

Of the two superior types of spiritual being the most important and powerful are the *kami*. These numinous presences have been the principal objects of worship in the Shinto cult since pre-Buddhist times. They are difficult to describe, because they are elusive, enigmatic, heterogeneous. They are best understood perhaps as hierophanies, manifestations of sacred power in the human world. Motoori Norinaga, the great eighteenth century scholar of the Shinto Revival, remarked that anything which was beyond the ordinary, other, powerful, terrible, was called *kami*. Thus the emperor, dragons, the echo, foxes, peaches, mountains and the sea, all these were called *kami* because they were mysterious, full of strangeness and power. *Kami* may thus be descried in certain people, in certain trees and stones, mountains and islands; in the excellence which overshadows the practice of certain crafts, in the continuity and protection which attends a family stemming from a remembered ancestor. In all of these things there shows through, as though through a thin place, an incomprehensible otherness which betokens power.[1]

Sometimes this manifestation of power goes unnamed, supine, scarcely recognised except by the occasional passer-by with second sight. More often it gathers itself together, is given a name, attaches itself to a particular group of human beings. It is no longer simply a window indicating another world beyond, but a being endowed with power, impinging closely on human life and requiring treatment of an elaborately special kind if it is to remain friendly. It is conceived to dwell in a world or dimension of its own, hazily related in a geographical way to ours.

Elusive, shadowy, largely formless though these beings may be, in their disposition and status they are many and variable. Some are great *kami*, with names recorded in the mythical chronicles, who exercise power over a wide area of man's life. Sickness, fire, seasonal rain and marital happiness may all lie in their gift. Others of humbler status confine themselves to narrower spheres, specialising in easy childbirth, good fishing catches or cures for diseases below the navel. Some are remote, static, slow to take offence. Others impinge closely upon our world and are quick to react to the treatment they receive here. Some may exist in a close tutelary relationship with a particular village. Others exert the same protection over a particular family or a particular individual. Others again are prepared to consider in a benevolent light anyone who takes the trouble to make the pilgrimage to their shrine. Despite this variety of nature and potency, however, all *kami* possess certain characteristics in common which enable the shaman, with his special powers, to communicate with them.

In the first place they are able, freely and voluntarily, to cross the barrier which divides our world from theirs. This they may do of their own accord, irrupting suddenly and unexpectedly into our lives from another plane. Or they may come in response to due summons. Certain musical sounds—a koto twanged, a bowstring tapped, a drum thumped—certain songs or certain dances will cause them to leave their own world and visit ours.

Once here, in our alien dimension, how do they manifest themselves? A variety of forms and shapes have been recorded as seen by the clairvoyant eyes of the shaman.

The testimony of these people is apt to vary a good deal, but the shapes most commonly reported are those of a snake and of an old man dressed in white, with long white hair and beard.

Miss Ishida, however, a clairvoyant medium practising in Tokyo, told me in the summer of 1972 that for her the appearance of a *kami* was usually preceded by sounds. She would hear the sound of footsteps approaching with long strides, or the sighing reedy music of the *shō* or the *hichiriki* or sometimes the harp. Then the *kami* himself would appear and speak. Sometimes she could see only his feet or the hem of his robe, sometimes only his mount, the animal on which he rode. The rest of him was hidden in mist.

Miss Ishida went on to say that certain kinds of flowers, trees, birds, stones or metals were more *reiteki* or 'spiritual' than others. These things were closer to the *kami*, partaking more easily of the *kami's* nature, than the rest of their kind. Among birds, for example, white birds like the seagull or shiny black birds like the crow were more spiritual than others. Among trees, the cryptomeria was the most spiritual, and among stones, the agate and lapis lazuli.

Mrs Hiroshima Umeko, an experienced ascetic living in the Suishōji temple at the foot of Mt Miwa, also declared that *kami* appeared to her clairvoyant eyes in many forms. She had seen them in the likeness of flowers, of animals, or human beings. And Mrs Jin, an ascetic based on Mt Iwaki in Aomori prefecture, told me that most of the ascetics in the area, including herself, had seen a vision of the deity Akakura Daigongen. This numen was apt to appear in a variety of forms. His *shōtai* or true form was that of a tall man with long black hair, hairy all over and carrying in his hands a flute and a staff with jingling metal rings. But he also frequently appeared in dragon form, and in the form of a white-haired old man.

It is relevant to note here that in the Nō plays, many of which we should rightly regard as mystical literature deriving from rituals for calling up a numen or a ghost, overwhelmingly the most frequent form in which the *kami* appear is that of an old man. In *Awaji*, for example, the god Izanagi appears as an old man. In *Hakurakuten*, Sumiyoshi

Myōjin appears as an old fisherman. In *Shiga*, Shiga Myōjin appears as an old woodcutter. Sometimes a pair of gods may appear as an old man and an old woman, as in *Ema*, *Gendayū*, *Kuzu* and *Takasago*. It is possible that we see here some confirmation of Yanagita's theory that most *kami* had their origin in the figure of the divine Ancestor, of which the prototype is the beaming figure of the *okina* or old man.

More often, however, it is to the sleeping eye rather than to the waking one that the *kami* reveal themselves. Dream is apparently an easier medium than waking consciousness for the *kami* to manifest themselves to the human mind. In a *reimu* or divine dream, the *kami* may himself appear in the guise of an old man or a beautiful woman, often delivering an answer to a problem perplexing the dreamer. Indeed, it seems to have been a widespread custom in medieval times for a man beset by trouble and anxiety to pass a vigil in a shrine in the hope of having the answer to his problem vouchsafed to him in a dream. In such dreams the deity, in the manner of the Greek incubatory oracle, appears and speaks, sometimes bestowing on the dreamer an object— a jewel, a dagger, a wooden spoon—which is invariably to be found by the dreamer's pillow when he awakes.

Many tales of such dreams occur in the medieval collections of Buddhist tales. Sometimes a figure, in the guise of an old man, a tall priest or a 'strange visitor', appears to the sleeping pilgrim. Sometimes the dreamer sees no figure at all; he only hears a voice of terrible and awe-inspiring resonance reciting a poem in the classical metre. Thus Taira Munemori passed a seven-night vigil in the Usa Hachiman shrine in Kyūshū. At last he was vouchsafed a dream in which he saw the door of the shrine burst open and heard from within an awful and hair-raising voice chanting the thirty-one syllables of a poem. Terrified though he was, Munemori was able to summon up the wit and courage to murmur a suitable old poem in reply.[2]

Again, the dreamer may see not the *kami* himself but his *tsukawashime* or messenger. These spirits, who may take the form of animals, birds or boys, are the intermediaries whom the *kami* employs to visit our world when he is disinclined to traverse the barrier himself. Thus Taira Kiyomori, passing a vigil night in the Itsukushima shrine in the year 1178, dreamt that the door of the shrine flew open and that there appeared two boys, their hair neatly dressed, who delivered a message from Itsukushima Daimyōjin, the deity of the island. They gave him as a sign a silver dagger, which he found on his pillow the next morning when he awoke. A similar dream is recorded as coming to Sashōben Yukitaka. He too saw the door of the shrine burst open and two boys emerge who delivered to him an important message from the god Hachiman. Other messengers frequently encountered in dreams, and sometimes seen even in waking life, are the fox sent by Inari, the deer sent by Kasuga Daimyōjin, the doves sent by Hachiman. Fudō Myōō too has a large retinue of thirty-six boys whom he employs as messengers to our world in a variety of ways.[3]

The belief that the *kami* have any permanent or 'true' form which they can manifest to human senses is, however, late and derivative from Buddhist iconography. In the early cult a *kami* had no shape of his own, his occasional visionary appearances being temporary disguises only. In order to manifest himself in our world he must rather be provided with a suitable vessel or vehicle. This vehicle he could be persuaded by magical sounds to enter and 'possess', and through it to communicate with the human village.

These vessels, seats or temporary abodes of the *kami* were sometimes known as *kura*. Thus the place-name Iwakura, rock-seat, is even today commonly found on sites at the foot of holy mountains. The deity had, it is thought, to be lured down from his abode at the top of the mountain to the rock-seat below, where he could temporarily reside for the duration of the ritual. Again, the old word *mitegura*, hand-seat, represents an object held in the shaman's hand to induce divine possession, as a branch, a wand or a marionette.

The term *yorishiro* also describes a wide variety of objects used as temporary vessels for the *kami*. Many *yorishiro* were long and thin in shape—as a tree, a banner, a wand—as though the numinous presence, like lightning streaking down a conductor, could be induced by such means to descend from his higher plane to ours.

Thus trees, particularly pine trees, have always been a

favourite vehicle for the *kami's* descent. Tall pine trees are constantly found in the neighbourhood of a shrine, and innumerable place-names survive which associate trees with a numinous presence. Stones, too, frequently served as *yorishiro*, stones of the invitingly long thin shape, impressively huge rocks, boulders of suggestively phallic form. The peculiar outcrops of rock on the slopes and summit of Mt Miwa, for example, known as Nakatsu-iwakura and Okitsu-iwakura, which suggest a sudden volcanic explosion spewing gobbets of rock into clearings in the forest, contain a good many such holy boulders. To judge from the archaeological finds of ritual tools at these sites, these have been the object of cult attention since prehistoric times.

An extraordinary conglomeration of stone *yorishiro*, artificially worked, may likewise be seen on the summit of Inariyama at Fushimi and in the hamlet of Fukakusa at the foot of the hill. These strange regiments of oval stones, each inscribed with the name of the deity dwelling therein, each girt with the belt or cravat of tasselled straw, were set up, I was told, at the request of the deities themselves, transmitted through dreams, to be worshipped in that particular vessel.

Honda Yasuji believes one of the oldest forms of *yorishiro* to be a combination of these two forms: a pole, flag or spear standing upright on a rock or mound. Many place-names. he avers, survive to suggest the antiquity of such sacred sites: *hoko-iwa*. spear rock, *hatazuka*, flag mound, or *hokotateiwa*, rock with a standing spear. On a smaller scale the same pair of shapes, which Honda recognises as representing the joining of two sexual symbols, may be found in the rice-cake or sack of rice impaled by a bamboo or willow frond. The same image on a magnified scale may be seen when an entire mountain or island becomes the vehicle or the *kami*, its conical or thickly tree-covered appearance being seen to invite the numinous descent.[4]

Artefacts used as *yorishiro* included banners, pillars and wands, while the earliest dolls and puppets were made not for decoration or amusement, but for the sacred purpose of housing the divinity. Mirrors, swords and the mysterious curved stone called *magatama*, found in profusion in the great tombs of the third and fourth centuries, also served as temporary vessels for the divinity. The *Kojiki*, for example, tells of a *sakaki* tree with its branches hung with strings of *magatama* beads, lengths of blue and white cloth and a large mirror. A tree decked in this manner became, by manifold inducement, the temporary abode of a deity.[5]

In the early stage of the cult the *kami* remained inside his tree, stone or wand for no longer than was required for the duration of the ritual. He was summoned, worshipped, petitioned, and at the end of the rite 'sent back' by appropriate magical words to his own world. At a later stage, however, certain *kami* were believed to prolong their stay. Some would remain for the greater part of the year in a vessel known as the *goshintai*, provided in the holy recess of the shrine. These more permanent abodes for the *kami* were usually of a shape similar to, if not identical with, the temporary *yorishiro*. A stone, a mirror, a sword, a spear—all these attest to the continued attraction that these particular shapes were believed to hold for the divinities.

Some *kami* would remain in the *goshintai* for all the months of the year save the tenth, when they were believed to repair to the Grand Shrine of Izumo. Others, notably the mountain god, *yamanokami*, would remain in the village for half the year, from the spring sowing to the autumn harvest, returning to their own world on the mountain for the winter months.[6]

Others take up their abode of their own accord, not in a prepared vessel in a shrine, but in certain natural objects. These objects usually by their very shape proclaim that something numinously 'other' lies hidden within. A camphor tree of unusual age and hugeness, for example, a cryptomeria tree of vast girth, a pine tree with its roots twisted into peculiar contortions, a stone of unmistakably phallic shape—all these are clearly vessels through which an inherent numinous presence shows as though from another world. Objects of this kind are usually distinguished by certain outward signs and emblems. The *shimenawa*, for example, or straw rope with tassels, found wound like a girdle round the tree, the rock, even the island, indicates that the object it embraces contains sacred power. Small cash offerings too testify to the awareness that a sacred presence dwells within. On a shelf in a tea house in Nachi in 1959, I was puzzled to see a miniature landscape in a china bowl, in front of which lay a substantial heap of small coins. It was soon apparent, however, that the reason for the offerings lay in the suggestively phallic, and therefore sacrally powerful shape of the principal rock. Another dwarf landscape nearby, which boasted no such rock, had received no offerings at all.

Kami can therefore possess trees and stones, mountains and islands, mirrors and swords. They can also possess human beings of a special kind and can furthermore borrow their voices in order to transmit their utterances. These special human beings are of course the *miko*, already exemplified by the sibyl Teruhi. Without the *miko* the *kami* is voiceless, save in dreams, and further divinatory steps must be taken—the tortoise shell, the deer's shoulder blade, the horserace—to assess his will.

Another relevant characteristic of the *kami* is his essential amorality. His nature is ambivalent; it is neither good nor bad, but can manifest itself as benign or destructive to human interests according to the treatment it receives. Treat him correctly with the proper worship and cult attention and with the right and appropriate offerings, and the *kami* can reasonably be expected to bless, protect and succour the village, to see that the harvest ripens, to ward off flood and drought, to forestall fire and pest. Offend him, on the other hand, either by neglect or by exposure to the pollutions of blood and death, and at once his benevolence will turn to rage which will smite with fire, sterility and sickness.

The treatment which all *kami* find pleasing consists of assiduous worship, correct offerings, and above all ritual purity on the part of the worshipper. Frequent visits to the shrine, copious offerings of dried fish, rice-wine, fruit, lengths of cloth, swords, spears, horses, are all calculated to win his favour.[7]

Of paramount importance, however, is the ceremonial purity of the worshippers who approach the *kami's* presence. More offensive than neglect to these numinous beings is pollution, *tsumi*. In ancient times a complex variety of acts and states rendered a man unclean in the sight of the *kami*. The full list is set out in the ritual known as the *Ōharai*, and included such diverse acts and conditions as birth, the consummation of a marriage, menstruation, bestiality, disease, wounds, snakebite, and breaking down the divisions between rice fields. Most of these acts, it will be at once remarked, carry no moral guilt whatever; indeed, they are the unavoidable concomitants of the human cycle of life. Men and women in such conditions, however, could not expect to approach a shrine until a stated length of time had elapsed and unless they had undergone the approved methods of purgation and catharsis.[8]

In practice today the complex list of pollutions set out in the *Ōharai* is ignored. Two sources of pollution only need be reckoned with, death and blood. Anyone who has been in contact with a corpse, even be it a dead dog or cat, must refrain from visiting a shrine for a stated number of days. Anyone who has eaten food cooked on the same fire as a person polluted with death is likewise rendered unclean, though for a shorter space of time.

Blood, the other principal source of pollution, comes in its most abhorred form as menstrual blood and birth blood. The reason why women were prohibited until the late Meiji period and in certain cases even today from climbing holy mountains or entering the portals of certain shrines lay in their liability to the 'red pollution' of menstruation. Blood drawn from wounds likewise caused uncleanness, though for a shorter time.[9]

Pollution is thus directly antipathetic to sacred power. It is the principal source of magical weakness, of the depletion of power. He who would cultivate power must therefore first purify himself from pollution. Only thus can he acquire the bottom of strength which will enable him to accomplish his task. The *miko*, if she is to be possessed by a deity, must by catharsis make herself a fit vehicle for him. The ascetic, if he is to approach the world of numina, must likewise rid himself of the unclean hindrances which make his presence unwelcome.

So much therefore for the *kami*. They represent power of a mysterious and numinous kind over human life. Their nature is non-moral, ambivalent, perilous, unpredictable. Their world is both away from ours and behind it, showing enigmatically here and there through the familiar shapes of nature. To maintain contact between their world and ours special people are necessary, endowed with the special power of effecting the required rupture of level. This task the *miko* and the ascetic accomplish in their complementary ways.

We turn now to the second category of superior spiritual being with which the shaman in Japan is called upon to deal. These are the quiet ancestral ghosts, the spirits of the dead who, through the performance of the correct requiem obsequies, have been successfully brought to rest and salvation.

Spirits of the dead are known in general as *tama*, a word which can without misrepresentation be translated as 'soul'. The *tama* is an entity which resides in some host, to which it imparts life and vitality. Thus it may dwell in the human body, in animals, in trees (*kodama*). It may even dwell in certain words and sounds (*kotodama*), imparting to them a particular magic absent from other sounds. Once let it leave the body in which it resides, however, and its host will become enfeebled and sick and eventually die.

The *tama* is capable of detaching itself from its host and wandering about the country unanchored, occasionally revealing itself in the form of a large shining jewel or ball, to which its name proclaims its association. The ancient ritual of *tama-shizume*, or pacifying the *tama*, was thus a means of preventing or dissuading the *tama* from leaving the body of the sick person. Likewise the *tama-furi*, or shaking the *tama*, another rite of great antiquity, is considered to have been a means of rousing or activating a sluggish *tama*. By waving or shaking an object in which a *tama* was believed to reside, it was possible to stir up its magic power and hereby transfer it to the person for whom the ceremony was performed.[10]

When the *tama* finally and irrevocably left the human body at the time of death, however, it required certain nourishment if it was to achieve its proper state of rest and salvation. This state, usually known as *jōbutsu*, is one attainable only after it has received from its immediate descendents requiem obsequies and offerings over a prescribed period of time.[11] Thirty-three years is the interval usually considered necessary to final peace, though in some districts as many as forty-nine are required. When this period is accomplished, the saved spirit will slough off its individual personality and blend itself into the corporate spiritual entity, the Ancestor, in which all past forebears of the family are believed to be incapsulated. Henceforth the spirit needs no separate tablet in the family temple. One tablet suffices for all the ancestors included in this corporate being, a figure ofter represented by the beaming, anonymous and beneficent old man known as *okina*, who appears in the congratulatory and luck-bringing Nō play of that name performed at New Year.

Two kinds of benevolent ghost may therefore be distinguished: the corporate ancestor, and those spirits who have not accomplished the span of time necessary to attain *jōbutsu*, but who are rendered benevolent nevertheless by assiduous worship on the part of their family. Into this category therefore will come the dead grandfather, grandmother, father and mother of the family, still retaining some semblance of individuality, still responding to calls for advice, still ready to express their opinion, through a medium, on the conduct of their children and grandchildren. Provided the correct offerings are kept up, of rice-cakes and cooked rice, and provided that the correctly powerful requiem sutras are recited, these dead spirits will continue to act as mentors and monitors to their descendants until the time for their apotheosis is fulfilled.

These benign spirits have many points in common with the *kami*. Like the *kami*, they can traverse the barrier which divides their world from ours and return at stated seasons to visit their families. Like the *kami* too they can take possession of a medium and deliver an utterance through her mouth. Unlike the *kami*, however, they are not offended by the pollution of blood, nor of course of death, and the distinctively round shining shape in which they so often manifest themselves is entirely unlike any of the guises in which the *kami* appear. We may note in passing, however, that the round ball is not the only form in which benign ghosts may be seen. Miss Ishida told me in 1972 that to her they usually appeared in the likeness of the person they had been while alive, though frequently they wore an archaic form of dress of pale green or white. Mrs Hiroshima, on the other hand, declared that to her dead spirits differed in the form they manifested according to their *kurai* or rank. The higher they advanced and the nearer they drew towards salvation, the more they tended to resemble shining balls. Her mother, Mrs Hiroshima Ryūun, an ascetic renowned throughout the Kansai district for her powers of healing and exorcism, described in her ascetic diary several cases in which dead spirits appeared to her clairvoyant eyes. Sometimes these were clearly recognisable as the dead persons they formerly were. Sometimes, however, they were balls of light flashing like stars.[12]

The precise relationship between *kami* and the *tama* of dead spirits is still a matter of controversy among Japanese ethnologists. Oka Masao, for example, believes that in ancient times the two kinds of spirit were entirely separate and required separate modes of worship. Yanagita Kunio, on the other hand, firmly believed that all *kami* had their origin in the dead ancestral spirit, and were merely superior and proliferated forms of an original deified ancestor. Both Origuchi Shinobu and Matsumura Takeo likewise believe that the *tama* was an older and more primitive form of spiritual being, from which the *kami* in the course of time developed. Their theory is certainly supported by a number of enigmatic references in the chronicles to *kami* who possessed, or consisted of, two or more *tama* of opposed natures. One of these, the *nigimitama*, was gentle and benign; another, the *aramitama*, was rough and destructive. The one seems to have been capable of detaching itself from the other and appearing as an *altera anima* or exterior soul unrecognisable to its counterpart. Thus we have the curious passage in the *Nihon Shoki* which relates how the deity Ōkuninushi saw his own counterpartal soul floating towards him over the sea, how he interrogated it and held converse with it,[13] and how it declared itself to be his own lucky and wandering spirit.

In shamanic practice today, however, the two kinds of

spiritual being, *kami* and *tama*, are treated differently. The calling of a soul or ghost into the body of a medium requires a ritual different from the summoning of a *kami*, and often a different season of the year. In districts of the north-east, for example, it is specifically forbidden to summon ghosts in the lunar fifth month, when the mountain god is expected to descend from his winter retreat to supervise the work in the rice fields. If he should encounter ancestral ghosts on the road, it is believed, a quarrel would certainly ensue. In other northern rites, however, it is customary to call myriads of *kami* to the scene of the séance before summoning the ancestral ghost with which one wishes to speak: much as in a spiritualist séance in the west the medium's 'control' must be summoned before contact can be made with what Professor Broad called the 'ostensible communicator', that is to say, the ghost.

Certain specific seasons of the year have, however, been set aside since very early times as auspicious times for the recall of ancestral spirits to their old homes. Anciently these appear to have been two, New Year and Bon. Although New Year, *shōgatsu*, has now lost its character of a celebration of the return of the dead, Yanagita has shown us that the figure of the New Year deity, *toshigamisama*, bears so strong a resemblance to the benevolent ancestral old man as to leave us in no doubt as to the original character of the festival.[14]

Bon, however, which on the lunar calendar falls towards the middle of the seventh month, July or August, still retains its character of a welcome to the dead. At this time both kinds of benign ancestor, the corporate figure as well as the individual ghosts, are expected to return to their old home. Altars with appropriate offerings must be arranged in the house for each category of spirit, together with one for the homeless wanderers, the *muenbotoke*, next to be described. In some mountain districts paths are cut in the long grass to enable the spirits to make their way the more easily from their mountain realm to their old homes, and Yanagita believes that a horse may sometimes have been led up this path into the mountain to meet the spirits. He recalls how his own father used to put on his best clothes to go to the door of the house to welcome the spirits on their arrival. He remembers a samurai family too in which the wife, also dressed in her best clothes with the family crest, would prostrate herself at the door with exactly the same courteous formulae on her lips as she would extend to exalted living guests. In language of the most honorific possible she would apologise for her poor and inadequate hospitality, thank the ghosts for their visit and beg them to come again in a year's time.[15]

In other mountain districts the special flowers reserved for Bon—feathery, fragile, redolent of the coming autumn— are gathered from the summits of the hills and brought down into the houses. They are believed to be the *yorishiro* or vessels in which the spirits can inhere for the duration of their visit. Bonfires too, kindled at the tops of hills, are a means of lighting the spirit guests back to their own world. So also is the custom of *tōrō-nagashi* or floating lanterns loosed in the darkness of the last night over the lake at Matsue. When in the summer of 1972 I reached the lakeside, the lanterns were already streaming past, thousands of dim flickering lights over the dark water. Each with the family name written on one side and a valedictory formula on the other, they floated slowly past, uncannily like a great host of spirits, and gradually receded into the darkness of the other side of the lake where one by one they quivered and went dead and black.

We shall find that in the north this season for the return of the dead is celebrated with particularly intense shamanic activity. Unless the ancestral spirits are called at this time into the body of a medium and encouraged to speak, it is believed that their progress towards salvation will be seriously hindered, and that they will appear in dreams to their descendants to complain of neglect.

This brings us to our third category of dead ancestral spirit, the discontented, wandering or angry ghosts.

If the ancestral dead are not correctly treated by their descendants, if the offerings or the obsequies necessary to their nourishment are neglected, then with frightening suddenness their nature will change. The kindly old grandfather, the sympathetic father, the loving mother will turn in an instant into a vicious and capricious tyrant, punishing the neglectful family with curses. The spirit has slipped, without warning, from its position in our second category into our third. From a superior and benignly disposed being, it has become less than human, malevolent, spiteful, in need of succour and restitution.

Of these malevolent ghosts, several different kinds are recognised. There are those in the first place who, during the thirty-three year period between death and the attainment of *jōbutsu*, suffer neglect from their descendants. The necessary nourishment of water, rice and potent sutras is denied to them and in their starved rage they will attack their surviving relations in a variety of painful ways. Once the correct cult attentions are resumed, however, they will usually revert to their former tranquil benevolence.

A second class of discontented ghost may be seen in the *muenbotoke*, spirits of no affinity. These are the ghosts of those who have died with no surviving descendants to accord them the nourishing worship they require, who die childless and without kinsmen or lost and friendless in the course of a journey. They are therefore rootless, wandering, starved, desperate of hope for rest and peace. In their misery they will attack any passing stranger whose condition, through sickness or weakness, lays them open to spiritual possession. In many families, therefore, the custom still persists at the Bon festival of providing a separate altar for these homeless 'hungry ghosts', whose sufferings may thus be temporarily assuaged.[16]

Most dangerous of all, however, are those ghosts whose manner of death was violent, lonely or untoward. Men who died in battle or disgrace, who were murdered, or who met their end with rage or resentment in their hearts, will become at once *onryō* or angry spirits, who require for their appeasement measures a good deal stronger than the ordinary everyday obsequies.

Many examples of such furious ghosts and the havoc wrought by their rage can be found in the literature of the eighth, ninth and tenth centuries, when terror of such spirits rose to a curious crescendo. The Prince Sawara, for example, who died a horrifying death in the year 785, starved, degraded, exiled and finally poisoned, was later credited with a series of calamities which included a general pestilence and the sickness of the Crown Prince. The usual prayers were offered at his grave but these proved ineffectual. It was only when the posthumous title of Emperor was conferred on the dead prince, his body exhumed and reinterred in a grave of the rank of Imperial tumulus, that the disasters stopped.[17]

Even greater havoc was wrought by the angry ghost of the learned minister Sugawara Michizane. Unjustly exiled to the wilds of Kyūshū in the year 901, he died two years afterwards in lonely disgrace. Thereafter another succession of calamities, flood, drought, lightning, pestilence was attributed to the work of his furious ghost. Again extraordinary measures were needed to pacify the spectre. Only when its full apotheosis was brought about, its transformation into a superior *kami* under the name of Kitano Daimyōjin, was its enmity appeased.[18]

Usually, we may note, it is into a *kami* of relatively modest rank—*reijin, mikogami, ōjigami, wakamiya*—that such ghosts are content to be transformed. Yanagita, however, records an exceptional case of the ghost of Yambe Seibei of Iyo which was not satisfied with the title of *reijin* and continued its baleful activities until accorded the much higher rank of *daimyōjin*.[19]

As to the shape assumed by these discontented ghosts, a variety of testimonies present themselves. Miss Ishida told me that she could in fact *see* no distinction between them and their benign counterparts, though she had noticed that angry ghosts often carried an unpleasant stagnant smell. These she would see against the background of their lives. Their home, the history of their death and the reason for their malice, unfolded about them as though a long scroll painting were being unrolled. Koike Nagahiro points out that it is not until late in the Heian period that ghosts are depicted in art or literature as assuming the shape they had while alive. Before that time their presence was manifested in a variety of odd ways. Raigō Ajari, who died of rage and starvation, appeared as a horde of magical rats. Sugawara Michizane appears to have taken the form of lightning and thunder. In the Nō plays, however, of later date the figure who appears resembles his living counterpart so closely that it is only when he announces that he is a ghost that his true nature is recognisable. Nō ghosts may also take the form of ordinary men and women, only revealing themselves in their full panoply of horned mask and long red wig in the second half of the play.[20]

All these varieties of malignant spirit are capable of possessing a human being and inflicting upon him sickness, enfeeblement and mental derangement of numerous kinds. In the laying and restitution of these unhappy spirits the ascetic, as well as the medium, plays a prominent part. We shall find indeed that he first rose to prominence as virtually the only specialist capable of ridding the community of the threat from these spectres, of healing those whom their malignant possession had made mad or sick, and transforming their evil power into one for good.

One more variety of lower, malign spiritual being, with whom the ascetic is likewise called upon to deal, remains to be described before we can proceed to the next stage of our investigation. These creatures, whom I call witch animals, are, however, of sufficient complexity as to require a chapter to themselves.

3
Witch Animals

The witch animals of Japan are creatures believed to be
capable of assuming a discarnate and invisible form, and in
such guise of penetrating inside the human body and
inflicting upon it a variety of painful torments.

Yanagita Kunio, the great authority on Japanese ethnology
and folklore, distinguished two broad categories of witch
animal: a snake, and a four-legged variety usually known
as a fox or a dog. The snake, known as *tōbyō, tombogami* or
simply *hebigami*, covers a relatively small area, being found
only on the island of Shikoku and in the Chūgoku district
of the main island. The distribution of the four-legged
creature is far wider. As a fox, it is found all along the Japan
Sea coast, in both the Kantō and the Kansai districts of
the main island, and over most of Kyūshū. As a dog, *inugami*,
it is found in much the same areas as the snake, that is to
say Shikoku and the Chūgoku district. Under the name of
izuna, it abounds over much of the Tōhoku district, Aomori
and Iwate prefectures. And again, under the peculiar
name of *gedō*, meaning a Buddhist heresy, it appears in the
old province of Bingo in Hiroshima prefecture.

Even here our problems do not end, for the fox itself,
kitsune, falls into a baffling number of sub-species. In Izumo,
for example, it is known as *ninko*, man fox. In southern
Kyūshū it is known as *yako*, field fox. In the Kantō regions
it is known as *osaki*, and in Shizuoka, Nagano and Yamanashi
it sports the name of *kuda*, pipe fox.[1]

Surely, it will be objected, these various names must
indicate different species of animal. Apparently not so.
When asked to describe what the creature actually looks
like, they will tell you in all these districts, regardless of
what name they give it, that it is long and thin with reddish-
brown fur, short legs and sharp claws. Clearly we have the
same creature appearing under a variety of names, none of
which, incidentally, seems particularly appropriate. The
creature described does not in the least resemble a fox or a

51

dog, but rather a small weasel or large shrew. Nor indeed does the name 'snake' seem very appropriate to the animal described. Yanagita's informants in Bitchū told him that it was short and fat, resembling a squat earthworm or small bonito.[2] Indeed, this peculiar separation of name from thing is one of the odd features of the belief.

The first question which comes to mind is, why should these creatures wish to enter the body of a human being, causing him pain and distress? Of what possible benefit could it be to a fox or a snake to take up its abode in so alien a species?

Two clearly distinct answers present themselves.

First, the creature may enter the body of the sufferer through its own volition. Its motive may be *urami*, malice. It possesses its victim in revenge for some slight; killing one of its cubs, for example, or startling it out of an afternoon nap are reasons frequently alleged. Another motive may be greed or desire. The creature wants something which it cannot obtain in its ordinary shape. It may want a meal of red rice or fried bean curd, delicacies irresistible to foxes, but which they are unlikely to come across in their usual form. Or it may want a little shrine set up to it and worship paid to it every day, and can make this wish known only through a human mouth. I have spent several mornings listening to exorcisms of possessed patients in Buddhist temples of the Nichiren sect, and have been astonished at the way in which time and again the same motives are alleged by one possessing creature after another.

What concerns us here, however, is not so much the incidence of voluntary possession as the cases in which the animal attacks its victim because it is compelled to do so by certain baleful persons known as fox-employers, *kitsune-tsukai*, or fox-owners, *kitsune-mochi*.

These people are believed to have fox familiars at their beck and call. They feed them every day, and in return for their commons the foxes are compelled to exercise their supernatural powers in the service of their masters. They thus correspond with what in the west is known as either a witch or a sorcerer.[3]

These sinister figures fall at once into two distinct groups.

First we find the solitary sorcerer, a single lone figure who 'employs' a fox or a dog in order to gain power or wealth, or in order to harm those whom he dislikes. As we shall see, he often turns out to be a degenerate priest or exorcist. Second and more commonly met with today are families who are believed to be the hereditary owners of foxes, and to transmit this evil power from generation to generation in the female line.

These two kinds of witch figure are not found together in the same district. In the regions where the belief in hereditary fox-owning families is still strong, the solitary witch is not to be discovered. His territory lies chiefly in the north-eastern districts of the main island, where the fear of fox-owning families so far as we know has never existed. We must therefore give these two types of witch separate treatment.

The solitary 'employer of foxes', *kitsune-tsukai*, is a figure which invites immediate comparison with our own witches and their cat or toad familiars. In the Japan of today, however, he is rarely met with, though stories of such people were reported as late as the 1920s. Here is an example recorded in the journal *Minzoku to Rekishi* of 1922 by a Buddhist priest of the Suwa district.

A woman came to him, he writes, complaining that every night she was assailed by deathly feelings of suffocation and waves of inexplicable bodily heat. Suspecting a case of possession, the priest sat her down in front of his household shrine and caused her to recite several powerful prayers. At once her babbling speech and the convulsive shaking of her clasped hands proclaimed her to be unmistakably in the power of a fox. The priest at once began the *mondō* or dialogue which is one of the standard methods of exorcism.

'Who are you?' he asked, 'and why are you molesting this woman?'

'I have nothing against her myself', replied the fox, 'but I am compelled by a certain person to torment her and if possible to kill her.'

'Who is this person?' demanded the priest.

'He is an ascetic', replied the fox. 'Another woman paid him three yen to send me on this errand. I am sorry about

53

it, but I have to obey orders if I am to receive my daily food.'

The possessed woman, it soon transpired, was the mistress of a certain man, whose legal wife had naturally become jealous. She had paid the ascetic to use his power over the fox to have the woman killed.

'How did you fall into the power of this man?' the priest asked.

'I used to live under a rock on the mountainside', the fox answered. 'One day the ascetic found me and offered me some delicious fried bean curd if I would go on errands for him. I refused. I wanted nothing to do with the man. But alas, one of my cubs ate the bean curd. From that day I found myself in his power, forced to obey his commands in return for my daily food.'

The priest, after threatening the fox with a portrait of the Emperor Meiji, which reduced it to an abject state of shame and terror, eventually cajoled it into leaving the woman's body by promises of a place in the retinue of the deity Inari. The fox professed itself delighted with the arrangement, promising thereafter to protect the poor woman rather than molest her.[4]

This story, recorded of course as circumstantially true, is instructive in many ways. The description of how the ascetic first acquired power over the fox, finding it in its lair, tempting it with food, is the standard account which has been repeated over and over again for several centuries. Compare it, for example, with what in the works of the Tokugawa period is called the *Izuna-hō* or Izuna rite, the magical means whereby power may be gained over fox familiars. The late seventeenth century work *Honchō Shokkan* contains a much-quoted account. Magicians have recently appeared in Japan, it runs, who employ foxes by means of the Izuna rite. For this rite you must first find a pregnant vixen in her lair. You feed her and tame her, taking particular care of her at the time when her cubs are born. When the cubs are grown up, the vixen will bring one of them to you and ask you to give it a name. Once you have done this you will find that you only have to call the young fox by name for it to come to you in invisible form. Then

you can ask it any questions you like, on any matter however secret, and always it will be able to find out the answer
for you. Other people cannot see the fox in its invisible
form, so when you show them that you know of these
hidden things they will all think that you possess divine
power.[5]

This peculiar rite, described in almost identical terms in
several Tokugawa works, seems to be a degraded vestige of
something which in early medieval times was a religious
rite of heretical but not very evil character. The Izuna rite,
as de Visser has shown us, was at this period another name
for the Dagini or Daten rite, much performed by warriors,
noblemen or priests anxious for power or wealth. It was by
dint of performing the Dagini rite, the *Gempei Seisuiki* tells
us, that Taira Kiyomori rose from obscurity to be virtual
dictator of the land. It was by causing a priest to perform
the Dagini rite for fourteen days that the Kampaku Tadazane
gained his heart's desire. It was through performing the
Dagini rite for thirty-seven days that the Zen priest Myōkitsu
Jisha gained everything he ever wished for. References
throughout medieval literature are legion to the successful
performance of this rite by perfectly respectable people.[6]

But always the Dagini rite, although it appears to have
been a ritual of the pattern usually found in esoteric
Buddhism, was in some way associated with a fox. The
figure of Dagini might appear as a fox; or the *shirushi*, or
sign as to whether the rite had proved efficacious, was given
by a fox. The seventeenth-century account of the *Izuna-hō*
is clearly a degraded version of this medieval ritual.[7]

In modern times this solitary sorcerer seems to have been
usually a debased religious figure: a *yamabushi* or mountain
ascetic, a *kitōshi* or exorcist who has allowed the desire for
money to corrupt him. In the manner described by our
Suwa priest, he may employ the fox, in return for a fee, to
prosecute other people's hatreds and grudges. Or on the
face of it he may be a respectable exorcist, making an
honest living by *curing* people of fox, snake or ghost possession,
as well as by finding lost things and giving advice on
marriages and business transactions. But underneath, it is
he all the time who has set the fox to molest its victim, in

order that he should be paid, all unwittingly, to remove the nuisance.

Since the war, however, little seems to have been heard of such evil men. Far more common are the cases in which the foxes or snakes are commanded by the people known as *tsukimono-suji*, hereditary witch families.

In a few districts of rural Japan, most notoriously along the coast of the Japan Sea, certain families are still subject to a peculiar form of ostracism. It is alleged that for generations they have kept foxes, snakes or dogs in their houses, and that thanks to the malign powers of these creatures they have not only become extremely rich, but also are able to revenge themselves on those whom they dislike by setting the creatures to possess them. The stigma of fox-owning is regarded first as a kind of contagion; you can 'catch' the contamination, for example, by living in a house occupied by a former fox-owner, or by buying his land after he has gone bankrupt.[8] But it is also a hereditary pollution, transmitted, it is interesting to note, largely in the female line.

If you wish to avoid the stigma, therefore, you must eschew all business dealings with fox-owning families. You must not visit their houses, you must not borrow money from them or buy land from them. You must avoid giving them offence. But above all you must see that neither you nor your kith and kin marry any of their girls. To receive into your family a bride who is even remotely associated with the fox-owning stigma is to risk acquiring the stigma in full measure yourself. In some places it was believed that the foxes, even to the number of seventy-five, accompanied the girl when she went to her bridegroom's house. Henceforth that house, and all the ramifications and sub-branches of the family, would be contaminated. Thus it used to be said that when a marriage was arranged in these districts the first question to be asked about the bride's family, even before making sure that it was free from tuberculosis, insanity and shortsight, was whether or not the slightest suspicion of fox-owning attached to it. If such was found to be the case, negotiations were broken off at once.

The creatures, whether foxes, dogs or snakes, are believed to be kept in the houses of their masters and to receive daily rations of food. In return for their board and lodging they hold themselves ready to obey the behests of their masters, using their powers of invisibility and possession to molest those whom he happens to dislike. Not only will they inflict on their victims all the approved symptoms of possession—pain, hysteria, madness—but they will also quietly remove the valuables of their victims to the houses of their masters. Hence the fox- or snake-owners are believed to be one and all extremely rich. In the case of the fox and the dog, the number kept in their master's house varies considerably. Sometimes ten, I was told, sometimes twenty, sometimes as many as a hundred have been counted. But a common number is seventy-five, though the reasons for preferring it are far from clear.

In the case of the snake, only one at a time seems to be the rule, and that is kept in a pot in the kitchen, fed on the same food as the family gets, with a tot of saké occasionally thrown in. If a snake-owner in Sanuki happens to quarrel with anyone, Yanagita informs us, he is believed to say to the snake, 'All these years I have been feeding you, so it is time you did me a good turn in exchange. Go at once to so-and-so's house and make things as unpleasant for him as you can.' The snake then sallies forth and possesses one or more members of the marked family. In this part of Shikoku the principal symptom of snake possession is a sudden and unbearable pain in the joints, similar to acute rheumatism.[9]

A couple of centuries ago these unfortunate families were subjected to a fairly ruthless persecution. Banishment from the fief and extirpation of the family line within the fief were not uncommon measures during the feudal period. Motoori Norinaga mentions a case in 1747 in which the *daimyō* of the Hirose fief ordered the extirpation of a family accused of fox-owning.[10] Their house was burnt down and the entire family banished from the fief. Only rarely, however, were the unhappy victims condemned to death, and never, so far as I can discover, death by burning.

During the past century, however, it is rare to hear of violence of any kind directed against the accused. Cold and implacable ostracism is rather the rule.

As a result of surveys done in the early 1950s, Professor Ishizuka has designated four districts in Japan where he considers the fox-owning superstition to persist particularly obstinately, and where in consequence the families branded as 'black' are particularly numerous. The first two are in Shimane prefecture, where the prevalent animal is the fox. They are the district of Izumo and the island of Oki. In the last two, a district in southern Oita prefecture in Kyūshū and another in Kōchi, Shikoku, the stigma was not for fox- but for dog-owning. Both these last districts showed peculiarities of distribution. Out of eleven *buraku* or villages investigated in the Kyūshū area, three proved to consist entirely of dog-owning families; but next door to one of them was a village with no dog-owning families at all. Again, out of ten *buraku* investigated in the Shikoku district, one was composed entirely, save for a single household, of dog-owning families; yet next door was a village with no dog-owning families at all. The obvious inference was of course that the ostracised families had sensibly congregated in their own villages and intermarried among themselves, with their own schools and social groups.[11]

Let us look at one or two examples of the misery perpetrated by these obstinate beliefs. As late as the 1950s several cases were reported in the newspapers whereby *jinken*, human rights, were claimed to have been infringed by the belief in hereditary fox-owners. In 1952 the Shimane edition of the *Mainichi Shimbun* reported that a young couple had committed a double suicide because the young man's parents had forbidden him to marry a girl on the grounds that the fox-owning stigma attached to her family.[12]

In 1951 a case of malicious slander came before the Bureau of Justice in Matsue. A month-old baby in a family called Mita suddenly fell ill and died. The child's father declared that its death had been caused by demoniacal dogs, sent to bite it from the dog-owning family of one Abe. The rumour spread, with the result that Abe was soon ostracised by the neighbourhood. His daughter's engagement was broken off, and all the workmen in his building company left so that the business came to grief. Investigation proved that the Abe family had recently come into money, was unpopular in the district, and had quarrelled with Mita over a plot of land. When Mita's baby died, an exorcist called Myōkō told him that the cause of death was a demoniacal dog from the Abe household.[13]

Which brings us to the problem: how did these unfortunate families originally receive so extraordinary a stigma? Outwardly they are no different from their neighbours. What has earned them their reputation for evil witchcraft?

As the Mita–Abe story illustrates in all too melancholy a way, many have fallen into this unhappy state of social ostracism through little more than untested slander: an accusation made by an exorcist in a state of trance, perhaps, or even by the patient herself. In 1922 a case was reported from Bungo province of a girl who rushed out one night and fell unconscious outside a house belonging to a man named Genjū. Her parents pursued her, and on no other evidence concluded that she was possessed by a dog sent by Genjū. Reviling Genjū in the strongest terms, they beat the girl violently on the back for a quarter of an hour, after which she recovered. After this incident Genjū and his family suffered great misery from slander and ostracism. His sister, who had been happily and prosperously married, was divorced on account of the scandal. At length, in desperation, he brought an action for libel against the girl's parents and was awarded suitable damages.[14]

To our question, what have these families done to be thus singled out as witches, the answer one is likely to receive in the district is a simple one: because they do in fact keep foxes in their houses. In the winter of 1963 I visited a temple called Taikyūji, not far from Tottori, which since the Meiji period had been a renowned centre for the exorcism of fox-possessed patients. The priest was an elderly man who had served in the Russo–Japanese War, and he was certainly well-educated. But he had been the incumbent of the temple for twenty years and had exorcised a great many fox-possessed people. It is easy to tell, he told me, who are the fox-owning families, because you can see the foxes sitting on the eaves of their roofs. Time and again during his evening stroll he had seen them playing outside the houses of the marked families, or sitting in a row on the eaves, shading their eyes with their paws. Often they would rush up to him, snarling and snapping at his robe. Nor was he the only one who could see them. Everyone in the village could do so.

Again, a Mr Ikuta, a schoolmaster in Tottori whom I met in 1963, told me that he had spent a great deal of time lecturing in various villages in the area, exhorting them to abandon the evil superstition of fox-owning. But he had made little headway. After his lecture he was usually challenged by one of the villagers: how could an outsider know anything whatever of the matter? The whole village knew which families were the fox-owning ones because they could see the foxes outside the houses.

Detached investigation has, however, yielded one or two more likely solutions to our problem. Mr Hayami Yasutaka in his interesting book published in 1953, *Tsukimono-mochi meishin no rekishiteki kōsatsu*, describes how he himself was brought up in a family with the reputation for fox-owning in a village near Matsue. Having suffered mockery and inconveniences of various kinds during his childhood, he eventually, after the war, carried out a number of investigations in the Izumo district which formed the nucleus of a thesis on the fox-owning superstition. His principal conclusions were as follows:

1. That as late as 1952 10 per cent of the families in the Izumo district bore the stigma of fox-owning.
2. That the belief arose during the middle Tokugawa period, at the end of the seventeenth and beginning of the eighteenth centuries, at a time when the money economy was beginning to penetrate into the countryside, bringing in its train a new class of *nouveaux riches* landlords.
3. That the fox-owning families originated in these *nouveaux riches* landlords, through accusations of fox-owning first brought through the jealous slander of the older inhabitants of the village, ousted and impoverished by the newcomers.
4. And that the superstition was inflamed and exacerbated by Shingon priests, *yamabushi*, exorcists and suchlike people who would be likely to make money from the discovery of such witchcraft and the exorcism of its effects.[15]

These conclusions agree by and large with those of

Ishizuka's surveys of the fox-owning districts. His investigations pointed to the fox-owning families being the *nouveaux riches* of about a century ago. They were neither the oldest families, that is to say the descendants of the founders of the village, nor the most recent settlers. They were the middle layer. Ishizuka too attributes the origin of the accusation of witchcraft to the jealousy of the impoverished older settlers.[16]

These explanations, however, account for no more than the grounds for hostility; they in no way explain its nature. They do not tell us why so extraordinary an accusation should be levelled against the intruders. You may hate and dislike someone, and a new, hardfisted, intruding landlord is an understandable object of dislike. But you will not necessarily accuse him of having acquired his wealth and power through the medium of witch animals. There must have existed in the district, deeply rooted in its beliefs, some prior conviction that fox witchcraft was possible and dangerous. We must therefore try to look even further back to see in what possible context this fear originated.

Several Japanese ethnologists, including Yanagita Kunio, have attributed its origin at least in part to the *ku* magic of China. Let us look into this.

The practice of *ku* magic is apparently of great antiquity. The character *ku* appears on the oracle bones (1500 B.C.) and gives its name to one of the hexagrams of the *I Ching*. But what exactly the word meant does not become really clear before the sixth century A.D. Here, in a work called *Tsao shih chu-ping yüan-hou tsung-lun*, we find the first clear descriptions of how the *ku* magic is performed and the poison manufactured.

You take a pot and put inside it a variety of venomous creatures, snakes, toads, lizards, centipedes. You then let them devour each other until only one is left. This survivor is the *ku*. 'It can change its appearance and bewitch people', the work continues, 'and when put into food and drink it causes disease and disaster.'[17]

This *ku* creature, be it snake, toad, centipede or caterpillar, can be used by its master both for enriching himself and for killing his enemies, very much as we have seen the fox or snake to do in Japan. But its mode of activity seems altogether different. It does not possess its victim so much as poison him. The *ku* creature is introduced into the food and drink of the sorcerer's enemies, causing death in a variety of horrible ways. Sometimes they simply die in terrible pain spitting blood. Sometimes the fish and meat they have just eaten come alive again in the stomach, and they not only die but their spirit becomes a slave in the house of the sorcerer. The *Sou shen chi*, a fourth-century collection of supernatural tales, has a story of a monk who went to dinner with a family who made *ku*. All the other guests died spitting blood, but the monk took the precaution of reciting a spell before beginning his meal, and saw two black centipedes a foot long crawl away from the dish. He ate his dinner and survived unharmed.[18]

A favourite form of *ku* creature from the Sung period onwards is the *ch'in tsan* or golden caterpillar. But here the procedure is rather different. You do not invite your enemies to dinner and put the golden caterpillar in their food. You leave it on the roadside wrapped up in a parcel with pieces of gold and old flowered satin. A stranger will then pick up these rich and glittering things, to find himself cursed with the caterpillar. In a manner not clearly explained the caterpillar will slowly kill its victim, at the same time removing all his valuables to the house of the sorcerer, who suddenly thus becomes extremely rich.

At the same time, once you have such a caterpillar at your command it is extremely difficult to get rid of it. You cannot burn it or drown it or hack it to pieces with a sword. The only sure defence, indeed, both against its attack and against the risks of ownership, seems to be moral virtue. Several Sung works tell stories to illustrate how scholars were protected by their moral virtue against *ku* magic. They pick up mysterious parcels on the roadside, only to be persistently haunted by frogs, snakes or caterpillars which cannot be killed. Eventually, to the dismay of their families, they eat the creature. But they do not die, as everyone expects. They live happily ever after, both rich and free from *ku* haunting.

The *Yi chien san chih*, for example, tells of a brave scholar in the district of Ch'ang-chou, so brave in fact that there was really nothing that he was afraid of. One day he was walking with some friends when he saw on the ground a parcel wrapped in silk. The friends were too afraid even to look at it, but the scholar laughed and said, 'I am a poor man, so why shouldn't I take it?' He opened the parcel then and there, to find inside several rolls of silk, three pieces of silver and a *ku* frog. Saying to the frog, 'I don't care what you do; it is the silk and the silver that I want', he took the things home. His family were horrified and wept bitterly, expecting a calamity to fall upon them at any moment. But the scholar told them not to worry; it was his business, not theirs.

That night he found two frogs in his bed, as big as year-old babies. He killed them both and ate them. His family were even more terrified, but he simply said he was lucky to get such good meat. He then got drunk, went to bed, and had an excellent night's sleep.

The next night he found ten frogs in his bed, though they were smaller than the previous ones. These also he cooked and ate. The next night there were thirty. Every night thereafter the frogs in his bed became more numerous, though they got smaller in size. At last the whole house was full of frogs and it was impossible to eat them all. Yet his courage never failed, and he hired a man to bury them outside the village. Finally, after a month, the thing stopped. The scholar laughed and said, 'If this is all that the *ku* calamity is, it does not amount to much.' Nothing more happened and everyone was filled with admiration for his bravery.[19]

Now on the face of it there seems to be little in common between these Chinese practices and the hereditary animal witchcraft found in Japan. Let us review the facts.

First, the *ku* creature is nearly always cited as a reptile, insect or batrachian. It is, in short, a creature of the scaly variety indicated by the radical classifier 142. The pot, after all, is a receptacle suitable only for such creatures. The only exception to this rule that I can discover is the story in the *Sou shen chi* which describes a man called Chao Shou who had dog *ku*, and how guests to his house were attacked by large yellow dogs.[20] And this from the description would seem more likely to be a case of hydrophobia than one of *ku*.

Secondly, there is no mention of the *ku* creature having powers of possession. It seems either to be administered as a poison in food, or to haunt its victim, as did the frogs in the scholar's bed. This is very different from the activity of the Japanese *tsukimono*, which enters into the minds as well as the bodies of its victims.

Thirdly, I can find only one mention of the *ku* animal being the hereditary property of a family. This is in the *Sui shu ti li chih*, the geographical section of the Sui dynasty history, where it is written that *ku* is handed down from generation to generation in a family, and is given to a daughter as a dowry when she marries.[21] But for the rest, there is no indication that possession of a *ku* creature or the ability to manufacture *ku* is something which runs in certain families, least of all that it is handed down in the female line.

On the other hand, several curious similarities do occur between the *ku* magic and the Japanese belief in snake witchcraft. In the first place, as Yanagita Kunio assures us, the snake is believed to be kept in a pot in the owner's kitchen. To possess one is by no means an unmixed blessing and many families are anxious to get rid of theirs. The only way in which this can be accomplished without bringing misfortune on oneself is to get a total stranger to kill it unwittingly.

A man once came to a certain village in Sanuki province on a building job. He lodged in a house in the village and every day went to work on the building site. One day he came back to find all the family out. He saw a kettle of water boiling on the stove, and thought that a cup of tea would be nice after his day's work. On the floor he saw a jar with a lid, and thinking that it contained tea he took the lid off. Inside he saw a snake coiled up like a lamprey. He poured some of the boiling water on it and replaced the lid. When the family returned he told them what he had done, and one and all rejoiced at their deliverance by a stranger from the curse which had plagued them for so long.[22]

But for its ending, this story is remarkably similar to one in the *Sou shen chi*. A family called Liao had manufactured

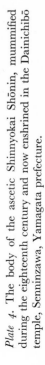

Plate 5. The great waterfall at Nachi as depicted on the thirteenth-century painting known as the *Nachisan Mandala* preserved in the Kumano shrine. The priest Mongaku with his two supernatural saviours is seen in the raging waters.

Plate 4. The body of the ascetic Shinnyokai Shōnin, mummified during the eighteenth century and now enshrined in the Dainichibō temple, Senninzawa, Yamagata prefecture.

Plate 6. Haniwa *miko* from Okawamura, Gumma prefecture, height 68.5 cm. Tokyo National Museum. She wears a ritual attire of jewels at her neck, wrists and ankles, while from her waist is suspended a metal mirror decorated with five small bells.

ku for a long time, and had become rich thereby. One of the sons married, but the bride was not told about the *ku*. One day everyone went out, leaving the bride alone in the house. She noticed a large pot, and on lifting the lid saw inside a big snake. She poured boiling water into the pot and killed the snake. When the family returned and heard what she had done they were all terrified. And soon after, sure enough, they all died of plague.[23]

Stories so similar must certainly have a common origin. The origin of the Chinese story, as also of the story of the yellow dog *ku*, is the fourth-century work *Sou shen chi*. This book we know to have found its way to Japan at least by the Tokugawa period, and its stories in a curious manner to have become absorbed in the oral tradition of Japan. Is it not more likely that the parallels are due to the dissemination of this book and others like it in Japan, rather than to common origin between the magical practices themselves? Knowledge of *ku* magic imported through books, moreover, is surely not enough to account for this widespread and tenacious belief in hereditary animal witchcraft.

Another suggested explanation is that the belief in fox witchcraft is a degraded survival of a former household or village deity in animal form.

There is abundant evidence that both the fox and the snake used to be, and in some places still are, regarded as benevolent protective deities of a family or village group. It is perhaps perilous to use the word 'totem' in view of the work of Lévi-Strauss, who tells us that the term no longer has any real meaning. Nevertheless, it still seems to me to be a useful one by which to designate an animal which lives in a special and mutually beneficial relationship with a particular family: an animal which, in return for food and the spiritual nourishment imparted by worship, will exercise tutelary protection over the family and reserve for them the benefits of its powers of clairvoyance and healing.

Examples still survive today of foxes enshrined in private houses, usually under the nomenclature of Inari and his messenger, which in return for the usual offerings and recitations will give useful supernatural information. In return for such 'worship', he will pronounce on the where-abouts of lost things and missing persons, on the prospects for the rice harvest or the fishing catches, on the cause of sickness or the advisability of marriage. Such information often used to be delivered in the form of a *takusen* or oracular utterance through a medium. So also is the snake found usually conflated with the deity Ryūjin, invoked as a benevolent family or village oracle in return for worship offered at a special little shrine.

Even in the districts along the coast of the Japan Sea where the fox-owning belief is still strong, there still survive indications of the fox as a benevolent protector. Ishizuka found several interesting cases of families with the fox-owning reputation but who were not hated or feared because they were so assiduous in their daily worship at the animal's shrine. In other words, we are back with the familiar Japanese belief that a spiritual being, whether numen, ghost or animal, will remain benevolent so long as it is treated right. Once neglect the nourishing rituals and the being will change its nature completely, becoming a source of curses rather than of blessings.[24]

But how did these originally benevolent and useful divinities become degraded into witch animals? The answer can only be conjecture. But perhaps we see here yet another example of the familiar psychology of the witch fear. It comes as an explanation of otherwise incomprehensible strokes of fate. Why should my baby die and not hers? Why should my back ache or my wife go mad? And again, why should *they* suddenly become rich and successful? The origin lies in the overwhelming necessity for finding an explanation of disaster, disparity, sickness, which will lay the blame on someone else and exonerate you. They surely could not have become so rich by their wits alone; they must have had help of some kind, non-human help. The fox they used to worship at once springs to mind, and accounts also very conveniently for the pains in my back and the sudden death of my baby.

Though the totem explanation accounts fairly satisfactorily for the hereditary character of Japanese witch animals, it does not explain why the great majority of them should be passed down in the female line.[25] The present hereditary family system known as *ie* is an overwhelmingly masculine institution; the bride is received and absorbed, but brings virtually nothing from her own family which will affect or modify her husband's. To look back to some distant period of antiquity when power may have been transmitted in the female line would be carrying speculation too far. This aspect of the problem still awaits solution.

A final problem is the hallucinatory one. The priest of Taikyūji was quite certain that he had seen the foxes outside the houses of the condemned families, not once but many times. He is only typical of large numbers of people in the district whose proof that foxes are kept in those houses is that they have actually seen them there. It would be easy of course to dismiss the whole problem as one of collective wishful vision. They see the creatures, as one rationally minded Japanese told me, because they wish to see them; much as those involved in African witch cults will swear that they have seen the witches with their phospherescent teeth flying on their malign errands. But I cannot refrain from drawing at least a tentative comparison with those families in this country which appear to possess a spectral attendant animal. These creatures usually appear as birds or dogs, though radiant boys are not unknown, but as a rule they do not manifest themselves unless a member of the family is about to die. The black dog of the Herefordshire Baskervilles and the birds of the Bishop of Salisbury are merely two among many instances of animal apparitions seen at such critical junctures.[26] If we are not inclined to dismiss these at once as 'mere' hallucinations, we may at least accept them as food for further speculation about survivals of former, closer relationships between a family and an overshadowing animal.

It thus seems reasonable to conclude that the practices we have discussed under the name of Japanese animal witchcraft are probably, in both their principal forms, survivals of former cult practices not in themselves evil. The Izuna or Dagini rite was a *gehō* or heretical ritual, but not necessarily an evil one. Neither was the worship of the fox or snake as a household guardian; the creatures were possessed of useful supernatural powers and, like a friendly watchdog or efficient mouser, would behave in general benevolently if kindly treated. That they should have evolved into uncanny, often atrocious instruments of evil is due to a shift of emphasis. The same set of symbols, which originally benefited one family, is now seen as primarily harmful to others. Their gain has become my loss.

4
The Other World

The question now suggests itself: where are we to look for this mysterious other world? It lies somewhere outside our own sphere, beyond a barrier which separates planes, but where geographically does it lie in relation to ourselves? In which direction is the ascetic to make his journey, and from which quarter will the numina and ancestral spirits, summoned by the medium, make their appearance? We must ask, therefore, what is the shape of the universe which accommodates both our own world and the worlds of the *kami* and the dead.

No sooner do we pose these questions than we find ourselves, like the people on Bunyan's enchanted ground, beset by confusions and ambiguous shapes. We shall find no neatly defined cosmos, comparable with those imagined by the Indians, the Babylonians or the ancient Hebrews, with a central axis, mountain or tree, round which are disposed layers of heavens, levels of hells, tidy ceilings and floors, and even walls and posts. We shall miss even the comparatively clear distinction to be found between the various realms of the other world in western myth and legend. For our ancestors, heaven lay above, hell lay below, and fairyland, though less predictable of access, was usually to be found inside howes or hollow hills which stood open on raised pillars on indeterminate nights of the year. None of these realms was easily confused with the other.

But in Japan the vision of the other world is riddled with ambivalence, like a piece of shot silk. Move it ever so slightly and what we thought to be red is now blue; another tremor and both colours flash out simultaneously. It is the same with the other world. No sooner do we see it across the sea, removed horizontally in space, than it dives down beneath the waves or beneath the earth. No sooner are we shown an eerie and verminous waste land, where prisoners are immured in chambers of centipedes and snakes, than again the shape shifts and we are dazzled by a magical palace under the sea, shimmering with pillars of jade and gates of pearl, and where carpets of sealskin and silk are laid out for the guest. And again, no sooner have we caught sight of the *kami* there, in their own world, than they are here, in ours, hidden invisibly within certain suggestive shapes.

Some of these contradictions may be attributed to the ambivalence which inevitably follows any attempt on our side to express the enigmatic strangeness of the other world. Its total unfamiliarity, its baffling otherness, can only be conveyed in our language by the devices of ambiguity and contradiction. But other anomalies can certainly be traced to the different intuitions of this elusive place to be brought to Japan in prehistoric times by different ethnic groups. Further still, as though this ancient mingling of ideas were not complex enough, we have also to take into account the projection on to these older beliefs of the Buddhist cosmos, with its gigantic axial mountain, its hierarchy of heavens and hells, and its island continents stretching into a middle sea.

Our task is therefore first to disentangle these various strands of other-world belief, and discover which apply most relevantly to the practices we are investigating.

We may begin by dismissing a cosmology which will in future concern us scarcely at all. This is the vertical, three-layered universe of the *Kojiki* myths. Here we are shown the human world as lying midway between an upper realm, located somewhere in the sky, in which the superior *kami* were conceived to dwell, and a lower world, the dark and polluted destination of the dead. Neither of these two realms is described in any detail in the texts. The upper world, Takamagahara, although the abode of discarnate *kami*, appears to be a place of almost gross physicality. It contains rice fields, which the deity Susanoo is able to ravage and lay waste, and houses with roof tiles. It has an earth floor, into which the goddess Amaterasu is able to stamp her feet in rage, but which yet can be pierced by an arrow shot from the world below. No ladder, road or hanging vine, no axial tree or mountain appears to connect this high realm with the one beneath it, though certain deities are able to make use of a floating bridge to accomplish their descent to the world below. Susanoo declares that he made his way up there on foot, through clouds and mist, but we are given no hint as to how or where he accomplished his climb. Yet the entrance, to judge from the Ōharai liturgy, would appear to be a rock door, which must be pushed open before the ritual words uttered below can be heard. Further than these sparse inferences, the essential nature of the realm, Saigō Nobutsuna assures us, must be understood to be that of a sacred world. It is light, bright, central, pure, unpolluted.[1]

In strong contrast stands the lower world of the dead, known as Yomi. Here is a place with all the complementary qualities: it is dark, defiled, disordered, peripheral. Its topography can be roughly inferred from the celebrated myth in the ninth chapter of the *Kojiki*. When the deity Izanagi followed his dead wife Izanami into the land of Yomi in an attempt to bring her back, she came out to greet him to the door of a hall. She then retired inside the hall in order to consult with the rulers of Yomi, adjuring Izanagi not to follow her inside. She was gone so long, however, that Izanagi grew tired of waiting and, torch in hand, entered the forbidden chamber. There he beheld the terrible sight of his wife's corpse alive with squirming maggots, while on her head, breast, belly, genitals and limbs sat eight kinds of thunder deities, probably in serpent form.

At this fearful prospect Izanagi turned and fled, hotly pursued by the ugly hags of Yomi. These spectres he managed to delay, however, by the device of throwing down his comb and the vine which bound his hair, and causing them to change into bunches of grapes and bamboo shoots. While the hags were eating these things, he reached the boundary between the two realms and closed the entrance with a huge boulder.[2]

The geography reflected in this account is thus minimal. There is an entrance to Yomi, described as a 'pass', which can be closed by a rock. There is an inner 'hall', pitch dark inside, connected with the entrance by what would seem to be a long passage. Several scholars, notably Gotō Shuichi, have noted the similarity between this topography and the structure of the great tombs, built on the Yamato plain in the course of the fourth and fifth centuries, which feature a stone passage leading to an inner stone burial chamber. Clearly, Gotō claims, the description of Yomi given in the myth is reflected in the structure of these tombs. The 'hall' into which Izanami retired and was later discovered in her decomposing state was the stone burial chamber, the entrance to Yomi was the mouth of the passage.[3]

It is tolerably clear, certainly, that the people who transmitted *Kojiki* myths and those who built the great tombs were one and the same, namely a ruling class who made their way from some northern part of the Asian continent into the district of the Yamato plain some time during the third century A.D. But they did not comprise the whole of the Japanese people, nor were their myths necessarily accepted by people dwelling in other parts of the islands.[4]

Neither the vertical cosmology of these myths, nor their segregated and polluted dead, can be in any way related to the shamanic beliefs we are considering. We shall not find the medium summoning any divinity from Takamagahara, nor any dead spirit from Yomi. Nor will the ascetic make any attempt to travel to these realms. Neither are the *kami* with whom the shaman communicates so separated from the dead as this vertical universe demands. On this scheme the lower world contains the source of all that is most offensive to the *kami*, the pollution of death. Yomi is a 'horrible unclean place', Izanagi exclaims as he cleanses himself in river water of the pollutions he has acquired there. The dead, whatever their merits, have clearly no hope of achieving any proximity to the *kami*, or any kind of apotheosis by which they may escape from their contaminated state. Among the sacred beings with whom the shaman communicates, however, there is no such rigid separation. The *kami* and the dead dwell in a similar place and in a similar direction, and, as we have already noted, there is much similarity between their natures and powers.

We have to conclude, therefore, that the cosmology of the builders of the great tombs was not transmitted to the beliefs we are investigating. We must look elsewhere for our other world.

Origuchi Shinobu advanced the theory that the oldest

cosmology known to the Japanese lay along a horizontal axis. Far across the sea lay a miraculous land known as Tokoyo, from which at regular seasons supernatural guests called *marebito* would arrive on the shores of our world in boats. These benevolent visitors, Origuchi contends, were the deified dead, returning from their abode across the sea at the appointed times of harvest and New Year to infuse life and energy into our world. It was the regular return of these divine guests which revitalised the spring, quickened the fecundity of the soil, and magically kept at bay the disasters which threaten during the stagnant winter months.

The evidence on which Origuchi reconstructs this picture of seasonal bringers of life-giving power is at first sight somewhat insubstantial. It is to start with entirely non-literary. No description of the benign guests exists in the ancient literature, and of the land whence they come only the most ambiguous references are to be found. For his proof of their existence Origuchi relies chiefly upon certain dramatic performances, dances, mimes, songs, which he claims to be survivals of ancient ritual impersonations of the visiting deities. In Japan itself these seasonal performances have all but vanished. Among the Ryūkyū islands, however, more convincing evidence may be found in the ritual dances and mimes still performed in a number of districts by men disguised to represent visiting gods.

In the Hachijōjima group of islands, for example, figures known as *mayanokami*, their faces hidden by masks or hats of leaves, make their appearance in boats at fixed seasons of the year. They are believed to be divinities from a land called Nirai which, like Tokoyo, lies far away beyond the horizon of the sea. They sing, dance, utter warnings, blessings and prophesies, and at length take their departure in their boats. In other islands the mysterious guests are known as *agama*. Often they appear in pairs, in the guise of an old man and an old woman. They too are disguised in masks, cloaks and hats, and they too dance, sing, admonish, bless and prophesy before taking their departure back to the land of Nirai.

In ancient Japan, Origuchi believes, ritual performances such as these, by men impersonating the divine guests, took place at stated seasons in many districts. What survive today, however, are vestigial remnants only. In the *okina* mask of the Nō plays, for example, in the beaming face of the old man who appears in the benedictory New Year play, we may well see the lineal descendant of the *marebito*, the Ancestor who returns on a brief visit from his long home. In the weird horned figures known as *namahage* too, covered with a coating of straw, which appear at New Year in the Akita and Aomori districts to call at people's houses to deliver blessings in return for refreshment of wine and fish, we may also see the remnant of an ancient visiting god. Their straw coat in particular recalls the travelling garb which the divinity naturally chose to wear for his journey from the distant land across the sea.

Until the Meiji period, furthermore, bands of strolling players used to make their appearance in many districts at the beginning of the year. These too would sing and dance, utter blessings, incantations and warnings. Unlike the Ryūkyū dancers, however, they were all of outcast status. They were accounted *hinin*, non-men, or *kawaramono*, dwellers on the dry river bed. They were not considered to be fully human. But this degraded status, Hori Ichirō contends, is in itself a telling argument in favour of a sacred origin. In ancient times these people impersonated deities. Their task set them apart from ordinary men, made them 'other' and remote, investing them with some of the perilously holy qualities of the beings they represented. In later centuries belief in these sacred beings waned, but the quality of otherness which first set their impersonators apart persisted. The numinous awe and horror which first surrounded the men who represented gods thus turned to revulsion and abhorrence. The players remained non-men, but on a level lower, not higher, than the ordinary villager.[5]

With this *marebito* theory, therefore, Origuchi gives us a picture of an other world across the sea which is at the same time a source of power. It is a place from which divine figures, at once deities and ancestors, bring to our world an infusion of life and strength. Does this picture conform any better than did the *Kojiki* myths with the other world with which the medium and the ascetic in Japan communicate?

In the conception of regular seasonal infusions of power, carried to the human community by divine figures from a source outside the human world, we see a pointer decidedly relevant to the other world we are seeking. The medium, we shall discover, summons both *kami* and ancestral spirits at regular seasons from their worlds, and conjures them to bestow just such an influx of life-giving power. But the direction from which the divine figures appear is not yet right. The medium summons neither *kami* nor ghosts from a land across the sea. Let us therefore look a little more closely at the position in space of Tokoyo, the land from which the *marebito* come.

We have seen Tokoyo to lie across the sea along a horizontal axis. Yet even as we descry it beyond the horizon it sinks down like Lyonesse beneath the waves. Tokoyo is thus spatially ambivalent. It lies both across the sea and beneath it. It is at the same time away and down under.[6] This underwater aspect of Tokoyo, though at first no more than one side of an innate ambivalence, soon refracts into an autonomous world of its own. With its own name and its own distinctive mythical structure, this water realm has come down to us in both folktale and legend as a powerful and persistent strand of Japanese other-world belief.

Can this downward and submarine direction help us in our search for the shaman's other world? Does the medium summon deities from water, or the ascetic travel to submarine lands?

The picture of a world of power beneath the water which has come down to us through oral tradition is a remarkably consistent one. The name Tokoyo, with its ambiguous overtones, soon gives place to the Chinese term Ryūgū, the palace of the dragon. In both folktale and legend, the elements which compose the mythical structure of this world appear with notable persistence, consistently related and juxtaposed. A woman, a snake, a dazzling underwater palace, a magical gift of power, an ugly and misshapen child—these elements are found constantly together and constantly associated with water.

Yanagita Kunio has classified a number of motifs under the folktale type he calls *ryūgū-iri*, visits to the dragon palace, but the purport of all of them is similar: an accidental visit by a man to the underwater elysium, his lavish welcome by the beautiful woman who presides there, the blissful interval of time he passes with her, and his final return to his own world bearing a gift of power which before long proves too perilous for human frailty. Tales of this type have been discovered over an unusually wide area of Japan, ranging from Kumamoto as far north as Iwate prefecture. An old woodcutter, to take an example from Kumamoto, unable to sell his bundle of firewood in the town, throws it instead into the sea, or into a mountain lake. At once there rises from the water a beautiful woman, who begs him, in return for his kind present, to pay her a visit in her underwater mansion. In these shimmering surroundings she presents him with a magical gift which, if he treats it in accordance with the simple instructions she gives him, will bestow upon him limitless wealth. The gift in this case takes the form of a hideous and misshapen child, who will, if a simple offering be made to him every day, execute all the desires of the old woodcutter's heart. Eventually, dazzled by his wealth, the old man fails to make the daily offering. His riches and the child vanish at once.[7]

A similar picture of fortuitous human communication with an underwater realm of wealth and bliss can be discerned in the field of folk legend. In the *wankashi densetsu* or bowl-lending legends, again widely scattered throughout Japan, the human visits to the bottom of the sea have ceased, but instead we have the motif of the treasures of the deep, in the form of a cup or chalice, temporarily lent to the human community.

According to these legends, certain pools, lakes, caves, ancient tumuli or tombs were thought to lead downwards to the miraculous underworld of Ryūgū. These entrances were guarded by a benevolent being—a snake in the watery places, a fox in the dry ones—who would obligingly lend cups, bowls and trays to anyone who wished to borrow them. In Hyōgo prefecture, for example, there used to be a celebrated bowl-lending pool. All one had to do was to go there the previous night, state the number of bowls one wished to borrow, and the next morning one would find them neatly set out on a rock in the middle of the pool. In the mountains near Toyama there was a bowl-lending lake where the service was even quicker. One stood on the shore and stated the number of bowls required, and immediately there would float to the surface of the water, and presently be washed ashore at one's feet, bowls of superior red lacquer exactly to the number ordered. In Yamanashi prefecture there was another such pool where the guardian required the order in writing. One wrote him a letter stating the number of bowls needed, and the next day they would be found neatly ranged on the edge of the pool.

Always, however, it was necessary to return the borrowed vessels as soon as one had finished with them, in perfect condition and exactly to the number lent. One bowl returned damaged or short, and the guardian would never again lend a single vessel. At the sites of these legends human frailty has invariably proved unequal to the gifts from the world below. Always, some time in the past, someone broke a cup or refused to return a bowl, so that the lending has always ceased. Yanagita tells us, indeed, that he several times came across a family who proudly preserved a bowl of costly red lacquer as a chalice from Ryūgū. It was of course a bowl which their ancestors had on one occasion borrowed, and failed to return to its rightful owner.

The watery entrances, the lakes and pools, were believed to lead downwards to the world of Ryūgū. Plunge deeply enough into the pool and you would find yourself standing before the magical palace with its jade pillars, its walls of fish scales and carpets of sealskin. The dry entrances, on the other hand, the caves and old tombs, were sometimes thought to lead to a hidden paradisal village known as Kakurezato. The vessels lent by the guardians of these places were believed to come from the hidden village, and had to be returned with the same care and precision as did the bowls from Ryūgū. They too were usually of superior red lacquer. It seems clear that the hidden village stands for no more than a waterless Ryūgū, a refuge devised by those who have no accessible lake or pool by which to reach the subterranean paradise in which they believe.[8]

In these legends, therefore, the communication with the

77

water world is a step less direct than in the folktales. No one is invited to visit the palace at the bottom of the lake. The magical gift has become a mere vessel, in which power was perhaps originally contained, but which now stands for no more than a useful receptacle. The gift, moreover, is no longer given, but lent for a short season only.

How much nearer to our goal have we been taken by this powerful tradition of a source of wealth and bliss in the depths of water? Is it from the bottom of lakes or the sea that the medium summons deities and the dead, and does the ascetic, like the old woodcutter, find himself in the course of his journey enticed into the magical underwater palace?

The answer we return must be no, though with reservations. There is much to be discovered in this underwater world which will haunt our researches in an enigmatic and tantalising way. Particularly we shall find ourselves dogged by the figure of the snake: the snake who is transformed into a woman, who becomes a woman, the snake who forcibly claims a woman as his bride, seizes and 'possesses' her, at times even kills her. We shall discover pointers relating this snake woman with our *miko*; indicating that the shamanistic cult of which she was the central figure was closely connected with this world of water, serpents and ugly but miraculous children. Such a cult has long since been overlaid, however, by other and stronger beliefs, so that in seeing in the snake woman a dim reminder of the ancient *miko* we are trying to revive a pattern of shamanistic practice which has long been lost.

We can see no connection, in any case, between this snake woman and the seasonal divine guests. There is no longer any traffic, let alone seasonal visits, from the water world to ours. The snake woman, though she may rise to the surface of her pool to thank the bestower of an accidental gift, and though she may in return reward him with lavish presents of power, does not bring these things at regular seasons into the human world. Rarely does she leave her water world to visit ours. Her treasures lie at the bottom of the sea, their discovery contingent on human accident or chance.[9]

If a downward and submarine direction has not revealed to us the other world of the shaman, what of the opposite quarter? Is an upward direction likely to take us any nearer to our goal?

Here at once we find helpful and pertinent guidance from Hori Ichirō. We are back with Tokoyo as it lies in its ancient position across the sea. But sometime during the late pre-historic period, Hori tells us, an important shift took place in the lives of the Japanese people. Both in their own dwelling-place and in their conception of the dwelling-place of deities, a transition occurred from sea to mountain. People who originally were shore-dwellers began to move inland. As they lost sight of the sea and found themselves surrounded instead by high hills, their imagination of the direction from which the life-giving power would irrupt into their world naturally altered. No longer could the divinities be expected to come from the sea. Inland, in their new abode, they beheld hills of strange and distinctive shape, high conical hills, low tree-covered hills, always rising suddenly from the flat land below as though breaking upwards into a different plane. What more natural, Hori argues, than that these people should have looked to the hills for their other world, imagined these hills to be the dwelling-place of the spiritual beings whose visits bestowed life and fecundity on the village.[10]

Here at last we arrive at a view of the other world which seems to be consistent with the one we are seeking: an other world in mountains. Here is the answer to our problem. It is from mountains that the medium summons both *kami* and the benign dead. It is likewise in mountains that the ascetic looks for the other world from which he can gain the powers he desires.

The belief that *kami* dwell in mountains can be traced back to prehistoric times. Archaeological finds of ritual tools have been discovered on sites at the foot of certain hills which unmistakably point to a cult of a deity dwelling on the summit. In several cases these objects when first discovered were supposed to be burial goods, and the sites where they were found to be graves. Ōba Iwao in several interesting studies has shown us that they were nothing of the kind. They are objects of the magically inviting shape believed to induce the *kami* to enter into them as a vehicle for his manifestation. They are early examples, that is to say, of what in an earlier chapter we saw to be *yorishiro*.

At a site near the foot of Akagisan, for example, there were discovered several stone replicas of swords, of round Chinese mirrors, and of the mysterious 'jewels', *tama*. These appeared in several stylised shapes, notably the *usudama* or mortar jewel, the *kudadama* or pipe jewel and the celebrated *magatama* or curved jewel. In all these objects we recognise shapes believed to embody the magical power of inducement, of cajoling the *kami* to descend from his own world and to manifest himself in ours. Objects of very similar nature were found in sites at the foot of Nantaizan, Miwasan and a number of other mountains long known to have been invested with holy qualities. In several cases the objects were discovered near a gigantic rock, or outcrop of rocks, which Ōba infers must have played a prominent part in the ritual. It probably served as an *iwakura* or stone altar-seat on which were displayed the objects into which the *kami* were enticed to enter.

The mountains themselves Ōba recognises as falling into two distinct categories. Some are high mountains, presenting the elegantly symmetrical form of a perfect cone. Isolated from surrounding ranges, they rise with spectacular suddenness out of virtually flat land. Akagisan, Nantaizan and of course Fujisan are examples of such hills. The other category of holy mountain, well exemplified by Miwasan near Nara, is lower and smaller, nearer to human habitation, and always thickly covered with trees. These hills too present the same symmetrically conical form. The quality which originally distinguished a mountain as holy, Ōba therefore infers, was not so much great height as an appearance conducive to the descent of the *kami*. The conical shape and pointed summit of the larger mountains, the thick covering of trees on the lower hills, both offer an inviting semblance of the *yorishiro* into which the *kami* is invited to descend.

The deity we must therefore imagine as dwelling at the top of the mountain, to which at some previous time, lured by the inviting shapes of the conical summit and the trees, he has descended from an even higher point in the sky. At certain seasons he responded to the ritual summons at the foot of the mountain to descend to the great stone altar-seat on which the stone shapes of swords, mirrors and jewels had been invitingly displayed. Scarcely ever, Ōba writes, would human beings at this period have been permitted to set foot on these mountains. They were holy ground, taboo and inviolable to human entry, the territory of the *kami* only. No man could have climbed their slope further than the ritual site at the foot.[11]

Though visible and potentially accessible to everyone, therefore, these hills represented the other world from which flowed the seasonal influx of power which former generations had believed to come from across the sea.

It was not only the *kami* who at this early date were imagined to dwell in mountains. The benign and hallowed dead were also conceived to travel to a destination in certain hills. For this belief in a world of the dead in mountains we have no evidence earlier than the seventh century. But for that period Hori has adduced interesting literary proof in the *banka* or elegies in the *Manyōshū*. This great anthology of poetry, though compiled as late as the eighth century, contains many songs of much earlier date. Hori has collected some 130 elegies, known to have been composed in the course of the seventh century, in which some indication is given as to the destination to which the poet believed the soul to have travelled. In the great majority of songs it is to higher ground, either among mountains or among the clouds in the sky, that the soul is stated to have 'hidden itself'. The poems which hint that the dead have gone either to islands in the sea or to a subterranean world, *meido* or *Yomi*, are decidedly fewer.

From this analysis Hori infers that the predominating idea of the destination of the dead was no longer across the sea or underneath the earth, but poised above the human world, in mountains or the sky.[12]

Concerning the destination of the dead, however, a further complexity must be considered before our picture of the other world is complete. This is the superimposition on to these ancient holy mountains of the Buddhist cosmos of heavens, hells and other realms to which sentient beings may be prescribed by their past karma to transmigrate.

With the introduction and spread of Buddhism the Japanese were given a far more complex cosmos than any they had previously imagined. A vast mountain formed the axial pillar of the universe; about it were disposed six different realms in which the dead, according to the merits of their past lives, might be reborn. Here for the first time, therefore, there appeared in the Japanese land of the dead the conception of what Dr Joseph Needham calls 'ethical polarization'. Hitherto all dead spirits, irrespective of the sanctity or wickedness of their lives, had congregated in the same realm. Now with the Buddhist doctrine of rebirth these realms had to multiply to accommodate people of different moral destinies: those whose past actions had propelled them into the hells, hot or cold, or the world of hungry ghosts, or the worlds of beasts or titans, or to any of the numerous paradises to be found far up the slopes of the mountain.

As it became popularly understood in Japan, however, this overwhelmingly vast universe was considerably simplified. Heavens and hells, the only destinations of the dead to assume real importance, were projected on to those very mountains which former generations had recognised to be the dwelling-place of *kami* or the dead.

The Kumano mountains, for example, with their ancient associations with an older other world and even more specifically with Tokoyo, became early in the Heian period associated with paradise. The Bodhisattva Kannon's paradise of Fudarakusan was to be found there, or alternatively, for those who followed the sutra which stated that this paradisal mountain lay on the south coast of India, it was to be reached *from* the Kumano mountains, across the sea by boat. Likewise the Buddha Amida's paradise was to be found among the Kumano mountains, and pilgrimage there would ensure entry into the Pure Land in one's next life. Hence the enormous popularity, particularly during the tenth and eleventh centuries, of the *mitake-mōde* or pilgrimage to these mountains. The Emperor Shirakawa is said to have performed it nine times, the Emperor Toba twenty-one and the Emperor Go-Shirakawa no less than thirty-four times. So overwhelming, indeed, grew the numbers of pilgrims that they were frequently compared with swarms of ants. We shall see in a later chapter how in the doctrine and practice of the Shugendō sect of ascetics these mountains still stand not only for paradise but also for the whole cycle of Six Realms through which a sentient being is liable to transmigrate, and that they are powerfully invested, both in name and symbol, with a journey through other worlds.[13]

Again, in medieval times, the high mountain Tateyama in Etchū, also with pre-Buddhist associations with the other world, became strongly associated with an entrance to hell. Several medieval collections of tales contain stories of this place. They relate how a priest, climbing the mountain or dwelling in ascetic seclusion on its slopes, met a girl who told him that she had emerged momentarily from the hell that lay inside. She recounted her torments there, and begged him to recite requiem sutra to shorten her time. Or again, travellers on the mountains heard cries from beneath the earth. They were the wails of the damned in the hell below.[14]

The northern mountain Osorezan likewise has early associations with a world of the dead. Here, however, it is not simply heaven or hell which has been projected on to the landscape but other realms too which in both Shinto and Buddhism are accounted destinations of the dead. Here can be found Sainokawara, the dry river bed where dead children are believed to go, Sanzunokawa, the river which divided the worlds of the living and the dead, a place labelled Gokurakuhama or the beach of paradise, another called Chikushōdō or the realm of beasts, as well as features such as the lake of blood and the mountain of swords which derive straight from the landscape of hell.

The dry river bed called Sainokawara, which like the river itself is felt to represent a boundary between worlds, may incidentally be discovered in many holy places throughout Japan. In the precincts of many Buddhist temples it may be seen just at the spot where the mountain leaps steeply upwards towards the inner shrine at the top. A dry white gash of stones in the middle of the forest, it clearly divides a higher and more holy zone from the ordinary world beneath. Over this white stony tract there usually hangs a red arched bridge, an exquisite and largely unrecognised symbol for the joining of two worlds which we shall meet again.

The conversion of these mountains to Buddhism involved not only a change of name and a multiplication of destinations for the dead: it brought also an important change in cult practice. Hitherto the holy mountain was probably inviolable to human entry, sacred ground on which no human foot could tread for fear of the *tatari* or curse of the deity presiding there. With the spread of Buddhism to the mountains this taboo disappears. The holy mountain may now be climbed, by those in a suitable state of ceremonial purity, and the ascent of it will help to confer upon the ascetic the power he seeks. In climbing the holy mountain he crosses the same barrier between worlds, achieves the same rupture of level, as he does on the rarer occasions when his soul, separated from his body, is taken on the magical flight through the cosmos.

These holy hills, then, will be the other world to which the ascetic will make his journey and from which the numina and ancestral ghosts will be summoned. They are the abode both of the *kami* and of the dead. But here again, as Ōbayashi Taryō reminds us, the ambivalence, the janus-faced quality of the other world still persists. These hills may be the destination of the dead, but they are at the same time a source of life. They are the home of the mountain god Yamanokami, without whose aid human birth may not be safely accomplished, and where this deity may be discovered, in the likeness of a woman, enduring the pangs of childbirth in the depths of the hills.[15]

5
Ascesis

One more question of a preliminary and general kind remains to be discussed. How does the shaman in Japan acquire his special power?

We shall find that two modes of entry into the sacred life are open to the medium and the ascetic in Japan. Either he is 'called', summoned by a deity in a dream or a possession to leave his old life and begin a new one, closer to the sacred world; or he may of his own volition, with no supernatural election or persuasion, decide that the life he has hitherto led is meaningless and insupportable, and that he must seek another kind of life for which new powers and gifts are needed. Whether the impulse comes from his own will, however, or from some apparently external spiritual being, whether he is what Hori calls the 'quest type' or the 'vocation type', he can only acquire the special powers he needs to bridge the gap between the two worlds by certain ascetic practices.

These measures are known in general as *gyō*. In so far as they are painful, exhausting or wearisomely repetitive, in so far as they remove both body and mind from their accustomed habits, in so far as they require very great strength of will to accomplish, they may properly be described as ascetic. The same practices are performed indiscriminately by both the medium and the ascetic. Whether it is the medium's power of trance or the ascetic's power of banishment and transformation that is desired, the same disciplines are invoked. They are the means of building up a store of power, which can then be channelled into the required direction. Continuous application to these disciplines is needed, moreover, if this store of power is to be maintained. Once let the shaman relax his ascetic effort and his power will dwindle, grow flabby and eventually disappear.

These disciplines can be broadly classified into three: fasting, cold water and the recitation of words of power.

Let us start with food and the abstention from food.

Dietary restrictions, the avoidance of certain foods believed to be antipathetic to the acquisition of power, have been recognised as a potent austerity since the earliest appearances of the ascetic in the eighth and ninth centuries. *Nikudachi* or abstention from meat, *shiodachi* or abstention from salt, *kokudachi* or abstention from the Five Cereals, *hidachi* or abstention from cooked food, all these are described in the tales and biographies of celebrated ascetics in the early medieval period. They are still essential prescriptions in the shaman's ascetic regime today. Faith in the efficacy of these abstentions, therefore, has persisted for more than a thousand years.

These dietary prohibitions derive an interesting variety of sources. Abstention from meat may be traced equally to the Buddhist or the Shinto tradition. Either the Buddhist revulsion at the taking of life or the Shinto abhorrence of the defiling nature of blood, particularly the blood of four-footed animals, may account for the conviction that the eating of meat is antipathetic to the holy life.

The abstention from cereals, on the other hand, can be traced to a Taoist source. The repulsion in which the holy man should hold the Five Cereals derives from the Taoist doctrine of the Three Worms. The human body was believed to harbour by nature three parasitical worms, whose activities would in due course shorten human life. The favourite food of these creatures was the Five Cereals. Abstain from all rice, wheat, millet, barley and beans, therefore, and the worms would be compelled by starvation to leave the body and find a home elsewhere, thus allowing the life of their host to be prolonged.[1]

Early medieval literature contains a number of peculiar tales of ascetics who acquired their notable powers by the abstention from cereals. Ryōsan, for example, retired into one of the fastnesses of Mt Kimpu, where he abstained from all cereals and salt and ate only leaves. Day and night for ten years he recited the Lotus Sutra in his mountain retreat, never once relaxing his diet. So holy and powerful did he become as a result of this discipline that the demons who had come expressly to disturb his practice were quickly overawed, and instead brought him offerings of fruit and berries. Likewise bears, foxes and snakes, fascinated by the holy recitation, brought him daily presents of food.[2]

The ascetic Yōshō went to even greater lengths of austere abstention. First he gave up all cereals and ate only greens. Then he gave up greens and ate only nuts and berries. Then he reduced his diet to a single grain of millet a day, after which he stopped eating altogether. He then vanished, but was later seen flying through the air like a unicorn or phoenix. All that was left of him was a hairy skeleton.[3]

These ancient practices are still observed today in widely separated districts of Japan. The blind mediums in the northern parts of the main island, ascetics from Kyūshū and Shikoku, Kyōto, Nara and Kumano, have all testified that the regime of ascesis which they underwent included periods of abstention from cereals, meat and salt. Mr Mizoguchi for example, an ascetic living near Mt Miwa, assured me in 1963 that for many days he had subsisted entirely on pine needles. These were unexpectedly nourishing, and conducive to the development of second sight and clairaudient hearing.

To fill the gap left by the abstention from cereals there arose the practice known as *mokujiki* or tree-eating. Give up rice, wheat, millet and barley and you substitute nuts, berries, bark or pine needles. The title Mokujiki Shōnin, Saint Tree-eater, has been applied to a number of ascetics since medieval times, its most celebrated bearer being the eighteenth-century carver of wooden images whose work, since its discovery in 1923 by Yanagi Sōetsu, has achieved wide acclaim. Mokujiki Shōnin died in 1810 at the age of ninety-three, having passed some fifty years of his life in continuous tree-eating. Thirty-eight of these years, moreover, were spent in constant travel on foot throughout Japan, in the course of which he left behind him at least a thousand carved wooden Buddhas. Many of these figures, with their characteristic archaic smile, have become prized collector's pieces.[4]

The practice of *mokujiki* acquired unusual notoriety during the last decade with the discovery, in the remote valley of Senninzawa in Yamagata prefecture, of several surviving examples of *sokushimbutsu* or self-mummified Buddhas. One of these bodies, that of Hommyōkai Shōnin enshrined in the Chūrenji temple, dates from the seventeenth century. That of Tetsumonkai, in the same temple, is of the nineteenth century, while that of Shinnyokai in the Dainichibō temple is of eighteenth century origin. Two more mummies can be found enshrined it the Shingon temple of Kaikōji in the nearby town of Sakata. One, Chūkai, dates from the eighteenth century, the other, Emmyōkai, from the early nineteenth century.

These brown and desiccated figures, gruesomely arrayed in the brilliant robes appropriate to a Buddhist abbot, cap on head, rosary in hand, are seated in their temple in the position customarily reserved for the Buddha image. This seat of of honour is accorded to them in recognition of the great power they have accumulated during their long and terrible period of the tree-eating austerity.

We cannot here expand in detail on this interesting and now extinct cult. Suffice to say that these men, all of whom were members of the ascetic order based on Mt Yudono, made a vow to perform the tree-eating austerity for the period of one thousand, two thousand or even three or four thousand days. During the first part of the discipline their diet consisted of nuts, bark, fruit, berries, grass and sometimes soy in fair abundance. The quantity of these things was then reduced, until by the end of their allotted period they had undergone a total fast of many days. Ideally, if the discipline were properly calculated, the man should die from starvation, upright in the lotus posture, on the last day of his avowed fast. His body should have been reduced to skin and bone, all flesh and visceral contents having long disappeared. He was then placed inside a wooden coffin, and buried underground in a stone sarcophagus for a period of three years. When exhumed at the end of this time he was found, if all had gone well, to have become a mummy. Such skin as remained on the body had not decomposed, but had desiccated into the brown, scaly substance familiar to us from the mummies of the Egyptian tombs. Unlike the Egyptian mummies, however, no chemical embalming agents of any kind were used in this process.

If by an unlucky chance the body had not completely

dried, it was then smoked by burning beneath it candles, incense and leaves. Chūkai and Emmyōkai, moreover, are said to have elected to enter their coffins while still alive. Hence, though supplied with a bamboo tube which gave them the means of breathing, they were in effect buried alive. When exhumed at the end of three years, however, they too were found to be mummified.

The appalling sufferings entailed by this austerity of self-mummification are well attested by the numbers of inscribed stones, scattered throughout the valley of Senninzawa, which mark the graves of men who died before their vow could be accomplished. Some of these inscriptions are illegibly weather-worn. On others, however, we read of Ishinkai, who died in 1831 before he could complete a two-thousand-day fast; of Tetsuzenkai who died in 1838, Ryūkai who died in 1840 and Zenkai who died in 1856 in the midst of a thousand-day fast. The motive which prompted these men, most of whom seem to have been peasants of local origin, to embark on so fearful an austerity, was apparently the disinterested desire to turn the power they had accumulated through their disciplines to the benefit of mankind after their death. The torments they had undergone would endue them with power such that prayers addressed to their mummy were sure to be efficacious.

It was alleged too, however, that such people did not suffer death. What appeared to be death is in fact the state of suspended animation known as *nyūjō*, in which condition the soul may await the coming, millions of years hence, of the Future Buddha Maitreya.

The most recent mummy is that of Tetsuryūkai, enshrined in the temple of Nangakuji in Tsuruoka. He embarked on a three-thousand-day period of tree-eating towards the middle of the nineteenth century, but before his time was up, in the year 1868, he fell sick and died, lamenting to the last his inability to fulfil his vow.

Legend has it, however, that he announced before dying that he had determined, despite his premature death, to achieve mummification, and that after the necessary period had elapsed his friends must dig his body up. The new Penal Code, however, introduced in the early Meiji period, made it a criminal act to exhume a corpse. Tetsuryūkai therefore appeared to several people in dreams, begging to be dug up despite the legal prohibitions. At least on a stormy night two men from the temple secretly exhumed the body, to find to their chagrin that it was only partially dried. The insides of the corpse were therefore taken out, and the body stuffed with lime. To this day the body shows clearly the marks where the cuts have been sewn up, and is still stuffed with lime, the only mummy in the area which owes its preservation to chemical agents.

The cult of mummies was only brought to the notice of ethnologists in 1960, when a delegation of professors from Tokyo travelled north to examine the relics. Two of the bodies they were permitted to take to a laboratory in Tokyo to be cleaned, X-rayed and examined. Other mummies they discovered to be infested with rats' nests and moth, and these too they cleaned and set to rights. All are now back in their former positions in the temples, still the object of veneration in the district on account of the power which accrued to them as a result of their fearful regime of starvation.[5]

Before we leave the subject of dietary restrictions, a word must be added on the practice of total fasting. The total fast, *danjiki*, of a stated number of days is understandably less practised than the abstention from particular foods. It is nevertheless exceedingly productive of power. A notable example of such a fast is included by the ascetic branch of the Tendai sect of Buddhism in the regime of austerities necessary to qualify a man for the title of Ajari. The Ajari Enami Kakushō, the incumbent at the time of writing of the Mudōji temple on Mt Hiei, described to me in 1961 the nine-day fast he had undergone in the course of the ascetic exercise known as *kaihōgyō*. For nine days he had performed without a break, in an enclosed and sealed hall, a continuous series of *goma* fire ceremonies. Not once had he descended from the *goma* platform and not once had food or drink passed his lips. He showed me the photographs of his ceremonial emergence from the hall at the end of the nine days. Emaciated, pale, so physically weak that he had to be supported on either side by stalwart assistants, he was

yet so imbued with sacred power that the crowds which lined
the path prostrated themselves in reverence on the ground
as he passed by.[6]

So much then for the austerities of fasting and abstention.

The next category of ascesis which is considered indispensable to the acquisition of power is cold water. To stand
under a waterfall, preferably between the hours of two and
three in the morning and preferably during the period of
the Great Cold in midwinter, is believed to be an infallible
method of gaining power. If no waterfall is conveniently
to hand, the practice of *mizugori*, by which wooden buckets
of cold water are tipped over the head and body at stated
intervals of time, is considered almost as efficacious. We
shall meet in the following chapters several examples of cold
water regimes which reach a pitch of severity scarcely
credible. The blind girl in the north, on the brink of her
initiation into mediumship, must pour over her head every
day for a week no less than a thousand buckets of icily cold
water. The young men who aspire to become ascetics of the
Nichiren sect of Buddhism are required to undergo a bout
of *mizugori* seven times a day every day for a hundred
winter days.

Suigyō or the water austerity appears less frequently in the
medieval accounts of ascetics than do feats of fasting and
abstention. It is clear, however, that the Nachi waterfall at
Kumano was even at that time considered a powerful means
of accumulating power. This celebrated waterfall is now,
especially after heavy rain, of such weight and force that to
stand beneath it is a scarcely credible feat. The *Heike
Monogatari* tells us, however, that Mongaku Shōnin vowed
to remain up to his neck in the icy pool beneath the torrent
for thirty-seven days. Before a week was out, however, he
lost consciousness and was washed downstream. At once
from the top of the waterfall two divine boys descended and
revived him by rubbing him all over with their warm and
scented hands. Thus strengthened, Mongaku completed his
vow of thirty-seven days without difficulty. Even discounting
the legendary accretions in this story, we may gather that
the *Nachi-gomori* or ascetic seclusion at Nachi was a frequent
ascetic practice in the twelfth century.[7]

Both the fasting and the cold water exercises were originally conceived as cathartic in intention. They were means of
cleansing, of removing hindrances to the holy state. By
avoiding foods thought to be antipathetic to sacred power,
the ascetic removed obstacles likely to impede his approach
to the sacred beings and participation in their state. By
subjecting himself to long bouts of cold water, he likewise
rid himself of the defilements repugnant to the *kami* and
which thus hindered him from approaching them.

Today, however, the ascetic credits these practices with a
more positive efficacy than is implied in a mere removal of
hindrances. Clarity and concentration of mind are the
virtues frequently cited as resulting from both fasting and
cold water. It is true that, as several ascetics pointed out to
me, these practices often weaken the ordinary physical
strength. I have heard more than one confession that the
midwinter waterfall brought on an attack of pneumonia,
and that the digestive system was not only 'purified' but
disorganised, if not shattered, by the long abstentions and
fasts. But ordinary physical strength is of a different order
from *reiryoku*, sacred power, which cannot be acquired
without hazards. Miss Kataoka, whom I met in 1959 undergoing a solitary period of *gyō* in the Hongū shrine at Kumano,
told me that the week of total fasting to which she regularly
subjected herself every spring and autumn left her always
with an unparalleled clarity of mind and clairvoyance of
vision. Likewise the water austerity which she performed
every Great Cold—ten three-gallon tubs of icy water
poured over her head and shoulders three times a day—no
longer felt in the least cold to her. It rather promoted an
unrivalled concentration of mind, *seishin-ittō*, which formed
the very basis of her ascetic power.

A further positive efficacy of a subtle and little-recognised
kind can also be attributed to the cold water exercise. In
the following chapters we shall meet again and again an
overwhelming emphasis on the endurance of cold. Cold
water, cold food, unheated rooms, the deliberate choice of
the coldest part of winter in which to undertake any crucial
bout of ascesis—such are the stories which every ascetic has
to tell. Always he or she adds, however, that after a little

experience in these austerities they experienced no sensation of cold whatsoever. On the contrary, they emerged from under the waterfall, or from an early morning bout of *mizugori*, glowing with warmth.

Cold thus becomes, paradoxically, a means of rousing heat. By enduring cold the shaman in Japan is able to activate in himself that magical heat which with the shaman in so many parts of the world is the proof that he has risen above the ordinary human condition. By demonstrating that he is in the grip of this interior heat, the shaman shows that he is possessed of power, particularly of that power which Eliade singles out as distinctively shamanic in character, mastery of fire. When suffused by this mysterious heat, the shaman is impervious both to external heat and cold. He is capable alike of standing under a midwinter waterfall and of walking over burning embers, and emerging untouched. We shall meet in the following chapters many indications—symbols in both iconography and legend, remnants of rituals—which lead to the inference that in the past this ecstatic interior heat was a condition to which both the medium and the ascetic in Japan aspired for the practice of their powers. Today the quest for such a state seems to be less avowed. But we shall not be far wrong if we see in the feat of standing beneath the icy waterfall the same demonstration of power that the Manchu shaman shows when he dives beneath the ice, or the Tibetan ascetic monk when he dries wet sheets on his burning body in the snow.[8]

We pass now to the third and final category of ascetic practice in Japan, the recitation of words of power. Here the ascetic's world draws strongly on the magic of esoteric Buddhism.

Certain sounds are considered to carry power of a twofold kind. They embody first the magical power of spells in that their utterance can bring about a desired effect in the world. They will cure sickness, overcome demons, vanquish enemies, cause rain to fall and children to be conceived.

But also, if recited for long periods under the ascetic and purifying conditions of fasting and cold water, these same sounds can create power in the man who recites them. It follows, therefore, that they can only be recited effectively for their magical purpose by one who has first recited them in their ascetic usage.

The sounds which are believed in Japan to carry such power can be broadly classified into three types.

First there are words which are powerful because of their meaning. Power is conferred upon them because of the sense that they convey. Prominent among the words of power in this category is the *Kanzeon Bosatsu Fumombon*, the celebrated passage in the twenty-fourth chapter of the Lotus Sutra in which it is stated that a man only has to think of the Bodhisattva Kannon to be saved from every conceivable calamity. A man hurled into a fiery pit has but to think of Kannon for the fire to be quenched. A man floundering in an ocean of sea monsters has but to think of Kannon and he will neither sink nor drown. A man bombarded with thunderbolts has but to think of Kannon and not a hair of his head will be hurt. A man beset by goblins, demons, ghosts, giants, wild beasts or fearful fiery serpents has but to think of Kannon for these creatures to vanish.

This comparatively short passage is all that is left in popular ascetic practice of the Lotus Sutra, the *Saddharma Pundarīka* which in medieval times held so supremely important a place among holy and powerful texts. From the *Konjaku Manogatari* alone we can gather the unrivalled estimation in which this sutra was held in the twelfth century. Tale after tale is told of the ascetics known as *jikyōsha*, who through the power of the holy text which for years they devotedly 'held', recited and copied, saw into their past lives, reversed the effects of evil karma, fascinated wild beasts and demons, cured sickness and possession. Today, however, aside from the ascetics of the Nichiren sect, whose particularly severe ascetic regime we will describe later and whose entire stock of words of power comes from the Lotus Sutra, the *Kanzeon Bosatsu Fumombon* is all that remains in common ascetic usage of this powerful text.[9]

Here the power of the words clearly derives from their meaning, from the comprehensible statement that the Bodhisattva will rescue from every imaginable horror the person who takes the trouble to recite the sutra.

Very different is our second category of empowered

words. Here power resides in a succession of syllables from which all meaning has long been lost. These are the *shingon* or mantras of esoteric Buddhism, and the longer *dhāranī*. In their original Sanscrit these sounds carried meaning. By the time they reached Japan in the eighth and ninth centuries the original Sanscrit sounds were distorted beyond recognition. They are now incomprehensible to all save the rare scholar of Buddhist Sanscrit who cares to trace the sounds back to their original source.

Into this category of words of power fall the mantras of the various Buddhist divinities, devas, Bodhisattvas, wheel-bodies of the Buddha and Buddhas themselves. Each of these divinities, according to the doctrine of the Shingon and Tendai sects of esoteric Buddhism, carries his own mantra, his essence and nature as expressed in sound. When recited under conditions of ascesis these sounds confer power on the reciter, identify him on the level of sound with the divinity.

Thus in the twice-nightly rituals of the Haguro sect of mountain ascetics, a litany of eighteen mantras is prescribed, the recitation of which confers power upon the gathering of neophytes. Eighteen Buddhist divinities are thus invoked in sound form: Dainichi or Vairochana, for example, whose mantra is *abira unken bazara datoban*, Amida whose sounds are *on amiritateizei karaun*, Sambō Daikōjin whose potent mantra is *on kembaya kembaya sowaka*, and Fudō Myōō himself who is represented by a spell similar to that which we saw the Saint of Yokawa use in the Nō play:

> *Nama sammanda basaranan*
> *Senda makaroshana*
> *Sowataya untarata kamman.*

No meaning can be extracted from these syllables. Their magic lies elsewhere than in their sense.

In this same category of 'meaningless' words of power must be classed the spell most widely and frequently used today by ascetics of all sects, the *Hannya Shingyō* or Heart Sutra. This short, easily memorised scripture expresses the essence, it is said, of the extensive Prajnaparamita literature which forms so important a branch of the Mahayana

95

Buddhist canon. Its content is recondite, profound, not for the ignorant. Form and emptiness are the same, it declares. Whatever is emptiness is form; whatever is form is emptiness. In emptiness there is no feeling, consciousness, sound, smell or taste. In emptiness there is neither ignorance nor extinction of ignorance, neither death nor the extinction of death. The bodhisattva, dwelling without thought in this emptiness, at length enters Nirvana, and the Buddhas of the Three Worlds awake to the uttermost enlightenment.[10]

So far the choice of this sutra, not only as a vehicle of power but also as a spell productive of worldly benefits, seems a paradoxical one. Towards the end of the sutra, however, the reason for its popularity becomes clearer. The Prajnaparamita, it declares, is the great spell, the utmost spell, the unequalled spell which will allay all suffering. The magic syllables are then recited: *Gyate gyate haragyate harasogyate bochi sowaka Hannya Shingyō*. To the Japanese reciter these sounds are as meaningless as the mantras. It is only when we turn back to the original Sanscrit that we discover that their sense is: 'Gone, gone, gone beyond, gone altogether beyond, what an awakening, hail.'

These potent syllables can be heard gasped and spluttered under waterfalls, shouted from the tops of mountains, chanted for long hours through the watches of the night, droned in forests before images of Fudō, gabbled at breakneck speed until trance intervenes. The sutra is indispensable to the ascetic affiliated to either sect of esoteric Buddhism, to either sect of Zen, to any branch of the mountain order known as Shugendō. Of all sutras and spells it is acknowledged to possess unrivalled *arigatami*, virtue and power.

Lastly in this category must be mentioned the *dhāranī*. These, like the mantras, are successions of syllables deriving originally from the Sanscrit but whose meaning has long been obliterated. They tend to be longer than the mantras, but like them dedicated to a particular Buddhist divinity.

The cult of the *dhāranī* or *ju* appeared in Japan as early as the eighth century, the early prototype of the ascetic, the *ubasoku*, deriving his holy power from the constant repetition of a particular *dhāranī*. En-no-Gyōja, later hailed as the presiding genius of all ascetics, is said in the later

Plate 7. A blind *itako* at Osorezan, 1959. She delivers a message from the dead husband of one of her audience, rubbing her rosary in time to the chant.

Plate 8. The medium's rosary, *irataka-juzu*, at Osorezan, 1959, with pendant loops of the bones, claws and horns of male and female animals.

Above, Plate 9. The central image of Zaō Gongen in the Zaōdō temple, Yoshino. *Photograph courtesy of Joan Martin.*

Right, Plate 10. Eleven-faced Kannon by Enkū, the ascetic peripatetic carver of Buddhist images.

accounts of his life to have gained his strange powers from the recitation of the *Kujaku Myōōju* or Peacock Dhāranī. Mongaku Shōnin relied on the *Jikunoju*, one of the *dhāranī* of Fudō Myōō, to enable him to pass his thirty-seven days under the Nachi waterfall. Nichizō Shōnin is said to have been rescued from a river full of huge snakes by a black shiny figure with long red hair who was an emanation of the *Senju Darani*, the spell of the Thousand-handed Kannon.[11]

As a final category of words of power we may mention the *hōgō* or names of divinities. The mere invocation of the divinity's name, several times repeated, is held to be power-giving. Thus in the nightly rituals performed during the autumn retreat of the Haguro sect of ascetics, the names of fourteen deities are recited at speed, three times each. Here are invoked in the same breath a motley and miscellaneous host: deities of the three holy mountains of Dewa, the deified founder of the order, local emanations of the Bodhisattva Jizō and of Fudō Myōō. The mere calling of their names—Hagurosan Daigongen, Gassan Daigongen, Yudonosan Daigongen, Arasawa Emmei Jizō Daibosatsu—is held to be productive of power.

One further point remains with regard to words of power. The traditional Buddhist view of the mantra or *dhāranī* is that power resides in the sound itself, irrespective of whom it may be who recites it. If the sounds are correctly made according to the rules, the stir made by their utterance will bring about the desired result. The very word *dhāranī* derives from a root meaning 'to hold'. The words are therefore holders or vessels of power, knowledge revealed originally to mankind by the Buddha in a state of deeply absorbed trance.

As they are recited in Japan, however, these Buddhist words of power are not in themselves sufficient. Recited by a person inexperienced in ascesis, ordinary and unempowered, their efficacy will be diminished, if not nullified. To release the latent power within the words they must be recited by a person practised in the fasting and cold water austerities. This feature appears in Japan in the earliest records of ascetic practice. En-no-Gyōja's recitation of the Peacock Spell, for example, was activated by *shū*, ascetic practice.

The holy text is thus not truly powerful unless combined with ascesis.[12]

Techniques of breathing, it will be noticed, have found no place in this catalogue of power-giving practices. That devices of breath control, so important a part of Indian spiritual practice and of Taoist discipline towards the attainment of the transubstantiated body of the Immortal, should be almost entirely absent from the ascetic tradition of Japan is difficult to explain. The *Nihon Ryōiki* tells us that every evening En-no-Gyōja would practice the *yang-sheng* or Taoist vitalising breath in a garden of flowers.[13] But this is merely one of the several details in which the life of En-no-Gyōja, in the semi-legendary accounts which have come down to us, does not stand for the prototype of the ascetic in Japan. It is odd that although the Taoist abstention from the Five Cereals has become an accepted part of the Japanese ascetic regime, its important techniques of breathing are conspicuously absent.

There remain two more subsidiary ascetic disciplines to be described, both of ancient origin and both still practised today. At first glance they seem oddly contradictory.

The first is known as *komori*, and means seclusion, preferably in the darkness of a cave, in a temple or shrine or in a room of one's own house specially prepared and purified. The second consists of a continuous walking pilgrimage from one sacred place to another, usually along a route which describes a circle.

The power-giving qualities of seclusion in darkness have been interestingly explained by Origuchi Shinobu. Sacred power is often manifested in Japan, he writes, inside a sealed vessel. In the darkness of this vessel it gestates and grows, until eventually it bursts its covering and emerges into the world. This principle is well illustrated in myth and folktale. A supernatural child appears out of a fruit or plant, as Momotarō emerges from a peach or Kaguyahime from a segment of bamboo. The small deity Sukunabikona is said in the *Kojiki* to have appeared from a gourd. This quality of containing a supernatural principle is known as *utsubo*. Thus the gourd is an *utsubo* vessel and so is the fruit. Nor is the stone the solid impenetrable substance that its appearance suggests. It too is an *utsubo* vessel, for it surrounds and contains a sacred force which grows. Here, incidentally, lies the explanation of the strange idea of growing stones. Stones grow over the years, from pebbles to rocks, because the supernatural principle inside them swells. May your reign, runs the poem addressed to the Emperor which is now the Japanese national anthem, last for thousands of years until pebbles have become moss-covered rocks.[14]

Before sacred power, as manifested in a being from the other world, can burst its skin and appear in our world, it must pass a period of gestation in the darkness of a sealed vessel. Likewise the ascetic who wishes to acquire sacred power undergoes a period of gestation in the nearest he can find to an *utsubo* vessel, a cave or darkened room. In this womb-like stillness he undergoes his fasts and recites his words of power, emerging only to stand beneath his waterfall.

Medieval lives of the ascetics make frequent mention of sojourns in caves. En-no-Gyōja becomes once more the prototype of the ascetic when he leaves his garden to recite the Peacock Spell and eat pine needles in a cave. Dōken Shōnin before his ecstatic journey to the Six Realms, to be described later, spent long months fasting in the Shōnoiwaya cave on Mt Kimpu.[15]

These ancient practices are still continued today. Near many waterfalls on holy mountains will be found a *komoridō* or seclusion hut, windowless, where the ascetic may dwell between his periods under the torrent. In many shrines and temples associated with the ascetic tradition, men and women can be found undergoing *komori* in a darkened room. The ascetic may also seclude himself in his own house, with the separate fire so necessary to the purity of his diet, emerging only to perform the water austerity at stated times.

Complementary to the still seclusion of the cave is the continuous journey on foot to a prescribed series of holy places. At each of these spots the ascetic pauses to offer recitations of appropriate words of power. Three *Hannya Shingyōs*, for example, may be the requirement, or even seventy-five; ten Fudō mantras or a hundred invocations to the deity presiding over the particular spot. At each of the holy places on his route, therefore, he both gives and receives power.

The route followed by ascetics both ancient and modern may consist of an apparently haphazard journey from one sacred mountain to another. The *Hokke Genki*, written about 1043, contains many accounts of such travellers. Shamon Giei, for example, travelled round 'many mountains' in search of the Buddha's law, Kumano, Omine, Kimpu and countless others. Kairen Hōshi climbed Tateyama and Hakusan, and visited many holy places performing severe austerities the while. Chōen Hōshi attained miraculous powers from the austerities he performed while journeying through the mountains of Katsuragi, Ōmine and Kumano. Isshuku Shamon Gyōkū went to even greater lengths of peripatetic austerity, making it his rule of life never to stay more than one night in the same place. In consequence 'there was not one of the sixty provinces which he did not see'. The *Heike Monogatari* tells us that Mongaku Shōnin, having completed his thousand days of seclusion at Nachi, set out on a long journey which took him three times up Mt Ōmine, twice up Mt Katsuragi, and thereafter to the holy mountains of Kōya, Kogawa, Kimpusen, Hakusan, Tateyama, Fuji, Izu, Hakone, Togakushiyama and Hagurosan.[16]

That the climbing of as many holy mountains as possible, fulfilling the while the ascetic requirements of abstention and cold water, brought the practitioner an immediate reputation for power, is well attested by a passage in Sei Shōnagon's *Pillow Book*, written about the end of the tenth century. No sooner does the word go round that you have climbed this or that mountain, she remarks, than you never get a moment's peace. All day and night messengers come rushing for you begging you to come at once to houses where there are sick people whom only your spells can cure. But when, from sheer exhaustion, your voice begins to weaken and flag, no one has the slightest sympathy for you. You are simply upbraided for incompetence.[17]

Sometimes the route followed by the ascetic is not a haphazard one from one mountain to another but describes a circle round one particular mountain. In the *kaihogyō* exercise of the ascetic branch of the Tendai sect, the disciple follows a circular route 'round the peak' of Mt Hiei. At Iwayayama to the north of Kyoto the ascetic may circumambulate the mountain, pausing at thirty-three places on the way to recite invocations to Fudō, Kannon or Amida. At Inariyama at Fushimi a similar circumambulation may be made round the holy peak. On a larger scale the prescribed circle may cover hundreds of miles. The route through the Eighty-eight Places sacred to Kannon, much tramped by ascetic pilgrims, circumscribes the entire island of Shikoku.

Holy wanderers have appeared continuously in Japan since early medieval times. We have already mentioned Mokujiki Shōnin, who in the late eighteenth century spent thirty-eight years of his life wandering through most of the provinces of Japan, leaving behind him as he walked a trail of carved wooden Buddhas. Other similarly gifted holy travellers have left their mark. Enkū, for example, a century earlier walked over most of the main island of Japan and climbed many of its holy mountains. He too left behind him a trail of wooden Buddhas to mark his route. Nor should we forget the poet Bashō, whose accounts of his journeys in the seventeenth century are full of the *haiku* poems evoked by the beauty and holiness of the scenery through which he passed.[18]

These long wandering journeys are sometimes felt to be commanded by spirits or numina. Mrs Kawaii, whom I met in the course of the autumn retreat of the Haguro *yamabushi* in 1967, had left her home in Kyūshū at the single ghostly command, *Gassan e ike!* Go to Gassan, she had been ordered, the mountain lying next to Mt Haguro in the Dewa range of three. Since receiving this peremptory behest she had no home of her own, but had spent her life wandering alone from place to place and mountain to mountain, with the mortuary tablets of her dead husband and six dead children tied in a bag round her neck. Everywhere she travelled she was conscious of overshadowing spiritual guidance. Spiritual beings commanded her to go to a certain mountain or shrine, and saw to it that she had exactly the right sum of money for her journey. The money would arrive from an unexpected source, and she would find at the end of her journey that it had been exactly enough for her needs.

Many of these directions came to her through dreams, and she was not always sure whether it was a *kami* or a dead ancestor who was guiding her. Usually, however, the commands came from ancestors some of whom had scattered to widely dispersed mountains throughout Japan. Halfway through the retreat I begged her to tell me her life story in more detail, but she was reluctant. Her spiritual guides, she declared, had forbidden her to speak of her experiences. Skilful persuasion, however, induced her to consult them on this point once more. Turning to face the wall, she fell at once into the semi-possessed condition in which she was able to hold a colloquy with the spiritual being inside her. After uttering a few sharp cries, she was heard to say peremptorily, '*Dame dame*'. No, certainly not, were the words clearly proceeding from the spirit inside her. Then in a softer and more submissive voice, her own reply to the being within her, she said, '*Hai hai.*' Three times this performance was repeated. Three times the spirit forbade her to speak, three times she acknowledged its command. When she recovered from the trance she refused, with profuse apologies, to divulge anything more of her life.

Womb-like seclusion inside a cave in the depths of the mountains, continuous wandering from one holy place to another—these are the two principal forms in which we shall find the early ascetic practising his fasts and cold ablutions and reciting his holy text. We shall find too that these two methods of stillness and movement are still to be found among shaman figures in Japan today.

A final word is perhaps necessary on the efficacy of these practices. Apparently it is no mere fantasy or blind belief in traditional practice that produces the conviction that austerities lead to the acquisition of power. Both mediums and ascetics testify that it was just when they felt that cold, hunger and sleeplessness had brought them to the verge of collapse that they suddenly felt themselves flooded with a new and mysterious strength. With this access of power they felt themselves to be different people from those they had been in the past, possessed of new life and in touch with another plane of being, subject to spiritual guidance and protection. The source of such guidance, the shaman's guardian deity, his nature and mode of communication with the shaman, must be reserved for discussion in a later chapter. Suffice to say here that it is the overshadowing presence of this supernatural being which ultimately enables the shaman to derive power from these austere practices.

6
The Ancient Sibyl

The oldest shamanic figure of which we have any record is the Shinto *miko*. This powerful sacral woman—the term 'female shaman' conveys only feebly the probable majesty of her presence—served in shrines throughout the land in the late prehistoric period as the mouthpiece for numina of certain kinds. She was to be found in the Emperor's court, transmitting the admonitions and instructions of deities to the Emperor himself, as well as in villages remote from the central Yamato plain where she acted as the link between the local tutelary *kami* and the villagers under his care.

Reliable evidence of her cult is not abundant. We shall here try to reconstruct her probable appearance, the ritual by which she became the intermediary for spirits, and the kind of numina whose utterances she may have transmitted.

First, is anything known of her dress and panoply of magical instruments? Valuable information is afforded by the *haniwa* pottery figures found in the great tombs of the fifth and sixth centuries. These funerary objects of low-baked reddish clay range from simple urns and tubes to astonishingly vivid representations of houses, boats, horses, warriors in armour and women decked with crowns and bells. They were not, as were the Chinese grave figures, buried with the coffin. Apparently they stood in rows and phalanxes on the slope of the tumulus, probably forming a 'spirit fence' intended to guard the tomb against spiritual enemies from without as well as to contain the denizen of the tomb within.

Among the human *haniwa* figures so far excavated several have been confidently identified as 'female shamans'. One, discovered in Okawamura, Gumma prefecture, wears on her head a peculiar flat head-dress, like an oblong board. She sits bolt upright, her hands outstretched before her, an expression on her face of remarkable intentness and serenity, as though she were waiting and listening. Round her neck, ankles and wrists are tight double strings of round beads, while from the sash round her waist hangs an unmistakable representation of a round metal mirror ornamented at the rim with five small bells.

A second figure, also from Gumma prefecture, wears the same board-like head-dress and is likewise decked with what must be a ritual attire of jewels. Ear-rings dangle from her ears, and round her neck is a tight string of the mysterious comma-shaped jewels, *magatama*, so ubiquitous and so magically powerful in ancient Japan. Across her right shoulder she wears a broad sash decorated with a pattern of triangles. Her right hand resting on her cheek, her left outstretched, she would appear to be caught in the midst of a ritual dance. Her face too wears an expression of extraordinary concentration and peace.

Another figure assumed to be a female shaman, from Unemezaka in Kamakura, also wears the diagonal sash and a magnificent string of *magatama* beads round her neck. Though her arms and head-dress—in all probability the flat board—have been broken off, the expression on her face is remarkable for its solemn dignity.[1]

Further useful information about the appearance of the ancient *miko* may be gleaned from passages in the early chronicles. The memorable passage in Chapter 14 of the *Kojiki* which describes the fury of the goddess Amaterasu gives us a picture, Saigō Nobutsuna believes, not of the goddess herself, but of a medium possessed by the divinity. Hence when we read that the goddess tied her hair in bunches with a vine, wound round her arms and in her hair long strings of *magatama* beads, that she carried on her back and on her chest quivers full of arrows, that she brandished a bow, and that in her rage she shouted, stamped and kicked the earth, we are in fact seeing a medium 'seized' by the goddess and in the throes of a divine possession. We hence infer that the costume of the *miko* might include not only the flat hat, the jewels, the sash and the mirror with bells to be seen on the *haniwa* figures, but also a bow, quivers of arrows and strings of the mysterious beads twined about her arms and hair.[2]

There is a certain amount about this panoply to remind us of the costume worn by the Siberian shaman, each item of which is imbued with powerful and transforming symbolism.

First, the mirror with bells. We know that the copper mirror was an important item in the costume of the Tungusic shaman in northern Manchuria. It was a receptacle for a spirit, a vessel in which the shaman could see a dead man's soul. In ancient Japan too a mirror was a vessel for a spirit, one of the oldest *goshintai* or vehicles in which the *kami* could be induced to dwell. The mirror with bells is less commonly found, but Torii Ryūzō has no difficulty in finding a continental origin for its use in the *miko's* 'sacred wardrobe'. The north-east Asian shaman, he writes, wears a mirror with bells suspended from his waist, which gives off as he dances mysterious flashes and jingles. The Korean shaman too wears several such mirrors about her waist which likewise, as she dances in her possessed state, import into her performance a mystical effect of light and sound. Its presence round the *miko's* waist may have had a more specific intention: as she danced and stamped the clashing bells and glittering metal served to lure the *kami* to draw near and to enter into her body.[3]

The strings of *magatama* beads twined round the *miko's* neck and arms and in her hair are more difficult to trace to a north Asian origin. Their only continental appearance is in Korea. In Japan their ubiquitous presence in prehistoric sacred sites proclaims them to be also magical tools for attracting a divinity and sheltering him once he arrives. Used by a medium engaged in ritual summons and intercourse with spirits, these beads would act, like the mirror, as a powerful spirit-lure.[4]

The bow and arrows which the medium for the sun goddess wore about her person are likewise to be found in the panoply of the continental shaman. There the bow is not so much a weapon as an instrument of magical sound, a one-string zither which when twanged emits a resonance which reaches into the world of spirits, enabling the shaman who manipulates it to communicate with that world. For the *miko*, from ancient times until the present day, the bow has likewise been an instrument whose sound magically compels spirits to draw near. We have already seen how the sibyl Teruhi's catalpa bow successfully cajoled the presence of a malicious spirit. We shall also see in a later chapter that a similar bow is still used by the blind mediums of the north when they summon ghosts and *kami*.

For the ancient *miko*, however, it is likely that the bow had a further function. It was a *torimono*, an object which she 'held in her hand' as she danced, and which acted as a conductor along which the deity could make his entry into her body. To this day the bow, together with the sword, spear, bamboo wand and branch, numbers among the nine varieties of *torimono* which the *kagura* dancer may hold in her hand during a performance. We may recall in passing that the mad woman in the Nō plays usually carries in her hand a branch or wand of bamboo fronds. Now a stylised token of an abnormal mental condition, its presence in her hand still recalls its original function of inducing a state of divine and inspired madness.[5]

The arrow too in ritual situations on the Asian continent is less a weapon than an instrument which magically joins two worlds. Shot into the air, it will apprise a deity that a rite is about to take place. In considering the quivers of arrows which the medium still carried on her back in the course of her transport, therefore, we may recall that in Japan too the arrow had a similar function. At the beginning of the fire ritual known as *saitō-goma*, still practised by the mountain ascetics called *yamabushi*, an arrow shot in each of the five directions is the means of informing the Five Bright Kings who preside over the order that the rite is about to begin. The *miko's* arrows may have been put to similar use, to summon the *kami* and warn him that his descent is required.

Lastly, the *miko's* peculiar board-like hat. No similar head-dress has been discovered on the Asian continent, nor does anything resembling it survive in the costume of the *kagura* dancer in historical times. It is possible that such a hat may have had a function similar to that of the shaman's cap. In these magic caps, some of which resemble turbans covered with ribbons, some iron helmets with reindeer horns, some crowns decked with owl and eagle feathers, much of the shaman's power lay hidden. With his head thus covered he becomes an empowered person. The *miko's* flat board, however, is an unlikely shape for inducing the *kami's* presence and its function remains far from clear.[6]

Most of the *miko's* instruments may thus be seen as summoners of deities, as magical means of establishing contact with the spirit world and of luring the deity to descend into the sacralised space made ready to receive him. Her arrows apprise him, her bow twangs to compel his presence, her curved beads and her mirror invite his entry into her body. There is nothing, it is interesting to note, to suggest the bird symbolism which plays so prominent a part in the costume of the Siberian shaman, nothing resembling the feathers, wings and magical plumage which enables him to accomplish his mantic flight to the other world. Her costume draws spirits to her; it does not despatch her to them.

Can we now reconstruct anything of the ritual by means of which she was thrown into her trance and made the intermediary for the deity's utterance? Useful evidence can be found from two sources. First, there are descriptions of two such rites recorded in the early chronicles, the *Kojiki* and the *Nihon Shoki*. The accounts given in the *Nihon Shoki* are rather more detailed than the *Kojiki* versions, but clearly they are both intended to describe the same ritual trance, performed probably sometime in the middle fourth century A.D.[7]

Second, there are living examples of such divine trances, induced by ritual, still to be found in a few remote villages. The medium is thrown into her possessed state and induced to deliver the deity's words, by rites similar in so many respects to those described in the chronicles that we are justified in inferring them to be of ancient origin.

From the accounts in the chronicles we know that the rite was conducted in an enclosure known as a *saniwa* or sand-garden. This was clearly a temenos, a sacred and purified space, cordoned off from the profane world outside, into which a deity could safely be inducted. It may well have presented a roughly similar appearance to the sacred enclosure in which Shinto rituals are still performed: a 'fence' constructed of green bamboo poles at the four corners, joined by the straw rope which we have seen to surround and demarcate a sacred object. From this rope, at regular intervals, flutter the numinous streamers of white paper known as *gohei*.

Inside this temenos were three people. The first was a musician who played on the zither the magical tunes which summoned the god inside the enclosure and soothed and placated him once he had arrived. The second was an interrogator, known as *saniwa* or *saniwahito*, the 'person in the sand-garden', who put questions to the deity and interpreted the utterances made in reply. The third figure was the medium herself, through whose mouth the deity spoke.

The accounts tell us nothing of the manner in which the medium was thrown into her state of trance. We do not even know whether she was able to throw herself into this state or whether she required a second person to apply the necessary stimulus. In some of the seasonal rites which still survive, as we shall later describe, the medium depends entirely on the services of a member of an ascetic order to induce her trance by means of loud blasts on shell-trumpets, continuously jangling metal rings and shouted mantras. Though it is possible that the interrogator in this ancient rite may have performed a similar function, Nakayama Tarō is convinced that the medium threw herself into her possessed state by violent magical dancing and invocatory singing in the manner of the Tungus shaman.[8] The interrogator's services became necessary only when the time came to question the deity on the matters for which the rite was called, to interpret his utterances when they proved, after the common manner of oracles, to be enigmatic, and to send the deity back to his own world at the end of the rite. He also appears to have directed the ritual, and to have dealt with any emergency which might arise from this perilous contact with spirits.

The questions which the interrogator was required to put to the deity depended of course on the reason for which the rite was performed. From the surviving examples of trance oracles in village shrines we should infer that the rite took place at crucial seasons of the year—at the beginning of the year, at the time of rice-planting, after the harvest—and that the deity was required to prophesy on the fortunes of the community during the coming critical time. We shall later examine several such rituals, obviously old, in which the deity is required to forecast the exact amount of early rice, middle rice, late rice, red beans and black beans to be expected in the coming harvest, as well as to pronounce on the fires, robberies and sicknesses likely to plague the village. [9]

Yanagita, however, is convinced that it was not only at such fixed seasons of the year the *kami* was invoked in ancient times. So close and paternal was the relationship with him felt to be that the slightest pretext was enough to invoke his advice. Any extraordinary or mysterious occurrence, any dilemma in which the village felt itself placed, any problem which it was unable to solve, could immediately be referred to the *kami*. [10]

The accounts in the chronicles, however, describe rites performed not in a village shrine but in the Emperor's palace. The medium was no less a person than the Emperor's consort, the interrogator was the chief minister Takeshiuchi-no-sukune, and the musician was the Emperor himself. Here, therefore, the questions recorded as put to the deity were concerned with less parochial issues than the prospects of the rice and the black bean harvest. The accounts are far from clear, and the *Kojiki* version differs in certain details from the version in the *Nihon Shoki*. But the issue over which the Emperor wished to consult the deity in the first rite seems to be, is it advisable to launch an attack on the Kumaso aborigines?

This particular rite ended in an extraordinary and terrible manner. The deity's reply was to advise instead an expedition to a rich land in the west, full of gold and silver and treasures, which would be delivered into the Emperor's hands. But the Emperor, instead of thanking the deity in the customary manner for his council, committed the crime of what was known as *koto-age*, 'raising words' in opposition to the deity's expressed will. [11] He laid aside the zither on which he had been playing and declared: 'It is a lying deity. However high you may climb you can see no such land in the west. There is nothing but sea.'

For this rash speech retribution came as quickly as it did to Korah in the book of Numbers. The enraged deity pronounced the dreadful cursing words, 'Go straight in one direction!' The interrogator in great alarm begged the Emperor to continue playing on the zither. But it was too late. When they held up the lights they saw that the Emperor was dead.

After this dreadful event another rite was naturally carried out, first to discover what deity had wrought so powerful a curse, and second to enquire further into its wishes about the western land. The Empress again offered herself as medium, with the same interrogator assisting her, and although she had to wait seven days and nights before any answer was vouchsafed, this time no calamity occurred. The interrogator put the first question: 'What are the god's instructions?'

The answer came: 'The land in the west is to be ruled by the child in the Empress's womb.'

The interrogator asked again, 'What child is this who is in her womb?'

Again the answer came, 'It is a boy.'

Then once more the interrogator asked, 'What is your name?'

And again the answer came, 'This is the will of Amaterasu-ōmikami and of the three great deities Sokozutsu-no-o, Nakazutsu-no-o and Uwazutsu-no-o. If you wish to find this rich land, then make offerings to the deities of heaven and earth, mountains, rivers and seas. Make a shrine for our spirit at the top of the ship, put wood ashes into a gourd, make many chopsticks and flat dishes and cast them on to the sea.'

With these enigmatic instructions the account ends.[12]

This record is instructive in several ways. It is interesting to note in the first place that the custom of enquiring the name of the god, still alive in such rites today, is of such ancient origin. The *Nihon Shoki* account tells us that in the second rite the interrogator asked no less than four times what deity was present. Each time a name of extraordinary length and complexity was uttered, together with a description in poetic metre of the place where the deity dwelt.[13]

Secondly, it gives us some idea of the manner in which the god spoke through the medium at that time. Today there appear to be several recognised ways for the god to make his utterance. In some places, such as the Sakumatsuri performed in Sakata, it is conventional for the god to answer every question put to him in a single short shrieked word. Yes, no, four, seven, is his style of response to questions about the harvest and the storms.[14] Elsewhere a longer utterance is usual, though to be convincing it must be delivered with violence and even rudeness. But here, as Nakayama points out, we can detect in the god's speech the metre which from the earliest times has been fundamental to Japanese poetry, a metre of alternating seven and five syllables. The first deity to appear in the *Nihon Shoki* account announced its name to be: *Kamikaze no Ise no kuni momo tsutau Watarai kata no saku kushiro ni iru kami na wa Tsukisakaki-itsuno-mitama-amasakaru-mukatsuhime-no-mikoto.*

The seven–five rhythm, if not very regular, is discernible, as also are examples of the *makura-kotoba* or 'pillow-word', fixed epithets of possibly magical import which are found attached to certain words in early poetry. Hence Nakayama's contention that Japanese poetry made its beginnings in the utterances of a shaman in trance. Its metre and its poetic devices are not the work of man, but revealed from a divine source.[15]

So much then can reasonably be reconstructed of the principal ritual—the trance communication with a deity—which the early *miko* was required to perform.

What else can be reconstructed of her cult? Do we know anything of her manner of entry into the sacred life? Was she chosen for her task on hereditary grounds, for example, or because she was a natural shaman, spontaneously endowed with power?

Here useful comparative material may be gathered from those other districts in the far east where the 'female shaman' survived further into modern times than did the ancient *miko*; from Korea, for example, where the women called *son-mudang* are still to be found, and from the Ainu in Hokkaido, among whom the women called *tsusu* still survive. It is from the Ryūkyū islands, however, that the most instructive parallels may be discerned. Both Yanagita and Origuchi were convinced that much had survived in these islands which could shed light on the beliefs and practices which had long disappeared in Japan, and their researches have been confirmed by those of later ethnologists.

The feature which struck Yanagita most forcibly was the clarity with which the belief survived in the supernatural power of women. Magic power, similar to that inhering in the *kami*, was in the Ryūkyū controlled and invoked only by women. A man who required such power for the exercise of his office, and secular offices were usually held by men, was entirely dependent on a woman relative for its acquisition. Usually this woman was his sister: it was his sister who conferred such power upon him, and replenished it once it became depleted.[16]

Nakahara Zenshū believed that the women who originally controlled this power were shamans, who received their own power by supernatural gift, strengthened by ascesis and ritual seclusion. Today, however, this original shamanic woman seems to have split into two kinds. In the first place we have the *nuru* or *noro*, a majestic sacral woman, a priestess who exercises spiritual power over a village or group of villages. Until some sixty years ago her life was one strictly regulated by the demands of ritual purity. She was forbidden to marry, she avoided funerals and houses where a death had occurred. Even today she does not sleep with her husband during ceremonial periods, nor does she perform rituals during her period of menstruation. She possesses a personal *kami* who is in fact the apotheosis of her own ancestors, and who provides her with a direct link with the spirit world. Her residence is a shrine where these ancestors have their tablets, and where her special panoply of clothes, which includes a necklace of *magatama* beads and sometimes a bronze drum, are kept. In former times she used to travel to the villages under her jurisdiction on a white horse, accompanied by a male acolyte.

All these signs are immediately reminiscent of the ancient *miko*. In the *nuru* we glimpse a parochial Pimiko, secluded in her large and lofty wooden palace, attended by only a single man, her own brother. For some centuries, however, the *nuru* has exercised her sacral functions without any recourse to trance. Her communication with spiritual beings, and her exercise of the magic power deriving from them, is accepted as possible without any altered state of consciousness. The women who possess the capacity for trance, and who are consequently called shamans, are humbler personages known as *yuta*.

The *yuta* evince all the characteristic marks of the shaman. Before her supernatural call to the sacred life, she is afflicted by symptoms of sickness very similar to those of arctic hysteria. Loss of appetite, hallucinations, terrifying dreams, skin trouble, headaches, failing eyesight and periods of disassociation of personality are the usual lot of the incipient *yuta*. Once the supernatural call is made to them, however, and once they accept the new life which is thrust upon them, the symptoms disappear and give way to powers of clairvoyance, clairaudience and possession, all the equipment, in short, to discern the causes of human misfortune when these lie in the spirit world.

It is now considered that these two kinds of sacral women, the *nuru* and the *yuta*, were originally one. The shamanic woman in the Ryūkyū islands possessed both the dignity and majesty of authority and the characteristically shamanic powers of healing and divining through the medium of trance. When the office of *nuru* became a hereditary one, however, her faculty of trance passed from her, to be carried on by lowlier women who were endowed with the true shamanic sickness, initiation and subsequent gifts.[17]

The ancient *miko* may well have resembled the ancient *nuru* in the Ryūkyū. She was not only a majestic figure invested with spiritual authority, whose life was set apart and sealed off from the sources of pollution, separated from contact with the blood and death, childbirth and sexual intercourse which for ordinary people were the natural and unavoidable causes of ritual uncleanness. She was also a natural shaman, experiencing the characteristic initiatory sickness, supernatural call to the sacred life and subsequent magic powers which enabled her to act as a bridge between the human world and the world of spirits.

Oka Masao believes that the *miko* who served in village shrines were, whether their office was hereditary or not, all natural shamans. They were 'chosen by a god'. Power was conferred on them not because they sought it, but by an external and supernatural force. Yanagita and Hori likewise believe that there was no lack in ancient Japan of natural woman shamans, of women gifted with the peculiar temperament which culminates in the shamanic seizure; that Japan at that period was only one example of many peoples and cultures where the sacral woman, rightly designated a shaman, was the principal religious figure.[18]

Why shamanism of such a basically continental type, however, with so many links with the prototypal Altaic shamanism of central and north asia, should in these areas have become the monopoly of women, is still far from clear.

The question now presents itself, what kind of deities were they who in ancient times chose and possessed these shamanic women? The names given in the *Kojiki* and *Nihon Shoki* accounts are no guide to the kind of deity who may have appeared in remote villages to assume the task of instructing the community.

To answer this question Japanese ethnologists have drawn on a source of evidence less direct than those we have so far considered, the evidence of folktales and legends.

Such stories do not of course speak to us in plain language. They speak in symbols which must be interpreted, like a cypher which must be broken before its message is understood. They are, however, the only help so far available to us in the recovery of this otherwise lost level of shamanic practice.

The stories adduced as shedding light on the *miko* and her cult fall roughly into four groups or types. In all of them there appears with overwhelming persistence the figure of a supernatural snake. In some of the tales the snake appears as the woman's lover, visiting her mysteriously by night and getting her with child. In others the woman becomes not the bride of the snake but its victim. She is buried alive as a 'human pillar', sacrificed to the snake warden of a river or pool. In yet other tales she is rescued from this horrible fate at the last moment by a clever ruse devised by a passing hero. In others again the woman turns into the mysterious lady whom we saw earlier presiding over a shimmering palace at the bottom of the sea, and who in her turn becomes the snake guardian of a lake or pool. We are back therefore with a shamanic cult which looked to the water world as the source of power and wealth and of the miraculous help on which the community depends.

Let us review these stories.

The first two groups of tales, which Yanagita in particular saw as illuminating the ancient shamanic cult, are those known as *shinkontan* or divine marriage tales. These tell of a marriage between a human being and a god. In one group a human girl is visited by an unknown deity, who on investigation is discovered to be a snake. In the other group the goddess of the sea leaves her watery home to marry a human man, only to return to it in her true form of a snake when the man has violated a taboo.[19]

Both these types of tale are found associated with certain shrines, usually purporting to account for the semi-divine ancestry of the priestly family in whose hereditary charge they lie. The Miwa and Kamo shrines are the most celebrated examples, the Miwa shrine in particular having given its name to two sub-types of divine marriage legend, broadly known as *hebi-no-mukoiri*, or snake bridegroom.

That Japanese folklore is particularly rich in stories of marriages between human beings and animals is clear from a glance at Seki Keigo's *Nihon Mukashibanashi Shūsei*, in which a number of folktales are classified according to type and motif. Here are not only fish wives, frog wives, stork wives and fox wives, but also monkey bridegrooms, horse bridegrooms and spider bridegrooms. Most widespread and common of all, however, are the snake bridegrooms.

The Miwa legends, both of which appear in the *Kojiki*, recount two such tales.

The first, known as the *ninuriya* or red arrow type, is found also in the *Yamashiro Fūdoki* associated with the Kamo shrine. It tells how the Miwa god Ōmononushi fell in love with a girl called Seyadatarahime. He floated down the river in the likeness of a red arrow and struck Seyadatarahime in the genitals just as she was defecating on the bank. She took the arrow home and put it by her bed, whereupon it turned at once into a handsome young man who took her to wife. She in due course bore him a child called Himetataraisukiyoribime.[20]

The Kamo legend is almost identical, save that the girl's name is Tamayorihime, and that both the Kamo deity and the child whom the girl bears him are associated with thunder.[21]

Of closer import to our theme, however, is the second Miwa legend, known as the *odamaki* or hemp-thread type. Here the girl Ikutamayorihime is visited mysteriously by night by an unknown lover who gets her with child. Her parents, anxious to discover his identity, instruct the girl to sew a thread of hemp to the hem of his garment and to follow it the next morning to wherever it might lead. The girl did as she was instructed, to find that the thread passed through the keyhole of the door and led straight to the shrine of the deity of Mt Miwa. They accordingly knew that the girl's lover had been the Miwa deity Ōmononushi in snake form. The girl later bore a child, who became the ancestor of the family serving the shrine.[22]

This latter legend has proliferated into several variant forms, associated with different places and shrines, with an extraordinarily wide distribution throughout Japan. Seki Keigo alone records examples ranging from virtually all over the main island from Aomori to Yamaguchi, from all over Shikoku and all over Kyushu. This is also found widely distributed throughout the Ryūkyū islands. Frank Daniels's unrivalled collection of snake stories also includes examples from almost every prefecture in Japan.[23]

A number of variant forms appear also in literature, notably in the thirteenth-century works *Heike Monogatari* and *Gempei Seisuiki*. Here the figure of the snake appears more powerfully and emphatically than in the old and bald *Kojiki* legend. In the *Heike Monogatari* story, set not near Mt Miwa but in the province of Bungo in Kyūshū, the girl follows the thread for miles over the entire province until it disappears inside a deep cave. Standing at the mouth of the cave the girl calls into its depths that she wishes to behold her lover's face. A voice from within answers that were she to do so her heart would burst with fright. But the girl still begs to see him, so at last from out of the cave there crawls a monstrous serpent, quivering all over, with a needle stuck in its throat, so fearful in appearance that the girl faints with horror at the sight of it. The child which she eventually bore him, however, grew to be an enormous boy called Daida, who in due course became the greatest warrior in Kyūshū.[24]

In two of the stories just noticed, and in a significant number of similar tales associated with other shrines, the name of the girl seduced by the supernatural snake is Tamayorihime.

It was this name which first led Yanagita to suggest that the stories were originally connected with a shamanic ritual. The name, he argues, is a generic one for a *miko*, denoting a girl (*hime*) possessed (*yoru*) by the spirit of a god (*tama*). The story therefore points to a cult in which a *miko* was specially chosen to serve a deity connected with water and serpents. With this same cult Yanagita also associated the numerous shrines which are found dedicated to three deities, a mother, a child and a third deity who is the father of the child. The case of the Hachiman shrine at Usa in Kyūshū is a notable example.[25]

Other shrines boast a divine marriage legend in which the divine partner is not the man but the woman, a goddess who emerges from the sea in order to wed a human man. The prototype of this tale is usually taken to be the legend, again appearing in the *Kojiki*, of the sea-god's daughter Toyota-mahime. Having left her water realm to marry Ho-ori and bear his child, she bade him strictly not to look upon her during the time of her delivery. She thereupon retired to a parturition hut thatched with cormorant feathers. But Ho-ori, thinking her words strange, peeped into the forbidden chamber, only to see that his wife had reverted to her 'true form', and become a *wani*, crocodile or serpent, crawling and slithering about the hut. As soon as she realised that she had been seen, she at once returned to her water realm, closing behind her the barrier which separated her world from the human one.[26]

In both these types of divine marriage legend there can be

discerned the vestige of an ancient shamanistic cult in which a woman is chosen to serve a water-serpent god. In the *odamaki* stories we see a girl seized and forced to act not only as the mouthpiece of a god, but also as his bride. She is thus 'possessed' in a double sense, both spiritually by an oracle and sexually by a lover.

We are at once reminded of the similarly sexual relationship which obtains in many Siberian tribes between the shaman and his tutelary deity. Here, however, the sexes are usually reversed and it is a male shaman who finds himself visited by a goddess. Among the Goldi on the Amur river, Sternberg quotes a shaman as saying that his tutelary goddess, a beautiful woman who taught him the secrets which enabled him to shamanise, was at the same time the wife with whom he slept. When he shamanised he was possessed by this goddess, as his body might be permeated by smoke or vapour, and it was she who spoke through his mouth and drank the offerings of pig's blood. The Yakut shaman was also visited when asleep by a female spirit, and the Teleut shaman likewise had a celestial wife whom he visited in her abode in the seventh heaven.[27]

The *odamaki* stories suggest that a similar relationship, with the sexes reversed, was common between the early *miko* and her guardian snake.

In the forbidden chamber stories, which Matsumura Takeo reminds us have variants in China, Korea, Indonesia and as far away as Europe in the Melusina tale, the *miko* herself becomes divine. She now is not merely possessed by a serpent: she is one herself. Divinity has been conferred on her by her possession by her divine lover. We are back, of course, with the magical woman whom we earlier met in the palace at the bottom of the sea. The *miko* is thus assimilated with the water woman, whose world we saw to be a constant source of riches and power, and whose cult we saw shifting upward at some point of time to the summits of certain mountains. These tales may therefore be relics of a time when the shamanistic cult in Japan was directed principally towards an other world in the sea.[28]

Divine marriage tales are not the only stories which have been adduced as evidence of the close connection between a woman shaman and a serpent deity. Two further groups of tales must be considered, in both of which the woman is not the bride of the snake but its sacrificial victim.

In the *hito-bashira* or human pillar legends, again found scattered over a wide area of the country and in many places still believed to be true, a woman is buried alive as a propitiatory offering to the serpent presiding over the river or lake. A dam or dyke has been broken so many times by raging floodwater that the villagers realise that a sacrifice is necessary if it is ever to be successfully repaired. Sometimes a passing traveller was seized for this horrifying purpose, each shrine having its own rules for determining what kind of traveller should be seized, whether man or woman, whether the first, second or third person to pass through the village. In a remarkable number of examples, however, the buried victim is stated to be a *miko*. In a village in Rikuzen where the dam kept collapsing they seized a travelling *miko* who happened to be passing through the village and buried her alive. The dam was at once finished and they built a shrine to the *miko's* spirit on that very spot. In a village in Hitachi where a dyke in the river refused to be mended, they at length resorted to consulting the local oracle through a *miko*. The oracle pronounced that if the dyke was to be mended a woman must be sacrificed as a human pillar. The villagers thereupon seized the hapless *miko* herself and buried her alive under the dyke, which needless to say remained intact from that moment.[29]

Sometimes the victim is not merely a solitary *miko* but a mother with her child, affording an immediate link with the mother–child deity stories we have just noticed. The most celebrated example is the case of Tsuru and Ichitarō, worshipped at the Aibara shrine in Oita prefecture. This tale, which subsequently became widely diffused through the country, tells how a dyke controlling the water of the ricefields belonging to the Usa Hachiman shrine was constantly collapsing. A man named Yuya Danjō Motonobu was chosen to be the victim, but at the last moment a woman called Tsuru and her thirteen-year-old son Ichitarō offered themselves as human pillars in exchange. They were buried alive in the river and were afterwards worshipped as guardian deities of the place. Here the boy's name, Ichitarō, calls to mind the word for a shaman, *ichi*, so that here too lurks the suggestion of an ancient association with a *miko*.[30]

Matsumura contends that these legends are not based on fact but reflect an ancient and lost cult in which a woman was offered as a 'living sacrifice' to a water-snake deity; not, however, in the sense that she was murdered in the horrible manner described, but in the sense that she thereby died to ordinary human life. She was snatched from her familiar world and pressed into a sacred calling which represented death to her old manner of living. By becoming his bride she was indeed sacrificed to the deity.

The suggestion that none of these stories actually indicates that the *miko* was killed but rather removed from ordinary life, has been applied also to the second groups of human sacrifice stories, the *orochi-taiji* or serpent-killing tales. Here the woman designated to be the living sacrifice to the monstrous serpent who guards the adjacent pool or river is saved at the last moment by a clever ruse devised by a hero who luckily happens to pass by at the crucial moment and hear her lamentations. The prototype of this tale—which, needless to say, is the familiar Perseus and Andromeda motif of virtually worldwide distribution—is in Japan taken to be the narrative in Chapter 19 of the *Kojiki*. Here the god Susanoo comes upon an old couple lamenting that the last of their eight daughters, Kushinadahime, is soon to fall victim to a monstrous eight-headed dragon. The other seven have already died in this way. The dragon had eight heads and eight tails, and his body was covered with moss and cypress trees and blood. Susanoo instructed the old people to build a fence with eight doors, at each door to construct a platform, and on each platform to place a tub of strong rice wine. The old couple having done as they were instructed, the monster appeared, put a head into each tub, drank the wine and fell into a drunken slumber in which Susanoo was able to hack it to pieces.[31]

Here on the face of it we have a story of the familiar Perseus and Andromeda type. Not so, Matsumura Takeo avers. Whereas in the dragon-slaying myths found in other countries the girl is no more than a sacrifice to the dragon, in the Japanese versions of the tale there is more to be discovered about her. The story has certainly evolved from an earlier form in which the girl was no ordinary human being but a *miko*. Again, behind the figure of the victim we may discern the shaman.

The evidence adduced by Matsumura in support of his view turns on several points. The eight victims specified in the myth, the girl and her seven sacrificed sisters, point to the ancient custom by which a chapter of eight *miko* (*yaotome*) served a deity. The rice wine on which the monster was made drunk, moreover, was in ancient times not a brew to be drunk casually on ordinary days of the year. It was a sacred beverage consumed only on those days when the deity descended into the village. It was then offered to him for his own delectation, and partaken of by the villagers in order to facilitate their meeting with him. That the tubs of wine were placed on platforms, Matsumura continues, suggests that they were offerings to a deity, these platforms being devices for marking off a sacred area from the surrounding profane space.

All these considerations point to the conclusion that the story of the girl offered in sacrifice to the eight-headed serpent has grown out of an earlier form based on a ritual in which a *miko*, or a group of eight *miko*, offer the deity they serve his seasonal feast of eight jars of rice wine.

But why, it will immediately be asked, should this innocent ritual have been distorted into a myth of human sacrifice and dragon-slaying? Why should the tranquil offering of jars of wine to a visiting deity have been transformed into human sacrifice, and why should the deity have become a man-eating monster?

Let us return to the hypothesis of the *miko* serving the deity as his bride. Originally, Matsumura writes, this custom was accepted unquestioningly. Later it came to be hated and feared, especially by the families of the women. By rendering this duty to the god, the girl was no longer considered to be a chosen and favoured person but to be a victim. Further proof of this shift in attitude is afforded by the nature of the deity. He is a serpent, a deity controlling water, and hence the arbiter of the fortunes of a wet rice-growing community. But the force of water is highly ambivalent. It can nourish the crops, but it can also drown them in flood and tempest. Human attitudes to this god can be likewise ambivalent; the transition from love and welcome to fear and hatred is not difficult.[32]

All these human sacrifice tales may therefore be seen, both Matsumura and Origuchi believe, as supporting the view that the *miko* in ancient times served the deity who spoke through her as a bride. The deity as he 'possessed' her became her lover. She was wholly given to him, becoming in the process a divine figure herself, dead to her old familiar life and removed to a different mode of existence. They also support the hypothesis of a widespread and deep-rooted cult of the snake in ancient Japan, a serpent connected with water, controlling and emerging from it, and hence probably closely connected with wet rice agriculture. Matsumura sees the serpent deity as a transformation of the rice-field deity Tanokami, and Higo Kazuo too sees it as a magic creature presiding over water and hence over rice culture.[33]

We shall meet the figure of the snake again in our discussion of the ascetic and his tutelary deity. In connection with the early *miko* and her cult, however, it makes one more dramatic appearance. Hitherto it has been a watery serpent, lurking in rivers and pools, connected with thunder and giving birth to miraculous and ugly small boys. Now we meet the *miko* conjoined with another serpent, this time a creature not of water but of fire.

The suggestion that certain stories in which a woman is transformed into a fiery serpent can shed light on the manner in which the ancient *miko* exercised her sacral function comes from Torii Ryūzō. The watery snake stories, though they tell us something of the structure of the cult, tell us nothing about the manner of the *miko's* divine seizure, or the proofs she gave of her ability to transcend the ordinary human condition. In the Dōjōji story, however, Torii sees such proofs amply afforded. In this tale, with its celebrated versions for both the Nō and the Kabuki stage, we have only to strip away the obvious Buddhist accretions to find the following narrative.[34]

123

A priest in the course of a pilgrimage to the Kumano shrines stopped for the night in a certain house. During the night the daughter of the house saw him asleep and at once fell uncontrollably in love with him. She begged him to marry her but he recoiled, horrified at the thought of breaking his Buddhist vows, and consented only to make one more brief call at the house on his way back from the shrines. On the appointed day the girl went out to meet him, only to be told that the priest had already passed by and was well on his way back to his temple. Furious with anger she set off in pursuit of him, and as she ran flames burst from her mouth and the upper part of her body was transformed into that of a snake. The terrified priest was quickly ferried across the river and rushed for refuge into the nearby temple of Dōjōji, where the monks, aghast at his tale, let down the great bell over him so that he was entirely hidden from sight.

The woman, however, plunged relentlessly into the river after him, and as she swam she was entirely transformed into a snake. In this monstrous form she entered the precincts of the temple, and wound her body round the bell, coil on coil, until it became red hot. She then uncoiled herself and disappeared, but when the monks lifted up the bell to release the priest they found inside only a blackened skeleton.

Other stories may be found in which the human passions of lust, jealousy and hatred appear to take the form of a snake and in this shape to detach themselves from the sleeping body of their host. De Visser quotes several examples to illustrate this belief. The celebrated monk Ippen Shōnin was first driven into the religious life by the shocking experience of seeing his two wives dozing over a go-board. From the head of each of them reared a serpent, hissing fiercely at the other. The mutual jealousy and hatred of the two woman had assumed the form of snakes and detached themselves from the sleeping bodies of their hostesses. Again, we read of a wife's jealous soul detaching itself from her body, taking the form of a serpent and killing her husband while he lies with his concubine. And again, a carpenter engaged on a job on the summit of the holy mountain

Kōyasan, forbidden to women, was visited one night by a snake which subsequently proved to be the disembodied form of his wife's neglected sexual passion.[35]

In none of these stories, however, are the snakes associated with fire. It was presumably the fire in the Dōjōji story which led Torii to deduce the meaning that the *miko* in her possessed state became suffused with the magic interior heat which is so characteristic an accomplishment of the shaman.

We have already a brief reference to this condition in our discussion of the methods of ascesis which are traditionally believed to be productive of power. The stress on intense cold—cold water, cold food, absence of heating in mid-winter—we suggested may have been intended to produce that state of interior heat in which the practitioner is impervious to either heat or cold. He is, in Eliade's phrase, a master of fire. This heated state we shall meet again in our discussion of the ascetic and his tutelary deity. Here suffice to say that this shamanistic accomplishment may, if Torii is right, have been common among the ancient *miko*. When possessed by her serpent lover, and when in consequence she herself became a serpent and partook of his divine nature, she may have become suffused by an access of such mysterious heat. When in the grip of this afflatus, she became a terrifying figure, transformed into a demonic being before whom an ordinary man quailed and fled.

The snake which has so far been a cold and watery being now therefore shows a contrary face: it becomes a creature of fire, the symbol of the non-human condition of heat which descends on the shaman during his communion with spirits. Here is a clear representation of the Kundalini, the 'serpent power' which the Indian yogi experiences together with a burning sensation of heat, climbing up his spine from chakra to chakra until it reaches its destination at the top of his head. Whether the coincidence of images is due to a similarity of actual experience—you feel in that state *as if* a snake were climbing up your spine—or whether it is due to some hitherto unrecognised dissemination of images from India, is not a problem that can be treated here. We may simply draw attention to the possible relevance here of the snake mask in the Nō plays. The Nō mask of the snake bears no resemblance to that reptile. With its golden horns, its fierce golden eyes, its gaping red mouth opened to reveal rows of golden teeth, its wild red hair, it is a face virtually identical with the mask of the *hannya* or female demon. May it not represent also the face of a woman possessed by a supernatural snake and in the throes of a divine *furor*?

With these conjectures we must leave the shamanic medium so evidently powerful in ancient Japan and pass to her more modern counterparts. We have already seen that with the introduction of Buddhist and Chinese thought the *miko* as a mantic person was banished from the court and the large shrines and relegated to the 'little tradition' of religion in Japan. On this largely non-literate level, where the ritual and the supporting myths are passed down by oral means, we find that this majestic sacral woman is replaced by humbler figures, some of whom seem to derive from an altogether different tradition of mediumship.

7
The Living Goddess

We will not attempt to follow the history of the shamanic medium in Japan during the centuries between the late prehistoric period and today. It is clear that on the humble level of the folk religion she continued to put her powers at the service of the community in most parts of the country. Until the time of the Meiji Restoration in 1868 there were bands of *miko* to be met with virtually all over Japan. Many of these women were loosely affiliated to large shrines, and lived in enclaves known as *miko-mura, miko* villages. From these bases they would set out at stated seasons of the year on long peripatetic journeys, like strolling minstrels, delivering prophesies and messages from the dead in the villages through which they passed. The women known as Kumano-bikuni, for example, whose base was the Jippōin temple at Nachi and whom Kaempfer encountered in the course of his journey with the Dutch merchants from Nagasaki to Edo in 1692, were venerated as oracles all over the country. In the Edo district the women called *ichiko* were reported to travel great distances to make their seasonal calls, and near Osaka the women called Shinano-miko, with their base villages as far away as Nagano prefecture, were recalled as continuing their visits until the beginning of the Meiji period.[1]

These activities were summarily suppressed, however, by a directive from the Meiji government in 1873. Anxious to promote the 'enlightenment' of the country in accordance with modern rational principles and determined at the same time to purge 'pure' Shinto of all that savoured of Buddhism or of ancient superstition, the government decreed that all *miko* who deluded the people by professing to deliver messages from the dead were henceforth forbidden to practise their calling. The following year an even sterner directive was issued to the same effect.[2]

In theory this prohibition lasted until 1945, when General MacArthur's Religious Bodies Law allowed the Japanese

127

people for the first time for seventy years freedom to worship as they pleased, to form what religious bodies they pleased, and to carry on what religious activities they pleased. A good many *miko*, who had until then practised their calling only furtively and in secret, thereupon began to find their way back into the acknowledged life of the folk religion. The fact that they had survived at all, despite the legal prohibitions, bears witness to the strength of their position in rural Japan.

Today, thirty years later, their numbers are still more drastically depleted by the encroachments of modern life. Nevertheless, there still survive broadly four kinds of women who still practise the calling of shamanic medium. There are the blind mediums known as *itako* or *ichiko* who still act as mouthpieces for both *kami* and ghosts in the northern districts of the main island. There are mediums who serve in conjunction with an ascetic in the seasonal summoning of a *kami* in certain villages. Both these types we shall describe in later chapters. Neither, however, is thought to derive from the same shamanic lineage as the ancient sibyl described in the last chapter. The *itako* are thought to stem from some southerly, 'Polynesian' source, and the passive mediums, whose first appearance is recorded in the literature of the ninth century, are thought to have derived from certain occult practices of esoteric Buddhism.

A more convincing survival from the ancient *miko* is to be found in small numbers in the seven Izu islands. These women appear to be natural shamans of the same type as those found in the Ryūkyū islands and in Hokkaidō. They suffer from a neurotic complaint known as *miko-ke*, which culminates in a supernatural seizure. Thereafter they acquire a guardian spirit who enables them to serve the village by their powers of clairvoyance and possession.[3]

The most convincing link with the past, however, is to be seen in a number of remarkable characters whose shamanic qualities have only recently been recognised. These are the *kyōso* or Founders of the new religious sects which during the last hundred years and particularly since the end of the last war have made so dramatic an appearance in all parts of the country.[4]

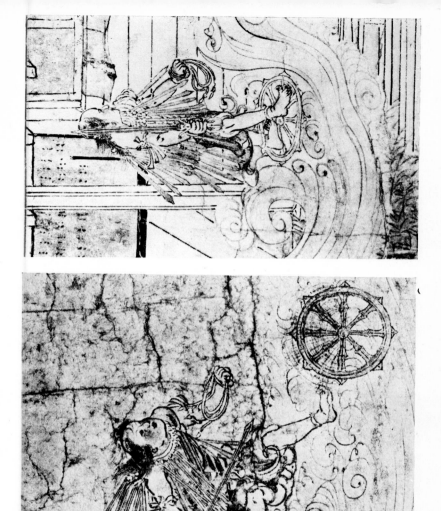

Right, Plate 11. The spirit boy sent by the ascetic of Shinano to cure the Emperor's sickness, as depicted by the late Heian handscroll *Shigisan Engi.* He flies to the assistance of the Emperor, a Wheel of the Law rolling before him and his collar of swords blowing backwards in the wind. The sword in his right hand and the noose in his left are reminiscent of Fudō Myōō himself.

Far right, Plate 12. The same boy enters the Emperor's palace.

Plate 13. The *yamabushi's* ascent of Mt Omine. The place known as Nishi-no-nozoki where the neophytes are dangled head first over a precipice and adjured to confess their sins.

These notable characters, among whom women are a good deal more numerous than men, exhibit in their personal histories a curiously uniform pattern. Nearly all of them in their early life betray symptoms of what could be called 'arctic hysteria'. They are sickly, neurotic, hysterical, odd, until a moment comes when, exacerbated by suffering, these symptoms rise to a climactic interior experience of a mystical kind. A deity, by means of a dream or a possession, seizes them and claims them for his service. Thenceforward they are changed characters. Their former oddity and sickliness give way to a remarkable strength and magnetism of personality, which is conferred on them, together with various supernormal powers, by the deity who has possessed them and who henceforth governs their lightest move. The exercise of these powers and the proclamation of the deity's message result in the course of time in believers gathering round and forming a new sect. That these people, in their powers and their life histories, showed unmistakable shamanic traits, was recognised by Hori Ichiro in 1964.

The phenomenon known as the *shinkō-shūkyō* or New Religious Cults has made three major appearances during the last hundred years. The first outcrop of such new sects occurred in the middle of the last century, at the time of the collapse of the feudal system and its replacement by the new centralised, industrialised state which came into being after the Meiji Restoration. During this period a number of new religious movements made their appearance, but the only ones to survive the restrictions imposed both by the feudal regime of the Tokugawa and by the new Meiji government were the thirteen groups which subsequently and misleadingly became known as the thirteen 'sects of Shinto'.[5]

A second period of sudden religious growth occurred during the 1920s and 30s, at a time of economic depression and increasingly totalitarian militarism.[6] The third and most remarkable outcrop of such new sects burst upon the scene immediately after the last war. No sooner were the legal restrictions on religious liberty abolished by General MacArthur's legislation of 1945 than an extraordinary number of new sects, movements and groups began to

proclaim their message. Though a good many were subsequently proved to be entirely fraudulent, no more than
commercial enterprises exploiting the loose wording of the
law of 1945 to masquerade as 'religious bodies' in order to
avoid paying income tax, and though others proved to be
too bizarre in their doctrines to survive for more than a few
months, the number of genuinely inspired new cults was
still, even by 1964, registered at the high figure of 378.[7]

The largest, richest and most successful of these groups
all owe their original inspiration to a Founder, to whom the
message of the cult has been divinely revealed, and whose
personal history conforms closely with the pattern already
outlined. They all exhibit traits of markedly shamanistic
character.

Let us examine the biographies of a representative few
of these Founders, and see how in each of the three periods
of religious growth the same pattern tends to persist. A
series of almost unendurable sufferings culminates in a
terrific experience of divine possession.[8]

Nakayama Miki, the Foundress of Tenrikyō, now the
largest and richest of the 'new' cults which survive from the
early nineteenth century, was dogged throughout her early
life by a series of appalling personal tribulations. Melancholy
and introspective by nature, she was married at the age of
thirteen to a man she disliked, and whose mother bullied
her unmercifully. She lived through the famines of the 1830s
and the disturbing phenomena of the *okage-mairi*, when huge
crowds of ecstatic pilgrims surged through her village on
their way to the Ise shrine. Her response to these anxieties
was to plunge herself even further into suffering. When a
neighbour's small boy fell gravely ill while under her care,
she petitioned the local deity to take the lives of two of her
daughters as substitutes for the boy. In due course the boy
recovered and her two daughters died.

Her next tribulation came in 1837 when her son Shūji
was suddenly afflicted with agonising pains in his legs.
Doctors and ointments were powerless to help, and it was
not until they called in a *yamabushi* by the name of Ichibei
to perform his rite of exorcism that the boy felt any relief.
Ichibei's method of treatment was the traditional one known

as *yorigitō*, which we will examine in greater detail in a later chapter. By reciting sutras and mantras he would force the malicious spirit causing the sickness to leave the patient and enter into a medium, through whose mouth it would announce its identity and its reasons for molesting the boy. Ichibei for this purpose usually employed a professional medium from a neighbouring village. One night in September 1838, however, the medium was unable to come, and Miki offered her services instead.

As the spells began to get under way Miki's face suddenly changed and she fell into a violent state of trance. To the question as to what deity was possessing her she answered, 'I am Ten-no-Shōgun.'

'What manner of god might Ten-no-Shōgun be?' they asked.

'The original true god who has descended from heaven to save all mankind', the deity answered through Miki's mouth. It then demanded that Miki's body should be given over as a shrine for its own use. Miki's husband, much taken aback, replied that such a request was impossible to grant, since Miki was the mother of four children, the youngest only a few months old. The god thereupon threatened that if its orders were disobeyed it would blast the whole family with curses.

For three days after this exchange Miki is said to have been in an uninterrupted state of possession, sitting bolt upright transmitting the god's answers to questions without touching a drop of water or a grain of rice. Eventually her husband saw no alternative but to capitulate, and formally renounce to the god his responsibility for his wife. At once Miki returned to her normal state of consciousness.

From that time she was frequently visited by further fits of possession, and her behaviour became increasingly eccentric. She began to give away to all and sundry, apparently in response to divine commands, all the family possessions and property. If restrained from such prodigal charity she would turn pale, fall into convulsions and refuse to eat until allowed to do as she wished. Eventually she gave away the entire family substance, even to the extent of insisting, with the usual convulsions if thwarted, on the family house being pulled down. She is said to have sung with joy during this operation and to have entertained the workmen with wine and fish.

These strange and violent experiences were Miki's initiation into her role of divine vehicle, whereby her body was chosen by the god to be his instrument for transmitting his revelations to the suffering world. Some years after the complete destitution brought about by such unusual behaviour, she was discovered to possess miraculous healing powers, particularly in the granting of painless childbirth. Her fame spread throughout the district and believers began to flock round. When in 1863 their ranks were joined by one Izō Iburi, who proved to be a devoted and entirely efficient and shrewd organiser, her cult began to make rapid headway. In 1869 she started to write the *Ofudesaki*, an enormously long poem in 1,711 verses, apparently divinely inspired and recorded largely in automatic writing. It took fifteen years to complete. In 1872, again in response to a divine command, she is recorded as having accomplished a seventy-five-day fast without the smallest fatigue or discomfort.

Persecuted by the authorities during the early years of Meiji and imprisoned several times, Miki died in 1887 at the age of ninety. Her cult, with its body of teachings based on her copious revelations, had already a large following, although it was not until the years after her death that it was finally given official recognition, somewhat misleadingly under the title of a 'Shinto sect'.[9]

The life of the Foundress of the Ōmoto sect followed a very similar pattern. Deguchi Nao was likewise possessed by a god in middle age as the culmination of a series of miseries. Born in 1837 in the midst of famine and unrest, she was sent out to work at the age of eleven owing to the extreme poverty of her family. Six years later she was married unhappily to a drunken and spendthrift husband, to whom she eventually bore eleven children. Of these, three died in infancy, one disappeared after attempting suicide, and one was killed in the Sino-Japanese war. Her husband died in 1887 after lying for three years paralysed by a stroke, leaving her with her three youngest children to pick up a bare pittance by selling rags and working long hours in a silk mill. In 1890 one of her married daughters suddenly became insane with puerperal mania, and the following year the same fate overtook her eldest daughter.

A few days after this latest and culminating disaster, in January 1892, Nao had a vivid dream that she was wandering in the spirit world. A day or two later she fell suddenly into a violent state of trance. Her body almost torn apart with the strain, she leapt up and down from a sitting position while loud roars like those of a wild beast burst from the pit of her stomach. In the course of this seizure an extraordinary dialogue is said to have taken place between her own voice and the terrible 'stomach' voice of the deity inside her. The god announced its name to be Ushitora-no-Konjin, and to have come into Nao's body in order that the present hideous state of the world should be transformed into a paradise.

After this first initiatory possession she often during the next year or so fell into similar states of violent trance, wandering round the town roaring at the top of her voice. Eventually she was arrested on suspicion of arson, and confined to a room in her house for forty days. During this period she became quieter, and began to scratch with a nail on the pillars of her room rough *hiragana* characters. These words were the beginning of the immense *Ofudesaki*, the transmission of her revelations in automatic writing which continued for the next twenty-seven years of her life and which eventually ran to more than 10,000 fascicules.

On being released from her confinement she was discovered to possess powers of healing. Sick people for whom she prayed seemed to recover. Inevitably therefore believers began to flock round her, and the cult which later became known as Ōmoto was born. When in 1898 her ranks of faithful were joined by the remarkable character Ueda Kisaburō, who later married one of her daughters and took the name of Deguchi Onisaburō, the movement was given an impetus which gained it national notoriety.[10] Deguchi's initiation into the sacred life, we may add, will be treated in a later chapter. It is one of the few examples to be found among the Founders of initiation by means of a journey of the soul to other worlds.

Let us now look at the lives of two founders of post-war cults. Okada Mokichi, the founder of the now flourishing sect of Sekai Meshiakyō or 'World Messianity', was born in 1882 of poor parents who made a precarious living from a wayside stall. As a young man he was shy, diffident and introspective. He seems to have endured an almost incredible number and variety of illnesses. Among other maladies he suffered from eye trouble, pleurisy, tuberculosis, cerebral anemia, typhoid fever, intestinal disorders, heart disease, rheumatism and nervous collapse. No doctor was able to help him. Every enterprise to which he put his hand failed, until the great earthquake of 1923 reduced him to complete penury. His initiation came in 1926, when for some three months he was almost continuously possessed by the Bodhisattva Kannon, who announced that she had chosen his body to be the vehicle by which all men might be saved and a new age brought into being in which all sickness should vanish. He wrote, under divine inspiration, a long account of the origins of Japan in remote antiquity and of the nation's destiny in the future after the new paradisal age had arrived. He was also granted the gift of a new method of healing, a dispensation which accounts for the special emphasis on healing in the cult which subsequently grew up round him. It now boasts a membership of 662,000.[11]

Lastly let us look at the dramatic example of Kitamura Sayo, the foundress of Tenshō Kōtai Jingukyō, more popularly known as the Dancing Religion. Ōgamisama, 'great goddess', as everyone called her, was married to a weak and colourless man, whose mother was reputed to be the greediest and stingiest woman in the district. She was in the habit of finding a bride for her son just before the busy farming season in spring, using the girl unmercifully as unpaid labour, only to divorce her as soon as the busy season was over. A few months later, when the autumn harvest-time approached, she would find another bride for her son, and divorce her once the harvest was safely in. Ōgamisama was the sixth bride to be chosen in this way in the space of three years. She rarely had enough to eat, and was reduced sometimes to eating tangerine peel and rotten pumpkins. Scarcely ever did she have more than three hours sleep a night. When the time for her confinement approached, her mother-in-law was too stingy to pay for a midwife, and refused to give any help herself on the score that she had a cold. Ōgamisama therefore had to give birth to the baby entirely unaided.

A crisis of conscience about her own unworthiness caused her to start various ascetic religious practices, which she continued for a couple of years until in 1944 she became aware that there was another being inside her body which conversed with her and ordered her about. This entity announced itself to be a snake by the name of Tōbyō. It explained many things to her, of the past and the future and of her previous lives. It also gave correct weather forecasts and lessons in laundering and cooking, together with useful advice on diet and vitamins. Its advice was always good, but if for any reason Ōgamisama were to disobey its commands she was immediately racked with agonising pains. She soon found that she only had to open her mouth for sermons and songs to pour forth from the being inside her. As she became increasingly governed by its will her character underwent a notable change. Her former modesty and politeness gave way to her celebrated coarseness of speech, in which she would frequently abuse her audience, irrespective of their social standing, as maggot beggars and traitors. The deity inside her announced itself shortly after the end of the war, to be Tenshō Kōtai Jingū, who had chosen Ōgamisama's body to be the vehicle for the salvation of the world.

So rough and unconventional was apt to be the language of this deity that for all her public appearances and particularly for her sermons Ōgamisama used always to wear a man's suit. It would look incongruous, she once told me, for such language to come from someone in female attire.

Her followers, who now number more than 325,000, worship her still, even after her death, as a divine messiah, the successor of the Buddha and Jesus. Her divinity, they claim, has been abundantly proved by countless miracles. She has cured sickness, raised people from the dead, diverted the course of storms and arrested the spread of fires. At her headquarters at Tabuse in Yamaguchi prefecture, which now boasts a gigantic concrete temple and preaching hall designed by Tange Kenzō, she delivered sermons several times a day until the day of her death. Her discourse was frequently punctuated by bursts of extempore song, which her followers, who listened with closed eyes and clasped hands, recognised to be the words of the deity inside her. She taught her followers to perform a dance, known as Muga-no-mai or the Selfless Dance. The believers glide to and fro with closed eyes, their faces wearing expressions like those of ecstatic sleepwalkers. In 1964 she accomplished a world missionary tour of the most taxing nature, visiting something approaching thirty-six countries and giving sermons unfailingly three times a day.[12]

Other examples of successful and flourishing new religions which made their beginning through the inspired possession of the founder by a deity include Konkōkyō, whose founder, a poor peasant by the name of Kawate Bunjirō, was possessed and elected in 1857 by the deity Konjin. The Reiyūkai, a powerful offshoot of the Nichiren sect of Buddhism, was likewise founded by a poor peasant woman, Kotani Kimi, who was possessed by spirits. The Risshō Kōseikai, another extraordinarily rich and flourishing offshoot of the Nichiren sect with a gigantic pink cathedral on the outskirts of Tokyo, had its beginnings in the possession of another poor peasant woman, Naganuma Myōkō, by various Buddhist deities.[13]

From these examples it is clear that the lives of the Founders tend to conform to a specific type, in which a number of distinctively shamanistic features are present. The sickly and eccentric personality of these people before their initiation, the shattering initiatory experience of election by a personal deity, the change of character which takes place after this initiation, the former oddity and feebleness giving place not only to an awe-inspiring majesty of personality but also to supernatural powers of healing and divination, the effusions of 'revealed' writing, often in metrical form—all these are traits which are found also in the lives of the Siberian shaman. In these remarkable personalities, therefore, whose activities have transformed the religious scene in Japan since the end of the war, 'there still survive some of the fundamental elements of genuine arctic shamanism'.[14]

It is plausible to imagine the ancient *miko* as people of

this kind, but supported and sustained by the ritual of a recognised and flourishing religious cult. They too were snatched into their holy calling by the sudden invasion of their bodies by a deity—usually, as we have seen, one connected with water and serpents. They too developed powers of divination and perhaps of healing, and the same dignity of personality. Though revealed writing was a gift not accessible to them in an age before the introduction of any script, yet Nakayama Tarō is doubtless right in ascribing to them a copious flow of oral revelation.[15]

It is true that the present-day Founders do not enter their entranced state by means of the magical dancing and music which we saw to be so important a preliminary to the ancient *miko's* ritual trance. Indeed, in the case of Ōgamisama at least, no external stimulus of any kind was necessary to encourage the deity within her to burst into prophesy and song. Her trance state enveloped her like a mantle at virtually any hour of the day or night. But here we see simply the result of the separation of the mantic function in Japanese shamanism from official religious ritual. The music and dancing which anciently acted as the beginning and elicitation of prophesy, remain, stylised, fixed and uninspired, in shrines where the oracles have long been dumb. To the genuinely mantic woman such stimuli are unnecessary.

It is true too that there seems to be no special connection between these shamanic founders and the snake deity which we saw to be in all probability the principal tutelary *kami* to elect and inspire the ancient *miko*. Save for Ōgamisama's Tōbyō, the deities who forcibly seize these people have nothing to do with snakes. We shall find in a later chapter, however, that among certain other natural shamans in Japan the snake is far from extinct. These people, though more properly classified as ascetics, nevertheless exhibit life histories very similar to those of the Founders. That the snake appears frequently as the tutelary deity of such people is ample proof that its connection with shamanism still persists.

Two more points of similarity may be adduced. First, it is noticeable that in the cults with a woman founder, the movement becomes a viable one when the Foundress is joined by a dedicated man. Had not Nakayama Miki been joined by Izō Iburi, Deguchi Nao by Ueda Kisaburō, or Kitamura Sayo by Nakamura Kimitake, it is doubtful if their powers would have reached beyond the narrow rural circles where they were first manifested. It was the combination of the inspired woman with the dedicated but extremely practical man which ensured the success of the cult as a missionary enterprise. A prefiguration of this situation may surely be discerned in the story in the Wei chronicles of the shamanic queen Pimiko, who remained unmarried but was attended upon in her closed and heavily guarded palace by a single man who transmitted her words; or in the relationship between the shamanic figure of the Empress Jingo and the rather mysterious minister Takeshiuchi-no-sukune, who acted as interrogator in the séance when the Emperor was struck dead for his unbelief.

A further parallel between present and past may be adduced from the extraordinary sense of a *monde à part* that pervades the atmosphere of the headquarters of these new cults. Step through the gate and one enters a separate world with its theocratic queen, surrounded by subjects who not only render her absolute devotion but also worship her as an *ikigami* or living goddess. The presence of the deity inside her has transubstantiated her into a divine person, much as the ancient *miko* through her possession by the water-snake deity became herself divine, slipping imperceptibly into the image of the magical lady at the bottom of the lake, the daughter of the dragon, even the dragon herself. Outside the gate of the cult headquarters lies the rest of Japan, but it is as irrelevant as the white mount surrounding a picture. For those within, the primary allegiance is paid not to the Emperor, nor to any government, nor to any set of abstract principles, but to the figure of the living goddess in their midst, whose clairvoyant eyes penetrate to their very souls, and whose utterances, coming straight from the divinity within her, give meaning and hope and purpose to their lives.

Two further points remain before we leave these unusual people. If shamanism was so widespread in prehistoric Japan, if an inspired woman could be discovered to serve in virtually every shrine in the land, how is it that today these natural shamans are so rare? That they manifest themselves only in times of crisis, anxiety and the collapse of tradition, and even then comparatively scantily? An answer is readily available. Were the conditions of modern secular life more propitious to the display of such powers, it is likely that many more women would exhibit them in Japan today than might be suspected. Many women appear neurotic, peculiar or even half-witted merely because these powers are repressed or disguised within them. A number of women do exhibit exactly the same life history as the Founders, the same symptoms of arctic hysteria, the same cataclysmic initiation. They do not become the leaders of flourishing religious movements because the attendant circumstances are not correct. No practical man, for example, appears to organise and manage. Such women tend to become *gyōja*, ascetics, employing their shamanistic powers more for the banishment and exorcism of malignant spirits than for the transmission of the oracles of benign ones.

We are led thus to conclude that the original, true natural shaman in Japan was a person in whom the powers of both the medium and the ascetic were combined. She was one who could at the same time transmit the messages of her tutelary deity and overcome malignant spiritual beings. The division of Japanese shamanism into two complementary parts, active and passive, emerges as due probably to the influence of ascetic and esoteric Buddhism. The Buddhist figure of the ascetic, in appropriating to himself the active, banishing side of shamanic practice, at the same time relegated the task of medium to one of mere passive, almost automatic utterance.

Before we examine the figure of the ascetic, therefore, we must describe one of these surviving types of passive medium. These women differ conspicuously both from the living goddesses and from their ancient forebears. But they deserve description because, in the first place, they are among the very few still living representatives of the shamanic medium who operates alone, unaided by a member of the ascetic order, and secondly, because they preserve in their ritual vestiges of ancient practices which have elsewhere been lost.

8
The Blind Medium

The blind mediums known as *itako* or *ichiko* are not considered by some authorities, notably Hori, to be true shamans. They exhibit none of the symptoms of 'arctic hysteria', the neurotic oddity and proneness to dreams and haunting that we saw to be the prelude to the sacred life among the living goddesses. They experience no call from the other side, neither in dreams nor in sudden possessions. Nor do they show any true power-giving relationship with a tutelary deity. The deity to whom they are formally 'wedded' at their ceremony of initiation seldom comes to their aid thereafter with the supernatural gifts we saw to be the strength of the living goddesses. Nor are they capable any longer of achieving a truly ecstatic state. What passes for a trance among them is seen on shrewd inspection to be mere imitation.[1]

They deserve treatment, nevertheless, for the vestiges of ancient experience and ritual which can still be discerned in their practice. We shall therefore in this chapter examine the manner in which these blind girls make their entry into the sacred life, and in which they ply their profession thereafter of calling ghosts and numina and transmitting their words.

These blind mediums are still to be found in most of the prefectures of the north-east of the main island. Elsewhere in Japan there is no trace of them. The practices of these women have fortunately been well described. Sakurai Tokutarō has given us careful studies of the *itako* and their practices in the Tsugaru district of Aomori prefecture, in Yamagata prefecture, and in the northern part of the old province of Rikuzen, now Miyagi prefecture. These studies, helpfully supplemented by those of Togawa Anshō for the Shōnai district of Yamagata and of Satō Shōjun for Iwate prefecture, give us an interesting picture of a basic uniformity of practice among these mediums over an entire area of the north-east. Her motive for entering the sacred life, the austerities which prepare her for her entry, her manner of exercising her profession thereafter—all these, irrespective of district, show a fundamental similarity.[2]

Recent studies of shamanistic practices in the north have drawn a sharp distinction between two different types of *miko* to be found there. The *itako*, they assert, must be clearly differentiated from the women known as *gomiso*. This distinction will not affect us in the present chapter. According to the classification we earlier defined, whereby the medium is primarily a transmitter and the ascetic primarily a healer and exorciser, the *gomiso* falls clearly into the ascetic category. It is only the *itako* who are mediums and will therefore concern us at this stage of our investigation.[3]

We have already noticed that the word *itako* is thought to be cognate with the Ryūkyū *yuta*, and with certain Altaic names for a shaman. The Yakut *udagan*, the Buryat *udagang* and the Tungus *idakon* are cited as evidence for the Altaic associations of the Japanese shamanic person.[4] Certainly the terms *itako* and *ichiko* are general throughout the north despite extra local appellations such as *onakama* in Yamagata and *ogamin* in Miyagi, and suggest an ancient contact with continental shamanism.

First let us examine the motive of the *itako* for entering her sacred calling. A girl is impelled to become an *itako* purely and simply because she is blind. Either she is born blind, or she becomes blind in infancy as a result of sickness or malnutrition. A number of occupations have been traditionally reserved for blind people in Japan, among which massage and lute-playing are prominent examples. In the north the profession of medium has also for some time been in the hands of such people.

The blind *itako* is not forced into her calling, as are the living goddesses, by an irresistible command from the other side. Her motive is voluntary and purely practical. By becoming a medium she will become a viable member of her community rather than a burden. It is in order to save her from the stigma of uselessness that her parents apprentice her to an older, already established *itako*, in whose house she may receive the necessary training.

It is her parents rather than she herself who take this decision, since she is seldom more than twelve or thirteen years old at the time. A firm belief prevails throughout the district that she must start her apprenticeship before the onset of menstruation. Sexual desire, it is alleged, is a hindrance to the practice of the necessary austerities and to the proper accomplishment of the initiation ritual. With a young girl the god will 'take' her without difficulty. With a girl trained over the age of puberty he may well be reluctant, and many attempts may be required before success is attained. Nor can an adult-initiated medium be trusted to transmit reliably the utterances of *kami* and ghosts. The rumour soon gets round that *yoku ataranai*, her transmissions are unreliable, and soon she has no clients. Hence the early age at which she is usually apprenticed to her teacher.[5]

For the period of her apprenticeship she commonly lives in the house of her teacher. There she stays for the two, three or even five years that may be necessary for her training, acting as maid of all work in the intervals between her lessons. During this period she must undergo an ascetic regime, the severity of which varies according to the district and the individual teacher.

Hasegawa Sowa, for example, an *itako* from the Tsugaru district of Aomori prefecture, aged sixty-five when interviewed, told Sakurai that her daily routine throughout the year of her training had been as follows. She got up before dawn and performed her morning cold water austerity. There followed a short service of chanting before the family altar, and after breakfast the morning lesson. Here she would have to repeat phrase by phrase after her teacher a number of sutras, ballads, *norito* and the psalms known as *wasan*. Over and over again she repeated these chants until she had them effortlessly by heart. The texts included the *Hannya Shingyō*, the Kannon Sutra, the Jizō Sutra and the *Jizō wasan*. After lunch she had to go over with the other two pupils in the house the phrases she had learnt in the morning. After supper there was more practice until the evening cold water austerity and bed. The teacher had been very strict, she recalled, and would scold her unmercifully if her memory was bad. If she was wilting with tiredness, the teacher would direct at her a short sharp yell which startled her so much that she often burst into tears. So unhappy was she that she once ran away.[6]

In Yamagata prefecture a similarly strict regime was the rule in the early 1930s. Suzuki Tsuyako, born in 1923, recalled a severe daily *mizugori* at crack of dawn, twelve buckets of cold water from the river to be poured over each shoulder. In winter this austerity was excruciating; the cold was so intense that often she nearly lost consciousness and only kept herself from fainting by focusing all her power and concentration on reciting the *Hannya Shingvō*. She had nothing to eat until midday. All the morning was spent in repeating, phrase by phrase after her teacher, various kinds of sacred text, including *norito* and invocations to Inari, Kōjin and the deities of the nearby mountains Gassan and Yudonosan. Her memory was bad, and her teacher often scolded her until she cried.[7]

Once the initiation ritual drew near, however, the austerities increased ferociously in intensity. For the week immediately preceding the rite, the girl was subjected to appallingly severe *gyō*, calculated to reduce the body to a pitch of exhaustion verging on total breakdown.

Suzuki Tsuyako, for example, described the ordeals which she underwent in 1935 at the age of twelve. The intensification of her *gyō* started a hundred days before her initiation, when every morning at 2 a.m., the spiritually powerful hour of the ox, she had to get up, grope her way to the river bank and pour twelve buckets of cold water over each shoulder. She then had to walk to the local Inari shrine, light candles and chant the *Hannya Shingyō*. Blind as she was and unaffected by the darkness, she nevertheless found the precincts of the shrine at that hour of the morning terrifyingly uncanny. During this period neither she nor her family ate meat or strong-smelling vegetables.

For the week immediately before her initiation the austerities were further intensified to an almost incredible pitch of severity. She had first to observe the *sandachi* of Three Abstentions. No cereals must pass her lips, no salt, nor any cooked foods. Nor, if the austerities took place in winter, must she ever go near a stove or any other form of heating. Every day she had to pour over her shoulders no less than a thousand buckets of cold water, each one counted on the beads of a rosary. At the same time she must recite a thousand *Hannya Shingyōs* and twenty-one Kannon Sutras. This appalling austerity lasted from crack of dawn until late at night, so that throughout the week she was allowed next to no sleep. The first two days of this fearful regime, she recalled, were almost unbearable. The intense cold, the sleeplessness and the semi-starvation brought her to the point of breakdown. Her joints ached so agonisingly that she could scarcely walk or lift the buckets over her head. But on the third day her pain suddenly vanished. She felt herself flooded with an extraordinary access of strength and enthusiasm such that she felt capable of enduring any ordeal in order to accomplish the final initiation.[8]

A similarly severe example of preliminary *gyō* was recorded for Sakurai by Mrs Chichii Yae, a celebrated *itako* from the Tsugaru district. For a week during the atrociously cold February of 1918 she lived in a small hut specially constructed for her near a well. From this well, seven times a day, she had to pour three large buckets of cold water over each shoulder, reciting sutras and mantras meanwhile at the top of her voice. Her diet was deprived of all meat, all bird and fish, all vegetables and all salt. For the entire week she was allowed no sleep at all. All night and all day, between her bouts of cold water, she had to recite over and over again the sutras and psalms she had learnt during her training. At one point she felt she was going to die under the strain of cold and exhaustion. But, forcing herself to carry on, she was given towards the end of the week a new access of strength, and of faith in the deity Fudō Myōō.[9]

Mrs Nara Naka, also from the Tsugaru district, underwent a similar ordeal before her initiation in 1918, in which intense cold, sleeplessness and abstention from her accustomed diet were the order of the day. She too was required to live for a week in a small hut specially constructed for her by her teacher. She too had to observe the Three Abstentions, from cereals, from salt and from hot food, and she too for the entire week was forbidden to sleep. All night long she must sit up reciting the texts she had learnt by heart, with no fire to warm her through the cold winter hours. Three times a day she had to make her way down to the river at the bottom of the valley, and on a special place on the bank, cordoned off with sacred rope, perform a strenuous bout of the cold water austerity. Thirty-three buckets of cold water must be poured over her right shoulder, thirty-three over her left, while she recited over and over again the invocation, '*Ōyama Daishi Fudō Myōō, namu Daishi Fudō Myōō.*'

During this week she was for most of the time entirely alone, but as she never knew when her teacher might call on her to supervise her progress, she could never allow herself to relax her efforts for a moment. Towards the middle of the week she became so exhausted from cold, sleeplessness and lack of food that she sank into a condition of semi-trance in which the figures of *kami* seemed to appear and disappear before her eyes. Towards the end of the week, however, an indescribable and mysterious strength seemed to well up and suffuse her entire body. Her physical exhaustion disappeared before this access of power from a source seemingly outside herself, and by the morning of the initiation she was well prepared to face the ordeal.[10]

In Miyagi prefecture the picture is much the same. The three abstentions are observed for three weeks before the initiation, with the water austerity night and morning. The night before the ceremony is due to take place—and a favourite time for the event is the 'great cold' just before New Year—must be spent in the continuous performance of the cold water exercise. It is alleged that in some districts the number of buckets poured over the head and shoulders during the night reaches the almost unbelievable figure of 33,333.[11]

Sleeplessness, semi-starvation and intense cold is thus the picture for the whole north-eastern district. Such strains would normally, in a profane context, reduce the body to the point of breakdown. In almost all the accounts before us, however, we read that just when the girl was on the verge of collapse, she felt herself flooded by a new access of strength which transformed her outlook on life. For the rest of the period a wave of enthusiastic determination to continue until the moment of her initiation made her impervious to pain and fatigue.

Here we are surely confronted with the underlying reason for *gyō*. Performed within a sacred context, with the prospect of a transformed life ahead, ascesis may open the mind to an influx of spiritual strength. By breaking down the ordinary human habits of living, by drastically altering the rhythms of sleep and eating, and above all by subjecting the body to extreme degrees of cold, the system is reduced to a point where mere collapse would usually ensue. Where the sacred world lies before one, however, these stresses become the means of opening a crack or vent in the hard carapace of human habit, enabling a new source of power to stream in.

The initiation rite itself comes, therefore, as a supreme climax of a period of ordeal. Again, accounts from the different districts of the north-east report a similar structure to the ceremony. Mrs Nara Naka, for example, recalled the rite, known in her district as *yurushi*, taking place in a room in her teacher's house. It was carefully curtained and cordoned with sacred rope to prevent the ingress of malign and hindering forces. An atmosphere of uncanny mystery pervaded the darkened chamber. A number of guests were invited to the ceremony, notably the girl's own family and all the former pupils of the teacher living in the district. An altar was constructed in the alcove of the room, on which stood three sacks of rice, the middle one implanted with a *gohei* wand. The girl's seat before the altar was surrounded with three more sacks of rice, one behind her and two on either side, while in front of her sat her teacher.

The older *itako* in the room then began to chant over and over again the sutras and liturgies which the girl had learnt by heart, meanwhile walking round and round the girl and her teacher. Eventually the loud rhythmic noise and the circumambulating movement caused Mrs Nara to feel as though innumerable *kami* were streaming into the room and that one of these was taking possession of her. At that moment she lost consciousness. When she came to herself she was lying in another room, her teacher telling her that the rite had been successful. While she was unconsious her teacher had asked, 'Who has come?' and the girl had replied in the approved manner with the name of the deity who was henceforth to be her tutelary *kami*.

The final step of the rite took the form of a wedding feast. All the girl's relations were present, with all the teacher's old pupils, and she herself changed out of the white garments she had previously worn into a brilliant kimono with long sleeves and a pattern appropriate to a bridal robe. She was now wedded and dedicated to the deity who had taken possession of her, and who now stood to her in the relation of a tutelary god. In later life she had married in the normal way, she recalled, but her wedding celebration had been on no scale comparable with that which marked her spiritual marriage with the deity.[12]

Very similar descriptions come from Yamagata and Miyagi prefectures. The curtained, cordoned and darkened room; the sacks of rice, the loud continuous chanting, the tremors, shivers and convulsive shaking which overtake the girl, culminating in a dead faint. When she recovers consciousness in the adjoining room, she is told by her teacher that the deity Nittensama, or Fudō Myōō, has satisfactorily taken possession of her and will henceforth act as her tutelary deity. The same lavish wedding feast follows, with red rice, whole fish, as much saké as can be afforded, and the girl in a red wedding dress to indicate her spiritual marriage with the deity.[13]

Here we have a rite of unmistakably initiatory character. A preliminary ordeal of an excruciating kind involving fasting, cold water and repetitive chanting; a rite in which tension is raised to the point at which the candidate faints dead away. Dying to her old self, she is reborn in the dazzling garb of the bride of the deity implanted in her at the moment of death and with whom she will henceforth stand in a close tutelary relationship.

An important final step in the initiation ritual in all districts is the *dōgu-watashi* or transmission of instruments of power. These are the tools without which the girl cannot accomplish the tasks of summoning *kami* and ghosts and inducing them to take possession of her. All over the Tōhoku district the instruments used for these purposes are of three principal kinds: a bow or one-stringed lute used for summoning ghosts, a pair of puppets known as *oshirasama* for summoning *kami*, and a rosary used indiscriminately for invoking both kinds of spirit.

The catalpa bow with its hempen string is now less often seen in the north than its variant, the *ichigenkin* or one-stringed lute. In the past, however, it was clearly in wide-spread use. The literature of the Edo period contains many references to *miko* who, tapping the string of their catalpa bow with a bamboo rod, deliver a terrifying lament from a ghost in hell. That the use of this bow as a summoner of spirits is ancient is testified by the use of the word for catalpa bow, *azusayumi*, in the great eighth-century anthology of poetry *Manyōshū*. Here it appears many times as the *makura-kotoba* or fixed epithet of the word *yoru*. *Yoru* is a verb meaning either 'to approach' or 'to possess'. From the close association between the two words we infer that when the bow gives forth its sound, spirits are compelled to approach and possess the waiting medium. Both the bow and the one-stringed lute are probably simpler forebears of the *koto*, which we saw at the time of the Empress Jingo already to be the instrument used to summon deities.[14]

The second instrument of power handed to the *itako* after her initiation is the long rosary known as *irataka-juzu*. The rosary is originally a Buddhist device to aid concentration of mind during meditation, to count repetitions of a sacred formula, or, the beads rubbed together with a dry rustling noise, to accompany the chanting of sutras. Most of the Buddhist sects use a rosary of 108 beads. In the hands of the *itako*, however, the rosary is lengthened and elaborated into a heavy chain of 300 black soapberry beads, sometimes barbarically festooned with the teeth, claws and horns of wild beasts. A notable example which I saw in use at Osorezan in 1959 was decorated with two pendant loops. One of these was 'male', and was strung with the horns of a stag, the tusks of a boar, the claws of male bears and falcons and the jawbone of a male fox. The other chaplet was 'female'. This was likewise strung with cow's horns, a vixen's jaw, sow's tusks, cowrie shells and old coins of the Tempo period with a square hole in the middle. Rosaries as potent as this one are now increasingly rare. Either 300 or

180 black shiny beads are the examples most often seen. Of the derivation of the peculiar name of the rosary, *irataka*, nothing is known. Hori points out, however, that it was probably borrowed by the *miko* from the ascetics of the Shugendō order. The fourteenth-century work *Taiheiki* mentions an *irataka-juzu* as worn by a *yamabushi* of the time.[15]

The last instrument recorded in all districts as handed to the *itako* after her initiation is the curious pair of puppets known as *oshirasama*. These are sticks about a foot long, with bulbous ends roughly carved to represent the heads of a woman and a horse, and covered with layers of cloth. Some examples are luxuriously clothed in glittering gold and silver brocade. More often they are drably clad in rough cotton dyed to peasant blues, browns and dirty whites. A new layer of cotton is added every year, so that it is easy to discover the age of any particular pair of *oshirasama* by counting the layers in which it is clothed. Several of the examples in the Folk Museum on the outskirts of Tokyo have as many as ninety to a hundred layers, the undermost ones rotting away with age. In some parts of the north, notably Iwate prefecture, the head of the stick with its rude carving pokes through a hole in the layers of cloth. Elsewhere the cloth covers the head and, tied round the neck with a string hung with bells, gives the impression of an enigmatically faceless marionette.

In origin these puppets were probably ancient examples of *torimono*, objects which the *miko* held in her hand as she danced herself into a trance, and which acted as a conductor by which the god could enter into her. Most *torimono* seem to have been a single object, the *sakaki* branch already noticed, for example, or a bow or a wand. The double *torimono*, however, an object held in either hand, seems to have been common in the north. Today they are used by the *itako* in exactly this manner. As she summons the god and delivers his message, she waves, jerks and flourishes the puppets in her hands in a manner suggesting a remote forebear of the modern puppeteer.

As she manipulates the puppets, the *itako* recites the curious tale known as *Oshira-saimon* which purports to explain their origin. This tale, which exists in Japan in ten main variations, is an essential part of the repertory which the girl must learn by heart during her training. It recounts how, from an unnatural passion between a girl and a horse, silkworms were first born.[16]

I give it here in bare outline, shorn of all detail. A certain man had a daughter called Tamaya-gozen, and a beautiful chestnut horse called Sendan-kurige. Every day Tamaya-gozen used to feed the horse with her own hands, until one day, struck by his beauty, she said, 'If only you were a man I should like you for my husband.' From this moment the horse conceived a burning passion for Tamaya-gozen, so consuming that he could neither eat nor drink.

The rich man called in diviners to discover what ailed the horse. When they told him that the horse was sick for love of his daughter the rich man in a rage had the horse killed and skinned. Tamaya-gozen went to say a requiem mass over the skin, when it suddenly wrapped itself round her and carried her up to the sky. Presently there fell down a shower of black and white insects, which alighted on the mulberry trees and began to eat the leaves. As they ate, they gave out a fine thread. They were the first silkworms, and in consequence the rich man became the greatest silk merchant in the land.

This peculiar tale clearly originated in China, where a legend attributing the beginning of sericulture to an unnatural passion between a horse and a girl is to be found in the fourth-century work *Sou shen chi*. In China, however, it remained a folktale only, unconnected with any ritual. Through its association with the *itako*, it has spread throughout the north of Japan in the form of a *saimon* or sacred ballad. Its transition from a plain folktale to a sacred text is to be explained probably as an example of the potency of recalling origins. To recount the origin of a god is to remind him of his nature and its attendant powers. To describe a beginning is to go back to that beginning, thereby renewing the power that was born at that time. The tale also picks up the peculiar structural connection, appearing again and again in Japanese myth, legend and ritual, between a horse, silkworms and sexual potency. Its relationship with the *itako's* summoning of *kami*, however, of the local tutelary deity, for example, unconnected with silkworms, has so far baffled folklorists.

Two subsidiary instruments of power used by the *itako* may be mentioned in passing. A fan-shaped drum is used to summon both *kami* and ghosts by *itako* with affiliations with the Nichiren sect of Buddhism.[17] And the mysterious box known as *oi*, so often mentioned in descriptions of *miko* at the beginning of the century, is now virtually extinct. This box purported to contain an object, often an animal's skull, in which the *miko's* power over spirits was incapsulated. Deprive her of her box, therefore, and her power vanished. The whole principle of the *oi*, however, Nakayama avers, is foreign to the tradition of the *miko*, which requires that her power reside within herself, as a result of training and initiation. There is no doubt, however, that during the Edo period many *miko* were habitually associated with such a box and its gruesome contents.[18]

Once a girl is fully initiated and possessed of her instruments of power, what tasks is she expected to perform? In all districts of the north-east her duties fall into two broad categories: *kamioroshi* or bringing down *kami*, and *hotoke-oroshi* or *kuchiyose*, summoning ghosts. She is expected to deliver utterances from both kinds of spirit on the problems which beset the human community.

The ritual and treatment which she offers to each kind of spirit tends to differ in different areas. An elderly *itako*, for example, who was called in for the evening to the house in Tanabu in which I was staying in 1958, declared herself equally capable of summoning either *kami* or ghosts, but not both on the same day. Always she had to sleep before making the transition from one to the other. Both types of spirit, she declared, were helpful in solving human problems, though ghosts were slightly better in advising on the personal difficulties of their surviving families.

The methods she employed to invoke each kind of spirit were nevertheless very similar. Whether she was summoning the family ancestors that evening, or the local *kami* the following morning, she banged repeatedly on a fan-shaped drum, rubbed her black rosary and recited sutras and invocations, many of which seemed to be identical. In the summoning of ghosts, however, and the delivery of their messages, she always used a special vocabulary of taboo words. For 'father', for example, she said *tsugi-no-yomboshi-sama*, and for 'mother' *tsugi no kara no kagami*. For 'grand-father' she said *toshiyori-yomboshisama* and for 'grandmother' *toshiyori-kara-no-kagami*. These were the only names, she declared, to which the dead spirits would respond.[19]

Further south in Miyagi prefecture, however, the calling of *kami* takes a different form altogether from the invocation of dead spirits.

The *kami* are called by means of ritual performed in the local shrine, apparently very similar to the one we tried to reconstruct for the ancient *miko*. It is performed at crucial seasons in the calendar when supernatural advice about the future is particularly welcome. At New Year, for example, at the time of the rice planting and at harvest time, the god is petitioned to reveal what are the prospects for the village in the way of storms, monsoon rains, sickness and fires, as well as of the rice harvest itself. The ritual is so similar, both to the ancient model and to those performed with the assistance of an ascetic which we shall deal with in the chapter on village oracles, that it would be repetitive to describe it in detail here. Suffice to say that in Miyagi prefecture and in Yamagata as well, the blind medium is the intermediary for a seasonal call to the local deity for his advice and help.[20]

More important and more time-consuming than the calling of *kami* is the task of *kuchiyose*, or the calling of dead spirits.

Sakurai is his account of the *ogamisan* of the Rikuzen district gives us an extremely full and interesting description of the manner in which ghosts are summoned. Unlike the rest of the north-eastern area, two distinct processes are here observed. One relates to 'new ghosts', the spirits of those who have died within the last hundred days. The other relates to 'old ghosts', whose death took place before this period.

The calling of new ghosts should properly be performed during the period of forty-nine days after the funeral. In some districts it is incumbent to perform the rite on the third or fifth days after the coffin has left the house, in others on the day immediately afterwards. Always it is performed in the house of the bereaved family, where the *ogamisan* is expected to reside for the duration of the ceremony.

The structure of the ritual is an interesting one. The first step is always to summon myriads of *kami*, ranging from superior deities with names down to anonymous village and household divinities. Always, before a ghost can be invoked, these *kami* must be summoned to the scene of the séance. They act as wardens or guardians of the ritual, in a manner which recalls the practice in spiritualist circles in the west, whereby the medium's control must be summoned before any 'ostensible communicator' can be induced to speak.

Before a newly dead spirit can be reached, however, another preliminary step must take place. This is the summoning of the Ancestor of the family, a ghost at least fifty years old who acts as the *michibiki* or guide. This Ancestor must make seven utterances in response to a fixed order of seven questions relating to the condition and abode of the new ghost. Where is the spirit now, is it satisfied with the offerings supplied, is it happy?

At last the new ghost itself comes through and addresses each of its relations in turn. To parents, children, brothers, sisters, grandchildren, uncles, aunts, it speaks just as it might have done when still alive, save that it always addresses them by means of the taboo words. Everyone present sobs and cries during these utterances, and the atmosphere is said to be indescribably uncanny. In a large family, where the ghost has many relatives to address, this stage of the rite may well go on for eight or nine hours. A 'new calling' which starts at nine o'clock in the morning may well continue until nightfall.

The next stage is therefore a short rest, enabling the *ogamisan*, who has been talking continuously all this while, to refresh herself with a little tea. The final step is of the nature of an envoi. The new ghost is despatched to its own world, and the Ancestor is requested to show it the way back. Finally the myriad *kami* summoned at the beginning of the rite and who have been present all the while are in their turn sent back to their own abode.

Sakurai witnessed a 'new calling' in 1966, in which an *ogamisan* from Ishinomaki transmitted the utterances of the eldest son of the house, killed a hundred days before by a fall from a bridge. The spirit addressed all its relations, neighbours and friends, making in all no less than seventy-three speeches through the mouth of the *ogamisan*. To his mother, whom he addressed by the local taboo term *ainomakura*, he apologised for all the trouble his early death had caused her, told of his feelings in his new condition and his hopes for the future. His wife's elder brother, whom he addressed as *oyakatasama*, he urged to keep an eye on his wife and family now that he was no longer there to look after them. A large number of friends, each addressed in turn, he begged to come often to his house to see that his family was all right. I am now your guardian, he added, and will see that you are safe and happy, so please be extra careful of accidents between August 27th and September 10th.

After each speech an old coin was put by the *ogamisan's* side as a tally to reckon the number of utterances the spirit had made and hence how much the *ogamisan* should be paid. In 1966 the rate was 25 yen per utterance. After seventy-three speeches, therefore, the *ogamisan* received 1,825 yen, and with the addition of 350 yen for the calling of the preliminary *kami*, made a total of 2,175 yen for her day's work.[21]

Whereas there are no taboos or restrictions on the season at which new ghosts can be called—on the contrary, it is strictly incumbent on the relatives to call the spirit within a hundred days of the funeral in whatever season its death may have taken place—with the calling of old ghosts, attention must be paid to auspicious and inauspicious seasons. The seasons in which it is proper and propitious to call an old ghost are the spring and autumn equinoxes, the Bon period, and the 1st, 3rd, 7th, 13th, 23rd, 27th and 33rd anniversary of the person's death. If old ghosts are not called at the equinoxes and Bon, it is thought that they will be offended and appear to their families in dreams to complain of neglect.

The seasons at which it is not propitious to call an old

ghost coincide with the months in which *kami* are particularly active. These are the first, fifth and ninth months of the old lunar calendar. The fifth month is unsuitable because the deity Tanokami is believed to descend from his mountain to supervise the work of the rice fields at that time, and might quarrel with the Ancestors if he met them on the road. The tenth month, on the other hand, is an excellent month in which to summon the ancestral dead, since the *kami* are all believed to flock to Izumo leaving their shrines empty and untenanted.

Another propitious date for the summoning of old ghosts is the 24th of the old sixth month, the feast day of the Bodhisattva Jizō. It is on this day that the notable gatherings of *itako*, later to be described, take place at certain temples throughout the north.

Sakurai describes an old ghost-calling which he witnessed at the spring equinox of 1966 at the village of Kisennuma in Miyagi prefecture. Ten women of all ages were crowded into a six-mat room, one of whom acted as *toiguchi* or interrogator to the medium. This assignment was held to be an important one, since on the skill of the questioner largely depended the success of the medium's utterance.

As in the case of new ghosts, it was necessary to summon myriads of *kami* first, who were present in a tutelary capacity throughout the rite. Then, one by one, in due order of seniority, all the family's ancestral ghosts were summoned. First the corporate Ancestor was called, then the grandfather, grandmother, father, mother, children, grandchildren, brothers, sisters, uncles, aunts and cousins.

The interrogator called upon the Ancestor, '*Hai, senzosama, o-tanomi mōshimasu . . .*' Whereupon the Ancestor launched into a long admonitory speech. Always remember to be courteous to friends and relations, he advised. Don't neglect the mortuary tablets. Be extra careful on May 6th . . . If a member of the company sought his counsel on any particular subject—on building a house, for example, or arranging a marriage—she could put the question to the Ancestor through the interrogator.

When the Ancestor's speech was concluded, the interrogator called, 'Next, father-in-law!' The *ogamisan* then transmitted father-in-law's message: work hard, don't forget to pay attention to *us*, and be careful not to catch cold next month.

The interrogator then called, 'Next ghost, mother-in-law!' Through the medium, mother-in-law described her grief in leaving all her family and friends so suddenly, told her daughter-in-law to take care to bring up the children properly, and warned the company against colds and accidents on certain dates.

Thereafter ghost after ghost was called; the husband's sister, his young brother, his nephew, the wife's parents, brothers and sisters, the daughter's husband, the small nephew drowned at the age of five, and lastly the *muen-botoke*, any 'unrelated ghost' who might wish to speak.

Some of the ghosts were extremely talkative, their utterance continuing for some forty or fifty minutes. Others were briefer. But irrespective of the length of the speech, the medium received 30 yen for each one. The audience eagerly took notes of what each ghost had said. Most utterances, however, Sakurai recognised as falling into fixed types or *kata*, with which the audience was familiar.[22]

In the case of both old and new ghosts the medium is expected to go in person to the bereaved house in order to perform the calling rite. In the Ishinomaki district, however, a rather different system prevails. The mediums form a group or union, the younger and stronger of whom are elected to undertake a seasonal 'walk' round a prescribed series of villages. This walk, known as *debayashi*, takes place twice a year at the time of the spring and autumn equinoxes. Its purpose is to enable the inhabitants of remote villages to perform their equinoctial calling of family ghosts. A strict *nawabari* or beat must be observed by each itinerant medium, great resentment being caused if any member strays off her prescribed course.

Sasaki Kie recalled at the age of sixty-two her first *debayashi* performed at the age of eighteen. Her prescribed beat took her round various villages on the Ojika peninsula. Her father had come as far as the harbour to see her off, and thereafter, at every village she visited, *tebiki* or hand-holders were provided as blind guides.

In each village she was conducted to a private house, where a room was made over to her for the duration of her stay. Here an altar was arranged, on which were set offerings of salt, water, dried fish and saké, and where a sacred enclosure was constructed with straw rope and branches of *sakaki*.

The ritual she then performed, and to which a crowd of villagers flocked, was very similar to the village oracles which we shall discuss in a later chapter. The first step, as always, was to invite an enormous number of *kami* from all over Japan to descend to the place of the rite. The local deities were then questioned as to the fortunes of the village during the coming six months. Enquiries as to the weather, the rice harvest, the fishing catches, accidents, fires and sicknesses were put to the deities, whose answers through the medium's mouth were duly noted down.

The first day having been devoted to the *kami's* predictions of the general fortunes of the village, the following day was set aside for the calling of the ancestral ghosts of individual families. The medium undertook to call both old and new ghosts, according to the family's need. Again the rite started with the summoning of the household *kami* (*yashikigami*), of which some families possessed more than one. These divinities then pronounced on the family fortunes, predicting the exact days on which illness or accident might be expected. These taboo days, *imibi*, were noted down on paper and stuck up on the porch of the house. In some families the danger of such days was treated so seriously that no one would leave the house.

The calling of ancestral ghosts in due order of seniority then followed. It is believed in this district that unless ghosts are called at the spring and autumn equinoxes they cannot achieve salvation, but will wander round the house and village inflicting a variety of curses on the inhabitants. It is therefore absolutely essential to have them 'called' at these seasons and encouraged to speak of their condition.

If there are many families in the village and hence many ancestors to be called, the work of the medium may continue all night and well into the following day.[23]

Further west in Yamagata prefecture the customary

treatment of ghosts differs. The strict differentiation found in Miyagi prefecture between new and old ghosts is not observed here. Both kinds of spirit are treated alike, with the reservation that new ghosts are not expected to speak until a hundred days have passed. Nor is it usual to call them until then. Here Yamagata resembles the Tsugaru and Nambu districts of Aomori prefecture, where again no ghost is called in less than a hundred days.

In these parts ghosts differ considerably in their degree of loquaciousness according to the age at which they died. Child ghosts are expected to talk much and boisterously. Aged ghosts, on the other hand, are much quieter because they leave the world with less resentment.

In every case, whatever the age or condition of the ghost, the medium must always ask, 'Is there anything you specially want?' This question is necessary because some ghosts are haunted and oppressed by remorse for the things that they were unable to accomplish because of their untimely deaths. Children who died before they could go to school, for example, are tormented with longing for school and remorse that they never went there. Young men and women who died before they could get married are desperate to remedy their single state. Very sensibly, however, these ghosts will always tell their relatives exactly what to do to assuage their remorse. The child will ask to have a votive picture painted of itself sitting for the school entrance examination, and that the picture should be taken to the Okunoin or inner shrine of the great temple Yamadera. The unmarried girl will tell her parents to search in a particular direction for her fiancé. This they must do until they find a suitable candidate. They must then obtain a photograph of the young man and put it in a frame next to that of the dead girl, and present it at the Okunoin of Yamadera with suitable requiem sutras. The spirit's remorse will by this means be assuaged so that it can peacefully await its due attainment of salvation.

The ritual for the calling of ghosts in this district resembles the one performed in Miyagi prefecture. The medium, beating time with a bamboo rod on the string of her catalpa bow, first calls the Ancestor of the household. Only then can she summon the dead spirit whose utterance is particularly desired. The spirit addresses each of its surviving relations in turn, starting with close relatives and continuing to distant cousins and friends. In a large family with many relatives, so many speeches are often necessary that the medium is required to continue her chanting all night long and well into the following day.[24]

Finally, let us look at the custom which still survives in the north for the *itako* to gather together at certain seasons and places for a grand communal summoning of ghosts. The most celebrated of these gatherings is that which takes place on the 24th of the old sixth month, the feast day of the Bodhisattva Jizō, at the temple known as Osorezan.

This temple, which stands on the edge of a lake halfway up the Shimokita peninsula and whose name is of Ainu derivation, is a notable example of those places in Japan on to which the geography of the other world has been projected. Just as Mt Tateyama with its sulphur springs was thought to be the entrance to hell, and the Kumano mountains to represent various realms of paradise, on the slopes of Osorezan are to be found almost all the countries of the other world to which the dead are expected to go. In a white gash on the mountainside from which bubble a number of sulphur springs, hell may be viewed. A little further on is a grey stony strand; this is Sainokawara, the dry river bed which is the boundary between worlds and the place where the ghosts of children can be heard sobbing by night as they make their little piles of stones. Walk on a little more and you come to the Sanzunokawa, the river which divides one world from another, and a little further yet and you reach paradise itself.

In the precincts of Osorezan, therefore, can be found many lands of the dead, who are thought to haunt the spot all the year round but to be particularly grateful for a 'calling' at the Bon season. At this time, therefore, some twenty *itako* from all over Aomori prefecture make their way to the temple and, sitting in a row beneath the eaves of the Main Hall, hold themselves ready for three days and nights to call the dead ancestors of any clients who may present themselves.

In 1959, when I observed the proceedings, there was a

fixed charge throughout the company of 30 yen for each ghost called. For the three days that I stayed in the temple, the row of blind women under the eaves were scarcely ever silent. At least a thousand peasants from the surrounding countryside arrived in busloads, and were accommodated with their bundles on the floor of the Buddha Hall. All day long and for much of the night they would pass from one medium to another requesting that this or that dead ancestor be called.

The *itako's* procedure was as follows: rubbing the beads of her rosary together, she cited the posthumous name of the dead person and the date of his death, together with the invocations needed to summon the spirit. These preliminaries over, she would pause and ask, casually in a low voice, a number of leading questions. What relation was he to you? Was he your father, your brother? Did he die in an accident? Or after a long illness? How many children had he, and how old is the youngest? All these questions were eagerly answered by the client, who was often an old woman.

Having thus ascertained into which type the dead person fell, the *itako* launched into a rapid singsong chant lasting five or ten minutes. It was not difficult to see that not a single one of the *itako* were in any state resembling trance. They exhibited none of the usual symptoms of stertorous breathing and convulsively shaking hands. The chants they recited, moreover, were easily seen to fall into different fixed forms. Soldiers killed in the war, for example, always said the same thing: that despite their misery at being killed, they found some repose in the Yasukuni shrine in Tokyo. Children always said the same thing: that they were constantly chased by red devils on the dry river bed of Sainokawara, but took refuge under the robe of the Bodhisattva Jizō. Grandfathers likewise had their fixed forms of words, so did mothers and grandmothers. All spirits spent a great deal of time in repeating over and over again how glad and grateful they were to be called, how sweet was the moment of respite which the calling gave them from the gloom and misery of their present existence.

Clearly the *itako* were simply reciting the most suitable among a repertory of fixed chants learnt by heart in the

Plate 14. The autumn retreat on Mt Haguro. The party arrives at Kōtakuji, where the retreat is to be observed, and receives instructions from the *dōshi* about moving in.

Plate 15. The *daisendatsu* at the Haguro autumn retreat wears the *ayaigasa* hat, which symbolises the placenta covering the embryo in the womb.

Plate 16. The autumn retreat on Mt Haguro. The pilgrimage climb to Sankozawa on the fourth day.

Plate 17. A *yamabushi* climbing the ladder of swords: Festooned with holy white *gohei*, the ladder of razor-sharp swords represents a passage to heaven which only the initiated can ascend.

course of their training as purporting to come from the dead. Their performance belonged to the category of *geinō* or folk drama, and at the same time functioned as a *kuyō* or requiem comfort to the dead.

On their audiences, however, the effect of these hackneyed effusions was pathetically touching. Round each *itako* was to be seen a little group of sobbing women, old and young, their faces screwed up with emotion, paper handkerchiefs pressed to their eyes. Here and there I noticed women sitting in rapt attention, as though at the theatre, and eagerly begging with proffered coins for 'One more!' as soon as the *itako's* chanting stopped.

By the afternoon of the second day the air resounded with a hubbub of high-pitched chanting and the dry rustle of rubbing beads. When night fell and the moon rose over the lake, some of the crowd drifted indoors and fell asleep on the floor of the Buddha Hall, so tightly packed together that arms, legs and heads were pillowed on other bodies. The crush in the Main Hall of the temple was just as bad. By midnight most people woke up and rings of the Bon dance started on the white shore of the lake. Harsh reedy voices rose and fell in the moonlit air to the Bon tune, hands clapped and feet stamped, while under the eaves a few *itako*, a candle flickering in front of each blind face, continued to recite messages from the dead.[25]

To conclude our account of the *itako* we may add that though some may be affiliated, with their drums, to the Nichiren sect of Buddhism, others used to apply for certificates of proficiency to the Tendai temple of Hōonji near Hirosaki. When I visited this temple in 1959 it was sadly dilapidated: its straw mats were dark yellow-brown and frayed, its paper walls torn, its roof in disrepair, its woodwork broken. A very old man who served as acolyte in the temple told me, in the absence of the priest, that the connection between the temple and the *itako* went back to the days of the *biwa-hōshi*, the blind priests who played on the lute. These blind priests had been given grades, by the temple, called *kengyō* and *kōtō*, for their prowess as musicians and reciters, but gradually, as their numbers dwindled, their place had been taken by the blind *itako*. *Itako* thus affiliated with the Tendai sect were required to be blind, and although the musical side of their performance had entirely died out there were still certain rules and conditions which the sect required them to fulfil before it would issue the certificate. These conditions seemed to be too difficult for the modern *itako* to meet, for no one had applied for a certificate for more than twenty years. The temple had not ceased to issue them; there had simply been no applicants for nearly a generation.

We infer then that the decline of the truly shamanic medium in the north came about when the profession became the monopoly of the blind; when it was not so much a religious call that propelled a woman into the occupation of spirit medium, as the need to find one more gainful occupation for the increasing numbers of blind girls. Hori is therefore right when he declares that the blind *itako* as they survive today are not shamanic persons. Equally surely, however, their practice betrays that they perpetuate, without inspiration or supernatural gift, practices which go back to antiquity. They have replaced women who fulfilled more closely the requirements of shamanic inspiration; whose call to the life was a truly religious one, through dreams or possession, and who achieved for the deliverance of the spiritual messages a genuine state of dissociated trance.

With the blind girl, the power which the religious call confers must be found artificially from a regime of austerities. The *itako* in their sixties whom Sakurai interviewed all recalled a fearfully severe ascetic course of training which successfully culminated in a rite of initation; which provided the ordeal through which the candidate must pass before he experiences the death and rebirth of the initiation itself. From so excruciating a degree of ascesis some mantic power might be expected to come to them. All too often today this is not the case. Even the mantic gift comes to be artificially simulated, and the messages which used to burst from the mouth of a truly entranced medium now become stereotyped utterances, classifiable into different *kata* or types, which the medium in the course of her training learns by heart. That such utterances should still strike the sobbing audiences as convincing communications from the dead argues a suspension of disbelief of the same order as that which sees the invisible world behind the sacred drama, the ritual mask or the recital of a myth.

Those women in the north who still experience a genuine religious call, who are propelled into the religious life by the appearance of a deity in a dream or in a sudden possession, now tend to become not *itako*, but *gomiso*. These people are not mediums, however, but ascetics, and will be treated in a later chapter.

The *itako*, dilapidated though they may be as mantic persons, are nevertheless the only representatives left in Japan of the professional shamanic medium who operates alone. We shall later find examples of the passive, untrained and unprofessional medium who still offer his services in seasonal rites both for healing and benediction. But with these blind women we may at least see the husk of a genuine shamanic ritual and practice which until only recently survived in the north of Japan.

9
The Ascetic's Initiation

We now turn to the active partner of the two shamanic practitioners in Japan, the ascetic. He first appears on the scene in the late Nara or early Heian period, that is to say in the late eighth or early ninth century, known variously as an *ubasoku*, a *hijiri* or a *shamon*. All these names carry a Buddhist connotation. They indicate a man who has taken Buddhist vows, but chooses to retire to the fastnesses of certain mountains rather than to reside in any recognised temple or monastery. There he undertakes a regime of the austerities we outlined in an earlier chapter. Abstaining from cereals, salt and of course meat, he devotes himself under the guidance of a guardian divinity to the recitation of a particular holy text. If a waterfall happens to be nearby he stands beneath it. He also makes, in either visionary or symbolic form, a journey to the other world. These experiences act as an initiation. They endow him with the supernatural and holy power by which he can vanquish malignant spiritual beings and transform them into powers for good.[1]

Hori distinguishes two principal categories of *hijiri* during this early period. One is a solitary hermit, dwelling in either a cave or a grass hut on the slopes of a holy mountain. There he avoids human company, fasts and devotes himself night and day to the recitation of one particular holy text. Usually this is the Lotus Sutra. Many of the earliest *hijiri* and *ubasoku* are recorded as devoting their lives to the constant repetition and contemplation of this holy text, their voices as they recite achieving in time an unearthly quality of holiness which makes the hair of all who hear it stand on end, and which draws monkeys, bears, foxes and deer from the surrounding forest to listen in front of the cave.[2]

The favourite place chosen by these recluses for their retreat was the range of mountains south of Nara, stretching from Mt Kimpu near Yoshino down the Kii peninsula to Kumano. We are told of many hermits who retired to Mt Kimpu itself, to the neighbouring mountain Ōminesan, to

Mt Katsuragi nearby and to the Kumano mountains further south. But also even at this early period we hear of recluses further afield, on the slopes of Ibukiyama, Atagosan, Hōki Daisen, Tateyama and Hakusan.

The ascetics in Hori's second category lived entirely different lives. Instead of dwelling in solitary and unmoving seclusion in a cave, their days were spent in a continuous walking pilgrimage from one holy place to another. Some wandered constantly among holy mountains; others, as we have already noticed, evolved from their journeys specific pilgrimage routes which usually described a rough circle. The villages through which they passed on their travels were always benefited by their holy powers. Ghosts were brought to salvation, sick persons were healed, bridges and dykes were built, problems of disharmony with the spiritual world were solved.

Today the spiritual descendants of these early ascetics are still to be found in many places in Japan. They appear, however, in a number of different guises. Some are men, some women. Some are fully ordained Buddhist priests living in a temple or monastery; some are solitary hermits with only a nominal connection with any Buddhist sect. Four such types of ascetic may be usefully distinguished.

First, a fully ordained Buddhist priest of the Tendai, Shingon or Nichiren sect may be discovered fulfilling exactly the requirements of the ascetic life. After a long and severe regime of austerities performed directly under the aegis of this sect, he dedicates himself to the task of healing spiritual maladies. The Ajari of the Tendai temple Mudōji, on the slopes of Mt Hiei, is a notable example of an ascetic in full Buddhist orders. So are the Nichiren priests of the Nakayama branch who, having accomplished the fearful regime of the hundred days *aragyō*, settle down as incumbents of temples whose principal occupation is the exorcism of cases of demoniacal possession.

Next, the ascetic is well exemplified by the members of the order called Shugendō. These men, known as *yamabushi*, are dedicated to the performance of rituals and ascetic and occult exercises in mountains, through which efforts they eventually acquire power over spirits. They are the most direct lineal descendants of the ancient *hijiri* of the eighth and ninth centuries. The solitary *hijiri* with their rather haphazard austerities began towards the end of the twelfth century to form themselves into groups, and thereby to work out certain rituals whereby the power they sought could be most effectively acquired. The Shugendō order was the result. The ritual and symbolism used by the order is largely derived from esoteric Buddhism, but the 'symbolic action' which constitutes its practice takes place against a background of the more ancient belief in the holiness and other-worldliness of certain mountains. The hills where the *yamabushi* carry out their rites and practices, therefore, are those very ones which in pre-Buddhist times were believed to be the world of the dead or the dwelling-place of numina.[3]

The Shugendō order was proscribed in 1873 under the legislation by which the Meiji government sought to destroy all religious cults in which Shinto and Buddhist elements were mixed. Like other bodies nominally dissolved at this time, however, the order survived, principally by dint of the various groups of *yamabushi* linking themselves more closely with the Shingon or Tendai sect of Buddhism. After religious liberty was restored to the Japanese by General MacArthur's Religious Bodies Law of 1945, several new groups made their appearance under the title of Shugendō. Some of these have preserved fairly intact the ascetic exercises in mountains which were the order's ancient prescription for the acquisition of power.

The other guises in which the ascetic may still be found today are more or less derived from this order. There is the woman ascetic, for example, who is a professional healer and exorcist. She lives all the year round in her own house which is at the same time a temple to her tutelary deity, leaving the place only to make a seasonal visit to the headquarters of the Buddhist sect to which she is affiliated and perhaps take part in a seasonal mountain climb. In her own house every day she receives the stream of patients who come to her complaining of a variety of symptoms, physical and mental, which they attribute to malignant spiritual possession, and which they expect her, as a result of the austerities she has undergone, to cure. An enclave of such women lives in the southern suburbs of Kyoto, in the district of Sagano. Others congregate round Mt Miwa not far from Nara. Others, under the peculiar name of *gomiso*, are to be discovered further north in Aomori prefecture, in the district of Mt Iwaki.

Again, in contrast to these static ascetics, there can still be found a few men and women who spend the greater part of their time in peripatetic wandering. Visiting their home only rarely and for short rests between pilgrimages, they accomplish most of their healing in the course of long wandering journeys. Sometimes these follow the prescribed course of recognised pilgrimage routes, the Eighty-eight Places of Shikoku or the Thirty-three Places of the Western Provinces. At other times they set out, allegedly at the behest of their tutelary deity, without any idea of a goal or a preordained route, walking every day where they feel their guardian numen will take them. These people, now less commonly found than the static type, can be regarded as the spiritual descendants of the early peripatetic *hijiri*.

With these four appearances in mind—a Buddhist priest, a *yamabushi*, a woman exorcist either static or travelling—I propose in the next four chapters to enquire into the following problems. First, what motive impels a man or woman to enter the sacred life, to give up the familiar human round for the privations of starvation, cold water and sleeplessness? Second, what part is played in this initiatory process by the ascetic's guardian deity? And third, what is the nature of the powers which the ascetic deploys as a result of his initiation? Under these headings we shall discuss the ascetic's journey to the other world, in either visionary or symbolic form.

First, then, the motive which drives the ascetic into the shamanistic life. Two clearly differentiated kinds present themselves. First, there are those people who do not take the decision for themselves. They are impelled by what seems to them to be an external and supernatural force to enter the religious life. And secondly, there are those who of their own free will choose to abandon their ordinary life and begin an entirely new one.

Let us look first at the 'natural' shamans who, like the living goddesses but unlike the blind mediums, are forcibly chosen by a spiritual being. These people, often as the culmination of a prolonged period of suffering, find themselves suddenly snatched from their ordinary mode of life by a shattering interior experience, a kind of psychic convulsion which appears to them to be unmistakably of supernatural origin.

This interior experience tends to take broadly three different forms in Japan. First, it can come as a supernatural dream, in which a deity appears to the future shaman while he is asleep. Second, it can come as a sudden *kamigakari* or divine possession, of the kind we noted in connection with many of the living goddesses. And third, it can come in the form of a mantic journey to other worlds, in which the soul is guided for all or part of the way by a guardian divinity. All these experiences, therefore, involve contact with a particular divinity, with whom the shaman lives henceforth in a special relationship and who is the source of his enhanced power.

Let us consider the supernatural dreams.

Dreams which are accounted of divine origin in Japan fall into several types. There are healing dreams, some of which are of the 'incubatory' kind due to sleeping in a holy place, there are prophetic dreams, and there are the initiatory dreams which we are considering. In all of them, however, the characteristic which is immediately apparent is that the sleeper is completely passive. A single figure appears as he lies and speaks to him. Sometimes he is able to answer, as earlier we saw Taira Munemori do. More often he simply lies and listens, a passive spectator. Occasionally he does not even see the figure, but only hears a voice of awe-inspiring and hair-raising resonance speaking to him. Here seems to lie an interesting parallel with the dreams in Homer as described by E. R. Dodds. There also a single dream-figure, a god, a ghost, a dream-messenger, or an *eidolon* or image created specially for the occasion, enters the sleeper's bedroom and delivers its message, withdrawing as soon as this is done.[4]

Like the Homeric dreams also is the apparent objectivity

of the Japanese divine dreams. The sleeper is convinced that the apparition which confronts him is not the construct of his imagination but an objective fact. It is a being of a different order from those perceived by our usual faculties, an order, in fact, of a subtle kind which can only be perceived when these faculties are in some sense withdrawn. It is nevertheless entirely objective, and frequently demonstrates its objectivity by presenting the sleeper with some object, which is found like a kind of apport by his bed when he awakes. The silver dagger which we earlier saw presented to Taira Kiyomori is an example of such dream-gifts which are still alleged to occur today.

The distinctive feature of the initiatory dream, however, is that the figure who appears to the sleeper is a spiritual being who afterwards functions as his guardian numen. Sometimes it is a dead ancestral spirit, the sleeper's dead father or grandfather. More often it is a recognised deity from the Shinto or Buddhist pantheon, of a kind we shall presently describe. This figure informs the sleeper that he must now leave his former life and enter a new one, with new powers conferred upon him from this divine source. It then prescribes a course of austerities which the sleeper must perform, at the end of which his new life will begin.

An example of such a dream initiation occurred to Mrs Sasanuma, whom I met in August 1972 in her temple in the village of Fukakusa at the foot of Inariyama at Fushimi. As a child she had been ailing and sickly, but had nevertheless succeeded in marrying when she grew up and in bearing a son. This child at the age of five developed what was apparently an incurable sickness. All the doctors having given up hope of his recovery, Mrs Sasanuma in desperation began a round of pilgrimages to various shrines. None were of the slightest avail. The child made no progress at all, and she was on the point of total despair when one night she experienced a radiant vision of the goddess Kishibojin, resplendent in a silver crown, who promised to save the boy. The next day the boy had totally recovered, all trace of sickness having vanished.

Mrs Sasanuma then found herself completely taken in charge by Kishibojin, who prescribed a series of arduous austerities which she dared not disobey. At the command of Kishibojin she made pilgrimages on foot to temples and shrines all over Japan, and practised *zazen* or Zen meditation for a time in a remote country temple. She even undertook the fearfully severe regime of austerities prescribed by the Nichiren sect, later to be described, which continues for a hundred days of the winter and involves stringent fasting, lack of sleep, continuous recitation of the Lotus Sutra, seven periods in the day of pouring buckets of cold water over the head and shoulders, and a particularly agonising practice with the *bokken* or magic castanets which must always be wielded with a straight arm.

At long last the goddess relented and allowed her to go home and settle down. She had accordingly built her temple to Kishibojin, founded a cult to the goddess and collected a body of disciples. Kishibojin continued to appear to her in dreams at all times, with instructions and encouragement, and the gifts of clairvoyance and prophesy. Once a month she repaired to a mountain near Kurama for a bout of austerities, and occasionally she took parties of disciples on walking pilgrimages. For the rest of the time she lived quietly with the small granddaughter she had designated her successor, serving the goddess from day to day. Kishibojin would appear to her frequently in snake form, with such vividness that she sometimes felt that she had become a snake herself.

Initiation by dream is common among the group of ascetics living near Mt Iwaki in Aomori prefecture known as *gomiso*. One of these people, a Mrs Jin whom I met also in August 1972, told me that both she and her mother had been granted their supernatural power by means of a dream in which the deity Akakura Daigongen had appeared to them. She herself had been visited by this deity while she was asleep, in the likeness of a tall man with long black hair. He had commanded her to undertake a regime of austerities on Mt Iwaki which consisted of a thousand recitations of the Heart Sutra, a week of fasting, a week of sleeping on the mountainside and a week of total silence. At the end of the prescribed period she had found herself possessed of powers of clairvoyance and divination. People now came to her with questions which baffled them, and the answers came to her at once.

Her mother's story was very similar. During a period of intense anxiety she had begun to experience a recurrent dream. She saw before her a vision of Mt Iwaki with its three volcanic peaks. From the left-hand peak there arose a dragon who flew towards her, dived through the roof of her house and came to rest by her pillow. There it turned into a woman who bade her repeatedly to 'go to the mountain, go to the mountain'. At the time she had no idea who the deity was and where the mountain might be to which she was bidden. She therefore consulted a diviner in the district who told her that the mountain was Mt Iwaki and the deity Akakura Daigongen in dragon form. To confirm the affinity with him she must seclude herself in the shrine at the foot of the mountain and observe the austerity of silence for a week. In the course of this week, despite a terrific snow storm which lasted for three days, the god appeared to her again in a dream and presented her with three scrolls, inscribed with mysterious writing. And when she woke up, lo, there in the manner of Bellerophon's golden bridle were the three scrolls by her pillow.

After this last vision she found herself possessed of powers of clairvoyance and insight into hidden things, which enabled her thereafter to become a professional *gomiso*.

Lastly Mr Ikoma, an ascetic living near Mt Miwa, told me in 1972 that his own initiation had come to him at the age of eleven in the form of a recurrent dream of a dragon reared upright on its tail blocking his path. In whichever direction he turned the dragon was always there blocking his path. Five years later he began to hear a voice every night which called to him, 'Kinasai, kinasai', come, come. Night after night the voice continued until eventually he fell ill with the nervous strain of it. The sickness continued for three years until they took him to the celebrated exorcist Mrs Hiroshima Ryūun, who prescribed the waterfall five times a day. This he carried out by his own efforts, and in a week the trouble vanished. After this he became the disciple of Mrs Hiroshima, accompanying her on her pilgrimages round Shikoku, and had eventually become a professional ascetic.

With some ascetics the contact with the tutelary deity is made not through dreams but by *kamigakari*, the sudden entry of the god into their bodies. Here the future ascetic does not see the figure of his guardian, but rather becomes a channel for his utterance.

Of the initiatory *kamigakari* pure and simple, we have already encountered several instances among the biographies of the Founders of new religious cults. The experiences of Nakayama Miki and Kitamura Sayo are typical of the kind which, in the absence of the other factors necessary for the birth of a new cult, may serve as an initiation into the life of an ascetic. It is also found, however, in combination with a dream, and of such double interior experiences we may cite the case of Mrs Hiroshima Ryūun, as related to me in July 1972 by her daughter Mrs Hiroshima Umeko, herself an ascetic residing in the Suishōji temple at the foot of Mt Miwa.

Mrs Hiroshima Ryūun was a celebrated ascetic belonging to the category of peripatetic wanderers. During the war and the years immediately preceding it she travelled on foot throughout virtually the length and breadth of Japan. The shrine to her spirit kept in an upstairs room of the temple contained a map of the journeys she had accomplished, which could be seen at a glance to include not only the accredited pilgrim routes of Shikoku and central Japan, but also long, apparently haphazard journeys throughout much of the rest of the main island. Her dramatic cures through exorcism were particularly celebrated in the district of Nara and the Yamato plain.

This powerful woman *gyōja* was first called to the religious life by a vision of the archetypal ascetic En-no-Gyōja. Ringed staff in hand, he stood by her bedside and adjured her to take it upon herself to save those suffering from sickness in the world. Thereafter for three years, always under the direction of En-no-Gyōja, Mrs Hiroshima undertook a regime of austerities in which the local waterfall figured prominently. Often, her daughter assured me, she would stand under the waterfall in the middle of winter for the length of time it took her to recite a hundred Heart Sutras.

At the end of three years these strenuous efforts culminated in a terrific divine seizure. For a whole week, without a single pause for rest, she was in a continuous state of divine possession. She neither ate nor slept, and only salt water passed her lips while deity after deity from all over Japan came into her body and spoke through her mouth.

After this extraordinary experience she found herself in possession of powers of healing and of clairvoyant vision of the spiritual beings which caused sickness. She found also that En-no-Gyōja ceased to be her tutelary deity, his place being taken by a mysterious spirit called Magotarō Inari. When first possessed by this divinity, Mrs Hiroshima had no idea who he was. She had never heard his name in her life before. She found his shrine only after a long search, a small and unobtrusive place in the precincts of the Yakushiji temple near Nara. He was wont to appear in various forms, a fox or a small boy, but his real shape, only seldom manifested, was that of a snake. Thereafter, as we shall see in a later chapter, it was entirely through the power of Magotarō Inari that Mrs Hiroshima was able to perform the dramatic cures which made her famous throughout the district.

Our third mode of interior initiation, the mantic journey, is of sufficient complexity to warrant a chapter to itself. It is possible to regard these 'out-of-the-body experiences' as a variety of dream or vision. But because they are felt to be a particular kind of objective experience, they are better treated separately. Here suffice to say that the future ascetic is visited by a Messenger or Guide, who separates his soul from his body and takes it on a long and terrifying journey through different realms of the cosmos. His body meanwhile remains behind in a state of cataleptic trance. When at the end of his journey his soul rejoins his body he is found to be a changed person, in the same manner that Mrs Sasanuma was changed by a dream or Mrs Hiroshima by a possession.

In all these kinds of interior initiation, therefore, the ascetic is brought into contact with a superior guardian. It is he who forces him into his new life and confers on him the necessary powers.

The presence of such a supernatural figure is likewise

necessary for those ascetics to whom the gift of a dream or possession is not vouchsafed, and whose decision to enter the religious life is therefore made of their own free will.

Such people usually begin from a state of despair or disgust with their ordinary human life. A succession of miseries and calamities reduce them to the condition known in Japanese as *happō-fusagari*, all eight directions blocked, or *yukizumari*, the feeling that you are up against a brick wall. The death of a husband or a child, a long and debilitating illness, hopeless alcoholism and its attendant financial ruin, miseries such as these are often cited as the *dōki* or motive which convinced them that their lives as hitherto lived were inadequate and meaningless and drove them to seek another kind of life in religion.

Mrs Matsuyama, a healer and exorcist living on the outskirts of Kyoto, told me in 1963 that at the age of twenty-two she had contracted what the doctors told her was an incurable sickness. Someone then told her that although medicine could not help her, the supernatural power of Fudō Myōō could. She must undertake under the tutelage of Fudō a regime of austerities on a mountain near Nara. To this place she accordingly repaired and threw herself, sick though she was, into a course of fasting and cold water exercises. At the end of the prescribed period she was not only cured, but had found an entirely new centre and direction to her life. She had accomplished a close bond with Fudō, who in the course of the austerities had conferred powers upon her, and who thereafter supervised her life down to the smallest detail.

Mrs Matsuyama's history may be taken as typical of the voluntary ascetic. If the gift is not given to them they may, with sufficient drive and will power, set out to find it for themselves.

Let us now examine more closely the kind of divinity who spontaneously appears as guardian to these people, and whose tutelage and overshadowing presence is so essential to their success.

Two broad categories of divinity seem to appear in this capacity.

First, there are Buddhist divinities of the classes known as

Myōō, bright kings, and Gongen, figures which are theoretically supposed to be 'temporary manifestations' of Buddhas or Bodhisattvas. The two characteristics which immediately strike the observer about both these classes of divinity are their ferocious raging visage and the halo of flames which surrounds them. Secondly, in the role of guardian there appears once more on the scene the figure of the supernatural snake.

Of the Buddhist angry, fiery deities the most frequent to appear in the role of guardian is Fudō Myōō. Fudō is the central and paramount figure in the group of divinities known as the Godai Myōō or Five Great Bright Kings, who in esoteric Buddhism stand as emanations or modes of activity of the Buddha. Where the Buddha exists static and immovable, withdrawn from activity, the five Myōō act a his agents and messengers. Each presides over one of the five directions, the centre being the domain of Fudō.

Though never so horrendous in appearance as the Tibetan angry deities, the face of Fudō is nevertheless startling to those accustomed only to the gentle and compassionate iconography of the Buddha and Bodhisattva figures, and even more so to those such as the sixteenth-century Jesuits who associate fury with the diabolic order. He is usually found represented as blue, red or black. One eye glares downwards, the other squints divergently upwards. With one upper tooth grasping his lower lip and one lower tooth grasping his upper lip, his mouth is twisted into a peculiar snarl. His long hair hangs in a coil over his left shoulder. His right hand grasps a sword and his left a rope, and he stands not on a lotus or an animal mount as do many Buddhist divinities, but on an immovable rock, which rises sometimes from curling waves. Always he is ringed round with fire. The celebrated Red Fudō at Kōyasan, dating probably from the tenth century, is encircled with leaping flames of the same fierce scarlet as the deity's body. The Blue Fudō in the Shōrenin temple in Kyoto is likewise surrounded by flames of vermilion, cinnabar and black which contrast vividly with the azurite blue of the deity's body.[5]

This is the divinity whom the great majority of ascetics

look upon as their guardian, who appears to them in dreams, who directs their austerities, who endues them with vitality and confers upon them their powers. In the doctrine of the Shugendō, as we shall later see, he is regarded as the image of the perfect nature residing latently in every man and waiting to be released by the proper religious exercises.

A similarly raging fiery deity who since the ninth century has been acclaimed as a potent guardian and guide to ascetics and *yamabushi* is Zaō Gongen. This divinity, unlike the Five Myōō, has no place in the official pantheon of esoteric Buddhism. Attempts have been made to associate him with the figure of Kongōzō Bosatsu who occupies a seat on one of the mandalas, but it is plain from a glance at their faces that the resemblance goes no further than name. The legend accounting for his first appearance gives us a better clue as to his real nature.

En-no-Gyōja, the *Konjaku Monogatari* tells us, in the course of a hundred-day seclusion on the slopes of Mt Kimpu, used his magic power to conjure a deity out of the ground. A divinity rose from the earth in the compassionate likeness of the Bodhisattva Jizō. At this mild apparition En-no-Gyōja shook his head. So tranquil a deity, he declared, would be useless for the saving of sentient beings. A second divinity then rose out of the earth. This time its face glared with demon-quelling rage and its right hand grasped a thunderbolt. This terrific apparition was exactly what En-no-Gyōja had desired, and he concealed it for safety behind a curtain. [6]

Thereafter Zaō Gongen presided over the holy mountain Kimpusen as the tutelary deity of the ascetics who retired there for seclusion and austerities. Like Fudō, he guarded them, directed their ascetic exercises, inspired them with vitality and determination to fulfil their avowed period, and occasionally, as with the priest Nichizō, acted as psychopomp and guide to the top of the golden paradisal mountain.

That he was much invoked as a guardian by ascetics in the ninth and tenth centuries is suggested by the archeological finds of mirrors excavated from sutra-mounds on the mountain. The precise use of these mirrors is not yet accurately established. They may be votive mirrors (*nōkyō*) of the kind found in profusion at the bottom of a pool on

Mt Haguro, or, as in esoteric Buddhist practice, they may have been put to some use of a ritual kind. But on the back of several of them is an engraved figure which has been clearly identified with Zaō Gongen.[7]

The most celebrated representation of this divinity, however, is probably the three wooden statues enshrined in the great temple Zaōdō at Yoshino. Behind a lattice screen, huge and obscure, the deity appears in his Past, Present and Future forms. Peer up through the curtained gloom and you see glaring down upon you an enormous dark green face, the red mouth gaping open in an angry snarl to reveal golden teeth and tusks. Chaplets of bells cover the chest, and tiger skins hang from the waist. The right hand brandishes a thunderbolt, while the fingers of the left stab downwards in the sword mudra, *tōken-no-in*. The right foot is upraised to stamp. Locks of hair stand stiffly on end like flames, and the huge head is ringed round with a halo of fire. So full of furious energy is the figure that we seem to see it caught and momentarily immobilised in the midst of whirling movement. Look away for only an instant and the dance will continue. The feet will stamp, the fingers stab, the gaping mouth release a deafening shout.

Fudō and Zaō are therefore supreme examples of the angry Buddhist guardians with their haloes of fire, who elect and supervise the shaman's work.

The second category of guardians is already familiar. They are deities who are either snakes in their 'real form' or who appear frequently in a snake transformation.

The deity Ryūjin, a dragon in his own right, is frequently cited, especially by women ascetics, as the guardian presiding over their welfare, their source of power and upholding guide. So likewise are an extraordinary number of deities who choose to appear to the ascetic in snake form. Inari, or Kōjin, or Kōbō Daishi appeared to me in a dream, they will declare. What did he look like, you ask. The answer comes with surprising frequency, a snake or a dragon. We have already seen how Akakura Daigongen chose to assume dragon form in his appearances to Mrs Jin's mother. Mrs Hiroshima's guardian Magotarō Inari likewise turned out to have a 'real form' which was a snake. And to Mrs

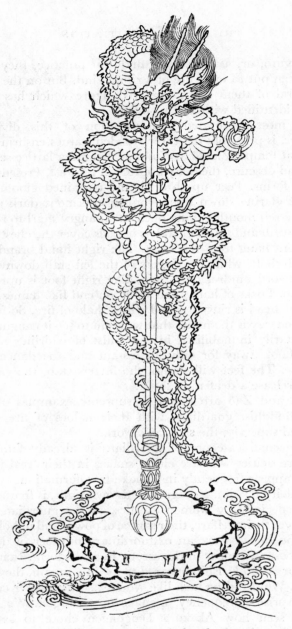

Fudō's sword and the dragon
Talismanic charm issued by the Dainichibō temple.
Yamagata prefecture.

Sasanuma, even a goddess so apparently remote from the animal world as Kishibojin chose a serpent form for her manifestations.

Nor are these two classes of guardian, the furious fiery ones and the serpents, so dissociated from each other as might first appear. Fudō himself is frequently represented by his attribute, an erect sword, twined about by the dragon Kurikara. The sword stands upright on its thunderbolt hilt, its point inside the mouth of the dragon who has flung its coils round the shaft. Here is Fudō unmistakably linked with the serpent, and at the same time providing a bridge between the two categories of guardian deity.[8]

Can anything be inferred from these persistent characteristics, the raging face, the halo of fire and the serpent?

Surely we have, once again, the vision of the magical interior heat which the shaman must rouse in himself before he can be proved to have access to the sacred world. The halo of flames which surrounds Fudō and Zaō is the same fire which the ascetic must kindle in himself. The raging face with which the images of Fudō and Zaō glare down on the appalled viewer reflects the hot rage which the ascetic must activate in himself if he is to appropriate his sacred powers. Only when he is properly 'heated' can the ascetic discern spirits, hear their voices and exercise power over them, pass freely from one world to another. The guardian deity, worshipped first as an exterior power, must eventually be roused from within. The disciple must become Fudō, must discover in himself the attributes of his guardian.

The link with the serpent thus immediately becomes plain. Just as we found the serpent persistently haunting the ancient miko, so again he reappears as the guardian of the ascetic. Here again is surely a reminder of the Kundalinī snake which as it rises up the spine of the yogi confers upon him heat and transformed sexual energy. As it writhes spirally upwards round Fudō's erect sword, we see the shakti or feminine energising force in its traditional serpent aspect. Once again we meet with this mysterious coincidence of images, so far unexplained, between India and Japan.[9]

From the tutelary deity who elects, guides and supports the shaman, we pass to the assistant spirits whom this deity sometimes confers upon him. Many shamans on the Asian continent have their spirit helpers. These familiars, bestowed on him at the time of his initiation, often take the form of animals. Among the Siberians and the Altaians, for example, they appear in the form of bears, wolves, stags, hares, eagles, owls or crows. These spirits accompany the shaman in his journeys to the underworld, or act as messengers who bring answers from the deities. The shaman has only to summon these spirits with his drum for them to come at once to his aid.

The Yakut shaman too is given an animal helper, a bull, horse, eagle, elk or bear, and the Eskimo shaman in northern Greenland may control as many as fifteen familiars which appear in the likeness of foxes, owls, bears or sharks. Among the Golds of the Amur river too, Sternberg tells us, the shaman is presented by his tutelary deity with a strange retinue of helpers. An old and celebrated shaman, gifted with the superior power of guiding souls to the other world, possessed a monstrous retinue, reminiscent of Comus's rout, composed of a mad dog, a mad fox, a dwarf, a headless man and a woodcock.[10]

These familiar spirits are the source of the shaman's power. Bereft of their aid he is reduced to ordinary human helplessness.

The ascetic in Japan at first appears to accomplish his feats of healing not through the aid of spirits placed at his disposal, but through powers innate in himself which his disciplines have released. But a closer perusal of the biographies of medieval ascetics reveals a remarkable number of stories in which a holy man is assisted and served by a supernatural boy known as *gohō-dōji*. Again and again, without comment or explanation, the enigmatic figure of a boy appears by the holy man's side, serving him with food, drawing water for his bath, keeping his anchoritic hut in the depths of the mountains clean and neat, rescuing him when he is lost or in danger, and lastly acting as the magical agent who accomplishes for him his feats of healing.

The priest Butsuren, for example, was served by two spirit boys who every day gathered firewood and heated the water for his three daily baths. The priest Jōzō had a guardian boy who brought him flowers and water during his periods of seclusion and spiritual exercises. The priest Yuirembō, carried off by an evil *tengu* to a lonely old house in the mountains, was finally rescued and restored to his temple by two boys dressed in white and holding branches in their hands. Divine boys also came to the rescue of the turbulent priest Mongaku when he stood up to his neck in the icy water of the great Nachi waterfall. Again, when a renowned ascetic from Shinano was implored to come to the capital to cure the Emperor's sickness, the holy man sent as his agent and messenger a spirit boy 'clothed in woven swords'. Three days later as the Emperor lay dozing he saw enter the room the glittering bright figure of a boy wearing a collar of swords. At once he began to feel better, until soon not a trace of his pain and sickness remained.[11]

Numerous other references to spirit boys attending a holy man, serving his daily needs and accomplishing his magical tasks of healing, invite us to compare these figures with the assistant spirits sent to the aid of the Siberian or Eskimo shaman.

In some of the tales no explanation at all is offered for the presence of the boy. In others they are stated to be transformations of certain converted demons in the Lotus Sutra. More often, however, we are told that they are members of the large retinue of supernatural boys who attend upon Fudō Myōō. Fudō's full complement of boys is thirty-six. Of these, however, a suite of eight are more frequently called into service, of which again two, Kongara and Seitaka, are most constantly employed. It was Kongara and Seitaka, for example, who rescued Mongaku from his icy death beneath the Nachi waterfall.

The length of time during which they are sent out on such errands, however, varies considerably. After his ordeal at Nachi we hear of no more good, to use the words of the Cauld Lad of Hilton, done to Mongaku by supernatural boys. The pair apparently returned to their master Fudō after only a short spell of service. In other cases, however, the boys appear to stay permanently at the beck and call of the holy man. The ascetic whom Giei discovered in the depths of the mountains, sitting in a trim hut surrounded by an exquisite garden, reciting the Lotus Sutra in an impressively holy voice, had lived there for more than eighty years, served day and night by three supernatural boys.[12] The ascetic of Shinano who sent the boy with the collar of swords to the aid of the sick Emperor, likewise seems to have had this helper permanently at his behest.

In the biographies of many other notably holy ascetics, however, no mention at all is made a supernatural boy, or of any other assistant spirit. Nor have I come across a single instance of an ascetic in modern times who intimated that his powers depended on a spirit helper. His sole source of strength lies in his guardian deity.

Before we pass on to the third mode of initiation open to the ascetic, his characteristic journey to the other world, we must mention one more supernatural connection. In curious contrast with the associations we have noticed between the ascetic and the snake are the frequent references in medieval legend and literature to a link between the *yamabushi* and that traditional enemy of the serpent, the bird. The bird, it is true, is no ordinary one. It is the complex and uncanny creature known as the *tengu*, half-man and half-hawk, with a large beak, long wings and glittering eyes, but a man's body, arms and legs.

It is deceptively easy to dismiss this harpy-like creature as a mere subtle enemy of the Buddha's law. Again and again, in the legends and stories of the eleventh century onwards, it is described as setting fire to Buddhist temples, kidnapping Buddhist priests and tying them to the tops of trees, feasting them on what appears to be delicious food but which afterwards turns out to be dung, implanting thoughts of greed, pride and delusion in their minds.

But to understand the *tengu* as a mere hindrance to Buddhist piety is to oversimplify him. In other tales he appears more nearly to embody the perilous, ambivalent, non-moral forces of nature. He is seen as a warden of forests, a guardian of huge trees.[13] Mr Higashibaba, who was well over ninety when I met him in the summer of 1972, had lived all his life in a village on the slopes of Musashi Mitake. In the woods on this ancient holy hill, he informed me, there were still *tengu* to be seen when he was a boy. They appeared to haunt the great cryptomeria trees which in those days abounded on the mountain, and indeed appeared to be the guardians of these trees. One of the reasons why there were no more *tengu* in the woods was that the great trees had recently been ruthlessly felled. But eighty years ago he remembered some charcoal-burners telling him that they had been woken up from their midday nap by a *tengu*, who clearly resented their having cut down a large cryptomeria to make charcoal.

In the stories of children kidnapped by *tengu* too we can glimpse the same elusive Pan-like figure. These boys usually return either as halfwits or as miraculous persons. Hirata Atsutane in his *Kokon Yōmikō* cites a number of tales of children abducted by *tengu* in the guise of golden eagles, who are reared in hollow trees by their captors. They return to the world of men to become renowned ascetics gifted with supernatural powers. More often, however, the kidnapped boys are unable fully to return to the human world. It is as though some perilous and terrifying force has dragged them out of their humanity, taken them to an 'other kingdom' from which they are never able completely to escape. To other men therefore they appear as fools, undirected and halfwitted.

This man-bird warden of forests appears time and again in the guise of a *yamabushi*. He wears the small round cap on his head, the neckband with six coloured tufts round his neck, the baggy tunic and trousers which are such distinctive items in the *yamabushi's* costume. When a *tengu* makes an appearance in the world of men, he commonly disguises himself as a *yamabushi*. The children kidnapped by *tengu* declare afterwards, if they have the power of speech, that two *yamabushi* took them by the hand and flew to the top of a high mountain, or even further afield to China or the far depths of Tartary. The marvellous dancers whom the *Taiheiki* describes as appearing suddenly in the Regent's palace, and singing and dancing with extraordinary excellence, all turned out to be *tengu* in the guise of *yamabushi*. A court lady hearing their strange singing peeped through a crack in the sliding screens, and saw that the dancers all had curved beaks like kites, long wings and the distinctive garb of *yamabushi*. She called for help, and the dancers suddenly vanished, leaving on the straw mats the dirty footmarks of birds.[14]

Occasionally a legend appears which hints that this beaked and winged figure is not so remote from the snake as might be supposed from the traditional antagonism between bird and serpent. The eighteenth-century work *Sanshū kidan kōhen*, for example, contains a tale in which the *tengu* appears to be closely assimilated with the snake: the whole mythical structure surrounding the serpent has been lifted out of the water and deposited in the middle of a forest. A man fell asleep in the midst of a forest. When he awoke dusk was falling and he saw stretching before him a path. He followed it, to find that it led him not out of the wood, but ever deeper into it. Eventually, in the very heart of the forest, he came upon a mysterious palace. There he was welcomed by an old man, and later lavishly entertained with music and dancing by the two masters of the palace attired as *yamabushi*, who presented him with pearls and a dragon head. Just before daybreak the two *yamabushi* retired, and the old man informed the bewildered guest that they were the essential spirits of beasts of the mountain and river. When day broke the palace and all its inhabitants vanished, and the man found that the pearls dissolved into drops of water and the dragon head was worthless dross.[15]

Not even Yanagita has properly explained why the *yamabushi* should have come to be identified with this peculiar goblin. We may simply surmise that after weeks spent in the forests and caves of high mountains, the *yamabushi* returned to the world of men with some of the ferocity, the wild strangeness, the perilous otherness of a wild animal or bird. It was as though, through his ritual garb, there could be discerned a beak and feathers. Nor is this impression entirely a thing of the medieval past.

On an afternoon in November 1963 I went to the Kurama temple with the intention of walking over the top of the mountain and down the other side to Kibune. A little way down from the summit I heard from among the trees a strong hard voice reciting what sounded like mantras. I left the path and followed the voice, until in a clearing in the forest I saw an enormous cryptomeria tree, its huge trunk girdled about with the belt of straw rope, and before it, with her back to me, a woman seated on the ground reciting. The hard base voice continued for several minutes, through a number of invocations which were unfamiliar to me, while the woman sat perfectly motionless with a long rosary in her hands. Suddenly I heard some words I understood. Over and over again she called upon the *daitengu* and the *shōtengu*, the large *tengu* and the small *tengu*, at the end of her invocation turning towards the forest and clapping her hands.

Venturing to approach her, I asked if there were still a good many *tengu* to be found on the mountain. She turned to face me, a brown face peculiarly like an old bird, with an expression fierce yet remote and a pair of extraordinarily glittering eyes, brightly sparkling like steel.

'If you do *gyō* like me you can see them', she replied abruptly.

I asked again if the *kami* in the great tree was very strong.

'Ask it anything you like. The tree is more than a thousand years old', she replied, and without another word and without looking behind her she plunged rapidly down the mountainside until she disappeared among the dark green trees and yellow leaves.

Only after she had gone did I remember that the *tengu* were traditionally believed to have brightly glittering eyes, and hence realise that the woman was extraordinarily like a *tengu* herself.

The Visionary Journey

Occasionally the ascetic makes his entry into the religious life by means of the experience of a mantic journey to the other world. His soul is forcibly separated from his body and carried off on a frightening voyage through a number of cosmic regions, notably heaven and hell. This experience seems to be complementary to that of the *kamigakari* or divine possession. Here it is not the numen who bursts into our world and makes a forcible entry into the body of the shaman: it is the shaman who is compelled to travel to the abode of spirits.

This experience now seems to be of comparatively rare occurrence. The case of Deguchi Onisaburō, later to be described, seems to be the only example to be found among the biographies of the shamanic founders of new cults. Several ascetics have told me, certainly, that out-of-the-body travel, up to the sky and down into the earth, is for them a common occurrence. Mr Ikoma, for example, told me in 1972 that he had frequently felt his spirit leave his body and travel upwards to heaven and downwards into the depths of the earth. He was reticent, however, over the details of his adventures, refusing to describe more than the *tennin*, angels, he had encountered in the course of his journey upwards. On the whole the experience seems today to be regrettably infrequent.

Certain evidence exists, however, which suggests that it may have been more common in the past than it is today. This evidence is of two kinds. First, we have certain narratives, scattered throughout the medieval collections of Buddhist tales, which describe the journeys made by Buddhist priests to heaven and hell. And second, we have the legend known as *kamigakushi*, still told 'for true' in certain mountain districts as late as the Meiji period, which relates how a boy is kidnapped by a deity and carried off on a mysterious journey to strange lands.

Let us first examine the Buddhist stories. Here we should

expect to find a Buddhist cosmos, with the realms of the other world disposed according to the Buddhist cosmological scheme. The traveller ought to see in the course of his journey the huge mountain, Mt Meru, which runs like an axis through the universe, and disposed about it the Six Realms into which sentient beings may be reborn according to the deserts of their past karma. Deep down near the roots of the mountain he would expect to find the layers of hells, hot and cold. He should next pass through the realms of Hungry Ghosts, Beasts and Titans. Finally, high up the slopes of the mountain and well past our own human world, he should contemplate the multiple layers of heavens.

The full journey through the Buddhist cosmos should properly include all six of these countries, and the Buddhist shaman should therefore accomplish the *rokudō-meguri* or round of the Six Realms. A classical example of such a traveller can be found in the Buddhist canon itself. In the *Mahāvastu* we are told how Maudgalyāyana, an exalted disciple of the Buddha, journeyed as an unaccompanied spectator to the various quarters of hell, to the realms of ghosts, beasts and titans, and to the successive layers of heavens. From each visit he returned to warn an appalled audience of the terrible fate to which the force of karma would condemn all who failed to lead the holy life.[1]

In the medieval Japanese tales, however, not a single example occurs of a traveller who passes through all six of the transmigratory realms. In several stories, certainly, the traveller is described as accomplishing the *rokudō-meguri*, but in no case are all six countries systematically visited and described. Indeed, at no period of Japanese literature can we find a narrative in any way comparable with Dante's visits to Paradise and the Inferno, or even with the Chinese *Hsi Yang Chi*, in which Professor Duyvendak discovered so many motifs enigmatically similar to those found in Dante. The dramatic theme of the full cosmic journey has apparently been neglected in Japan. The tales which here concern us fall into two types only: descents to hell and ascents to heaven. The descents to hell, being vastly more numerous, will be examined first.[2]

In the collections of Buddhist stories such as the *Nihon*

Ryōiki and the *Konjaku Monogatari*, a remarkable number of tales can be found which describe a priest who falls sick and dies. For one reason or another his funeral is delayed, and after a period of usually three, seven or nine days he suddenly comes back to life. He has meanwhile been on a long and strange journey, he tells his astonished disciples. Two grisly messengers came to fetch him and forced him to hurry along a dark and dreary road. They crossed a dismal river, usually by a ford, and eventually arrived at a glittering palace. 'Here he is', the messengers shouted, and a voice from within replied, 'Bring him inside.' Within he saw Emma-Ō, the king and judge of the underworld, and round about him a multitude of the newly dead, crying piteously, being hurried away by frightful looking guards to the realms of hell or the hungry ghosts.

What happens next to the terrified priest may be one of several possibilities. He may be subjected to a series of ghastly ordeals, from which he is restored to life chastened and changed. Or, like Mu-lien in the celebrated Chinese story, he may find himself called upon to rescue his dead father or wife from terrible torment in one of the worse quarters of hell. Or again, he may himself be condemned to suffer such torments, only to be rescued at the last moment by a diminutive priest with a crozier in his hand, who turns out to be the Bodhisattva Jizō.

A few examples of these stories will show that embedded within each of these types can be discerned a substructure of vision. Of the type in which the priest undergoes terrible ordeals, a good example may be found in the eleventh-century collection *Nihon Ryōiki*.

A priest called Chikō, who had led an otherwise blameless life, was suddenly seized by unworthy feelings of jealousy for the saintly priest Gyōgi, on whom the Emperor had recently lavished favours. Soon afterwards he fell sick, but warned his disciples that if by chance he were to die, they were to wait nine days before cremating his body. Sure enough he died, and the disciples accordingly locked his body up in a room. At the end of the nine days they opened the door, to find that he had come to life again.

Two messengers had come for him, Chikō told his

disciples, and they had walked along a road to the west. Ahead lay a golden palace, with two awful figures on either side of the door, clad in armour with red vines bound round their foreheads. 'Here he is', said the messengers. 'Go along that road then', replied the guards, pointing to the north. Chikō walked northwards with the messengers, and soon felt a scorching heat burn his face, though he could see neither any fire, nor any light of the sun. Before him there appeared a red hot pillar of iron. 'Clasp that pillar', the messengers ordered. Chikō did so, and at once all his flesh was burnt away so that only his skeleton remained. After three days the messengers came back with brooms[3] and brushed the pillar crying, 'Come back to life, come back to life.'

Chikō revived, and again they journeyed northwards, until before them rose another pillar even hotter than the first and this time of brass. Terrible though it was, Chickō felt a strong desire to clasp it. So when the messengers ordered him to throw his arms round it he did so, and again all his flesh was burnt away. After three days they came back again and brushed the pillar with their brooms crying, 'Come back to life.'

Once again he revived and they continued their journey northwards until they came to a fiery cloud, so hot that birds fell down dead when they touched it. 'What is this place?' Chikō asked. 'The Avīci Hell where you are to be burnt', the messengers replied, seizing him and hurling him into the fire. There he stayed for another three days until the messengers returned and brought him back to life, and this time they turned back and retraced their steps. When they reached the golden palace the two figures at the gate said to Chikō, 'The cause which brought you here was your jealousy of Gyōgi Bosatsu. We summoned you here in order that you might wipe out that sin. Gyōgi is soon to be reborn here and we are awaiting his coming. Do not eat of the food of the land of the dead, but return as quickly as you can.' Chikō set out again eastwards with the messengers, until he arrived back in his temple to find that exactly nine days had passed.

When he had recuperated from his ordeal, Chikō visited

Gyōgi, confessed his former jealousy, was forgiven, and thereafter led an exemplary life.[4]

Another type of story which recurs many times describes how a man is summoned to hell and bidden to rescue his dead father, mother or wife from frightful torments there. Here we have a type which clearly has parallels in China. The celebrated tale of Mu-lien, who made many attempts to take food to his mother as she starved in the lowest realm of hell, eventually rescuing her by performing a ritual prescribed by the Buddha himself, is only one among several Chinese examples of this theme.[5] In the *Nihon Ryōiki* again we find the tale of Fujiwara Hirotari, who died suddenly while recuperating in a mountain temple from a severe illness. His family were summoned and preparations were made for his funeral. But on the third day he came back to life and told them the following story.

'Two men came for me wearing armour over their crimson garments and carrying swords and spears in their hands. They struck me on the back and hurried me away, saying that I was to appear at once before the king of hell. The road ended at a deep river, black as ink and dismal to look upon, with a row of trees to mark the ford. The messenger in front warned me to follow close behind him as we waded across, and thus we reached the other side safely. Ahead stood a lofty tower, many storeys high and dazzlingly bright. One of the messengers ran inside and said, 'He is here.' 'Bring him inside then', came a voice from within. I went inside and a voice from behind a screen asked, 'Do you recognise the person behind you?' I looked behind me and saw my wife, who had died in childbirth some three years before. 'Yes', I replied, 'it is my wife.'

' "It is at her request that we summoned you", they said. "Of the six years that she must suffer here, she had already endured three. Those three remaining years she wishes to pass with you, because it was with your child that she died." '

Hirotari went on to tell how he offered to rescue her from further torture by copying and reciting the Lotus Sutra. 'If he will do as he says', his wife declared, 'I will forgive him and let him go home.' The pact sealed, Hirotari was just passing out of the gate of the tower when he thought to ask the name of the being who had summoned him there. 'My name is Emma-Ō', the personage replied, 'but in your country they call me the Bodhisattva Jizō.' With these words he touched Hirotari on the forehead and told him that the mark he had received would preserve him from disaster. Thereupon Hirotari came to life again, realising that the judge of hell and the saviour from its torments were one and the same person.[6]

Into this category of journeys to rescue or alleviate the sufferings of those in hell comes the voyage of one of the most prominent of the medieval mantic travellers, the priest Nichizō. Nichizō, formerly known as Dōken, is stated in several medieval works to have accomplished the full cosmic journey, visiting every one of the Six Realms, under the guidance of the Bodhisattva Kongō Zaō. Characteristically, however, only his journey to hell and his ascent to heaven have been described. His visit to hell is stated in the *Jikkinshō* to have taken place during the eighth month of the year 934, during a period of ascetic seclusion in the Shōnoiwaya cave on Mt Mitake. His body left behind in the cave, his soul travelled to a dreary waste where he saw a hut of reeds lying among mountains of iron. In this hut he found the Emperor Uda, with only a single garment to hide his nakedness, condemned for the sins he had committed during his lifetime to years of torment among caves of iron. Nearby were three of his ministers, stark naked upon red hot coals, ceaselessly wailing in their agony. The Emperor beckoned to Nichizō to approach. 'Make no reverence to me', he said as Nichizō prostrated himself. 'In hell there are no distinctions of rank.' He then begged Nichizō to tell the Empress to recite sutras efficacious in the wiping out of bad karma, which the priest, weeping bitterly, promised to do.[7]

Here we see the traveller acting not as the immediate saviour from hell, but as the salvationary messenger. It is he who carries the tidings of what he has seen and heard to the relatives of the sufferer, whose responsibility it is to perform the correct nullifying obsequies.

A similar case can be found in the fourteenth-century work *Taiheiki*. An itinerant priest found himself summoned by a *yamabushi* to a certain temple, and told to recite the eighth book of the Lotus Sutra, and to continue reciting the holy text, however terrible the sights that might appear before him. Past midnight there was manifested before his eyes a vision of the Avīci hell, in which he saw his wicked kinsman Yūki Kōzuke Nyūdō subjected to unspeakable torments. Time and again he was killed in an agonising manner, and brought to life again by means of a winnowing basket. Go at once to the man's wife and children in the north, the *yamabushi* told the horrified priest, and instruct them to recite the Lotus Sutra every day. Only thus can he be saved. Dawn then broke, and the priest found himself alone on a dewy moor. The prospect of hell and the *yamabushi* had both vanished. At once he made his way to the man's family and related his vision to them. At first they were incredulous, not yet realising that the Nyūdō was dead. But a day or two afterwards a messenger arrived with the news of the Nyūdō's terrible end. They therefore lost no time in reciting the prescribed sutra every day for the space of forty-nine days. The salvation of this wicked man was thus accomplished ultimately by the power of the Bodhisattva Jizō, of whom the *yamabushi* was a transformation, but effectively by the itinerant priest who carried the message of the vision.[8]

The appearance here of the Bodhisattva Jizō brings us to what is perhaps the most persistently recurring theme in these stories of journeys to hell: the rescue of the traveller himself by this benign Bodhisattva. We have here a version of the theme of the harrowing of hell.

The priest Ashō, the *Konjaku Monogatari* relates, had spent a blameless life devoted to the performance of ascetic exercises in mountains. One year a terrible pestilence ravaged the land, and on his way back to his temple one day Ashō was struck down by the sickness and died. His disciples, terrified of the infection, abandoned his body by the roadside. A couple of days later, however, Ashō came to life again and told the following story to a chance wayfarer.

He had found himself walking along a wide road towards the north-west. Soon he came to a tall tower, like a court of judgment, with a great crowd of people standing outside

Plate 18. The Shugendō *saitō-goma* or magic bonfire rite at Minoo. The Traveller arrives with his train and is interrogated at the gate of the sacred enclosure.

Plate 19. Arrows are shot into the sky to apprise the deities of the five directions that the rite is about to start.

Plate 20. Minoo *saitō-goma.* The pyre is lit.

Plate 21. Tanukidani *saitō-goma.* The smouldering ashes of the pyre are raked out to make a cursus for fire-walking.

whose sins were being weighed by rows of officials. Most of these people were eventually seized, tied up and sent off to hell, and the sound of their screams was as loud as thunder. Ashō was dumbfounded at the sight, and his hair stood on end with horror. Then he caught sight of a small priest, attended by a single beautiful boy, hurrying to and fro with a staff in one hand and a scroll in the other. Ashō asked the boy who the small priest might be. 'Don't you know?' said the boy. 'That's Jizō Bosatsu.' Overcome with awe, Ashō prostrated himself on the ground, whereupon Jizō came over to him and said reassuringly, 'You will soon be out of this place.'

He took Ashō in front of the officials and said to them, 'This priest has spent his life in performing austerities for the sake of the Law. He has been round all the mountains, Hakusan and Tateyama and many others, and written full descriptions in his ascetic diary. You must let him go at once.'

'Well', said the officials, 'if what you say is true, then certainly we will let him go.' The small priest dragged the weeping Ashō out of the tower and said, 'Go back home and never come to this place again.' With these words ringing in his ears, Ashō came to life again. [9]

The same theme is repeated again and again with sinners far greater than the innocent Ashō. Extortioners, hunters of fish and game, robbers and lecherers are saved from the brink of hell and sent back to their former bodies, chastened and affrighted, by the intervention of Jizō. Always the relations and friends who listen to the terrible tale are guided thereby to lives of greater holiness and moral effort.

On the face of it, therefore, these tales appear to be moral warnings to the ignorant of the terrible karmic penalties of sin, or of the salvationary power of various holy scriptures or bodhisattvas. Chikō's fearful experiences were undergone ostensibly to wipe out the karmic consequence of one particular sin of slander. Those who die in childbirth, like Fujiwara Hirotari's wife, or with unexpiated sins of slaughter or lechery in their lives, may expect to pass years in hell unless steps are taken to save them.

In nearly all the tales, however, beneath the accretions of

Buddhist morality there seems to lie a bottom or sub-structure of vision. The sinister messengers, the journey westwards or northwards, the barrier of dark water, the glittering palace, the ordeals of death and resuscitation from a skeleton, all these are reminiscent of the initiatory schema. The drama too of the rescue of the soul from hell is one which appears frequently in the initiatory vision of the shaman. There is rarely any superior Guide in these dark regions, it is interesting to note, nor is there any horse to carry the traveller along the road, nor any boat or bridge to take him across the river. Nor yet is there any clear notion of descent; the dark road does not plunge downwards. But the baffling ambivalence which we have seen to be so characteristic of the other world persists. The king of hell is apt to shift from the inexorable prosecutor to the benign saviour; King Emma is at the same time the Bodhisattva Jizō. The palace too, which appears so constantly at the other side of the river, is at the same time hell and paradise. It is the court of judgment where sinners are condemned to hell, and at the same time the paradisal palace where Gyogi Bosatsu is to be reborn.

We come now to the second principal type of other-world journey to be found in these medieval tales, the ascent to heaven. These stories are fewer, shorter and less dramatic than those describing visits to hell. Some, moreover, must be ruled out of court as probable literary borrowings from the Buddhist canon. The description of the paradise to which the priest is taken follows so closely the canonical account of the Land of Bliss in the two Sukhāvatī Vyūha Sutras as to make any visionary basis of the story improbable. Other tales of ascensions to paradise can be found, however, in which the schema of the initiatory vision is unmistakable.

Take the account of the priest Nichizō's journey to heaven, for example, as related in the *Fusō Ryakki*. This experience occurred thirteen years earlier than the visit to hell we have just described, at a time when this priest still bore the name of Dōken Shōnin. After several years of ascetic seclusion on Mt Kimpu, the *Fusō Ryakki* relates, culminating in thirty-seven days of complete fasting in the Shōnoiwaya cave, Dōken Shōnin suddenly felt his body suffused with a parching interior heat. His throat and tongue grew burning and dry and the breath stopped within him. His spirit then rose out of his body and left the cave. Soon he met a priest, holding in his hand a golden bowl full of water which he gave to Dōken to drink. Its taste was so miraculous that it seemed to penetrate his very bones and marrow. Twelve divine boys then appeared, who offered him food and drink on large lotus leaves.

Another priestly figure then appeared who caught hold of Dōken's hand and carried him far up the mountain into the snows. When they reached the top, Dōken saw the whole world stretched out before him bathed in dazzling golden light. To the north lay a golden mountain, and on its summit a throne made of the seven jewels. His guide sat down upon this throne and said, 'I am Zaō Bosatsu, a transformation of the Buddha. The land you see before you is the paradise of Mt Kimpu. You have not much longer to live, so struggle with all your might to lead a holy life.'

Dōken asked his guide whether any magic formula might prolong his life. The Bodhisattva then presented him with a small plaque, on which were inscribed eight mysterious characters.

A dazzling five-coloured light then shone upon them, and a deity by the name of Daijō-itokuten appeared in great majesty at the head of a huge retinue of followers. When he saw Dōken he offered to conduct him to his palace. Dōken was thereupon given a white horse, on whose back he travelled hundreds of leagues with the deity until they arrived at a great lake. In the middle of the lake was an island, and on the island was a square altar. On the altar was a lotus flower, and on the lotus flower stood a jewelled tower. Inside the tower was enshrined the Lotus Sutra, with two mandalas hanging on either side. To the north Dōken saw a shining palace which was the deity's dwelling-place.

The deity then told him that he was the spirit of Sugawara Michizane, and that in his hands lay the power to determine disaster and disease. He promised to allow Dōken a longer spell of life provided that he practised his religious disciplines with all his might. He then explained the meaning of the eight mysterious characters on Dōken's amulet, and instructed him to change his name to Nichizō, the first two characters written there. Thus armed with insight into the nature of disaster, Dōken returned to Mt Kimpu and thence back to his body in the cave.[10]

Much the same schema appears in the tale of Otomo-no-Yasuko in the *Nihon Ryōiki*. He too died, but rose from the dead after three days and described how he had travelled upwards along the path of a rainbow until he came to a shining golden mountain. There he was welcomed by the superior figure of Shōtoku Taishi, who conducted him to the summit. There a boy gave him a magical elixir in the form of a jewel which afforded him protection from murder by the sword.[11]

In both these narratives heaven is situated at the summit of a golden mountain, a cosmic, axial mountain the top of which is the soaring summit of the whole universe. Another more complex ascent, through several layers of heavens, is attributed to En-no-Gyōja.

We have already seen this mysterious figure, represented in iconography as wearing a pointed beard and a Mithras cap and carrying in his right hand a staff adorned with large rings, hailed as the archetypal and perfect ascetic, and the founder of the Shugendō order. Several accounts of his life have come down to us, in the *Shoku Nihongi* and the *Nihon Ryōiki*, for example, increasing in elaboration with the passage of time. In the *En-no-Gyōja Hongi*, however, we find a longer account of his life and miracles which includes an ascent to one of the heavens.

When En-no-Gyōja was twenty-five, it tells us, he climbed to the top of Mt Minoo in Sesshū province. There he disciplined himself to a deep concentration of mind. At once he rose up to the paradise of Nāgārjuna, where a man asked him, 'Who are you?' On giving his name, he was conducted inside a dazzling temple, vast and solemn, with tall towers and flowers of lapis lazuli, lakes covered with many-coloured lotuses, rows of magical trees and a strange bird whose marvellous song chanted forth the Buddhist law. Here, to the music of bells, gongs and drums which emitted sound of their own accord, he ate of the sweet dew of heaven. Seated crosslegged on a jewelled lotus was the

white figure of Nāgārjuna, a crown on his head, a thunderbolt in his right hand, a jewelled box in his left. There,
while miraculous boys poured fragrant water over his head,
Nāgārjuna conferred upon him the most secret 'seal', a
spell and a mudra of the hands. Thereupon he rose up
through the nine worlds until he reached the heaven of
Marvellous Enlightenment, where, having received the most
occult secret knowledge, he returned to his body on Mt
Minoo.[12]

From this account we can infer that the ascent to heaven,
and thence upwards through nine more paradisal levels, the
meeting with superior godlike beings, the eating of paradisal
food, the conferment of secret knowledge, was an experience
considered proper and necessary to the ascetic. En-no-Gyōja,
as the perfect model of the ascetic, must therefore have
undergone an initiation of this kind.

In all these stories, just as in the descents to hell, the
drama of the initiatory vision may be discerned. The ascent
up the mountain, the golden light, the benevolent and
superior Guide, the magical gifts, the occult knowlege, all
seem to pertain to a bright side of the initiation myth obverse
and complementary to the darkness and gloom which dogs
the previous tales. It seems likely, therefore, that these
stories were originally not the contrived moral tale or
admonitory allegory that they now appear. Beneath the
moral accretions may be perceived the account of a visionary
journey to other worlds.[13]

We turn now to our second source of evidence which
suggests that the experience of the mantic journey was more
common in the past than might be supposed today. It lies in
the field of folk legend.

Well into the present century there survived in many
districts a persistent legend known as *kamigakushi* or abduction
by a god. A boy or young man who unaccountably disappeared from his home was believed to have been kidnapped
by a supernatural being and carried off to the creature's own
realm. Appropriate spells were recited to compel the being
to bring the boy back, and frequently the whole village
would turn out at nightfall with lanterns, banging on drums
and bells and shouting, 'Bring him back, bring him back.'

THE CATALPA BOW

Quite often, it seems, these measures were fully justified by success. The boy would reappear, deathly pale, in some oddly inaccessible spot such as the eaves of the local temple or the cramped space between the ceiling and the roof of his own house. For several days he lay in a dazed stupor, but eventually he recovered consciousness and told as best he could what had befallen him while he had been away.

Sometimes, the stories run, the child was a halfwit when he recovered and was able to recount nothing of his adventures. But more often he told a tale along the following lines. A tall stranger with glittering eyes appeared while he was playing and carried him away. This figure is sometimes described as an old man, but more often as wearing the distinctive garb of the *yamabushi* or mountain ascetic. Sometimes, indeed, it is two *yamabushi* who, the boy relates, took him by the hands and flew up into the sky. They went on a long journey, sometimes down into underground passages and caves, sometimes up into the sky as high as the sun and moon, sometimes far away over mountains and seas as far as the Great Wall of China or the great lake in the middle of Tartary. At first he had enjoyed the flight, but after a day or two he began to feel lonely and homesick and to beg his kidnapper to take him back. Thereupon in a trice he had found himself deposited in the odd spot where eventually he was discovered by his relatives.[14]

The oral versions of this legend are always told 'for true', with circumstantial details of time and place. The boy was kidnapped, for example, 'on the evening of September 30th 1907, from Mr Kasaijima's house in the village of Damine in Aichi prefecture', the teller frequently assuring us that he knew the whole family well. Stories on remarkably similar lines, however, may be found in a number of literary works from the medieval period onwards. The story is substantially the same. The boy is carried away by *yamabushi* to a distant mountain where, after watching a number of strange sights, he is eventually restored to his home by a mysterious and benign figure, often absent from the oral versions, of an old man.

A peculiar story in the fourteenth-century collection *Shasekishū*, for example, tells how a boy disappeared from a

198

monastry. Several days later he was found on the temple roof in a state of stupefaction. When he recovered his senses he told them that some *yamabushi* had kidnapped him and carried him off to a temple deep in the mountains. There he had watched a band of *yamabushi* dance. They danced for a long time, until suddenly a net descended from the sky and drew itself round the dancers. In great terror they tried desperately to escape, but in vain. From the meshes of the net there shot forth flames which grew gradually fiercer until they were all burnt to ashes. After a while they all came to life again and began to dance just as before. Then an ancient priest appeared and said to one of them, 'Why did you bring this child here? Take him back to his temple at once.' Whereupon the *yamabushi*, looking very frightened, took the boy home and left him on the temple roof.[15]

In another story, related by a Mr Kurahashi, a friend of the celebrated Shinto scholar Hirata Atsutane, and presumably taken from an oral source, the boy is carried far away across the sea, first to the Great Wall of China and eventually to a region very far to the north, where it was very cold and where the sun could be seen at all times. There they found a wondrous palace, where five lords seated behind a screen. They told the boy that he would have to stay in that country for four or five days before they could arrange for him to be taken home, and during that time he sat in a large room where there were many other people who had also recently arrived in the place. They were pressing red hot lumps of iron against their bodies, or climbing into cauldrons of boiling water, always emerging unscathed. Eventually the boy was taken back to Japan, again flying through the sky, and left on the roof of a temple near his own house.[16]

In another tale, also recorded by Hirata Atsutane, a young man engaged in repair work to one of the temple buildings on Mt Hiei was forcibly abducted by a small priest and a man with wild black hair and a red face. They flew through the air past many magic mountains, and several times when he was particularly frightened a tall priest appeared and comforted him with spells from the

Lotus Sutra. When they arrived at their destination the young man begged to be sent home, to which his captors eventually agreed, giving him as a memento of his journey a magic herbal medicine and a prescription for a discipline which would make it efficacious.[17]

The most lucid and detailed account of such a magical journey to other worlds is certainly that told by the boy Torakichi to Hirata Atsutane in the year 1820. Hirata in the course of his antiquarian researches into the golden age of the gods before the beginning of history, had become interested in the various realms where supernatural beings were said to dwell. When he heard, therefore, that there was a boy in Edo who claimed to have been carried off to an other-world mountain by an elderly *tengu*, and to have spent several years there as the pupil of this being, his curiosity was at once aroused. He invited the boy to his house, and with a group of friends, most of whom were also scholars of the Shinto Revival, they plied the boy with so many questions about his stay in the other world that Hirata's record of his story runs to some two hundred pages.[18]

Torakichi's account departs from the more laconic prototype of the *kamigakushi* story in a number of ways. His captor, though a *tengu*, turned out to be an erudite and benevolent figure, who instructed the boy in swordsmanship, medicine, magic and cooking, sent him on errands to the Island of Women and the Land of Dogs, and taught him how to fly as high as the moon, which he described as covered with great muddy seas, pierced by two or three gaping holes, through which you could see right through to the other side. He also subjected the boy to a severe initiatory ordeal of a hundred days' complete fast. Torakichi was tied to a tree, and after several days' starvation felt as though he were dead. When he came to himself again he found that the hundred days were up, and that his little finger nail, pulled out before as a pledge of sincerity, had been restored to him.

Later cases of supernatural kidnapping have also been reported by persons of some education. During the Bakumatsu period in the middle of the last century a young priest called Kōan was carried off by a white-haired old man to

Mt Akayama, where he met many Immortals, and later to China and Siberia. He wrote a long description of his journey. Seventeen years later a young medical student was carried to the magic mountain Akibasan, where he acquired supernatural powers. His story won him many disciples. Elsewhere the recorded instances seem to be largely of boys in mountain villages.[19]

It is worth noting, perhaps, that no woman is ever recorded, either in the medieval tales or in the *kamigakushi* legend, as undergoing this strange journey. It seems to be an exclusively masculine ordeal. There are stories, it is true, of women kidnapped by supernatural beings, but the pattern here is quite different. The girls are abducted by tall furry creatures known as *yamaotoko* or mountain men, covered with leaves or bark, with glittering eyes and long straggling hair. These terrifying creatures, the belief in which some Japanese folklorists think to have originated in an ancient, unfamiliar and hairy race of mountain-dwellers, keep the girls in strict durance as wives or concubines in their lairs in the depths of the mountains, never allowing them to return to their homes. They are never taken on the magic journey.[20]

In all the examples of the *kamigakushi* legend, therefore, certain elements tend to persist: the magical flight to strange places, the weird sights that the boy witnesses, the miraculous gifts of elixir, herb or jewel that are occasionally bestowed on him, the benign saviour, sometimes anonymous, sometimes taking the form of a Buddhist saint, through whose intervention the boy is restored to his home.

Many of these elements are reminiscent of the medieval stories of the journey to the realms of the dead or to the heavenly mountain. The two *yamabushi* captors are not unlike the two messengers from the underworld, while the glittering palace, the strange ordeals in which people are killed and brought to life, the magical gifts, the flight up a mountain, we have already met in the earlier stories.

May we not see in this oddly persistent legend another vestigial remnant of the *rêve initiatique*? True, it has been deprived of its power-giving qualities. Some of the boys found on temple roofs later became idiots, unable to endure the 'otherness' of the experience they had undergone. Far from returning enhanced, empowered persons, they were afterwards diminished, maimed ones. Others, such as Torakichi himself, disappeared into obscurity, leaving scarcely a memory behind, let alone a line of disciples pledged to perpetuate their revelation. Though the vision remains it has lost its transforming power. No longer acknowledged to be a religious experience, it survives obscurely on the periphery of the religious world as a folk legend.

With this review of the evidence for mantic journeys in past centuries in Japan, let us now turn to the modern evidence. Direct testimonies of such adventures are few, but one spectacular example can be cited. This is the case of Deguchi Onisaburō, one of the founders of the flourishing religious movement known as Ōmoto.[21]

Deguchi appears to have been a sickly youth, haunted by visions of ghosts. He also affected the low company of gamblers and drunkards, who in the spring of 1898 beat him up so severely that he was nearly killed. After recovering from this ordeal he suddenly disappeared, and for a week nothing was heard of him. Then he reappeared, and, like the kidnapped boys we have just noticed, sank for several days into a comatose sleep. When eventually he recovered consciousness, he declared that he had gone to a cave on Mt Takakuma in order to undergo a period of ascetic fasting. There his soul had been separated from his body and carried off, under the guidance of a variety of divine figures, to all the quarters of heaven and hell. In the course of his journey he had been granted supernatural powers, including clairvoyance and clairaudience. He had seen back into the past as far as the creation of the world, and into mysteries such as *kotodama*, the occult soul of words. His family called in exorcists, thinking him to be suffering from fox possession. But he soon made a good recovery, and proceeded to embark on the career which was later to bring him the fame and notoriety of a remarkable religious leader.

The full account of his adventures was not published until 1921. By then he was already a celebrated figure. The religious group he had founded, Ōmoto, had already received its first blow of government persecution, whereby, on the charge of *lèse-majesté* against the Emperor, its buildings were savagely razed to the ground and its leaders imprisoned. It was on emerging from prison on bail that Deguchi embarked on the narrative of his adventures in the other world twenty-three years before. He is said to have dictated the story of his journey in a state of trance in which he relived vividly the whole cycle of his adventures. When he described travelling through icily cold regions, for example, he himself shivered so violently that he had to be wrapped in coats even though it was a hot day. As he dictated he was apparently impervious to fatigue; for many hours on end he continued to speak to a series of amanuenses who one after another retired exhausted.

The account of his journey to hell and his subsequent ascent to heaven is too long and complex to relate in full. A few scenes only from each journey will have to suffice to exemplify this remarkable narrative.[22]

His account begins with a description of his austerities in a cave on the holy mountain Takakuma. For several days neither food nor water passed his lips. Day and night he sat crosslegged on a painfully jagged rock, his body pierced by an icy wind, while blood-curdlingly uncanny sounds reverberated over the mountainside. There then appeared a messenger who summoned his soul from his body and carried it off hundreds of leagues through the air, his body meanwhile remaining behind crosslegged in the cave.

They descended at last to see before them a huge river, which the messenger told him was the barrier of the other world. They waded across, and as they did so Deguchi noticed that his blue garment had turned white. When they reached the opposite bank he looked back and behold, what he had thought to be no more than flowing water had become a writhing mass of thousands of snakes, their heads raised to spit forth fiery tongues. And following behind, apparently unaware of anything more than the water of the river, came a host of other travellers. Their clothes as they made their way across were all changed to different colours, black, yellow or brown. They were harassed and chivied by several frightful-looking guards, who called out their names and attached labels on their garments.

Soon Deguchi and his guide came to a courthouse, where

they were taken into the presence of the king of the under-world. A white-haired old man with a beautiful gentle face, he talked to them amiably until it was time for him to go to the court room to preside over the tribunal of the multitudes who had waded across the river. Seated upon his throne of judgment, the king's aspect suddenly underwent a terrible change. Gone was the gentle and dignified old man. What Deguchi saw now was a bright red face, eyes huge and staring like mirrors, and a mouth, split open as wide as the ears, from which there spurted forth a long tongue like a flame. One by one the travellers were called by name and, the judgment read out, were dragged off by the guards to the prescribed quarter of hell. When Deguchi's turn came, however, he received special treatment. Hence-forth, the king told him, he was to become the messiah between the two worlds. He must therefore see for himself what the other world was like. He was given to aid him on his journey a magic spell, which, as we shall see, was to prove on many occasions indispensable.

We see him first walking along a narrow road choked with dead weeds as sharp as icicles. On either side lay a deep ditch filled with loathsome worms and insects. Above loomed a black cloud from which a terrible face glared down at him. Behind, a demon in a red jacket was trying to prod him with a sharp spear. Ahead of him he soon came to a deep river full of blood and pus, with no bridge, in which countless people, their bodies covered with leeches, were writhing and screaming. In this desperate position he murmured the words of the spell he had been given, and at once found himself on the other side of the river.

Here he is again, sliding down an icy road, down and down into cold black depths, all round him a sickening stench of blood and the sound of indescribably agonised screams. Down and down he fell, until his face and body were cut to pieces on the sharp rocks. He managed to gasp out the words of the spell, however, and at once it grew lighter, his wounds vanished, and he found himself in the midst of a great crowd of people on the edge of a lake.

The lake was full of hairy caterpillars and horned snakes, and over it, as far as the opposite shore, stretched a slender bridge of ice. Goaded by demons with sharp spears, the people were struggling to climb the bridge. Already several had slipped into the lake, to be bitten and squeezed by the snakes. Again Deguchi recited his spell, and lo, the lake disappeared, the demons and snakes disappeared, and he found himself on a wide plain surrounded by thousands of dead people, their faces full of joy, greeting him by name as their deliverer.

Further on we see him again before a tall building as high as the clouds. At the gate stood two fierce guards, looking in all directions with eyes like mirrors. Then there appeared a band of soldiers driving before them a throng of tormented dead people. The women and children rushed towards Deguchi, blood streaming from their mouths, snakes twined round their necks and spears sticking from their stomachs. Deguchi went to meet them murmuring his spell, and at once the tall building, the soldiers and the blood disappeared, a brilliant light filled the sky, and benevolent spirits like stars took charge of the dead people. For a moment the air was filled with joyous voices. Then they faded into the distance until at length all that Deguchi could hear was the sound of the wind.

There follow in his narrative many more such scenes, shifting, enigmatic and dreamlike. Time and again he is killed, split in half with a sharp blade like a pear, dashed to pieces on rocks, frozen, burnt, engulfed in avalanches of snow. Once he was turned into a goddess. Time and again, by means of his spell, he was able to rescue tormented dead people.

At length, however, he was told that he had seen enough of the quarters of hell, and that it was time for him to pass on to his journey to heaven. After a short respite in his body in the cave, he was again snatched out of it, as though by an enormous hand, and set down at a double crossroads. From there he made many attempts to walk along the road to paradise. At each attempt, however, he found himself caught up in an enigmatic and dreamlike scene.

He saw running before him along the road, for example, a strange woman with a pitted face, a long hanging tongue and sunken, glittering eyes. Soon she plunged into a thick wood, and Deguchi felt impelled to follow her. Eventually, after a long pursuit, he emerged on to a green plateau to see the woman, who now had a long thick tail, surrounded by goblins. With her tail the woman killed the goblins and, with an expression of rapture on her face, began to lap up their blood. As she drank, horns sprouted from her forehead, her body swelled, her mouth split open as wide as her ears and her teeth turned to tusks like swords. Paralysed with horror, Deguchi murmured his spell, and at once found himself back again at the crossroads.

Realising that he had gone astray, he set out once more, to see before him a large black snake with the face of a woman, writhing in agony with bloodshot eyes. She plunged into the sea and swam frantically away. Deguchi attempted to follow her, but at once the sea and the snake-woman vanished and he found himself once more back at the crossroads.

Two more scenes and we must leave him. At length he found himself at the centre of the world, at the summit of the huge axial mountain Sumeru. Here he was vouchsafed a sight of the creation of the world. Below him stretched the entire universe, formless and shapeless like a muddy sea. But as he looked through his telescope he descried in the distance a golden pillar which spun round to the left. Faster and faster it spun, until the mud churned and scattered into lumps which took their place in the sky as stars. Another pillar then arose, silver and spinning to the right. As it spun it scattered seeds in all directions which became mountains and plains and rivers.

This vision ended, he found himself again walking along a road. At last he came to a great river, beyond which was paradise. Over it hung a great arched bridge made of gold. Many travellers were gathered at its foot, amazed at its steepness and dazzling beauty. There was no railing and the golden surface was very slippery, so that he had to take off his shoes and cast away everything he was carrying before venturing to step upon it. Many travellers slipped and fell into the river, but Deguchi, though dizzy and faint, reached the other side safely. There he saw before him, standing on a vast lotus, a marvellous palace made of gold and agate and the seven jewels. On to the lotus he climbed and saw all round him ranges of blue mountains, and a great lake rippling with golden waves. Among the waves rose innumerable islands, covered with pine trees with cranes' nests among their branches. Above the lake flew golden doves and crows, while on the surface of the water swam mandarin ducks and turtles with green fur.

With this vision of the islands of paradise we must leave Deguchi's narrative of his journey to the other world. We have followed him through only a few scenes of his first volume. His adventures continue through eleven more. But already we have seen enough to recognise many of the motifs of the initiatory journey. Ordeals which kill or transform, river barriers, perilous bridges, glittering palaces, the ambivalent ruler of the underworld, the obstacles on the road which ensnare or beglamour, all these are part of a familiar schema. But underlying the tale can be discerned the dissolving scenes of a genuine vision. This experience we know to have been a transforming one. Deguchi returned from his journey an altered person, gifted with powers and aspirations he had not possessed before.

Here then is evidence to show that the mantic flight to other worlds has been known in Japan for several centuries. As an initiation into the religious life, however, it occurs much less frequently than either the dream or the divine possession. That it was recognised as a power-giving experience, nevertheless, is proved by its survival in the 'symbolic action' of Shugendō ritual. To this symbolic mimesis of the other-world journey we must now turn our attention.

I I
The Symbolic Journey

For those to whom the experience of the other-world journey is not given in visionary form, it is possible to accomplish it nevertheless by the mimesis of symbolic action. If the soul will not detach itself from the body and travel to heaven and hell, it is possible to undertake, in body as well as soul, a journey to places which symbolise heaven and hell, enduring on the way penances which symbolise the ordeals to be encountered in these realms.

Such symbolic journeys through other planes of the cosmos have been made possible to the *yamabushi* since medieval times by means of the rites known as *nyūbu* or *mineiri*. During these ceremonial 'entries into a high mountain' at stated seasons of the year, certain austerities are enacted which symbolise the conception, gestation and birth of an embryo in the womb, and at the same time the passage of the Buddhist disciple through the Ten Realms of Existence.

Until a century ago such ritual climbs were apparently practised on many of the ancient holy mountains of Japan. Such hills, with their associations with the other world, were the ideal places on which to project symbolically the more sophisticated cosmology of esoteric Buddhism through which the *yamabushi* was required to pass. These mountains now represent not only the ancient other world of spiritual beings, but also the mandala, that powerful Buddhist symbol for isolating and enclosing holy space, and at the same time the womb where the disciple is newly conceived, grows and emerges into the world with the cry of a newly born child.

Today, however, the only places where these ceremonial climbs are practised with any recollection of the old symbolism are the two holy mountains of Ōmine and Haguro. On August 1st the Shōgoin branch of the Shugendō still carries out its *Ōmine-shugyō*, the remnant of what used to be the long pilgrimage from Yoshino over the hallowed Mt Ōmine down the Kii peninsula to Kumano. During the week from August 24th to 30th the Haguro branch of the Shugendō still performs its *akimine* or autumn peak, comprising a ceremonial entry into Mt Haguro and a subsequent sojourn on its slopes during which the aforementioned rites of passage are enacted.

The ascetic ascent of Mt Ōmine, also known as the *okugakeshiki*, has been since the earliest days of the Shugendō rule one of the principal power-giving practices of the order. A story in the thirteenth-century collection *Kokonchomonjū* describes how the celebrated Buddhist poet Saigyō Hōshi begged the *yamabushi* to take him with them on their ascent of Mt Ōmine. Before long he was reduced to tears of pain and exhaustion by the severity of the discipline, and it was only when the leader of the band explained to him that by undergoing the penances of starvation, beating and carrying heavy loads he was in fact passing through the horrors of hell, the realm of Hungry Ghosts and the realm of Animals, preparatory to entering paradise, that the meaning of his sufferings was made clear to him.[1]

Kaempfer heard something of the horrors of the climb at the end of the seventeenth century through the young man whom he instructed in 'Physick and Surgery'. This youth had undergone a 'very rude Noviciate' before being admitted to the order, which included a week of eating nothing but herbs, and of making 780 prostrations and seven cold water austerities a day. Should anyone set out on the climb without first having duly purified and prepared himself for it, he declared, he would run the risk of being thrown down the horrid precipices and dashed to pieces.[2] The climb itself was excessively dangerous, and freezing cold at the summit, and the only food allowed was roots and herbs growing on the mountain. Yet every member of the order was required to make the climb once a year.

The Jesuits too, a century earlier, were impressed by what they heard of the rigours of the exercise, which they interpreted as a pilgrimage to conclude a pact with the devil. Both Father Frois and Father Guzman were given a detailed account of the climb by a *yamabushi* who had performed it seven times, but who had subsequently been converted to Christianity. In order to demonstrate how blessed were those who carried the yoke of the Lord God rather than that of the devil, the fathers wrote a report of what they had heard.

The journey took seventy-five days, they wrote, a day being allotted to each of the seventy-five leagues of the route. A brutal discipline, including semi-starvation, was enforced the whole way by ferocious and mysterious people called 'Jenquis and Goquis'. These names in all probability refer to Zenki and Goki, the two demonic figures attendant on either side of En-no-Gyōja, from whom the inhabitants of such isolated mountain villages as Dorogawa claim descent. From the account it seems that the fierce mountain men of these villages emerged to guide and supervise the thousands of pilgrims, striking terror by the ferocity of their enforcement of the rules. Should anyone disobey orders or grow lax, he was tied by these terrible people head downwards to a tree overhanging a precipice, from which desperate position he was usually dashed to pieces in the valley below. Further on in the course of the pilgrimage, everyone was forced to sit for a day and a night with their legs crooked up and their knees touching their mouths, their arms crossed, hands on shoulders like an embryo in the womb. If any man from stiffness or exhaustion moved even a little, the Goquis came and belaboured his knees with a stick. If anyone fell ill on the way, he was left to die or to crawl home as best he could.[3]

These descriptions dwell on the ferocity of the discipline, the ardours and rigours of the climb. None explain the symbolic meaning of the penances, for the simple reason that in all probability the writers were told nothing of them. Such teachings were reserved until modern times for the oral tradition of the order, kuden, imparted in secret to those disciples only who had undergone the requisite initiations. It is only with the disintegration of the esoteric discipline of the Shugendō in modern times that such doctrines have been published for all to read. Today, however, we see that the sufferings endured on this climb were not undertaken with the mere vague intention of building up a store of power. They were invested with a symbolic meaning which conducted the disciple on a voyage into a new life.

The *yamabushi's* ascent of Mt Ōmine presents an interesting parallel to the climb which the pilgrim is intended to make of the enormous Buddhist monument of Borobudur in Java. Here we have not a real mountain but an artificial one. This huge stone temple is so constructed in a series of ascending terraces that the pilgrim as he makes his way to the summit passes through the Three Worlds of the Mahayana Buddhist cosmos. Starting from the lowest square terrace with its hidden foot, which represents the *kamadhatu* or world of desire, he passes through five more square but gradually diminishing terraces, each one flanked by bas-relief sculptures depicting scenes from the life of the Buddha. His ascent of this artificial mountain, through the Rupadhatu or world of Form, brings him eventually to a level where squares give way to circles, to a region where quiet rings of curious stone-latticed bells, each enclosing a Buddha image, surround a large central effigy representing ultimate Buddhahood. Here, encircling its enlightened centre, is the upper region of No-form.[4]

For the *yamabushi*, however, the mountain is a real one, and the worlds through which he passes are not depicted in sculpture but are reconstructed in symbolic action.

The symbolism of the Ōmine climb was first committed to writing, as Miyake has shown us, in the manuals of Shugendō instruction compiled from slips of paper on which were noted such points of doctrine as the disciple might not clearly remember from the oral teaching. Among these, Miyake notes as particularly useful the works of the early sixteenth-century *sendatsu* from Kyūshū called Sokuden, and of the veteran seventeenth-century *yamabushi* Gakuhō. The earliest, however, dates as far back as the thirteenth century. These works describe the esoteric symbolism to be observed in the journey from Yoshino over Mt Ōmine to Kumano, or conversely from Kumano to Yoshino. The chief mountains along this ancient route appear to have been quickly associated with the powerful Buddhist symbol of the mandala, particularly with the two complementary mandalas, the Diamond-world or Kongōkai and the Womb-world or Taizōkai, so fundamental to the doctrine of esoteric Buddhism. Mt Kimpu at the Yoshino end is the

Diamond world mandala, the three Kumano mountains are the Womb-world mandala, while the central and most holy peak, Mt Ōmine, combines both mandalas in itself, one superimposed upon the other. Alternatively it is likened to the eight-petalled lotus at the centre of the Womb-world mandala. Thus the whole Ōmine exercise, according to Gakuhō, becomes a *tainai-shugyō*, or exercise within the womb. The mountain is thus invested with strong symbolism both of a holy centre and of a matrix within which holy power may grow.[5]

In addition, these old books specify that a series of ordeals be observed during the journey through these mandala mountains, each of which corresponds to one of the *jikkai* or ten realms through which the Buddhist disciple must pass on his way to enlightenment. Six of these represent the realms which in the last chapter we saw to lie on the wheel of life, and thus to represent conditions into which sentient beings may transmigrate. Above these lie four more holy states, away from the wheel, occupied by the *śrāvakas*, the *pratyeka-buddhas*, the bodhisattvas and the fully enlightened Buddhas.[6] The rites which correspond to each of these realms are stated slightly differently in works of different date. Here, however, is the earliest example known to be committed to writing, from the *Shugen Hiōshō*, compiled as early as 1215 from a collection of thirty-three leaflets.

> First, the rite of Hell is weighing one's karma.
> Second, the rite of the Hungry Ghosts is fasting.
> Third, the rite of the Beasts is abstention from water.
> Fourth, the rite of the titans is wrestling.
> Fifth, the rite of men is repentance.
> Sixth, the rite of the devas is the Dance of Long Life.

What exactly is required to correspond with the next three holy states is not clearly explained, but the final and culminating stage of Buddhahood is suitably expressed by the baptismal *seikanjō*, water poured on the head, which figures so prominently in the initiation of the orthodox sects of esoteric Buddhism.[7]

The picture conjured up by this list, the items of which are amplified by more detailed description in works of later date, is therefore one of a ceremonial climb punctuated by austerities of varying degree. The climbers are forbidden to eat and to wash, and are subjected to the terrifying 'weighing of karma', in which they are seated on a kind of balance projecting over a precipice. The way is relieved, however, by a bout of wrestling and one of dancing, and culminates in a final baptismal initiation.

Today this ancient journey has been a good deal curtailed. No longer do the *yamabushi* traverse the traditional seventy-five leagues from Yoshino to Kumano. It is not now usual for the August party to walk further than the village known as Zenki-guchi. Even in the years since I have observed it, moreover, there has been a notable easing of the traditional rigours. Of old, the *yamabushi* would leave Kyoto in a long and magnificent procession, and wend their way on foot the forty miles from Kyoto to Yoshino, whence the exercise proper would start. Motoori Norinaga, the Shinto scholar, has left a noteworthy description in his diary of the spectacle presented by the procession as it left the capital in the year 1757. It was nearly six miles long and took several hours to file past the dense crowds of excited spectators who had got up in the small hours to line the route, and to watch particularly for the palanquin of the Imperial Prince who was accompanying the party. Though the blinds of his palanquin were drawn too far down for Motoori to see the Prince's costume, he was reliably informed that it was of pale blue satin with a figured pattern of *shinobu* flowers, in strong contrast, he noted, to the loutish and uncouth appearance of most of the other *yamabushi* in the procession.[8]

In 1961 the exercise started at 7 a.m. with a company of some fifty *yamabushi* in full regalia gathering at the Shōgoin temple in Kyoto for a short service of chanting and a valedictory address from the aged abbot of the order. A procession then formed outside the gate, which bravely marched through the roaring morning traffic, down the middle of Karasuma street past the banks and department stores as far as the station. It was entirely ignored, as though the brilliant medieval costumes were invisible, by the crowds on their way to work. At the station the party boarded a fast train as far as Yoshino-guchi, from which, in boiling midday heat, it ascended the path through the cherry trees to the hill town of Yoshino itself.

By 1972, however, even this preliminary austerity had disappeared. The entire party, resplendent in its yellow surcoats, brilliant six-tufted collars, strips of deerskin behind, coils of red rope and triton conches hanging from the waist, piled into a large air-conditioned bus. In this luxurious conveyance, complete with trim girl guide who kept up a continuous twittering commentary through a microphone on the scenery through which we passed, the company accomplished the entire journey to Yoshino, coming to rest in a large concrete car park at the top of the new motor road up the hill.

From Yoshino the business of the climb starts in earnest, for the party must pass through the first of the Four Great Gates which lie on the route. This is the Hosshinmon or Gate of Awakening. This enormous bronze *torii* has a narrow platform surrounding the base of each of its pillars. On these the neophytes, those undergoing the climb for the first time, must stand with a hand touching the pillar. As they shuffle in a compressed pradakshina round and round the pillar, the leading *sendatsu* loudly chants a poem in the classical metre:

Yoshino naru kane no torii ni te wo kakete,
Mida no jōdo ni hairu zo ureshiki.

'When I place my hand on the iron *torii* at Yoshino, how happy am I to enter the paradise of Amida.'

The gate therefore represents a boundary, a dividing line between this and that world, a threshold of paradise. It is also a boundary between life and death. As the neophyte passes beneath it he dies a symbolic death to his old life, and is not fully reborn to his new one until he reaches the end of his journey at Kumano.

After an afternoon of chanting at different holy sites in and round Yoshino, and a night spent in the Kizōin temple, the party rises at 2.30 a.m. After a maigre breakfast of rice and seaweed it sets out in the darkness, to a jingling of bells and clarion blasts on shell trumpets, up the path through the cherry trees which leads to Mt Kimpu.

At the ancient Kimpu shrine, which is reached after an hour's walk through the forest, a second symbolic action takes place. The neophytes are conducted into a small wooden hut with a thatched roof and a central pillar, known as the Kakuredō. The door is banged shut and they find themselves in total darkness. Not the smallest chink or glimmer of dawn light relieves the utter blackness with which they are surrounded. In 1961, when I numbered among them, I remember feeling at once a sense of suspension in space, of total loss of direction and of all idea of the beginnings and ends and edges of things. A booming voice instructed us to put a hand on the shoulder of the person in front, and to move forward round the central pillar. For several minutes we shuffled round and round, repeating phrase by phrase after the voice another magic formula:

> Yoshino naru shinzan no oku no kakuredō
> Honrai kū no sumika narikeri
> On abira unken sowaka.

'The Kakuredō in the depths of the Yoshino mountains, here has always lain the abode of Emptiness.'

The droning chant was interrupted with frightful suddenness by a deafening clanging on a bell, and at the same instant the door was flung open to flood the hut with dazzling morning light. The intended effect—which I was afterwards informed by the sendatsu was kyōgaku-kaishi, awakening by shock to the ultimate Emptiness of our natures—was completely successful. The combined burst of noise and light was startling in the extreme. The hut is also known as the Kinukidō, or the place where your spirit is drawn out, as a sword from its sheath or a cork from its bottle. The name recalls the belief that the soul can be driven by sudden shock to part company with the body.

From here the procession tramps up the mountainside to a spot where there stands a statue of Aizen Myōō and a stone pillar inscribed with the words, 'Kore kara nyonin-kinsei'—No women allowed beyond here. Here was the spot where until 1969 all the women of the party, even old and tried professional ascetics like Mrs Nakano, were forced to turn back. Thenceforward the mountain was too holy and pure to risk contamination by women. In 1969, however, the barrier was relaxed, and for the first time in the history of the mountain women were allowed to approach some twelve miles nearer to the ultimate summit of Mt Ōmine, as far as a place called Gobanseki.

In 1972 therefore I was privileged to see for the first time the deep ravines, the paths winding deeper and deeper into the hills, now through forests of pine and cryptomeria, now emerging on to open hillsides of bamboo shrub and long grass, from which could be seen layer upon layer of blue hills rising from a lake of mist as though to the edge of the world. At Gobanseki, whose name indicates some ancient barrier or stopping-place, the four women in the party were left behind to make their way down a steep rocky path, through thick undergrowth and bushes, to the village of Dorogawa. To this mountain hamlet a bus can now make an almost incredibly winding way, in and out of hills, for two hours from the nearest railway station. Until the road was cut, however, the village was one of those mysterious and utterly isolated mountain communities which claimed descent from Goki, one of the demonic attendants on En-no-Gyōja.

For the rest of the ascent of Mt Ōmine, therefore, I have to rely on the reports of men.[9] Above Gobanseki the party passes through the third of the Four Great Gates—the second, which used to lie inside the Kimpu shrine, is now destroyed—beyond which it is held to emerge into even more pure and unsullied regions of the mountain than it has hitherto passed. Nearby is the celebrated spot known as the Nishi-no-nozoki, from which each member of the party is dangled, head downwards and hands clasped above his head, over a precipice. In this desperate position he is required to confess all his sins, answering Yes to such questions as, are you dutiful to your parents? Are you working hard? Is your faith firm and strong?

It is at a spot near here that the legend expressed in the Nō play *Tanikō* is located. Any man of the party who falls ill in the course of the climb is not left to die, as the Jesuit writer understood; according to the 'great law' of the *yamabushi* order, he is thrown over the precipice into the valley below. There his body will be covered with stones and thus brought to life again. The purport of this ruthless story is probably the same one that lies within the rules of the Tendai *kaihōgyō* exercise. The *yamabushi* was urged to embark on his climb with the knowledge that it was not only a passage through death to a new life, but was also a narrow edge between life and death. Should he fall ill, or break his leg, or sprain his ankle, the valley would be his fate. Thus is imparted to the exercise that edge, that intensity of purpose which lifts it out of the realm of the mere endurance test which requires nothing beyond fortitude and determination to accomplish.[10]

For the rest of the journey today, however, little of the traditional symbolism seems to be enacted or even remembered. The growth of the embryo in the womb is recalled only in the names of certain spots on the route—a narrow crack between rocks through which one must squeeze is the *tainai-kuguri* or diving into the womb—and in the red and white strings which hang from the ceiling of the topmost shrine, which represent the mother's placenta and the child's umbilical cord. Little or nothing of this symbolism is now explained. Nor are the ten penances, which the old books prescribe as corresponding with the ten worlds through which the Buddhist disciple must ascend towards ultimate Buddhahood, any longer carried out with any understanding of their meaning. The dangling head-first over a precipice, it is true, seems to be a remnant of the penance of hell, as anciently prescribed. But it is no longer explained as such.

It is rather with the splendours and terrors of the climb that the disciple is preoccupied; with the precipitous drops, giant trees, green ravines, layers of forested hills, and deep caverns where once hermits secluded themselves for whole winters on end. Here may still be seen the celebrated Shōnoiwaya cave, where we have already seen Dōken Shōnin secluding himself for thirty-seven days before his visit to heaven and hell, and the Taizōkai cave where wooden images in the village below testify that the ascetic carver Enkū retreated from the world. These caves may clearly represent boundaries between life and death. But it is nevertheless on the this-worldly moral virtues of fortitude, unselfish cooperation and obedience to the acknowledged leader that the *yamabushi* today lay stress during their ascent of Mt Ōmine.

The recollection of the spiritual journey is better preserved in the *akimine* ritual still performed by the branch of the Shugendō based on Mt Haguro in Yamagata prefecture. Here the symbolism both of the growth of the embryo and of the passage through the Ten Realms is enacted with much more clarity.

The *akimine* or autumn peak is the third of the four seasonal rituals with which the year for the Haguro *yama-bushi* used to be punctuated. Now, however, the spring and summer peaks are scarcely performed, and the winter peak, known also as the Shōreisai, is less a journey into the mountains than a celebration to mark the emergence from ritual seclusion of two high-ranking *yamabushi*. It is only in the autumn peak that the symbolism of the spiritual journey is preserved.[11]

Traditionally, and apparently until the beginning of the Meiji period, this autumn seclusion in the hills lasted seventy-five days. This period, Shimazu informs us, 'represents' the 275 days during which the embryo was believed to gestate in the mother's womb. Today, however, the period has been reduced to a week, with the inevitable result that a good many of the traditional practices have had to be dropped or modified. During this week, however, a remnant at least of the former symbolic sequences is carried out, and ritual tools to aid their performance make their appearance at the start of the exercise.

Relating to the embryo symbolism, three important objects accompany the party into the hills, and appear constantly and at times inexplicably in the rites throughout the ensuing week. The first is a small chest or portable altar called the *oi*. It contains an image of the founder of the order, Shōken Daibosatsu, and represents the womb in which the company is to be transformed. The second is a peculiar hat, formed of a circle of straw folded in half and covered with round discs of white paper, and called the *ayaigasa*. It represents the placenta, the skin in which the embryo is covered in the womb, and throughout the week played an important if enigmatic part in the ceremonies, now covering the *oi*, now the head of the *daisendatsu* or leader of the company, now the head of one of his lieutenants. The third is a long pole called the *bonden*, decorated at the top with a fringe or mane of paper streamers. At times in the course of the week it seemed to represent a phallus.

Esoteric Buddhist symbolism, however, relating to the passage through the Ten Realms, also appeared in plenty.

It is to be seen first in the structure of the company's hierarchy. The party is commanded by a *daisendatsu* assisted by four *sendatsu*. These five figures correspond to the quincunx of five directions which, each with its appropriate colour and element, derive from the Five Dhyāni Buddhas of esoteric doctrine. Thus the *daisendatsu*, dressed in his proper colour white, corresponds to the position at the centre of the quincunx, over which presides Vairochana Buddha and the element earth. The officer known as *dōshi*, who is charged with a good many of the administrative tasks of the week's retreat, occupies a position corresponding to the north, with its colour black (he was actually dressed in purple which 'represented' black), its element water and its Buddha Amoghasiddhi. The officer known as *kogi*, or firewood, occupied the eastern direction, with its Buddha Akshobya and its element wood, and is accordingly dressed in green. The *aka* or water officer faces the west, with its Buddha Amitabha, its element metal and its colour red. Lastly the officer called *kari* faces the south, with its Buddha Ratnasambhava, its element fire and its colour yellow.[12]

At the same time the costume which the disciple wears consists of items which will not only serve him usefully during his sojourn in the mountains, but also contain in themselves transforming symbolism. They represent at the same time the attributes of the disciple's Buddha nature, which in accordance with Mahayana doctrine he seeks to release from its prison of ignorance, and with which he strives to identify himself. Usually sixteen such items of costume are listed, of which a few examples will suffice to indicate their double function. The *tokin* or small round hat perched on the forehead is divided into twelve segments which represent the twelve Buddhist links in the chain of causation. It is also considered to be a useful protection against swishing branches. The triton-conch trumpet serves as a practical signal during the climbs, sounding forth like a bugle the needful starts and stops; it also symbolises the blast which disseminates the Buddha's law throughout the world and which rouses the disciple from his sleep of delusion. The sword, which the *yamabushi* seldom carries today, was useful for hacking a path through the undergrowth, and at the same time for subduing the enemies of Buddhism, including the errors of greed, hate and delusion.

When he sets out for his week of transforming austerities, therefore, the Haguro *yamabushi* wears on his person and carries with him in his procession a number of objects which symbolically indicate his transformation from a profane to a sacred state.[13]

In August 1963, owing to the kind offices of Professor Hori and Mr Togawa Anshō, whose knowledge of the doctrine and practice of the Haguro *yamabushi* is unrivalled, I was allowed to join the *akimine* week as one of the dozen *shingyaku* or neophytes.[14]

On the afternoon of August 24th the procession which marched through the village of Tōgemura to the gateway at the foot of the mountain presented a brilliant sight. The five *sendatsu* wore checked surcoats displaying the colour demanded by their position in the esoteric quincunx. The *dōshi* wore the purple which stood for northern black, the *kogi* wore the green of the east, the *aka* the red of the west, the *kari* the yellow of the south, while the dignified figure of the *daisendatsu* Mr Shimazu, who rather resembled in appearance General Nogi, the hero of the Russo-Japanese war, was clad in the pure white required by his central and paramount position. The rest of the company were dressed in surcoats of large blue and white checks, sporting on the back a notable crest of a Chinese lion, baggy white pantaloons, tight white leggings, collar with six white tufts, small black cap on forehead.

The procession carried with it the ritual tools needed for the week's exercises. The powerfully symbolic *oi*, representing the mother's womb, was carried near the middle of the line, covered with the white folded hat. To the fore went the long *bonden* with its mane of white paper streamers, a large black wooden axe and a halberd. To the van and to the rear went the shell trumpeters who sounded the various signals for departure, and the halts for worship on the way. Over the heads of each of the *sendatsu* was held a large red paper umbrella, while perpendicular purple banners bearing the legend of the Haguro order also marched to the fore.

Before this brave procession passed beneath the red *torii* which represented the official gateway to the mountain, it paused at a small shrine called the Koganedō for a curious ceremony which, symbolically, marked the real beginning of the exercise. The white *daisendatsu*, with the *oi* representing the womb on his back and his face hidden by the strange *ayaigasa*, representing placenta, on his head, crouched at the foot of the wooden steps with the long *bonden* wand in his hands. After shaking it to and fro several times he flung it forward so that it clattered and banged up the steps.

No one explained this curious procedure until we made enquiries. It then transpired that what we had seen represented the act of conception. Having been corpses the previous night, we were all now embryos in the womb of the mountain.

The procession thereupon, to the accompaniment of blasts on conch shells, passed through the red gateway of the Haguro mountain. From there, pausing only to offer 'worship from afar' at stated spots to the other holy mountains in the district, it wound its way up an immense flight of stone steps, built in the seventeenth century and leading through several miles of forest up the mountain as far as the Haguro shrine at the top. Huge cryptomeria trees, likewise planted in the seventeenth century, formed an avenue on either side. At the foot of the shrine is a flight of ten steps which represent the ten stages on the path to enlightenment. Here, as was appropriate to their as yet ungrown, unformed, rudimentary state, the party made its act of reverence, chanting the Heart Sutra and appropriate mantras, at the bottom of this symbolic scale. Their corresponding act of worship at the end of the week was made from the topmost step.

From here the procession marched two or three miles further into the heart of the mountain, down a slippery path with a row of stepping stones like balls down the middle, to a spot originally opened and hallowed by the founder Shōken Daibosatsu. Here at the end of an avenue of stone images stands the temple of Kōtakuji which is the base from which the week's exercises are conducted.

At the entrance to the temple the procession halted, while the Dōshi delivered the necessary instructions for the party to settle into its new quarters. Having lain empty since the last retreat the previous August, it must be swept and garnished. The kitchen stores must be unpacked, the water must be pumped from the well, the altar must be dressed and made ready for the coming observances and the various ritual tools duly arranged. These included a long tassel of red and white cords suspended from the ceiling of the shrine room, which represented the veins and arteries by which the embryo was attached to the mother's womb.

Lastly the thirty members of the party must be allotted places to sleep. The company that year consisted of a number of heterogeneous elements. Besides the five *sendatsu* and a few other *yamabushi* living in the village at the foot of the mountain, there had joined the Haguro company several *yamabushi* from other centres, Nikkō and Sendai. There was a *karate* master from Osaka who was a part-time *yamabushi*. There were five women, all of them professional ascetic healers come to consolidate their store of power at the retreat, who were relegated to the only upstairs room in the temple. Another room was allotted to a group of veteran *yamabushi* who were farmers for the periods of the year when no ascetic exercises were taking place. The four 'students', together with one young boy, the *karate* master and the *yamabushi* from Nikkō, were allotted a narrow seven-mat room in which to sleep.

The Dōshi then explained that we had now entered the first of the three *shuku* or lodgings, into which the week was to be divided and which marked stages in the growth of the embryo. During these lodgings, certain rites and penances would be observed which marked the stages on the other symbolic system, the passage through the Ten Realms of Transmigration. The penance of hell, known as the *namban-ibushi* or southern smoking, would take place twice that night and twice more the following night. The penance of the Hungry Ghosts, observed concurrently, would continue for the first three days of the week; it consisted of abstention from all solid food. Tea would be allowed, but nothing else. Hence there would be nothing to eat for the rest of the day, and nothing the next day either. Likewise the penance of the Animal World would begin forthwith, but unlike the other two would continue for the entire week. By this penance we were forbidden to wash either body or face, to clean the teeth, to rinse the mouth or to shave.

These were the three lowest and most unpleasant realms to be negotiated. The remaining three of the six 'profane' realms, titans, men and gods, and the four 'holy' realms, *śrāvakas*, *pratyeka-buddhas*, bodhisattvas and Buddhas, would be enacted later in the week.

The afternoon having been thus spent in sweeping, pumping and unpacking, the business of the retreat started that night at eight o'clock with the *shoya-gongyō*, the first of the two nightly services, each lasting a couple of hours, which took place every night of the week.

The service, for which everyone had to appear properly dressed, was conducted in a large front room of the temple called the *toko*. It was lit by only an arch of candles over the altar at one end, and by five large dim lanterns, candles within translucent shades, one set on the floor in front of each of the five *sendatsu* as they sat ranged in their proper positions before the altar.

The service started with a roll-call called *toko-shirabe*, in which all the participants were called by the special names they had been given, ending with the syllable *bō*, together with the village where they lived.[15]

The chanting then started with a fast Heart Sutra and the name of the deity Sambō Dai Kōjin and his mantra, repeated three times:

> *Namu Sambō Dai Kōjin*
> *Namu Sambō Dai Kōjin*
> *Namu Sambō Dai Kōjin*
> *On kembaya kembaya sowaka*
> *On kembaya kembaya sowaka*
> *On kembaya kembaya sowaka.*

Then started the *Hokke Sembō*. It was very beautiful, on three wailing notes, with the Dōshī leading in with '*Shinkeirei*' and the other *sendatsu* responding with invocations to all the Buddhas of the Ten Directions, the east, the south-east, the south, the south-west, the west, the north-west, the north, the north-east, above and below.

> *Shinkeirei . . . tōhō sentoku fushin tōhō hakkai seishōfu*
> *Shinkeirei . . . tōnampō buyutoku fushin tōnampō hakkai seishōfu.*

There was a haunting quality about the chant which pursued me for days afterwards. I would wake up in the morning with it ringing in my ears, and it followed me in everything I did for at least a week after the retreat ended.

The chanting had continued for some minutes when without any warning the voices rose to a shout, and there was a deafening banging on the outer shutters of the room, like a sudden thunderclap crashing against the temple. Three times this happened at unexpected intervals, and at the first time the row of *shingyaku* or neophytes ranged down the left side of the room were considerably startled.[16]

Quite right that they should be, Mr Togawa afterwards explained. The sounds were supposed to bring home to you, with as much of a shock as possible, the chaotic state of your thoughts and passions at the beginning of the week. On the third day, when we had left the first 'lodging' and entered the second, the furious banging was replaced by a gentler sound, the faint crackle made by *shikimi* leaves fanned into flame over a brazier, suitable to the calmer condition into which our minds should by then have subsided.

The chanting of the *Hokke Sembō* then levelled out to one note, faster and faster until it sounded like the humming of bees. Then the voices swung into another tune, strange and beautiful like an old folksong, which was the Midasan or hymn to Amida.

There followed the *Fumombon*, then the mantras of eighteen deities, each repeated three times, then the *hōgō* or holy names of fourteen deities specially concerned with Mt Haguro, each one again repeated three times:

Plate 22. The ascetic and fire. Hōjūji *saitō-goma.*

Plate 23. The ascetic and fire. Indoor *goma* ritual in a temple at Uji. *Photograph courtesy of Dr Fosco Maraini.*

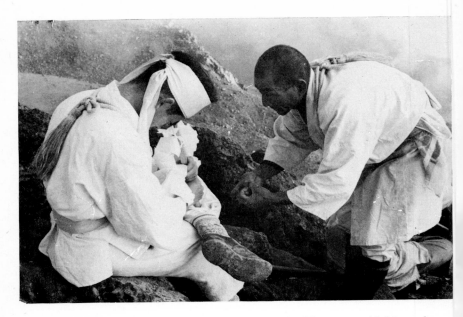

Plate 24. An *oza* séance on the summit of Mt Ontake. The *maeza* with his mudras and mantras brings the medium into a state of trance.

Plate 25. Another *oza* séance. Mr Ōmomo in 1963 controlling the violent trance of one of the mediums in his party.

Namu Tenshō Kōtai Jingū
Namu Hagurosan Daigongen
Namu Gassan Daigongen
Namu Yudonosan Daigongen.

and onwards through local emanations of Fudō, Jizō and the founder of the order Shōken Dai bosatsu.

There followed a *sengan-shingyō* or Thousand Heart Sutras. This was calculated to be adequately accomplished if every person present recited the whole sutra seven times and the dhāraṇī at the end forty times. With a company of between thirty and forty reciting, this somehow worked out at a round thousand.

There was then a short pause, and the Dōshi called '*Kamidoko e hibachi, shimodoko e hibachi*', 'braziers to the front of the room, braziers to the back'.

At once the outer shutters were thrown open and three *yamabushi* entered each carrying a long wooden brazier like a window-box, full of red-hot charcoal. These they set down to the front, middle and back of the room, and having closed the outer shutters tightly, took their places behind the braziers, each with a large red fan in his hand.

The Dōshi then called, '*Kamidoko e yakumi*', 'spices to the front, and at once the *yamabushi* manning the foremost brazier threw on to the red charcoal a tray of red pepper flakes, rice bran and a smelly plant called *dokudami*. A further call, '*Shimodoko e yakumi*', and the same was done with the two remaining braziers.

A thick cloud of smoke at once rose from all three, which the attendant *yamabushi* fanned vigorously with their red fans. Every few seconds, as the Dōshi repeated the command, more pepper flakes and bran were cast on to the charcoal until the room was quickly filled with a thick white smoke. So acrid and pungent was it that you had but to breathe in a whiff to start an uncontrollable paroxism of choking. Thicker and thicker rose the clouds of smoke until the figures on the other side of the room were blotted out, and even those near me were shrouded as though in a dense fog, and the Dōshi could only with difficulty splutter out his commands.

At last, after what I subsequently discovered to be only

four minutes, came the command, '*Tokoyurugi*', and the shutters were flung open. Some continued to sit bravely in their places, but most people rushed choking to the open windows and gasped for air. It was some time before I could stop coughing, and the peculiar smell and aftertaste of the smoke lingered over the entire temple for hours afterwards. The room where we slept was full of it when we got back, and only slowly drifted away through the open windows.

Exactly the same order of service was repeated at the *goya-gongyō* or late night service which started at 2 a.m. The Shakasan or hymn to Shaka replaced the hymn to Amida, but the haunting tune was identical. By four o'clock the worst of the smoke had drifted away, and we lay down to rest until 6.30. I slept badly, with the wailing chant of the *Hokke Sembō* ringing in my ears, with its *shinkeirei* and its Buddhas of the Ten Directions, and with bright visions before my eyes of an orchard of trees, now covered with white flowers, now with red leaves.

The smoking penance is known as the *namban-ibushi* or southern smoking because peppers were held to come from southern parts. The sufferings it entails constitute the austerity of hell, the lowest and worst of the ten realms to be negotiated on the way to Buddhahood. The choice of pepper smoke to symbolise the tortures of hell seems to be associated with the old belief that smoke burnt in the face of a possessed person will drive out the *jaki* or evil influence. In the old days when the retreat lasted for seventy-five days, the Dōshi informed us the next day, they used to do the *namban-ibushi* some forty times. Now it was reduced to only four, at the end of each of the two services on the first two nights. Before the war he had often seen people carried out unconscious. The smoke got down their throats, they tried to be sick, nothing came up because of the starvation diet, and after four or five violent reaches they fainted. With the recent modifications, however, nothing so drastic was seen today.

During the days that followed the remainder of the six profane worlds were negotiated at stated times. The starvation appropriate to the Hungry Ghosts was continued officially until the morning of the third day, though it was relieved on the 26th by a present of noodles, consumed midday, and on the 27th by another of beans and water melons. These gifts were made by the kind villagers of Tōgemura in return for our reciting, in our already spiritually strengthened state, the enormous Daihannyakyō or Larger Prajñāpāramitā Sutra, for the benefit of their dead ancestors. This huge sutra, it should be said, was not recited in full, but by the method known as *tendoku*. This feat, for which practice is needed to attain dexterity, consists of holding the volume of the sutra aloft in one hand and allowing its pages to cascade downwards in an elongated concertina into the other, reciting loudly meanwhile a short magic formula. Though the Daihannya Sutra occupies some scores of volumes, when divided among the thirty participants in the manner described, not more than a quarter of an hour was needed to extract from it the required effect.

Such *segaki* or offerings to the Hungry Ghosts apart, however, the fast continued until the morning of the 27th, when, with a ritual called *dan-biraki*, we were supposed to pass out of the realm of Hungry Ghosts. Thereafter two maigre meals were served a day, in the early morning and at midday.

The ordeal of the Animal World, however, not washing, not shaving, not cleaning the teeth, not even rinsing the mouth, continued until the end of the week and proved, in the hot weather of the comparatively low-lying Mt Haguro, to be a greater penance than the fasting.

The remainder of the seven worlds were negotiated, or celebrated, without any element of privation or suffering. The world of the Ashuras or titans, who are believed to be continually at war with one another, was celebrated by a bout of *sumō* wrestling. The human world was celebrated by a fairly strenuous exercise called *sange*, repentance, which consisted of forty prostrations, up and down from a standing position to one with the forehead on the floor and arms outstretched. These were performed in the middle of the third and fourth nights after the first service was concluded. The world of the devas, the topmost of the six 'profane' states, should by rights have been celebrated by the dance known as Ennen or long life, late on the night of the 28th after the *saitō-goma* was finished. When the moment came, however, it was discovered that no one among the company could remember how to execute it. Instead, therefore, the deva world was symbolised by some chanting in the Furukawa mode.

The four higher and sublime states of consciousness, off the prison of the ever-circling Buddhist wheel, namely the *shōmon* or *śrāvakas*, the *engaku* or *pratyeka-buddhas*, the bodhisattvas and the final Buddhas, were not celebrated by any rite at all. The *daisendatsu* explained their absence by the fact that such exalted states of consciousness were in any case 'formless', and hence not appropriately subject to symbolisation. Clearly, however, the traditional rites had simply been forgotten and fallen into disuse. There was therefore no final and triumphant culmination to this succession of symbolic rites of passage.

The concurrently enacted embryo symbolism was recalled throughout the week by a number of devices. The ceremony known as *Ninoshuku-hairi*, or entry into the second lodging, performed on the afternoon of the third day, clearly represented, with its two flaring torches pushed together end to end, some kind of sexual coupling. The curious 'staggered fence', known as *chigaigaki*, which also featured prominently in this rite, indicated, so the *daisendatsu* informed me, that the foetus had reached the stage of growth where it turned round in the womb. Likewise the passing of the white *ayaigasa* hat, representing placenta, from the head of the *daisendatsu* to that of the *dōshi*, indicated that the foetus had moved its place in the womb.

The tassel of red and white cords, moreover, hanging from the ceiling near the altar, underwent a significant change in the middle of the week. The red cords representing arteries, the white veins and the flaxen strings bones, these had for the first part of the week been looped up to a ring of three white fans in the ceiling which represented heaven. At the beginning of the third lodging, on the morning of the 28th, they were let down to dangle on the floor. This emblem likewise symbolised the movement of the foetus in the womb, and at the same time, in a manner not clearly explained, the disciple's ascent from a profane state to a holy one.

The rest of the time during the day was taken up with listening to lectures by the *daisendatsu* on Shugendō doctrine, practising such occult arts as the mudras, some of which represent lions, which accompany the nine magic syllables known as *kuji*, preparing and performing the important ritual of the *saitō-goma*, and with long pilgrimages known as *tosō* to remote parts of the Haguro mountain and district which had been originally hallowed by the Founder. The longest of these was to Sankozawa, reputed to be a cave set up in the cliff face where the Founder had for some time secluded himself in meditation.

The tramp to this place, which some people declared to be twelve *ri* there and back, some thirty miles, and others not more than three or four, was scheduled to take place at 4.30 on the morning of the 29th. The ceremonies following the *saitō-goma*, which included several small cups of celebratory saké, having only ended about three hours before, and this being the fourth night running in which we had had no more than three or four hours sleep, I was not at all sure, when roused, that I could manage the pilgrimage without collapsing. But after breaking one of the rules and washing my face, I felt much more clear-headed and decided to go.

The first lap of the journey was done in a bus bound for the top of Gassan, winding deeply into the mountains. At an indefinite spot on the way we got out, a smallish party of only a dozen led by the yellow *kari sendatsu*. Here he plunged straight into the undergrowth at the side of the road, and we followed him down a precipitously steep hillside, clinging on to the branches of saplings and the vines which covered them like a cloak. Down and down we plunged, swinging from tree to tree, until suddenly we found ourselves once more on level ground, on a flat stretch of rice fields winding like a green river into the hills.

The white line of *yamabushi*, resplendent in their collars with red and yellow tufts, then threaded its way for half an hour along the narrow paths between fields of rice. After half an hour it reached a village called Seba, full of large

L-shaped farmhouses. This was a *shugen-buraku* or *yamabushi* village, where every family, if it did not contain a *yamabushi*, was at least a faithful supporter of the Haguro sect.

Into one of these houses, with a garden full of yellow flowers and the shorter arm of the L, next to the entrance hall, occupied by the lavatory and a stall with a black cow, the party entered. Having recited the Heart Sutra and the mantra of Sambō Dai Kōjin in front of the family shrine, it then consumed the cold rice balls and slices of pickled cucumber provided for its breakfast.

Beyond the village a lorry carried us among crates of vegetables two or three miles along the course of a river as far as an electrical power station. There we scrambled down to the river bed, waded across a shallow ford, and climbed up the steep slope the other side through thick trees covered with red berries. There was a narrow path leading right into the heart of the mountains, looking down a couple of hundred feet below to an olive-green river with withered trees startlingly white on the bank. Sankozawa was somewhere over there, the *sendatsu* declared, beyond those folds of hills. In the old days before they made the dam for the power station the river had been much shallower, and instead of walking along this path above the course of the stream they had scrambled up the river bed itself, leaping from rock to rock. In the old days too, the cave where the Founder had performed his meditations could only be reached by the party gathering at the top of a precipice and lowering one man on a rope down the sheer face of rock as far as the cave. There he would recite the necessary observances before being hauled up again. Some years ago, however, a landslide had obliterated the cave, so that they now ended their pilgrimage at the top of the erstwhile precipice.

Suddenly the single-file procession came to a halt, and the *sendatsu* at the head called out that another landslide had crashed over the path and entirely destroyed it. With surprising equanimity the party decided that this was as far as they could reasonably get towards their destination. They produced a small image of Daihi Henjō Nyorai, the presiding deity of Sankozawa, and set it up in the middle of the path. A recitation of the *Sanjō Shakujō* and the name and mantra of Sambō Dai Kōjin, and the pilgrimage was considered accomplished. We walked back above the course of the river as far as the village, and thence the six or seven miles up the mountain back to the temple, which we reached, presenting bunches of wild flowers to the waiting *sendatsu* about three in the afternoon. I remember feeling surprised that throughout the day I had felt no suspicion of tiredness at all.

The final descent of the mountain was made on the afternoon of the 31st. The services the previous night had differed from those that had gone before in so far as the company had recited the *sengan-shingyō* or Thousand Heart Sutras no less than three times. This meant that each person must repeat the entire sutra twenty-four times and the final *dhāranī* 120 times. The petitions in response to which these recitations were made were read out by the Dōshi at the beginning of the service, and included the extra one for safety during the storms traditionally held to arise on the *nihyaku-tōka* or 210th day of the year, which according to the lunar calendar fell on that very night.

The packing, sweeping and necessary memorial photograph disposed of, a clamour of conch shell blasts and a stentorian voice calling '*Tatsu!*' announced our departure. The procession of five coloured *sendatsu*, the red umbrellas, the great black axe, the *oi* covered with the white hat, the purple banners followed by the rest of the blue-and-white company, marched down the stone steps of the temple and into the cryptomeria forest.

At the Haguro shrine the company now tramped up the ten wooden steps representing the ten stages on the path to Buddhahood, and at the top, having in symbolic experience passed through all ten, recited their mantras and Heart Sutra. The Dōshi, in the medieval speech in which all his ritual announcements were made, cried that the top of the steps represented our birth into the world from the mother's womb. We must therefore all give the *ubugoe*, the first cry of a newly born child, 'all together and as loud as possible'.

Everyone thereupon roared '*Wa*' at the top of his voice, and clattered down the steps.

The Dōshi then announced in his medieval speech that one more pilgrimage would be made to a holy spot called Akoya, and that everyone except the old and infirm should go.

Only a dozen people followed the yellow *sendatsu* as he plunged down an almost precipitously steep slope behind the Haguro shrine, clutching hold of the branches of tough saplings. At the bottom was a waterfall rushing down a sheer face of rock, and away among boulders. Under this waterfall the Founder had stood in the days of yore.

The usual sutras and mantras were recited, and then Mr Matsushita the *karate* master stripped off all his clothes down to his loincloth, tied a towel round his shaved head and stepped under the waterfall with his back to the sheer face of rock. As the water splashed off him his hands started to flash to and fro and his fingers to twist themselves into the complex mudras of the nine syllables. His pale naked figure against the wall of rock, the magically compelling movements of his hands, made him look strangely demonic, as though some extra power or grace had descended upon him through the splashing water. The mudras of his hands became more and more concentrated and ferocious, until suddenly they looked like the claws of a great bird, and I realised that they were now the *kata* or paradigmatic movements of his *karate* art. He then gave three or four tremendous *kiai*, a piercing abdominal yell which echoed among the rocks and trees. Then he stepped out of the waterfall smiling, rubbing himself down, and remarking how pleasant the cold water had been after a week of no baths. The demonic quality had dropped off him like a garment, and in an instant he was a human being once more.

By the time we had hauled ourselves up to the top again by the sapling branches, an extraordinary exhilaration had descended on the party. We almost ran, in fading light, down the hundreds of stone steps through the forest, and through the red gate at the bottom which marks the end of the mountain and the beginning of the village.

In deepening twilight the procession marched through the village, with lights going on in the houses and people coming to the gates to watch us pass. At the gate of the Koganedō there was a bonfire in the middle of the road, with people lined up on either side. The procession broke into a run, everyone leapt over the fire and ran straight into the temple where in front of rows of dully golden Kannons we recited once more the Heart Sutra and the name and mantra of Sambō Dai Kōjin.

There followed, in the big temple Shōzenin across the road, an address from the *daisendatsu* to celebrate the triumphant end of the exercise. He congratulated the company on its enthusiasm and fortitude, and presented each member with a beautifully inscribed certificate to prove that he had successfully passed through the ordeal.

There followed the exquisite pleasure of a hot bath, and an elegant vegetarian feast, with plenty of sesame sauce and saké, served on red lacquer trays round the perimeter of the room.

Thus was enacted, albeit in somewhat dilapidated form, two sets of initiatory symbolism. In a week, we had undergone death, conception, gestation and rebirth in the heart of a mountain which stood for a mother's womb. At the same time we had passed through the realms of hell, hungry ghosts, animals, titans, men, devas, *śrāvakas, pratyeka-buddhas,* bodhisattvas and finally Buddhas on a mountain which represented a mandala or sacred cosmos. After such an experience the company was in theory endued with powers beyond the ordinary human allotment. The professional woman ascetics retired to their temples convinced that they had received a new dispensation of strength to carry out their tasks of exorcism and divination. The professional *sendatsu* were raised a rank in the Shugendō hierarchy. Even the farmers declared an increase in *seishin-shūyō,* spiritual strength, as a result of their ordeal.

The tendency of the exercise today is nevertheless clear, and was confirmed four years later when I joined the *akimine* for a second time. It is to forget the other-worldly symbolism of the practices and to substitute for them moral virtues of a this-worldly kind. The various ordeals are no longer explained as symbolic means of entering another world or a new kind of life, but as virtues which will make you better fit to face life in this world. Fortitude, uncomplaining perseverance in the face of privations and fatigue, unselfish cooperation, cheerful obedience, versatile coping with emergencies, all these are virtues admirable in themselves. But they transform the ordeal from a passage to a new life to an 'endurance test' such as army cadets or the pupils of the Outward Bound School might undergo in the Welsh hills.

Having now reviewed the manner of the ascetic's initiation, the dreams, the divine possessions, the journeys to the other world whether visionary or symbolic, we are now in a position to take note of the particular powers which accrue to him in consequence of these experiences.

The Ascetic's Power

The powers which the ascetic attains through his initiation and subsequent austerities fall at once into two distinct groups. First there are those which are put to some practical use, either in the service of the community or in his own daily life. These are found practised by ascetics of all kinds, whether Buddhist priests, *yamabushi* or solitary professional healers. They consist principally of the powers necessary for the accomplishment of exorcism, but also include the power to 'open' a holy place, the founding of temples and shrines on holy spots and the sacralising of mountains for pilgrimage. Also in this category we may include the orphic power to fascinate animals and to communicate with them.

The second group of powers is practised only by *yamabushi* and consists not so much of practical accomplishments as of demonstrations of the magic art, undertaken to convince the community that the disciple has indeed risen above the ordinary human state. Until the end of the last century a fair number of these feats could still be witnessed in various parts of Japan. Today the repertory seems to have been reduced to three: *hi-watari* or fire-walking, *yudate* or sousing oneself in boiling water, and more rarely *katana-watari* or climbing up a ladder of swords. All these three feats, when closely examined, will be seen to point to the two characteristically shamanic accomplishments of mastery of fire and the magical flight to heaven.

First let us deal with the various methods whereby the ascetic overcomes the discontented ghosts and foxes which cause demoniacal possession, and the particular powers which he needs to carry them out. We will deal here only with those cases where the ascetic accomplishes this task alone and unaided by a medium. The techniques whereby the skills of both practitioners are combined will be examined in a later chapter.

Confronted by a sufferer complaining of aches, pains

hallucinations or compulsive actions which she suspects to be caused by some kind of possession, the exorcist's first task is to diagnose the trouble. He must discover first whether it is indeed caused by a spiritual agency rather than by indigestion or migraine or appendicitis, and second what kind of spiritual entity is responsible. For this task a good many ascetics rely on their power of *gantsū* or clairvoyant eyes. With this accomplishment the healer is able to see the inhabitants of the spiritual world, whether malignant or benign. Mrs Nakano, for example, a professional healer and ascetic from Shikoku who regularly appeared in full *yamabushi* costume in Kyoto on August 1st to join the ritual ascent of Mt Ōmine, told me that for her diagnoses she relied chiefly on her power of clairvoyant vision. Armed with this faculty, she was able to see at once the cause of her patient's malady. The image of a dog, a snake, a resentful ancestor, or an incident from the past which had preyed on the patient's mind, would appear vividly before her eyes. Equally clearly, however, would appear the image of an inflamed appendix, should that be the true cause of the malady. She could also see what had become of people who had disappeared without trace, and during the war had had to respond to many calls from relatives of soldiers at the front to discover if, when and how these men had met their death.

Likewise Mr Mizoguchi, an old man who had undergone a severe regime of austerities near Mt Miwa, including the aforementioned diet of pine needles near Kurama, was able to see the shapes of malignant possessing spirits. A man had once come to him, he told me in 1963, who had suffered from epilepsy for twenty-one years. On reciting the Heart Sutra and the Kannon Sutra there appeared before his eyes the forms of two unhappy ancestors of the man. One had been drowned, the other burnt to death in a mountain fire. Neither had been able to achieve rest. Both had therefore taken up their lodging, for want of another dwelling-place, in the body of their descendant. Mr Mizoguchi performed the necessary requiem mass, which brought the evil and unhappy spirits to their proper state of tranquillity. The patient from that moment had no more epileptic fits.

Mr Mizoguchi could also see through his faculty of *gantsū* the presence of a benign numen in certain trees and rocks. In the autumn of 1963 he kindly guided me to the summit of Mt Miwa, and as he walked up the path through the forest I noticed that certain cryptomeria trees and rocks wore the girdle of straw rope which, like a sacramental belt or collar, marks objects imbued with a numinous presence. To me these trees and stones appeared indistinguishable from those without the straw girdle. From a certain pile of stones, for example, two had been favoured by the straw rope, whereas the rest were bare. How was it possible, I asked Mr Mizoguchi, to tell which trees and stones were numinous and which were not. Entirely by the faculty of *gantsū*, was his reply. Those who had developed this faculty through the practice of austerities could see the deity inhering in the stone or tree. That ordinary dirty-looking rock, for example: he could see that the deity Hakuryūsan was inside it, though to me it would appear the same as any other boulder. His teacher had developed the faculty to an even greater degree. He could see not only when a deity had taken up residence in a stone, but also when one was about to do so. That tree, he would say, will soon be a sacred one. The deity is not yet properly settled inside it, but in another two weeks it will have done so. And after two weeks, sure enough, the *kami* would be there inside it.

Another power which proves useful in the process of exorcism is *mimitsū*, clairaudient hearing. Mrs Nakano told me that her practice of austerities had given her clairaudient ears as well as clairvoyant eyes. She would hear a voice clearly speaking in her ear and explaining the cause of the patient's malady. This voice she had always taken to be that of Fudō Myōō, her guardian deity, but lately, she informed me in 1967, she had had a strong suspicion that dead ancestors might be speaking to her as well.

Once diagnosed, the malignant possession must be overcome; either the cause of its misery and resentment must be removed or it must be brought to realise the error of its ways. Some living examples will best illustrate the methods customarily employed to this end.

Mrs Matsuyama, the professional ascetic healer living in

Sagano whose course of austerities was described in a previous chapter, told me in the autumn of 1963 that for the final banishment of the fox or ghost she relied on the power of Fudō Myōō himself working through her in a state of trance. She demonstrated her methods forthwith. Conducting me into the shrine room of her house, where in front of a large and glittering altar to Fudō was a *gomadan* or magic fire platform, she seated herself before it and began to recite in strong nasal tones the Middle Spell of Fudō:

Nōmaku samanda basarada
Senda makaroshana
Sowataya untarata kamman.

She then swung into the Heart Sutra, over and over again and constantly increasing in gabbling speed. Soon she began to make odd grunts and moans amidst the words of the sutra, followed by stertorous puffing sounds and one or two of the piercing magical yells called *kiai*, while her clasped hands shook violently up and down like a flail. Finally with frightful force she beat her stomach several times with her fists while bass roars burst from her mouth.

This violent seizure lasted about a minute. Then the chanting grew calmer and flatter, until suddenly, with a note on the gong, she was herself again, calm and businesslike.

That was Fudō who had taken possession of her, she announced. For her healing she would always invoke him into her body so that his power behind the words of the sutra would cause the evil spirit molesting the patient to capitulate. The sufferer would often fling herself frantically about the room, the fox inside her screaming that it was not afraid, that it was stronger than Fudō, sometimes even climbing up on to the roof in the effort to escape. But eventually it would capitulate and the patient would return to herself, dazed and astonished and remembering nothing of what had occurred.

About a month after my first meeting with Mrs Matsuyama I was privileged to watch her methods in practice. Our mutual friend Miss Nakagawa sent me a message to say that a neighbour of hers, a Mrs Fukumoto, was suffering from fox possession and would be visiting Mrs Matsuyama the next day for treatment. I was to go early to Mrs Matsuyama's house, and be there in a casual way as though I were a pupil when the patient appeared.

Mrs Matsuyama was ready waiting when I arrived, in a white silk kimono. Shortly afterwards the patient herself appeared, a robust-looking woman in her fifties. At once she burst into a torrent of animated talk. She was greatly troubled by a voice constantly talking in her ear. Sometimes it gave her useful information, such as which road to take at an unfamiliar crossroads. But usually it was a tiresome nuisance, keeping her awake at night asking questions.

Mrs Matsuyama arranged two cushions in front of the glittering altar, for herself and her patient, and rosary in hand slipped quickly into her violent trance. Her loud and stern Heart Sutras soon gave way to a succession of bass roars and barks and stertorous puffs, while she pummelled her patient on the back, rubbed the rosary over her body and traced with her finger some characters on her back. Finally she gave three or four piercing *kiai* yells, pointing her hands at the patient in the mudra called *hō-no-ken-in*, with two fingers outstretched like a sword.

Then with a shake she came to herself again and gravely addressed her patient.

'It is not a fox who is troubling you. It is your dead father. He died in the house of his concubine and hence has been unable to achieve rest. To get rid of the nuisance you must undertake the cold water austerity night and morning for twenty-one days.'

Mrs Fukumoto seemed appalled by this announcement and stammered that her husband would never allow it.

'In that case', Mrs Matsuyama replied, 'you must do the next best thing, which is to get up at half-past midnight every night for three weeks and recite the Heart Sutra a hundred and eight times. Have a rosary of a hundred and eight beads in your hand and count the beads as you recite.' It was not so quick a cure as the cold water, she added, but just as efficacious in the end.

Even this programme seemed daunting to Mrs Fukumoto, whose cheerful face looked dismayed as she asked whether it would really do her any good. Sternly Mrs Matsuyama assured her that it was the only way to get rid of the trouble. You must cast away all doubt, she said. Fudō has directed you to this course. Eat as little meat as possible and after three weeks come and see me again.

By these grave words Mrs Fukumoto seemed convinced, and took her departure looking much relieved.

Mrs Matsuyama's method of exorcism was thus to fall into a state of trance in which Fudō possessed her and used her voice to vanquish the fox or ghost. It is in fact rather an unusual one. The ascetic only rarely becomes entranced, even though in theory it is through the divine power of his guardian deity that he accomplishes his work. A more usual method is to overcome the foxes and ghosts by the power of the holy text which a previous course of austerities has activated.

This was the method practised by Mrs Ōnuma Myōshō, whom I met in 1963 and 1967 undergoing the rigours of the *akimine* on Mt Haguro. Like many priests and religious personages she was commonly known by the name of her temple, and was invariably addressed as Jizōin-san. To this temple near Sendai patients would flock all the year round for healing, but whenever these duties permitted she joined the *akimine* exercises in order to strengthen her powers with a bout of communal ascesis.

In 1967 torrential rains during the last week of August in Yamagata prefecture made much of the prescribed programme of the *akimine* impossible. The *saitō-goma* was cancelled and so were many of the pilgrimages to holy spots. Instead, for a whole day I listened to Jizōin's stories of possessed people whom she had helped with her special powers.

Diagnosing the kind of possessing spirit causing the trouble was no problem to her, for she could see not only the shapes of spiritual beings but their colours as well. The colours of ghosts differed according to their rank, that is to say their nearness to the state of salvation. All ghosts before salvation appeared to her round, but the newer they were the bigger and brighter they seemed. As they grew older and higher on the road to salvation their colour grew darker and sootier.

The word she employed for all possessing spirits was *zaishō*, a Buddhist term meaning the hindrance which sin and delusion place in the way to enlightenment. She spoke as though these sins, one's own and those of one's ancestors, became personified in the form of possessing spirits with a will and personality of their own. These entities would start to 'move' and cause trouble in certain circumstances.

There was the woman, for example, who at the age of about thirty joined one of the new religious cults. At once she became afflicted with terrible neuralgia. Furthermore, every night as she lay down to sleep the ghosts of her grandfather, grandmother and elder sister appeared a couple of yards away and asked, 'Are you in pain?' 'Yes', she would reply. 'Good', they all cried, laughing loudly. Then all three spirits would enter her body through the orifices of the ears, and rush up and down from the top of her head to the soles of her feet, causing her dreadful agony and making her body freezing cold.

Jizōin was called in to help, but whenever she went to the woman's house the ghostly manifestations ceased. She lived too far away to visit the house every day, so asked the *hotokesama*, the spirits of a dozen or so people who had lived near the woman's house, to let her know when she was needed. This they would do by making in Jizōin's house a tremendous noise of rushing feet, so loud that the pillars shook. There was of course nothing to be seen, and as soon as she prepared to set off to the woman's house the noises ceased at once.

Jizōin tried various methods of stopping the trouble, giving the woman amulets to stuff in her ears and prevent the spirits getting in. But none appear to have been very successful. The spirits continued to pinch the woman's face at night, tweak her ears and pull her hair, until at last she consented to give up her new and false religion. This done, the *zaishō* became quiet and all her troubles were at an end.

Then there was a dramatic story of a middle-aged woman afflicted with several possessing entities at the same time. She was frequently seized with violent labour pains, although she was not even pregnant. Likewise she was seized, on a bus or a train, with an overpowering and distressing desire for a man. These afflictions were caused, Jizōin discovered, by a wandering spirit, a *muenbotoke*, some three centuries old, of a woman who had been the concubine of a priest. She had been kept secretly in one of the temple outhouses, so that the villagers came to believe that she was a goblin. One of these, meeting her in the open one night, stabbed her to death with a spear. She was said to have been pregnant at the time; hence the nature of the pains which her unhouselled spirit caused.

At the same time, the poor woman who was Jizōin's patient was possessed by another *zaishō* in the form of a fox. This, on the contrary, made her so frigid, her body even feeling deathly cold to the touch, that her husband refused to sleep with her. He went and slept upstairs, eventually taking in a concubine so that the family fell badly into debt.

In desperation the woman made an appointment to visit Jizōin's temple for treatment. But the fox, foreseeing the danger, adopted every ruse that it could devise to prevent her from going. First it hid her purse so that she could not pay her bus fare. Then, when she went to the bus station and borrowed a ticket, explaining her predicament and being sympathetically understood, the fox held her up for a long time by hiding Jizōin's house from view, so that she was left helplessly wandering in the nearby rice fields. When eventually she reached the house, it took Jizōin half a day to vanquish the fox. For several hours it hurled rather clever insults at her, dancing round the room singing *naniwabushi*, before finally capitulating before the power of the Fudō Sutra which Jizōin continued to recite the while.

Finally let us look at a couple of the cases treated by Mrs Hiroshima Ryūun, whose ascetic journeys and whose dramatic manner of initiation we described in an earlier chapter. Some of the cures which she performed in the course of her travels were recorded by a pupil of hers in a manuscript book which in the summer of 1972 her daughter Mrs Hiroshima Umeko kindly allowed me to read. The manuscript is not dated, but internal evidence suggests that it was written shortly before the end of the war.

Among the many cures and exorcisms recorded in this interesting document, two examples will give some idea of

Mrs Hiroshima's methods. Here is the story of the *muenbotoke* or wandering spirits.

Mrs Hiroshima, respectfully referred to throughout the book as 'sensei', master, was summoned to the house of a Mr Morimoto near Nara, whose baby was suffering from an obstinate swelling on the shoulder which the doctors were powerless to cure.

Sensei at once began to recite the Heart Sutra in front of the sick child. Soon there appeared to her clairvoyant eyes three spirits flashing like stars.

'Who are you?' she enquired.

'We are spirits belonging to this house', they replied. 'We all died young and poor, with no descendants to care for us. We therefore made the Morimoto child sick in order to draw attention to our plight. Please tell the people here to recite requiem masses for us, and then we will let the child get well and act as guardians to it into the bargain. We are buried in the ground to the south of this house.'

When Mr Morimoto was told the tale, he remembered that some years before an uncle of his had been buried near the house, together with his two wives, who one after the other had died without children. Thus the family had died out, and no one had performed any of the necessary requiems for the dead spirits. It was quite natural, he realised, that they should call attention to themselves by making his baby ill. But as soon as the correct masses were said and offerings made, needless to say the child recovered at once.

A more unpleasant story is recorded under the title of 'The New Ghost's Wish'. Another family near Nara, also called Morimoto, was reduced to a desperate state of misery. The husband fell very ill with pneumonia, and despite the wife's devoted efforts to nurse him back to health and at the same time to earn enough to support the family, he was continually cursing her and upbraiding her for what he jealously imagined to be her unfaithfulness. At the end of 1942 he died. Soon afterwards his wife developed an appalling headache and had in her turn to take to her bed. Their kind go-between, realising that her sickness was outside the sphere of ordinary doctors, sent for Mrs Hiroshima.

Sensei entered the room to find the poor widow prostrated

near the altar to her dead husband's spirit. At once she began the *hyakugan-shingyō* or Hundred Heart Sutras, which takes two-and-a-half hours to recite. At the end of this powerful service she was able to address the spirit.

'Who are you?' she demanded.

'The new ghost', it replied. 'I have been waiting and waiting for you to come. Indeed, it was to get you to come here that I caused my wife to have this fearful headache. Magotarō, I died with great resentment in my heart and because of this I am wandering with nowhere to go. I died hating and loathing my wife because she was continually making me doubt her. If she marries again I cannot bear it.'

When the poor woman was told of this speech, she admitted that her husband had been continually jealous, and that nothing she did ever pleased him.

'Promise me now', sensei said, 'that you do not intend to marry again and will continue to honour your husband's spirit.'

The woman promised. Sensei thereupon recited with ear-splitting force the nine magic syllables.

'*Rin-byō-tō-sha-kai-jin-retsu-zai-zen*'.

And at that instant the headache which had been tormenting the woman for so long vanished.

There are a good many more rather similar stories in this book, which describe how Mrs Hiroshima not only healed the sick of maladies which the doctors could not touch, but also brought to rest many spirits who for one reason or another were lost, resentful, wandering or miserable, unable to reach their proper salvation. Buried images of Jizō who wished to be dug up, ghosts of those who had died with worries or grudges in their hearts, more ghosts who died without descendants to give them their required nourishment —all these inhabitants of the other world had called attention to their plight by causing pain or sickness to some human being. Mrs Hiroshima as she passed through the village on one of her long journeys was called in to help, and through her treatment she healed the sick person and at the same time comforted the unhappy spirit.

She is thus the modern counterpart of the medieval wandering ascetic. She reminds us too of that figure who appears so persistently in the Nō plays, the *tabisō* or travelling priest. In more than a score of Nō plays we see how the travelling priest may lay to rest spiritual beings who have suffered misery for years. We see a village, a mountain or a grave. All is still and familiar until a travelling priest arrives. With his appearance the ordinary, or what has appeared to be the ordinary, is suddenly burst open and transformed. The familiar scene disappears and the other world rushes through.

An old woodcutter or boatman or fisherman confronts the priest. On this spot, he says, a battle was fought, a warrior was killed, a girl was drowned. With strange emotion he describes the scene, until the priest is impelled to ask him who he is.

At once the scene shifts: the old man is not the ordinary woodcutter he had supposed. He reveals himself as the ghost of the warrior killed long ago and unable to find rest. He recounts his sufferings and dances.

But through the presence of the travelling priest and the efficacy of his prayers, calm is once more restored. Rescued from its misery, the ghost retires across the bridge and disappears into paradise. The place reverts to its accustomed quiet and the priest passes on.[1]

So much then for the powers which the ascetic requires for the performance of his principal task of exorcism.

Another power which the ascetic is able to put to practical use is his ability to 'open' a holy place. The history of a temple or sacred mountain often begins with its 'opening' by an ascetic who later becomes the founder of the religious sect or pilgrim clubs who worship there. Mt Haguro, for example, was opened by Shōken Daibosatsu, Mt Nantai by Shōdō Shōnin, Mt Ontake by the two ascetics Fukan and Kakumei, Mt Fuji by Kakugyō. Similarly, among the foundation legends of temples are many which recount that the spot was discovered, and its holiness sealed and activated, by an ascetic who wandered hundreds of miles before he discovered the paradisal mountain or holy site for which he was searching.

'Opening' a mountain or a temple site thus means releasing its latent holiness. All the time it has been a 'thin' place, through which the other world and its perilous power could show through. But until the ascetic arrives it has gone unrecognised and uncelebrated. By dwelling there and by practising meditations and austerities on the spot, the ascetic acknowledges its power, concentrates it into a centre from which worship can be conducted.

One more power of a practical kind with which the medieval ascetic is frequently credited, and which is still occasionally to be met today, is the ability to communicate with the world of animals. The ascetic can not only understand the language of animals: he can also tame them by his recitation of holy scripture. Thus Ryōsan, whom we saw retire to a cave on Mt Kimpu on a diet of leaves, soon found that his recitation of the Lotus Sutra brought bears, foxes and snakes to the door of his cave with reverent offerings of fruit and berries. Likewise the *kijin* or demons, who first approached with the intention of disturbing his practice, were soon overawed by the holy chanting and likewise brought him presents of food.[2]

Such feats are found illustrated from time to time in the *emakimono* or picture scrolls of the Heian period. The scroll painting *Kasuga Gongen Genkie*, probably of the twelfth or thirteenth century, which depicts the miracles surrounding the Kasuga shrine, includes a memorable scene of the Kōfukuji temple at Nara. By employing the technique known as *fukinuke-yatai*, or the 'roofless house', the painter enables us to look down as though through the roof of the temple, to see the abbot reciting a holy text before serried rows of monks. At the entrance of the hall, apparently bewitched by the holy sounds, crouch four spotted deer from the precincts of the Kasuga shrine.[3]

Again in the *Ishiyamadera Engi* scroll we see the ascetic priest Rekikai surrounded by an admiring audience of dragons. We look down, as it were from the top of a nearby hill, to see the priest Rekikai reading the Peacock Sutra on the shores of a lake. In front of him two dragons have risen to the surface of the lake to listen to the holy reading, while two more on his left and three more on his right listen attentively with clasped hands.[4]

That this communion with the world of animals is not an

entirely forgotten power was brought home to me by Mr Mizoguchi. His diet of pine needles on Mt Kurama, he informed me, enabled him both to understand the language of animals and to converse with them. Time and again he had been cheerfully accosted on the mountainside by friendly animals and birds. 'Going up to the top this morning?' they would enquire. They would often give him useful advice about the weather. Their language, when you listened to them talking, sounded just like Japanese.

With this short review of the powers with which the ascetic is armed in his practical everyday life, we turn now to the series of *genjutsu* or feats traditionally ascribed to the *yamabushi*, which are used less for the relief of suffering than for demonstrations of superhuman power.

Throughout the middle ages and well into the Tokugawa period, the *yamabushi* bore the reputation in the popular mind not only of an exorcist but also of a magician. The *Uji Shūi Monogatari* tells a sinister tale of the enraged *yamabushi* Keitōbō, who with his spells overturned a ferryboat whose boatman refused to take him on board. Elsewhere we find tales of the *genkurabe* or contests in the magic art, in which *yamabushi* were believed to indulge. The *Kokonchomonjū*, for example, tells how the celebrated priest Jōzō Hōshi once caused a white stone to bounce up and down like a football. His adversary Shunyū thereupon caused it to lie still. Jōzō then in a supernaturally resonant voice recited a passage from the Nirvana Sutra, at which the stone leapt up and split in half. Kaempfer too, who at the end of the seventeenth century encountered a good many *yamabushi* on the road between Nagasaki and Edo and learnt something of their practices from a young initiate to whom he taught 'Physick and Surgery', recounts their claims to 'dive into secrets and mysteries, to recover stolen Goods, and to discover the thieves, to foretell future events, to explain dreams, to cure desperate distempers, to find out the guilt or innocence of persons accused of crimes and misdemeanours and the like'.[5]

The old manuals of Shugendō teaching certainly contain a number of rituals and spells for the accomplishment of such feats as invisibility, flying, walking on fire, stepping into cauldrons of boiling water and climbing barefoot up ladders of swords.[6]

It is doubtful whether such feats were ever intended for practical use in the service of the community. Miyake is doubtless right when he points out in one of the chapters of his penetrating book on Shugendō ritual, that these spells were intended to prescribe symbolic rather than practical action. When the rites of fire-walking and boiling water are analysed, and the symbolic meanings of the mudras, mantras and visualisations which compose them made clear, it is at once apparent that their intention is to demonstrate that the disciple has acquired that characteristically shamanic accomplishment, mastery of fire. He has purified himself against evil spiritual attack, identified himself with his guardian deity Fudō Myōō, and with the divine power which thereby accrues to him he is rendered impervious to heat. Thus he can safely walk on red embers or immerse himself in boiling water.

Likewise with the feat of climbing up the ladder of swords. This is not so much a practical accomplishment— the necessity for performing such a feat is unlikely to crop up often in daily life—as a symbolic demonstration that the *yamabushi* has acquired the again characteristically shamanic accomplishment of magically ascending to heaven. The ladder of swords, as Miyake has shown, and as examples in other parts of Asia likewise indicate, symbolises the ladder to heaven, up which the ordinary human being cannot dream of climbing. Only one who has accomplished the *yamabushi's* initiation and ascesis can mount this perilous scale.

Symbolic though much of these rites may be, however, there still remains a core to them which has as yet to be satisfactorily explained. Like Isadora Persano's remarkable worm, they contain a bottom which is as yet unknown to science. Neither the salt which is ritually scattered over the site of the fire-walking, nor any possible hardening of the soles of Japanese feet, nor hypnotic suggestion, nor a collected mind, is sufficient to account for the fact that not only the *yamabushi* themselves but large numbers of ordinary lay people as well are able to traverse unscathed a twenty-foot path of red and smouldering embers. Likewise difficult to explain by any of these means is the *yamabushi's* immersion in boiling water or his climbing unshod up a ladder of swords.

The *katana-watari* or swoid-climbing is now seldom performed. Mr Percival Lowell witnessed a performance in 1895 and Miyake mentions a recent performance on Mt Haguro, but the art is apparently as good as lost.[7]

Yudate or the boiling water feat is more often seen, and Honda Yasuji's monumental study of the *kagura* performances throughout Japan mentions several which include a *yudate*.[8] The only example I have ever witnessed was performed not by the Shugendō but by the Shinto sect known as Shinshūkyō, strongly influenced by Shugendō practices, on 17 September 1963. In outline it seems to be similar to if not identical with the rite performed by the Shugendō: a sacred enclosure cordoned off with the usual straw rope and fluttering streamers of *gohei* paper, and with bunches of bamboo-grass at the four corners. In the middle is a large cauldron over a wood fire.

By the time the rite was due to begin the fire had been lit for some time, and the water in the cauldron was steaming and bubbling. The priest due to perform the rite was doing so for the first time, I was informed, having that very year taken over from an ancient man who had served for the last forty autumns. He stood, clad entirely in white, in front of the boiling cauldron, then proceeded to circumambulate it, striking sparks from a flint in each of the eight directions. He then repeated the pradakshina round the cauldron, this time laying salt on the rim in each of the eight directions. He then seized a *gohei* wand, a stick with two fronds of white paper symmetrically attached to it, and proceeded to stir the handle end in the boiling water so vigorously, again in each of the eight directions, that it slopped steaming and hissing over the side. At the end of each stir he gave a loud sharp *kiai*, 'Eee!'

Finally, seizing a long bunch of bamboo-grass leaves, he plunged it into the boiling water and swished it out so that a heavy spray of boiling water fell all over and round him, raising a cloud of steam. Moving once more round the eight points of the compass he repeated the performance eight times, swishing the leaves more and more vigorously in and out of the water so that his white clothes were quickly soaked and now and then he could hardly be seen for clouds of steam.

Then, no sooner was he round the eight points than he stopped, shook himself and walked nonchalantly out of the sacred enclosure while everyone clapped and thanked him.

The reason why the man was not scalded, I was informed, was entirely because the power of the *kami*, imparted to him through his ascetic training, had made him impervious to heat. It was the same with their fire-waking rite which they performed every spring. Neither the fire nor the boiling water felt hot because the power of the man's ascesis had abstracted the essence of the heat. Hence not only the priest himself but others also could walk with safety over the fiery embers. My informant Mrs Nakazawa, the daughter of the High Priest of the sect, told me that often in the midst of the fire-walking rite she had been cautioned, don't walk now because it is getting dangerous. The priest would walk once more over it and reduce the heat so that it was again safe for ordinary people like herself to do so.

Fire-walking, *hi-watari*, is the one feat in the *yamabushi's* ancient magic repertory which may still be seen practised in many places in Japan, particularly in spring and autumn, at the conclusion of the *saitō-goma* or magic bonfire rite.[9] The embers of the great conical pyre, the burning of which is a ritual of the greatest beauty and symbolic power but which it would be irrelevant to describe at this point, are raked out by *yamabushi* with long bamboo rakes to form a red and smouldering path about twenty feet long. A squadron of *yamabushi* draw up at the head of the path, loudly recite certain mantras, then stride firmly in procession down the smoking cursus. By this action, it is believed, they have so reduced the essence of the fire that it is not only safe but extremely beneficial for all and sundry from the profane world to traverse the path too.

When I first witnessed the rite in July 1963, it was performed by the *yamabushi* of the Tanukidani sect in a beautiful site in an armpit of hills north of Kyoto, with forest and a precipice of rock on two sides. A large crowd had gathered waiting for the privilege of traversing the fiery path: men and women, old and young, fat and thin, so many made a rush to walk in the *yamabushi's* footsteps that I decided it would be foolish not to go with them. The path was still alarmingly red and smoking by the time my turn came, but so effective apparently were the *yamabushi's* spells that the embers underfoot felt no more than pleasantly warm to the soles. I remain sceptical of explanations that the usual purifying libation of salt scattered over the embers will reduce their heat, that the Japanese sole is tougher than the western one or that a collected mind is required if one is to walk across unburnt. My feet are rather sensitive and my mind at the time was in turmoil, yet a mild warmth was all that I felt.

Whatever may ultimately account for either of these phenomena, fire-walking or hot water, their intention is clearly to demonstrate to the world that the *yamabushi* are masters of fire; that through their mortifications under waterfalls and their affinity with their fiery guardian Fudō, they have attained the state of interior heat which makes them impervious to any fire they may encounter in the external world.

So much then for the ascetic's initiation and the powers which thereby accrue to him. We pass now to the final stage of our investigation: those rites in which the ascetic's powers are used conjointly with those of the medium, and which are known in general as *yorigitō*.

13
Village Oracles

In the rituals known as *yorigitō* the task of making contact
with the world of spirits is accomplished by the combined
efforts of the *miko* and the ascetic. The *miko* no longer by her
dancing and music summons the spiritual beings to approach
and take possession of her. She is now a mere passive vessel
through whom the spirit speaks. The active task of invoking
the spirit, interrogating it and finally sending it back to its
own world is now accomplished by the ascetic.

Rituals of this kind have been practised in Japan since the
ninth century. For their origin we must clearly look to some
other source than early Shinto; the mere automaton who is
now the medium is a figure very different from the majestic
sibyl whom we saw presiding over village shrines in ancient
Japan. Suzuki Shōei suggests that it may lie in certain
esoteric Buddhist rites and spells introduced into Japan in
the early ninth century.[1]

These rituals instruct how a small child may be used as a
medium for divining the future. The most celebrated among
them is the *Abisha-hō*, brought to Japan from China in the
early ninth century by the eminent monks Kūkai and Ennin,
and hence practised by both the Shingon and the Tendai
branches of esoteric Buddhism. *Abisha*, the Sanscrit word
avesa, signifies the entry of a spiritual being into a medium.
The *Abisha-hō* or rite of *avesa* claims to be the method of
accomplishing this entry as taught by the god Maheshvara.
If you wish to know the things of the future, the text in-
structs, you must first find four little boys or girls, aged about
eight years old. They must have no scar or blemish on their
bodies, and must be of quick ear and quick wit. For a week
before the rite takes place they must eat only plain food.
Then, when a propitious day for the rite has been chosen,
they must be bathed, anointed with incense, dressed in
clean clothes, and a piece of camphor wood put in their
mouths. Then stand them on an altar of sandalwood and
scatter flowers before them. Burn Parthian incense over a

vessel of water and repeat seven times the mantra of the Great Mudra until the children begin to tremble. Then make haste to ask them anything you wish to know of the blessings and disasters of the future.

This rite is first recorded as having been performed in the year 861 by the Tendai priest Sōō in the presence of the Emperor Seiwa. Two little boys were entranced by spells as the text prescribed. The priest asked, 'Who are you?' 'I am Matsuo Myōjin', the boys replied. The Emperor then commanded Horikawa Sadaijin to question the boys on the matters which were perplexing him. They told him to his satisfaction all he wished to know.[2]

These rituals have been transmitted to us not so much by the orthodox schools of esoteric Buddhism as by their Shugendō branches. Rites similar to the *Abisha-hō*, which instruct how a deity may be summoned into the body of a child or a woman and caused to speak, appear in several places in Shugendō manuals of doctrine and collection of spells. Today, however, their practice survives only in a few remote villages and mountains. The originally Buddhist structure of the ritual has in many cases been modified by older village practices with which they have been assimilated.

Yorigitō rituals fall at once into two distinct categories. First, we have rites in which a spiritual being of a higher order, usually a *kami*, is cajoled to take possession of a medium and through her mouth to deliver to the community useful knowledge of hidden and future things. Second, we have rituals in which the spiritual being belongs to a lower or malignant order, a neglected ghost or spirit fox. Here it is compelled by incantations to leave the body of the patient it is molesting and to enter that of a medium, through whose mouth it is forced to name itself, to explain its motives and eventually to agree to terms which reduce it to submission.

In the following two chapters we will describe the rituals which summon a numinous being of a higher order. These, again, may conveniently be divided into two groups. First, the *yorigitō* ritual is found linked with a seasonal festival in a village. The descent of a deity into the human community, and the advice and warnings he imparts, comes as a fixed seasonal event in the agricultural year. In other *yorigitō* rituals the deity is accessible only on a particular holy mountain. This the faithful must therefore climb if they wish to establish communion with him.

We treat first the village oracles, known in general as *takusen matsuri*.

The number of *takusen matsuri* which survive today is very few, and has grown notably fewer during the last decade. Others disappeared during the rigours of the war, and others still were scotched by the proscription of such 'superstitious practices' by the Meiji government in the early 1870s. Those that survived long enough to be described by ethnographers, however, show us that we have here the vestiges of what was once a widespread cult. Further still, a number of *matsuri* still survive which bear unmistakable traces of having once included an oracular utterance through a medium. Sometimes the utterance itself has been lost: the medium appears and is thrown into a state of trance, but he remains dumb throughout the rite. A good example may be seen in the *matsuri* still observed in a couple of dozen shrines in Tosa; here a child is thrown into a state of trance resembling deep sleep, set upon a horse at the head of the procession, and kept in that condition all day until the festivities are over. The trance is induced by incantations, and by painting the face of the child white, for it is only when the white paint is removed at the end of the day that the child ' wakes up'. Clearly the child once, as in the Abisha-hō itself, acted as the medium for a deity, transmitting his answers to questions asked by the village. The oracle must long ago have been lost, however, because even in the manuscript of the 1730s, *Suien Sekiwa*, to which Yanagita draws our attention and which describes the rite much as it is performed today, no mention is made of any spoken oracle.[3]

Again, there are *matsuri* in which not only the trance utterance but even the trance itself has been lost. All that remains is the peculiar behaviour, enacted in mime, of what was once the inspired frenzy of the medium. An example is the *Kaeru-tobi Gyōji*, performed by *yamabushi* in Yoshino at the beginning of July. One of their number, disguised as a green frog, leaps and hops in a manner accountable only as a mime of what was once the odd levitation peculiar to trance behaviour in Japan. The moral tale which now 'explains' the rite is clearly a later invention.

The early numbers of the first folklore journal in Japan, *Kyōdo Kenkyū*, contain interesting accounts of *takusen matsuri* which have since disappeared. They conform to the same basic pattern of *yorigitō* discernible in those which still survive.[4]

This structure we will investigate by examining four examples of *takusen matsuri* which either still survive at the time of writing, or disappeared only in the last decade. We take two examples from each of the two principal areas in which these rituals survive, the *tōhoku* or north-eastern districts of the main island, and *chūgoku* or central region comprising the old provinces of Bitchū and Bizen and the present Okayama prefecture. In the north-east the Hayama Matsuri is still performed in two small mountain villages near Sōma in Fukushima prefecture, and until only nine years ago the Sakumatsuri was performed every February in a temple in the small port of Sakata in Yamagata prefecture. Likewise in the central regions of the main island, the Gohōtobi is still performed in a remote group of mountain temples in the Kume district of Okayama prefecture, while in Shimane prefecture, along the coast of the Japan Sea, the Ōmoto Kagura only recently ceased, for lack of a suitable medium, to be performed in certain villages every six or twelve years.

We turn first to the Hayama Matsuri. This autumn augury used to be performed in as many as thirty or forty villages in the mountains near Sōma. It now survives in only two. Both of these, Kanazawa and Ōkura, were observed and fully described during the 1950s by Iwasaki Toshio, on whose excellent work I shall later rely.[5] The *matsuri* at Ōkura was witnessed by me, in a disappointingly enfeebled state, in 1963.

The deity known as Hayama is found in many parts of Japan associated with mountains of the same name, on the summits of which he is believed to make his winter home. The *matsuri* in his honour takes place in the tenth month of the lunar calendar, on a date which marks the end of the summer and the safe ingathering of the harvest. It is in effect a farewell to the deity until the following spring, soliciting a prognostication from him as to the fortunes the village may expect during the coming year. The following day the celebrants escort him back to his winter quarters on the summit of the Hayama mountain. There he will remain until the following spring when, at the time of the rice-planting, he will again descend from the mountain and take up his abode in the village for the summer. In the Hayama deity, therefore, we see an example of the divinity, appearing frequently throughout Japan under many names, which alternates seasonally between mountain and village.[6]

The chief protagonist in the ritual is the *noriwara* or medium. He it is who transmits the answers of the deity to the stream of questions put to him by the village. Traditionally this duty has always been performed by a man, who appears spontaneously in response to demand from one of the families in the village. Unlike the professional mediums we have noticed, the *noriwara* required no particularly arduous training. No sutras or *saimon* need be learnt. All that was required of him was that he should purify himself for a stated period beforehand by the usual cathartic measures of the cold water austerity and avoidance of contaminating foods. For the rest of the year he worked in the fields like any ordinary farmer. Sometimes, like the *noriwara* known to Iwasaki, he manifested himself by falling spontaneously into a state of trance in the course of the *matsuri*. Sometimes he had to be sought out, in the manner of the Tibetan incarnate lama, in a direction indicated by the deity. In recent years, however, this spontaneous response from the village has failed. In the village of Ōkura, where in the past as many as four or five *noriwara* might appear at once and take turns to serve at the *matsuri*, no man capable of serving has appeared since 1955. Since then the village has had to resort to the services of a professional woman *miko* from Sōma.

The *noriwara* is thrown into his trance, and the questions from the village put to him, by a man with some ascetic training or affiliation with the Shugendō order. In Ōkura he was known as the *hōin*, in Kanazawa as the *sendatsu*.

He is assisted in his task by a group of boys, one from each family in the village, known as the *komorinin*. These, as their name implies, have undergone ritual purification and seclusion in a special hut or temple room. They have avoided

Plate 26. Medium in trance on the summit of Mt Ontake.

Plate 27. Another medium in trance on the summit of Mt Ontake.

Plate 28. Mr Ōmomo in 1967 at the conclusion of his trance.

Plate 29. Hotta Ryūshō Shōnin performing the water penance at the close of the Hundred Days' austerities on Mt Minobu.

Plate 30. Exorcism in a Nichiren temple. The Shōnin upbraids the fox who has been transferred from the body of the patient to that of the medium.

meat, strong vegetables and the company of women, and have cooked their maigre food over a separate pure fire. They have largely gone without sleep during the nights of their vigil. A special vocabulary of taboo words also used to be customary during the retreat.

In former times this seclusion lasted as long as a week in all the villages in the district. In Ōkura now the period has been reduced to two nights only. The boys, thus purified of defilements are in a position to form a company to welcome the deity and assist in the communication with him. It is they who consume the ritual meal of offerings made to the god before his utterance. These tributes, when I saw them in Ōkura in 1963, consisted largely of gigantic white vegetables. Huge white cabbages and giant radishes rose in a notable pile before the altar. Important also were the rice-cakes, ritually pounded by the boys at the beginning of the evening. The first of the batch were presented to the deity the following morning in his winter shrine on the mountain. The rest were eaten by the boys before the start of the evening ritual, served with a pink sour sauce.

The rite takes place at night, and in a sacralised enclosure which in some villages was on the top of the mountain where the deity spent his winters. At dead of night a procession of lanterns would wind its way up the hillside, and remain there until dawn in the freezing winter air, while the god answered questions about rice and silkworms, fires and sickness.

In Ōkura the ritual was performed in the main hall of the small Buddhist temple Fukuzenji, which at the same time was the place where the boys had passed their two nights of seclusion.

In 1957 Iwasaki observed and recorded the Hayama Matsuri as it was performed in the village of Kanazawa.[7] The night before the ceremony took place a preliminary séance with the medium was held in order to enquire whether the god had any instructions as to the conduct of the rite. The medium, seated before the altar with a white wand in each hand, was entranced by spells within ten seconds. The temple priest in deferential tones asked what time they should start the ceremony the following day.

'A bit earlier than usual!' was the god's first command.

257

'A man from the Ministry of Education is coming to watch the *matsuri* and says he wants to climb the mountain with us. Should we let him go right up to your shrine?'

'No. No further than the spot I told you about.'

'There is only one *noriwara* now, you know. Should we find another and begin to train him?'

'Yes. Find one for yourselves.'

'What ward will he come from?'

'The ward doesn't matter. You'll find he'll turn up from the east.'

Discussion then ensued as to who might be the likely candidate from the east. Two possible men were chosen on the spot and tested. The first was seated in front of the altar, bells rung in his ears, drums banged, the names of *kami* repeated. But he simply sat with closed eyes, making no movement of any kind. 'No good', everyone said.

The second candidate when subjected to the same treatment looked as though he were 'asleep' in ecstatic trance. He might do, people said, though those experienced in such matters declared that it might take years before a candidate of that kind would 'speak'.

The following night the ritual proper took place on the top of the local Hayama hill to the light of lanterns. A sacred place was cordoned off, and two mats placed inside for the medium and the shrine priest. The medium was entranced by *norito*, by jangling bells, and by a short invocation recited thirty-three times. He had two wands of red and blue paper in his hands. With the surrounding audience prostrated on the ground, the deity quickly took possession of the medium.

The order of questions put to the god was roughly as follows. First, a series of questions as to the yield to be expected in the coming year of barley, wheat, soy beans, small beans, millet, German millet, buckwheat, deccan grass, radishes, tobacco, silkworms and mulberry trees. All these were answered in terms of *bu*, five *bu* being considered the yield for an average year. Then followed another series of questions about possible threats to the welfare of the village—fires, robberies, sickness, frost. Finally a series of questions about the next rice harvest.

All questions about the harvest of any crop were answered by the Hayama deity himself. But enquiries in certain other spheres he advised them to refer to certain 'specialist' *kami*. Questions about sickness, for example, were answered by Shimmei.

'In February and March', he pronounced, 'there will be an epidemic of mild flu. Better worship at the Kuronuma shrine and Mizunokami'.

Next to appear was Suwa Myōjin, who was asked about robberies.

'Watanabe's house will be robbed', he declared. 'Nothing very serious. The thief will come in the daytime posing as a begger to see the lie of the land, and will come back at night to carry out the robbery. So take care! Otherwise no robberies in the village.'

Next to appear was Byakko Inari, who was asked about fires.

'There will be a fire in the Hokugō house towards the end of March, caused by children carelessly playing with matches. So take care!'

'Any others?'

'Nothing to speak of, though I do see a smallish fire breaking out to the south.'

'In whose house?'

'In so-and-so's.'

Finally, on the crucial question of the rice harvest, questions were asked about the relative proportions of early, middle and late rice, and how much to sow when.

'Early crop all right', was the answer vouchsafed by Hayama, 'but sow a bit more than usual in the middle season'.

The questions continued, Iwasaki noted, until five o'clock in the morning. From time to time the medium would become exhausted. The temple priest would then seize him, bring him back to normal consciousness and allow him to rest. The congregation would then raise their heads, bowed to the ground during the divine utterance, and also relax. So cold a night was it, Iwasaki noted, that the brush with which the scribe was noting down the god's answers was frozen stiff, together with the water in his inkstone.

Six years earlier, in 1951, Iwasaki witnessed and described the *matsuri* as it was performed in the village of Ōkura. Even when I visited it in 1963, Ōkura was still a small hamlet, accessible to the world outside only by two buses a day. It consisted of a school, a tiny shop, and a few farmhouses clustered in an armpit of hills and strung sparsely down the course of a stream. Mountains rose behind, and the Hayama mountain itself, a squat hill bristling with trees, loomed over the village from the other side of the river. The Buddhist temple where the *matsuri* took place was a small and unpretentious wooden building perched on the hillside.

The order of procedure here is similar to that which Iwasaki describes at Kanazawa, with the interesting addition of a fire-walking ritual known as *hitsurugi*. This office is roughly similar to the fire-walking ceremony known as *kashō-zammai*, already seen to be performed by *yamabushi* at the conclusion of their *saitō-goma* ritual. The medium and the ascetic, by traversing the fire, extract or nullify its heat, making it not only safe but positively beneficial for ordinary persons to walk across the embers. The unusual feature of the Hayama fire-walking is its position in the ritual. Usually a fire-walking is performed at the end of rite. The embers of the *saitō-goma* bonfire are raked out at the conclusion of the ritual, to make a path for the fire-walkers. At Ōkura it takes place *before* the oracular utterance of the god, appearing to stand as a purifying ordeal before the descent of the deity.

In 1951 the *noriwara* was the man Ōtani who had served for many years. He was brought to a condition of satisfactorily violent trance, flailing on the ground with his wand, his face convulsed, by the Heart Sutra and its concluding mantra; and also by a short invocation, chanted thirteen times, by the *komorinin* who sat in rows just behind the medium:

> *Sange sange rokkon daisho*
> *Oshime ni hachidaikongōdō*
> *Minami wa tombō jōruri seikai*
> *Yakushinoriko myōraishin raihaijin*
> *Ehō gakkō ehō ganjichibo*
> *Akai daisho kashikishuisho ichini raihai.*[8]

A short preliminary catechism then took place. The *hōin* asked, 'Who is it who has come?'

'Hayama', replied the *noriwara*.

'Will you give us a prophesy?'

'Do the fire-walking first'. These two answers from the deity are invariably the same.

There followed the *hitsurugi* or fire-walking, performed in an enclosed space near the temple, made ready with a cord of sacred rope, posts of green bamboo and a pile of brush-wood in the middle. The pile was set alight, and as it burned fiercely into flames the *noriwara* stood before it, waving his wand to and fro. When the flames died down to red embers, he gave three loud magic yells (*kiai*) and marched two or three times across the smouldering path. The heat of the fire having thus been removed, the *hōin*, the *komorinin* and the rest of the village then followed in its footsteps, deriving thereby, they believed, great benefits. Iwasaki, though he witnessed this rite many times, never once saw anyone burnt.

As soon as everyone present had traversed the embers, the *noriwara* gave another loud yell, signifying that the heat had returned to the fire and that it could no longer be crossed. The party then returned to the temple for the oracle proper. The protagonists and the *komorinin* resumed their former positions inside, while the rest of the village clustered round outside, peering in through the open shutters. The *noriwara* was re-entranced, and the dialogue proper began.

In 1951 Iwasaki recorded the following questions and answers:

'Should we plant early or middle rice next year?'
'Middle rice'.

'How big will next year's harvest be?'
'Seven *bu*.'

'Will the silkworms give a good yield next year?'
'Eight *bu*.'[9]

The answers were always very short and sharp, never exceeding two or three words.

More questions followed concerning the welfare of the village, its crops and the possible threats to its security. Then followed a number of questions concerning individual families and persons. When asking about marriages, journeys, lost things or other personal problems, people from Ōkura itself needed to give only their name. Anyone from neighbouring villages had to give his address as well. The crowd outside listened with bated breath, and flung in so many questions that the ceremony continued until dawn. Many of the answers contained reassuring phrases such as, 'Hayama will look after you', or 'Trust Hayama'.

When the questions came to an end, the *hōin* thanked the god and took a polite leave of him, and the *noriwara* returned to himself.

When I witnessed the Hayama Matsuri at Ōkura in November 1963, the conduct of the ceremony was pronounced by all to be disappointingly weak. Compared with Iwasaki's account of the rite twelve years before, and with what many present remembered of its conduct only five years previously, there was certainly a dispiriting lethargy about the procedure and sense of loss of contact with the deity.

The *noriwara*, in the first place, was no longer the impressive Ōtani, but a woman *miko* from Sōma. She was by way of being a semi-professional medium, working in the rice fields at times when calls were not being made on her mediumistic powers. The *hōin* was old, and the voice in which he recited the Heart Sutra so quavering and gulping that it was surprising that any deity responded at all.

The fire-walking, it is true, was performed with vigour, and, as I can myself testify, the heat was so effectively taken out of the fire that the red embers we traversed were reduced to a mild warmth. The *takusen* itself, however, was nerveless and unconvincing.

A feeble flap of her wand was the only sign the *miko* evinced of a divine possession. In answer to the first question, 'Who has come?', the voice in which she replied, 'Hayama Gongen' was so faint as to be barely audible. Very different, everyone afterwards declared, from the satisfactory bass roar emitted by the male *noriwara* in former times. Nor was this all. Her replies to the questions about the harvest were couched in language vague, uncertain and polite.

'I think that the early rice will be about nine *bu*, the middle rice about nine and the late rice probably about eight *bu*.'

'I imagine that you will need to take special care over the spring silkworms because of the threat of frost.' These faint and deprecatory replies were a far cry from the short, sharp answers the god traditionally delivered. Worst of all, when it came questions from individual families and persons, the *miko* made one or two bad mistakes. For a Mr Nakajima Katsuo, for example, she predicted that the year would be a thoroughly satisfactory one, in which all would go exactly as he wished. There was a doubtful pause before the *hōin* brought himself to say, 'But Mr Nakajima is at present very sick . . .' The *miko* in some confusion then said, 'Oh yes. . . of course. I think he'll probably be better in about forty days. Meanwhile he ought to take good care of himself'.

After this no more questions were put from the crowd, and the ceremony finished at the almost unprecedentedly early hour of 11 p.m.

The general verdict the next day was that the *miko's* performance had been so languid that it was difficult to realise that she was possessed at all. Five years ago the *miko* they had engaged for the occasion, women though she was, had flailed on the floor with her wand in a convincingly frenzied manner, levitating herself violently into the air and screaming answers to the questions put to her in an odd bass voice. So obviously genuine was her trance that the crowd outside had bombarded her with questions until dawn. But this strong woman had since left the district and become a nun, so that for the last four years they had had to make do with the present creature, despite her feebleness, because she was the only *miko* left in the entire area.

Even the strong woman was nothing, an old grandmother informed me, compared with the days when a male *noriwara* served. The violence of his behaviour was far greater than anything seen in recent times. If anyone came near the temple who was in any way ritually unclean, the *noriwara* would rush out and attack him. Since the last man ceased to serve, however, no other had appeared.

Later in the morning, although women were not usually allowed higher than the first *torii*, the *miko* and I accompanied the procession of *komorinin* to the top of the Hayama mountain to escort the deity back to his winter quarters. At the top, after an hour's climb, was a small shrine where offerings were made of the first batch of rice-cakes pounded the night before. The boys clustered round and recited their invocation thirteen times more. One of them then swarmed up the tree thought to be the tallest on the mountain and hence to reach nearest to the sky, and tied to its trunk, about twenty feet from the ground, the wand into which the deity had been summoned the night before. It would be left there until it rotted away. With this act, which I was given to understand must be of such antiquity as to antedate the establishment of shrines as fixed abodes for the *kami*, the deity was considered to be properly settled in his winter home until the following spring. The party descended the mountain and partook of a large *shōjin-otoshi* or non-maigre meal.

For our second example of a *takusen matsuri* we turn to the Sakumatsuri, performed until five years ago every February in the Buddhist temple of Kaikōji in Sakata. The existence of this *matsuri* only came to the notice of ethnographers a few years before its disappearance. It so happened that in Kaikōji were enshrined two of the self-mummified Buddhas, Chūkai and Emmyōkai, which were the subject of an extensive investigation in Yamagata prefecture in 1960. In the course of their examination of the two mummies in the temple, the party of ethnographers was apprised of the survival in that very place of a genuine trance *matsuri*. In 1962, therefore, Professor Hori was able to observe, record and even make a film of the proceedings. It is on his published account, and on the film which he kindly showed me on my return from Sakata in the summer of 1963, that I rely for the following description.[10]

Though similar in its fundamental structure to the ritual carried out at Hayama, the Sakumatsuri shows certain interesting differences. The medium is not, as at Hayama, an ordinary farmer or fishermen, appearing spontaneously from some unsuspecting family. He is a *yamabushi* of the order known as Isse-gyōnin, affiliated to the parent sect at Yudonosan. Before he can serve as medium he has to undergo a severe regime of *gyō*. For three successive winters he must carry out a thirty-day period of *kangyō*, cold austerities. Morning and evening he must perform the cold water austerity, and for a certain number of hours every day he must walk from house to house begging for alms.

Here is an anomaly. The part of the medium is assumed, most unusually, by a member of an ascetic order. Even more unusually, the part of medium and that of ascetic appear to be interchangeable by the same person. The man who has served to entrance the medium with his spells will afterwards take his turn serving as medium.

Again, as at Hayama, the rite performed at Sakata was only one among a large group of similar rites formerly performed in temples in the district having connections with the order of Isse-gyōnin. A trance ritual very similar to that of Kaikōji was performed at Nangakuji in Tsuruoka, for example, and at Hommyōji in Asahimura. The *matsuri* at Kaikōji was the last to survive.

The scene shows the medium, wearing the peculiar cap of the Isse-gyōnin sect, pulled so low over his eyes as almost to blindfold him. His feet are bound beneath him as he sits crosslegged on the floor. A short wand fringed with white paper streamers is put into his hands. A group of similar white clad figures, likewise ascetics of the Isse-gyōnin order, gather round him making loud and continuous sounds. Just behind his head they rattle iron rings, bang on drums, recite at the top of their voices the Heart Sutra and the familiar spell *Sange sange rokkon zaishō*.

After two or three minutes of this tumult the wand in the medium's hands begins to shake, and, his feet still bound beneath him, he begins to levitate himself violently into the air, sometimes to the height of nearly a foot. The wand in his hands furiously flails up and down, banging and slapping on the floor. Had not the precaution of the foot-binding been taken, it is clear that he would have flung himself out of the cordoned enclosure uncontrollably into the midst of the spectators.

As soon as the violence of his behaviour proclaims him to be fully entranced, the chanting ceases and an official interrogator calls out in resonant and impersonal tones a series of questions.

'How much will the rice harvest be this year? How much early rice? How much middle rice? How much late rice?'

Immediately on the heels of the questions, without a second's pause or hesitation, came the answer from the possessed man as he flung himself up and down, slapping the floor with his wand. The answers came always in a single word, screamed out in a strange voice:

'Seven . . . eight . . . yes . . . no . . . July . . . September.'

The questions, like those recorded by Iwasaki for the village of Kanazawa, came in a set, fixed order. After the rice, early, middle and late, came enquiries about soy beans, red beans, fleas, drought, winds, rains, floods, fires, sicknesses and fishing catches. To the questions about flood, fire or sickness, the man would answer *aru* or *nai*, yes or no. If the answer were yes, further questions would follow as to when the calamities might be expected and what deities might be invoked to prevent them. The answers were all carefully recorded with a brush by an official scribe.

When the questions pertaining to the welfare of the whole district were answered, each separate village took turns to ask questions about its own prospects, usually under the four headings of drought, wind, rain and pests. After the medium had replied for two villages he was allowed to rest. He was brought back to himself and another *gyōnin* made to take his place, similarly blindfolded, bound, and entranced by loud and repeated sounds. Each man who served as medium, and in 1962 Hori recorded that no less than twenty villages pressed their requests, necessitating several mediums, behaved in his trance in a manner exactly similar to the others. With similar violence each would levitate himself into the air, flail on the floor with his wand, scream single words in answer to the questions. It was astonishing to me to discover, as I watched Professor Hori's film, that one of the frantic figures was Mr Itō, the gentle and learned incumbent of the temple who that very afternoon had explained to me the history of the temple's two mummies.

The single screamed word which is the deity's customary answer at the Sakumatsuri is worthy of note. At the Hayama oracle Iwasaki noted the short, abrupt answers given by the *noriwara*. Here the replies are even shorter and sharper. Yanagita Kunio, many years before the existence of the Sakumatsuri was known to scholars, pointed out the possible significance of the name of the divinity Hitokotonushi, the master of one word, the divinity whom the Kojiki records as 'saying bad things in one word and good things in one word'.[11] The custom of delivering one-word answers to human questions may therefore have been widespread in ancient times. We shall meet it again in our account of the Ōmoto Kagura.

In former times, so many ascetics were qualified to serve as mediums that there was time and opportunity for questions to be asked by individual persons, as well as villages. The rapid decrease in men prepared to undergo the rigours that qualify them for the task made such proliferation impossible in 1962. With an accurately prophetic eye, Hori then wrote that the *matsuri* might soon, for lack of qualified mediums, disappear. Within four years of being written, his words had come true.

For our third example of a trance *matsuri* we turn south and west to Okayama prefecture. Here two groups of village oracles may still be seen. The Kōjin Kagura is still performed in villages in the Ōsa district, and the Gohōtobi in a group of temples in the mountainous district of Kume near Tsuyama.

The Gohōtobi, which I was able to observe in 1967 at the temple of Ryōsanji and the shrine of Ichinomiya Hachiman, was first described in the *Sakuyōshi*, a seventeenth-century guidebook to the western districts of Mimasaka province. In the Tendai temple of Iwamasan Ryōsanji, the account runs, *gohō* spells took place on the seventh day of the seventh month. For the office of medium they chose an ordinary simple person, and made him observe the rules of ceremonial purity for a stated period beforehand. When the day for the ceremony arrived, all the priests of the temple gathered round the medium and began to recite spells. Suddenly the man leapt to his feet and burst into a frenzied dance, howling and roaring like a wild beast. Superhuman strength was given to him, enabling him to lift huge rocks. If anyone happened to be present who was not ceremonially pure, the medium would seize him and hurl him away ten paces. They then gave him four tubs of water to drink, each of which contained about five gallons. When the man had drunk all four tubs he suddenly fell flat on the floor, and when he regained consciousness he remembered nothing of what had passed.

The *Sakuyōshi* further mentions a similar rite at the temple of Ryōsanji which on one occasion ended in tragedy. A samurai in an unpurified state came to watch the proceedings. Suddenly the possessed medium furiously leapt up and seized him. The samurai defended himself stoutly, but in the course of the struggle both fell over a cliff and were killed. A pine tree marks the spot.[12]

Today the Gohōtobi ritual is still performed in seven temples in this mountainous district, all towards the middle of the lunar seventh month. At Ryōsanji, Onshōji, Ryōsenji, Seisuiji and Ichinomiya Hachiman the rite takes place every year on the 14th, 15th or 16th of the month. At Bukkyōji it takes place in even years, and in Burakuji in odd years. The procedure at Ryōsanji is thought to preserve the rite in its most complete and ancient form.[13]

Here the medium is known as *gohōzane*, the *gohō* seed. As at Hayama, he is an ordinary village man whose only training for his task is a rigorous course of *gyō*. For a week before the day of the rite he must seclude himself in the small Gohō shrine at the back of the temple where there hangs a picture of the deity *gohō-zenshin*. He must eat only maigre food cooked on a separate pure fire, and twice in the morning and twice at night he must perform the cold water austerity twenty-one times, in the pond situated conveniently in front of the shrine. He must also circumambulate once a day the entire precincts of the temple, during which time he must speak to no one. After performing his final cold water ablution, on the night of the rite, he waits at the *gohō* shrine for the procession to arrive and escort him to the place where the entrancement is to take place.

The temple of Ryōsanji, which I visited in 1967 with Dr Tanaka of the Matsuri Society and several members of the Okayama Folklore Society, must be one of the most beautiful and numinous places in Japan.[14] So high is it situated on the mountainside that on a clear day you can see Hōki Daisen to the north and the islands of the Inland Sea to the south. On the night of the *matsuri* the moon was full, and looking from the gate of the temple it appeared to rise from far below, dark yellow and perfectly round through a fringe of pine trees. The roof of the Hondō or main building, dating from the Muromachi period, had remarkably deep eaves, like swooping wings, the veins and feathers of which were visible from below. Beside the Hondō stands a gigantic cryptomeria tree, said to be a thousand years old. Its remoteness and its height gave the place a true sense of a *monde à part*, and in the light of the rising moon it seemed still further enwrapped in an atmosphere of mystery and dream.

The procession which formed outside the temple to go to meet the medium was likewise a strange one. It consisted of seventeen conch-shell-blowers, eight torch-bearers, three drummers, several lantern-bearers, bearers of the medium's huge bamboo wand, the bearer of his large cap, a mat-bearer, and no less than twenty-nine 'waist-claspers' (*koshitori*) whose duty it was to see that the medium's frantic behaviour did not become dangerous. Some of the shell trumpeters, I noticed, were *yamabushi* from Ushiroyama; others bore no such insignia. There were also a dozen small boys known as *keigo*.

The procession, to a clamorous accompaniment of drums and conches, wound its way by lantern light through a dark wood up the mountainside as far as the *gohō* shrine. There the medium, dressed in white, was waiting to be escorted to the place of the rite. Hardly had he joined the procession than he seemed to slip into a condition bordering on trance. Walking immediately behind the bearer of his great white cap, and immediately in front of the bearers of his huge wand of bamboo fronds, he would from time to time leap high into the air, restrained sometimes by the waist-claspers. The *gohō* divinity, I was told, was now accompanying us, though it was not yet properly 'implanted' in the medium. The procession now wound its way back through the forest, to the light of round paper lanterns and of moonbeams filtering through the trees, until it reached the place near the gate of the temple where the 'god-implanting' procedure was to take place. This appeared to be a small shrine with an enclosed court before it.

The medium disappeared inside the shrine for a short time to change his clothes. When he emerged he was clad in a dark blue short coat with a white swastika front and back, tight trousers, and in his head the enormous white cap made of paper streamers.

All was now ready for the ceremony of *onoritsuke*, or implanting the divinity. This took place in the open court in front of the shrine, in an enclosed space duly sacralised by rope and green bamboo posts. In the middle sat the medium with the soles of his feet together. Between them was placed the great wand, a gigantic spray of bamboo fronds as much as six feet long and festooned with white strips of paper. Six waist-claspers crouched round him, like a six-pointed star, firmly clutching his feet.

A rhythmic clamour then started on drum and conch, in time to which the medium swished the great wand to and fro and back and forth. Gradually the rhythm grew faster and the swishing of the wand more violent, until the medium was plunging frenziedly back and forth, the long bamboo spray dashing wildly among the spectators, shedding its white streamers like autumn leaves. The six attendants meanwhile clung desperately to the medium's feet.

At the same time I was aware that the small boys who had accompanied the procession were running round and round the medium in circles. Had not the clamour of the drum, the conches and the swishing wand been so deafening, I was told, I would have heard the children shout '*Barōn sarōn*' as they ran.

As the movement reached a climactic pitch of violence, the rhythm on drum and conch slackened, and the plunging of the medium slowed down to a pause. This whole cycle, I was told, was called *hitoinori*, one spell, and it usually took two or three of such treatments before the medium was truly entered by the *gohō* divinity.

The procedure was then repeated. But as the plunging and swishing rose to a second climax, the medium suddenly leapt to his feet, burst through the ring of waist-claspers, and rushed at full speed down the steps from the shrine to a wide open space in front of the temple gate. Four waist-claspers followed hotly on his heels.

Up and down and round and round he ran, always trailing his pursuers behind him. At length, apparently exhausted, he collapsed on a large stone which stood to one side of the shrine. The four attendants rushed up and, chanting loudly in his ear, appeared to be massaging his body. These were measures, I was informed, to prevent the divinity from 'falling out', and the man coming out of his trance. After a moment or two the medium again leapt to his feet and began rushing to and fro as before.

This procedure was repeated twice more, the periods of wild rushing alternating with rests on the stone. It was known as *o-asobi*, the sport or play of the divinity during his visit to the human world.

After the last burst of 'play', the medium and his escort returned to the shrine. There they restored him from his trance by removing his white cap and dashing water over his head. He then changed from his dark clothes back into white ones and, at about 4 a.m., the rite was concluded. The cap, I understood, was subsequently cut up and the pieces distributed to believers.

The following night a similar rite was enacted at Ichinomiya. Although now a Shinto shrine, Ichinomiya was until the Meiji period a *matsuji* or subordinate temple of Ryōsanji. Its ceremony therefore resembles that of Ryōsanji, though on a more modest scale. The medium wore the same dark clothes, the same white cap, and his enactment of the divinity's 'play' in alternating rushes and rests was likewise similar. The same procedure is followed at Onshōji, Ryōsenji and Seisuiji.

At Bukkyōji and Burakuji, however, the only other temples where the *gohōtobi* rite still survives, slight variations are said to occur. The wand is not a gigantic bunch of bamboo fronds but a fan woven of maple leaves and twigs. The process of implanting the deity also boasts slight differences— seven short spells are recited seven times—and the posture of the medium as he rushes to and fro is said to be peculiar to these two temples. His rushes, moreover, are accomplished in three bursts, invariably of seven, five and three, along a fixed cursus between two fires.

Our final example of a *takusen-matsuri* is one which, like the Sakumatsuri, has recently disappeared, the Ōmoto Kagura. This ritual used to take place in a number of villages in the Iwami district of Shimane prefecture, at intervals of

271

either six or twelve years. The trance in this *matsuri* died out, Ushio Michio avers, because the medium was no longer prepared to undergo the strict period of *kessai*, purification, necessary for the proper performance of the task. Nor was the place of the rite always sufficiently sacralised, nor the interrogating ascetic always sufficiently experienced. In several villages attempts were made to revive the trance artificially, but always with untoward if not disastrous results. Either the medium failed to achieve a convincing trance, or someone other than the medium became unexpectedly possessed, or the medium became possessed not by the deity Ōmoto Daimyōjin, as intended, but by a spirit dog.[15]

Hagiwara Tatsuo, however, has left us an interesting account of the Ōmoto Kagura as performed in the village of Kida some time before—he gives no date—the demise of the ritual. In this village the rite was performed once every twelve years in a small shrine on top of a hill at the beginning of January.[16]

Before the trance took place a number of *kami-nō*, dance dramas based on the myths of the Izumo district, were enacted in a sacred enclosure in which were contained a large hawser known as the snake rope, and two sacks of rice with *gohei* wands stuck into them.[17]

At about 10 p.m., in the middle of the play known as Iwado-no-mai, a sudden commotion was heard in the corner of the room. One of the onlookers began to shout and roar in a strange harsh voice, and to manifest familiar symptoms of a divine seizure.

True to type, however, the possessed man did not immediately burst into the divine utterance. This could only follow the correct ritual procedure and the correct interrogation. First the 'snake rope' must be uncoiled and slung across the room. Next, the possessed man is tied up to it with bands of cotton, supported from behind by two assistants. Next, a long list of the names of all the *kami* in the district is read out, at the conclusion of which the *negi* or shrine priest begins his interrogation.

'Ōmoto Daimyōjin, how will the next seven years be with the village?'

Emitting loud roars and howls, the man answered, 'Uo uo, good harvests, good harvests.'

'Will there be any fires?'

'There will, there will.'

'In what direction?'

'West, west.'

There followed questions about floods and sickness. Then finally, 'Ōmoto Daimyōjin, is there anything you want?'

'Yes there is. Why have you stopped dancing? Dance, dance.'

'To be sure. We will prepare a dance at once for you to watch.'

'Uo uo.'

With the words, 'Now please return to your mountain', everyone burst into the special valedictory music that sends the god back to his own world.

They then untied the man from the rope and carried him into the next room, where for several hours he slept soundly. The whole of the next day he was in a state of dazed stupor, so furious had been his expense of energy. The rest of the company meanwhile resumed the performance of the Iwado-no-mai dance which had been interrupted at the moment of the man's seizure.

It is said that the effort of serving as medium is so exhausting that a man may never do so three times in his life, though he may succeed twice. In such circumstances it is not surprising that candidates for the office proved so few that the rite disappeared. On this occasion, apparently, three assistants had been chosen and subjected to preliminary measures of purification in the hope that the deity would make use of one of them. The sudden seizure of a member of the audience was unexpected though entirely successful.

It is noteworthy in this case that the interrogator was not a *yamabushi* but the *negi* or shrine priest. This feature points to the survival of an older practice, dating back to times before the office of interrogator was taken over by a *yamabushi*.

With these four examples of a trance *matsuri* before us we can deduce something of the general structure of such rites in Japan.

First let us consider the medium. Whereas in the groups of

miko we have so far observed the medium is almost always a woman, in these village *matsuri* alone the task is performed by a man. There is some evidence to suggest that in their older form these rituals employed children for the part of medium, in the manner suggested by the Buddhist Abisha-hō rite. The Tosa shrines where the child rides at the head of the procession, clearly impersonating the god, are, as Yanagita points out, certainly survivals of an older form in which the child served as the vehicle of augury and divination. It is possible, however, that the stringent requirements of the preliminary purification, with its cold water, its maigre food, its lonely seclusion, made the task in time more suited to a man than to a boy.

With the exception of the Sakumatsuri, where the same trained ascetic served indiscriminately as medium or as interrogator, the medium was always an ordinary man from the village, who left his work in the fields in order to serve as the vehicle of the god.

A good example of how such a task can fall to an ordinary farmer is given by Mr Ōtani, the *noriwara* of the Hayama village of Ōkura, who at the age of sixty-five spoke as follows to Iwasaki Toshio of his life of service:

'Every year since I was eleven years old I served as one of the *komorinin*. Then when I reached the age of seventeen I was reciting *sange sange* as usual when suddenly I felt my body begin to tremble and shake in a strange way. This was the first intimation I had of what it was like to be possessed by a god.

'As it so happened, just at that time the village had no *noriwara* of its own, and for the *matsuri* we always had to borrow a man from one of the villages nearby. This man had prophesied some years before that a *noriwara* would appear in our village about this time, so everyone was naturally on the lookout.

'So when I had my first possession it was decided that I should act as *noriwara* the following year. Since then I have served every year without a single break.

For the first three days after the god possessed me my ribs and feet were very stiff and painful owing to the unaccustomed violent movements I had made during the seizure.

I soon found that any god, not only Hayama, would come into me, and that this might happen at any time. Once it happened when I was alone on the mountain praying very intensely, and this frightened me so much that I tried not to think of the god when I was alone. Even now it is apt to happen whenever I get overexcited, so I have had to give up going to the shrine or thinking of the god very much. Once when I went on a pilgrimage to Mt Haguro and watched a *kagura* there, I thought the god was coming into me. But I avoided the attack by taking a firm hold of myself. They wanted me to become a *gyōja* on Mt Haguro, but that would have been no life for me.

'When the god comes into me I go into a kind of daze. I don't mean to say that I lose consciousness or go out of my mind, but I don't see clearly, and what I do is not done by my own will. At the fire-walking, for example, it is not by my will that I walk across the fire. I am moved by the god's will entirely.

'Nowadays the god has got rather quieter, but at first he was so wild and violent that all the skin of my legs would be rubbed off without my being aware of it. Nowadays all I do by way of preliminary purification before the *matsuri* is to have a good hot bath, but in the old days I was so afraid of being burnt at the fire-walking that I used to be quite carried away and do three times the usual number of cold water austerities'.[18]

Iwasaki also collected several tales from old inhabitants in villages where the Hayama rite had been discontinued. At Usuishi they remembered a *noriwara* who refused to serve one year on the score that he had a cold, and instead stayed at home by the fire. But when, at the shrine some distance away they started to recite the usual '*sange sange*', he fell into a trance in his own house and ran straight to the shrine. A similar story of a *noriwara* unwilling to serve because he was sick, but compelled to do so by the spells recited at the shrine, is also reported from the village of Higo. In this village too one man claimed to remember a *noriwara* who in the course of his entranced levitation leapt up, still crosslegged, five feet into the air. Stories of *noriwara* who flung themselves on spectators who appeared at the *matsuri* having recently eaten fish, are likewise numerous.[19]

In no case does it appear that the office of village medium is in any way a hereditary one. The man appears spontaneously, as though elected, as did Ōtani at Ōkura and the spectator at the Ōmoto Kagura. The only training that appears to be required is the preparatory purification, of which the essential seems to be *suigyō*, the cold water austerity. Without a preliminary period of cold water night and morning the deity will have difficulty in possessing the medium, or will 'fall out' quickly once it has done so.

Let us now consider the means by which the medium is thrown into his state of trance. In nearly every example we saw that loud, rhythmically reiterated sounds were the prominent devices used. Thunderous banging on a drum, deafening blasts on conch shell trumpets, clashing and rattling of iron-ringed croziers, clanging of bells and loud shouted chanting of familiar words of power are used in every case, with the modified exception of Hayama.

An interesting variation on these auditory methods is the device still used in some versions of the Kōjin Kagura, a trance *matsuri* still performed in certain villages of Okayama prefecture. Here the eye as well as the ear of the medium is bemused by what is known as the *nuno-mai* or cotton dance. When in 1963 I observed a demonstration performance of the Kōjin Kagura done for the benefit of the Okayama Folklore Society, the medium was an old man of eighty-three. A long length of white cotton was put into his hands, which in the course of his subsequent dance he caused first to describe serpentine movements in the air and then to wind itself round and round his body. At the end of the third of these dances he appeared to fall into the required trance, flopping over the huge straw snake which had previously, as in the Ōmoto Kagura, been slung across the room, and from this posture delivering a message of congratulation from the deity Kōjin.[20]

In this same category of visual methods of producing trance can be included the curious device used in the Gohōtobi rite whereby children rush round and round the medium shouting '*Barōn sarōn*'. Vestiges of such practices have been noted in other parts of Japan in the form of children's games. Both Yanagita and Iwasaki report that at the time of writing a game known as Jizō-asobi was still played in Fukushima prefecture. One child stood in the middle holding a branch in his hand, while the rest rushed round and round him until he began to speak. He was encouraged to say anything that might come into his head.[21]

In all these devices, both auditory and visual, there is much to be found in common, as Miyake has pointed out, with the recognised methods of inducing a state of hypnotic dissociation. Sudden shocks, through noise or gesture, continuously repeated loud sounds, are well-tried means of sending a suggestive subject into a condition of hypnotic sleep. That there may therefore be a strong element of hypnotic suggestion in these trances is highly likely.

A final word may be said on the behaviour of the medium in trance. In every case we noticed that a trance was approved by the village as 'good' and genuine when the medium's behaviour was violent, inhuman and strange. Behaviour ordinary or human—as in a decorous waving of the wand or a polite use of language—was instantly condemned as weak and unconvincing. To carry conviction the medium's behaviour must be inhuman; his voice must turn to a wild beast's roar or a bass unearthly scream; he must dash and flail his wand on the floor with a violence never seen in normal daily life; he must leap up and down from a cross-legged position on the floor, the higher into the air the better. Such are the fundamental symptoms of possession, recognised all over Japan. We shall meet them again on Mt Ontake.

In these village oracles, therefore, we clearly have an admixture in varying degree of two different kinds of rite. The ancient seasonal rite, in which the local guardian kami is summoned into the body of the village miko and induced to prophesy on the fortunes of the village, has been overlaid by another ritual of esoteric Buddhist origin. The nature of the prophesy is likely to be much the same as in pre-Buddhist times: the god still advises the village to plant more middle rice than last year, and Mr Yamamoto to take care not to drink bad water on March 15th. He will still demand from the village another dance, or a new roof to his shrine, and from Mr Tanaka that he should desist from building a new gate to his house. He still foretells the severity of seasonal hazards, pests, storms, and floods, and of perennial perils such as fire and sickness. He will still if he feels inclined give advice as to how these disasters may be averted. The Buddhist rite has simply given the figure of the ascetic a good deal more prominence than formerly would have been accorded to him. It has robbed the medium of much of her ancient majesty, of the music and dancing with which she formerly summoned the god, and raised up in her stead the ascetic with his shell, his iron-ringed stave and his distorted Sanscrit sounds.

14
Mountain Oracles

When Mr Percival Lowell climbed Mt Ontake in August 1891 he found himself, at a spot just above the eighth stage, the astonished witness of 'certain esoteric phenomena which turned out to be as unknown as they were peculiar'. Three young men dressed in the white attire of the Ontake pilgrim were engaged in fervent prayer before a small shrine. One then seated himself with his back to the shrine, his eyes closed and his hands clutching a *gohei* wand. A second man faced him intoning formulae, 'tying his fingers into mystic knots . . . accompanying each act with a gutteral grunt suggestive of intense exertion'. The third man stood and watched.

The man with the wand soon began to twitch convulsively, every moment with increasing violence, until at length he appeared to be in 'the full fury of a seemingly superhuman paroxysm'. The throe subsided, giving place to a continuous tremor, like a top when it settles at the apex of its spin. The other man, in an archaic and reverent form of speech, asked what deity had descended. 'I am Hakkai', the entranced man replied. The interrogator then asked a series of questions; what was the weather like at the summit of the mountain, how was the health of those at home, what would be the outcome of their pilgrimage? To all these questions the god replied briefly. At the end of the catechism the medium was thumped smartly on the back until he opened his eyes, 'like one awaking from a profound sleep'.

The trio then changed places. The interrogator moved into the seat of the medium, the onlooker took the place of the interrogator, while the medium retired to the post of onlooker. The whole ritual was then repeated with scarcely any variation; a similar entrancement, interview and awakening.

Once more the three men changed places, each now taking up the position he had not yet occupied, and for a third time the ritual was enacted. The party then put on their straw hats, seized their long wooden poles and continued their journey up the mountain. Mr Lowell subsequently encountered them at various spots on the summit engaged in an exactly similar ritual. The next day, having visited all the shrines on the various volcanic peaks and on the edge of the various volcanic lakes, they began their journey down the mountain and back to their homes 350 miles away. Most of this distance they accomplished on foot, and while they were on the mountain they ate nothing and drank only water.[1]

The esoteric phenomena which so impressed Mr Lowell, and which afterwards stimulated him to undertake further researches into the trance practices of Japan,[2] were the same *yorigitō* rituals which we saw in the last chapter performed in village temples and shrines. Here, though the circumstances are somewhat different, the basic procedure is the same: a deity is called into the body of a medium and cajoled to speak. But the séance now comes, not as a seasonal village festival but as an event in a mountain pilgrimage. In order to communicate with the deity the faithful must now climb the mountain where he resides. Nor are the faithful confined to a particular village or group of villages. Believers in the Ontake cult are usually members of the *kō* or pilgrim clubs, whose white-clad bands are in summer so prominent on the slopes of holy mountains.

These *kō* clubs can be found all over Japan, dedicated to the worship of notable holy mountains or celebrated shrines. Mt Fuji, Mt Haguro, Tateyama, Akibasan, Sagami Ōyama and Yudonosan all have their *kō*, which like Ontake came from all over Japan to pay them homage. Likewise the great shrines of Ise and Izumo have been since medieval times the object of widespread *kō* worship.[3]

In their numbers and distribution these *kō* clubs vary considerably. Some, scarcely larger than a family concern, consist of a mere dozen people; others may boast several hundred members. Some are confined to one village or to one particular quarter of a city; others may spread over several villages, or straggle over several wards of a city. All, however, have in common the dedication to the yearly pilgrimage. Once a year, between the middle of July and the middle of September, the club will set out, in the full panoply of the mountain pilgrim, for the slopes of its destined summit. If its numbers are small, all the members may go. If unmanageably large, then lots may be drawn as to who shall have the privilege. All are similarly attired: white trousers and jacket, with mystic signs stamped in red and black on the back, a large conical straw hat, rosary, straw sandals on the feet, and the long wooden pole called *kongōzue*, on which may be branded the names of the mountains that its owner has climbed. These are the figures who may still be seen in their thousands converging on the foothills of their mountains and wending their way, some lithely, some laboriously, to the most holy spot on the summit.

All likewise boast a leader, usually known as *sendatsu*. He it is who shepherds the flock up the ten stages which mark the route to the summit, who decides where they shall sleep, supervises their worship at the sundry holy spots on the way, who leads the chorus of chanting by which they ease the pains and fatigues of their climb. He should combine, therefore, the qualities of scoutmaster, courier and mountain guide.

The *kō* dedicated to the worship of Mt Ontake however, differ in their traditional structure from the *kō* to be found on the slopes of any other mountain.[4] In the first place they possess among their officers the persons necessary to the conduct of a *yorigitō* séance. Most prominent is the medium, known as *nakaza* or 'between seat'. Like the medium in the village oracles, he is usually an ordinary man with no professional pretensions, who has developed his powers of trance through a rigorous course of *gyō*. He is brought to his state of trance by the *maeza* or 'front seat'. Like the interrogator in the village ritual, he summons the deity into the medium's body, questions him and eventually sends him away. It is he who usually also fulfils the duties of *sendatsu* for the group, shepherding, supervising, paternally admonishing. Occasionally it is the *nakaza* who undertakes these extra tasks, and occasionally, again, a third person who plays no part in the ritual of the séance.

Four more figures make up the complement of officers of the Ontake *kō*. These are the *shiten*, named after the Four Kings of Buddhist iconography, whose duty it is to mount guard at the cardinal points during the ritual and prevent the ingress of evil influences.

The question at once presents itself, how did the Ontake *kō* come to possess this peculiar structure? Why did they, and no *kō* dedicated to any other mountain, become associated with the *yorigitō* ritual, and why did Ontake, alone of all the holy mountains, become the scene of such séances?[5]

The history of the mountain to some extent supplies the answer. During the eighteenth century, and possibly earlier, the Kiso valley at the foot of the mountain was inhabited by enclaves of ascetics known as *dōja*. These men carried out an annual ascent of Mt Ontake, in the lunar sixth month, preceded by a period of exceptionally severe seclusion and purgation. For as long as seventy-five days, in some cases even a hundred days before the climb, the ascetics were required to isolate themselves from the community in segregated huts. There they cooked their own maigre food on a separate pure fire, avoiding all meat, fish, poultry and strong vegetables, and performed frequent cold water austerities and long sessions of mantra chanting. Only after this dauntingly long period of ritual cleansing were they considered fit to set foot on the holy ground of the mountain.[6]

For the rest of the year they mixed more freely with the village communities in the valley, performing for them the tasks usually expected of an ascetic. Prominent among their methods was the *yorigitō* ritual. This they would perform on request in private houses, summoning and questioning deities associated with the mountain—Ontake Daijin, Tōriten, Marishiten—into the body of a medium, a young man known as *ichi*.

Towards the end of the eighteenth century a notable change in the cult of the mountain was brought about by two ascetics, Kakumei and Fukan. Each is credited with having blazed a new trail to the summit. Kakumei is said to have opened the route from the village of Kurosawa in 1785, Fukan to have done the same ten years later for the route on the southern side of the mountain from the hamlet of Ōdaki.

Through the influence of Kakumei several villages in the valley modified their rigorous rule of seventy-five days of preliminary seclusion to a more lenient twenty-seven days.

The ascent of the mountain thus became possible for many people to whom the prospect of two-and-a-half lunar months of isolation had proved too daunting. There quickly formed round the two ascetic figures a number of *kō*, dedicated, as had been the older groups, to a yearly ritual ascent of the mountain. Into the activities of these *kō* there naturally crept other survivals from the former groups of *dōja*, prominent among which was the practice of *yorigitō*. The *kō* therefore counted among their members a medium and an ascetic who, in the course of the annual ascent as well as at the club's meetings during the rest of the year, would summon the deities of the mountain and cause them to speak. The tradition of the séance, thus started, has persisted ever since.

Today Ontake *kō* are to be found in almost every province of Japan. From Aomori to Kyūshū white-clad parties converge during the two climbing months on the little town of Kiso Fukushima at the foot of the mountain, and proceed up the lower forested slopes by one of the two recognised routes.

Many *kō* have recently relaxed the strictness of discipline traditional to the Ontake cult. One which preserves the old ways more scrupulously than most, and provides us therefore with a useful example of former procedure, is the *kō* in the village of Kurogawa in the Kiso valley. When investigated by Ikegami in 1957 this large *kō* was found to number among its members no less than four *nakaza* and four *maeza*. And this despite the exceptionally severe *gyō* required in the training of both. On thirty consecutive nights during the coldest part of the winter, the future *nakaza* must repair to the river at nine o'clock and pour buckets of icy water over his head and body. He must spend many hours of the rest of the night learning by heart, and by the light of a single candle, a long succession of prayers and spells. Many candidates gave up the struggle before the five successive winters necessary to rouse their powers of trance were completed. A similarly severe regime of *gyō* was necessary to the training of the *maeza*: five consecutive winters of cold water and abstention were likewise required before he was able to evoke a deity and persuade it to speak. Both these offices, however, when eventually achieved, carried with them the posthumous title of *reijin*, miraculous person. The men who had accomplished these powers were believed to be apotheosised after death, and their souls to dwell on the slopes of the mountain. [7]

Those *kō* which today preserve so carefully the traditional disciplines of the cult are comparatively rare. Some indeed have so relaxed their former strictness that they possess no *nakaza* at all. No one of their members is prepared to undergo the severe *gyō* necessary to cultivate the capacity for trance. Mr Watanabe, the genial patriarch of the Mitakekyō 'sect', into which since the beginning of the Meiji period the various Ontake *kō* have been loosely federated, assured me when I first climbed the mountain in 1961 that few *kō* today observed the traditional precautions of purity. Some neglected entirely the usual preliminary purgation: they failed to avoid impure foods and neglected the cold water ablutions. Others observed a merely prefunctory couple of days before setting out. The older and more detailed requirements of purity—no leather to be brought on to the mountain, sandals to be of straw, purses of cloth, women altogether debarred—had long been forgotten. As a consequence of such laxity, the practice of trance had inevitably diminished.

On the three occasions when I climbed Mt Ontake, however, I found no shortage of trances. [8]

In the woodblock print of Mt Ontake which appears in the *Nihon Meisan Zue*, an illustrated guidebook to the mountainous districts of Japan published in 1807, we are shown a lofty soaring peak, towering numinously and precipitously above the streams and farmhouses huddled below. No rival mountain is to be seen anywhere near. It is a single high place, endued with divine symmetry and precipitancy, a single ladder to heaven. [9]

Here we see the superiority of the painting over the photograph. A painting shows us not the objective appearance of the thing but the manner in which it is seen by the painter. The anonymous artist whose sketches became the woodblock prints of the guidebook saw Mt Ontake not as it actually appears but as the image of an ideal holy mountain. He painted the mountain as he conceived the other world, the abode of numina, beautiful and perilous.

In fact Mt Ontake, seen from a distance, has little of the improbable and fearful symmetry of Mt Fuji or Mt Ibuki. Its summit is squat and jagged, any symmetrical cone it once possessed having long ago disappeared in a succession of volcanic explosions. These have left a circle of five craters, each filled with the green waters of a lake. In height it rises to no more than 9,000 feet. Like other holy mountains in Japan, the routes to the summit are divided into ten stages or *gōme*, each marked by a hut where rest and refreshment may be had. Provisions to the huts are carried up on the backs of porters known as *gōriki*, who may be seen plodding upwards bowed down under immense loads of tinned fish, bags of rice, cans of beer, jars of bean paste and tea, or running precipitately downwards, sure of foot with empty loads.

The recognised routes both start from hamlets in the foothills, Ōdaki and Kurosawa. For many miles upwards from these villages the old trackway is flanked on either side by curious avenues of carved megaliths. Like giant chessmen, these stones now coalesce in strange throngs and clusters, now dwindle into straggling lines. But always, until the fifth or sixth stage is reached, they stand as silent guides to the direction of the old road. All are inscribed, in ornate characters dug out of the stone, with the posthumous name, ending in *reijin*, of the ascetic they commemorate. These multitudes of stones are in fact memorials of former *maeza* and *nakaza*, who climbed the mountain many times, led bands of faithful to the summit, and are now believed to dwell, apotheosised and available to summons, on the slopes of the mountain.

In their lower stages both routes wind up through forests of pine and cryptomeria. Here there are waterfalls, under which the faithful may stand. Shintaki, for example, on the Ōdaki route, drops down from a height in a concentrated jet, in front of a dark cave full of inscribed stones. The force of the water on the bare head of the believer is stunning. Three Heart Sutras, I was told, is the longest anyone may stand it. From the sixth stage the tall trees diminish into the 'crawling' variety of pine tree, *haimatsu*, which spreads itself like a dark green bony lichen over many acres of mountainside. From the eighth stage the trees and all other vegetation cease. The mountain rears itself steeply upwards in a barren waste of lava rocks and cinders, the path punctuated at intervals by stone images of the deities of the mountain. Furious figures from the esoteric Buddhist pantheon, with stiffly erect hair and stamping feet, may be seen side by side with bronze Shinto pigs, their backs transfixed by *gohei* wands.

On the summit the landscape is lunar. Two shrines, one with an antlered roof, the other and altitudinally higher one a stone enclosure surrounding a curious throng of stone images, are separated by a neck of loose white rocks. Beyond the higher shrine a precipice drops down several hundred feet to a dry crater, ringed with a collar of jagged rock. Beyond this, another and larger crater, filled with the green waters of a lake. On this water's edge stands a hut, where the soup is good, and a stone image of the dragon woman. An expanse of rock and waste land to one side of the lake, dotted with odd piles and pyramids of stones, is called Sainokawara, the dry river bed where dead children are believed to pass centuries making little piles of stones.

As on other mountains, the weather changes with startling suddenness. In a moment the landscape is blotted out in a white mist, through which loom only the grey and eerie outline of rocks, pyramids of stones and the antlered roof of the shrine. All distant sounds are deadened. There is only the flapping of a flag placed as an offering on a nearby pile of stones, or the indrawn breath and clapping hands of someone in prayer by the water's edge. A moment later the mist clears and the mountain bursts into strong sunshine, revealing the jagged hills and the green lake below.

Almost anywhere along the route to this summit, in front of one of the statues or inscribed megaliths, one is liable to come across a group of crouching white figures. In their midst, with his back to the statue, stiffly sits a man with a white paper wand in his hands. Strange gasps and bursts of sound may come from his mouth, to which the crouching figures reverently respond. Sometimes his voice is resonant and booming. Sometimes it is a muttered gabble, so low that the man facing him must put his ear close to his mouth to hear what is said. The wand he holds is usually quivering. Sometimes it swishes back and forth like a flag.

Such a sight always betokens an *oza* séance. One of the deities of the mountain, Ontake Daijin, Hakkaizan Daijin, or one of the dragon deities from the lake, Hakuryūsan or Ryūjin, has been called into the party's *nakaza* and induced to speak. Sometimes the utterance takes the form of a dialogue. The deity is asked what weather the party should expect during the next stage, where they should stay the following night, whether all is well with their families at home. A village *kō* may ask about the coming rice harvest, or the typhoons to be expected in the early autumn. A city *kō* may ask how prices may behave in the coming month. Sometimes, however, there is no dialogue; the deity thanks the party for having taken the trouble to come, and delivers a general message of benediction and advice.

Such séances often take place at night in the huts. Many times I have lain awake in the hut by the lake, listening to the sounds, from the room above, of constantly repeated trances; the swish and flap of the medium's wand, the murmur of questions, the strangled groans in which the divine answers are delivered, and the sudden sharp shouts—'E', 'Hyun!' 'Shin!'—with which, again and again in the course of the night, the medium is entranced, restored and reentranced.

The most impressive trances, however, always took place at Kengamine, the topmost shrine. Here among the rocks is a stone enclosure in which stands a curious cluster of stone images. One, with an elongated face reminiscent of the great heads on Easter Island, another, said to represent Sukunabikona, carved with a cloak of feathers. Two or three, more conventionally clad in the tall hat and high collar of court dress, represented various high-ranking deities.

The rocks at the feet of these images are a favourite place for parties to hold a séance. When I first reached this place, in the early afternoon of August 7th, I found the enclosure filled with white figures and the cold air resounding with the clanging of bells and with loud chanting of the *Hannya Shingyō*. Silence suddenly fell, and I saw that one of the party, a muscular young man with curly hair bound round with a white towel, had seated himself with his back to the feathered image, a wand of paper streamers in his hands. In front of him crouched a thin and intense young man, who soon burst in fierce and vibrant tones into the *Hannya Shingyō*, pointing his hands meanwhile in stabbing mudras at the medium's solar plexus. The rest of the party crouched round with bowed heads. The wand in the medium's hands soon began to tremble, and his eyes turned up into his head so that only the whites showed. He then burst into jerky speech. Much of what he said was inaudibly mumbled, but certain passages were not difficult to understand. The divinity seemed to be proffering rather banal advice about the party's journey home. 'Be careful not to slip on the steep places', I heard him say, and 'Take extra care near the eighth stage not to get lost in the mist'. The thin young man, his head bowed, made deferential noises such as a retainer might make on receiving the behests of his lord, while the crouching company murmured from time to time a chorus of thanks for the advice vouchsafed. The muscular medium at length ceased his utterance, only to be seized by the thin man, vigorously thumped on the back, jerked in the joints, and shouted at in sharp monosyllables. Flopping about under this treatment for two or three minutes like a drunken man, the medium eventually stretched himself and stood up. The séance was over. The party burst into a final *Hannya Shingyō* before trooping down the long flight of stone steps and away down the mountainside.

Their place was soon taken by another party, whose *nakaza* was a little old man. He was helped up on to a rock at the feet of one of the images, and hardly was the wand put into his hands than his wrinkled face was convulsed in writhing contortions. His mouth twisted sideways and downwards, his eyes alternately screwed tightly shut or opened staring wide so that only the whites showed. He began to gasp out words, but so low that his followers had to put their ears close to his mouth to hear what he was saying. Finally he seized hold of a young man, pummelled him vigorously on the back, and fell forward inert. When they pulled him to his feet he seemed to have regained consciousness.

The following morning I walked up to the shrine again just before sunrise. The sky was already growing light, with a band of red to the east. All round the mountain lay a sea of dove-grey clouds tossed up into billows and waves, out of which rose, like magic islands, the darker grey forms of other mountain peaks. As the sun rose above the bank of clouds the crowd gathered on the summit began to chant and clap their hands, and in a moment the scene was transformed. The grey air became brilliant and golden, and the mountain islands below turned blue, layer on layer, dark blue turning paler the higher they rose from the clouds, as though a brush dipped in ink on one side had painted them in a single sweep.

I turned from this enchanted view to see inside the shrine a scene of unexampled strangeness. In the dawning light the stone enclosure was thronged with people, and on every rock, in every space between the images, sat a man in a trance. These were not mediums prophesying before a group, as I had seen the day before. They appeared to be working in pairs. Each medium had standing over him a *maeza*, through whose shouts, mantras and mudras he was brought into a trance. I counted among the rocks and stone images seven of these strange pairs working simultaneously.

One pair, poised on the edge of a precipitous slope down to the lake, was particularly remarkable. The *maeza* stood close to the medium, twisting his hands with ferocious intensity into the nine mudras known as *kuji*, repeating as he did so the nine accompanying magic syllables:

Rin-byō-tō-sha-kai-jin-retsu-zai-zen!

At the last syllable his voice rose to a sharp yell, while with two fingers stiffly outstretched he made the nine strokes of the gate, four vertical, five horizontal, through which no evil influences may pass.[10] He then thrust his fingers fiercely forwards towards the medium's stomach in the pointed sword mudra, shouting meanwhile in sharp grunting tones the syllables 'A-UN-A-UN!' These, the first and last letters of the Sanscrit alphabet, are believed to encompass between them the entire universe. He then passed into the Lesser Spell of Fudō:

Nōmaku samanda basarada!

And, several times repeated, the inevitable *Hannya Shingyō*.

The medium, a sickly-looking young man, responded by growing paler and paler, turning his eyes up into his head, and shaking the wand in his hands with increasing violence. His utterance was eventually delivered in so faint a voice that the *maeza* had to put his ear close to the medium's mouth in order to hear. For a minute I was witness to the strange spectacle of several pairs of men seemingly clasped together in close embrace on the craggy edge of the precipice.

The message delivered, the *maeza* restored the medium to consciousness by pulling his joints, pummelling his back, pointing the sword mudra at his stomach and giving vent to loud roars ending with the single syllable SHIN. Then, with curious casualness, they both rose, stretched themselves and strolled away. None of the lay Japanese climbers who had made their way up to the shrine to see the sunrise took the slightest notice of them.

I walked back to the hut by the lake, where I soon fell into a dose. I was woken by strange howls and wails coming from outside, and on looking out of the window saw a trance of great violence taking place by the side of the lake. A woman in white was flinging herself to and fro on the ground, in the throes of what seemed to be an excruciating seizure. Her voice rose to a strangled shriek, while with terrific violence she lashed and flailed the ground with her white wand. A young man appeared to be responding to her shrieks and controlling the direction of her movements. A moment later he himself gave a loud roar, pounded her on the back and jerked her joints. With great ferocity he then performed the Nine Mudras and recited the accompanying syllables. A moment later the women emerged, quiet and smiling as though from a refreshing sleep.

The young men next turned his attention to another woman in the party. Scarcely had he pointed his fingers at her in the sword mudra than she gave a loud shriek and began to writhe to and fro, dashing her body backwards and forwards and flailing the ground with her wand. I heard the young man ask, 'Who is it who has come?' but her reply was an incomprehensible scream. She then gave several remarkable leaps, six or seven inches into the air from a kneeling position, and began to splutter forth words. The only word I could make out was *arigatō*, repeated over and over again, which I took to be the deity thanking the party for having come. After a few minutes of such violent utterance the young man sent the deity away with the usual thumps on the back. It was astonishing to see the woman, after so agonising an expense of energy, come to herself as though she had woken up from a quiet afternoon nap.

I approached the party, which I saw to consist of the young man and twelve women, oddly reminiscent of a witches' coven, and enquired what deity it might be that had possessed the last woman. It was difficult to tell, the young man replied, but it seemed to be the dragon divinity Ryūjin; this was a *kitsui kamisama* or severe deity, who might well produce violent paroxisms if the kind we had just seen. His own name, he informed me, was Ōmomo Yoshio, and he and his party had come all the way from Niigata.

Four years later, entirely by chance, and in the same rocky place by the lake, I met Mr Ōmomo again. He had grown so considerably in stature that I scarcely recognised him. He was both taller and larger. His party too had grown. It was no longer the odd coven of twelve women, but a more conventionally mixed group of some two dozen people. In a couple of hours' time, he informed me, the party would hold an *oza* séance at a place near the topmost shrine called Sanjūrokudōji, the Thirty-six Boys.

At the appointed time, therefore, I made my way to the place. It was a peculiarly lunar spot, set among lava rocks, with a precipice dropping down on one side to invisible depths from which tails of cloud, like volcanic smoke, kept mysteriously rising and vanishing. To the other side lay the flat basin of a crater, ringed round with craggy rocks, and beyond it a second crater, with a green lake and a patch of unmelted snow.

Against this unearthly background the party crouched down among the rocks, with Mr Ōmomo, a wand in his hands, prominently to the fore. For several minutes they recited loudly. Then, suddenly and without the slightest warning, Mr Ōmomo whipped round to face the party. His face was scarcely recognisable. His eyes had disappeared into his head, and the wand in his hands swished to and fro. In a resonant booming voice, and in a high literary speech like the language of the Nō plays, he began to speak.

There was no dialogue, for there was no *maeza* to bring Mr Ōmomo into his trance and put questions to him. Instead, the divinity addressed each member of the *kō* in turn, delivering warnings and advice. One by one each man or woman approached, prostrated himself before the entranced figure and for two or three minutes received a personal message.

The voice continued to resound among the rocks for nearly half an hour. It was the longest trance I had ever witnessed. Eventually by massage and thumping Mr Ōmomo was restored to himself, and the wand was with some difficulty extracted from his convulsively clutched hands.

Puzzled at first as to why he should have changed from the role of *maeza*, which he had performed four years before, to that of *nakaza*, I soon realised that in an unusual manner he combined in himself both roles at once. As a medium he was incomparably more majestic and powerful than the passive and nondescript figures so often seen. At the same time he was his own *maeza*. He had brought himself into his trance, and was clearly the undisputed leader of the party.

I enquired what deity it was that had spoken for so long. Gakkai Reijin, he replied, a former *sendatsu* of the Ontake cult who had died some twenty years before. Nearly always the deity who possessed him was Gakkai Reijin, for with this spirit he stood in a relation of close affinity. His first 'call', seventeen years before, had been a spontaneous waking vision, overwhelmingly powerful, of the inscribed stone set up to Gakkai Reijin at the fifth stage of the climb. At that time he had never climbed Mr Ontake and never heard of Gakkai Reijin. But a month or two later he had made the pilgrimage and lo, there was the inscribed stone standing just as he had seen it in his vision.

His *kō*, he told me, met for a séance four times in every month, when usually it was Gakkai Reijin who appeared to guide and instruct them. But Mt Ontake itself they climbed only once a year.

Another interesting *kō* which I encountered in the hut by the lake was composed entirely of actors and musicians. Their leader was Yoshimura Ijurō, the greatest living exponent, I was told, of the *nagauta* style of chanting, whose work had been honoured as a 'formless national treasure'. Several tall and good-looking young men in the party were his pupils. The party's *maeza* was an ancient man of eighty-four with a long beard but a physique of extraordinary strength and agility, who had made the climb no less than fifty-one times. The medium was the old man's daughter. She was very accomplished and strong, they told me, taking only thirty seconds to become possessed. Their deity was Hakuryūsan, a dragon who lived in the third lake. He was infallible, one of the young men assured me, especially in his weather forecasts. Only the day before he had warned them to hurry as quickly as they could to the sixth hut or they would get wet. Sure enough, hardly were they safely inside the hut than it began to rain heavily. Never, he declared with great intensity, would he dream of taking any important step in his life without first consulting Hakuryūsan. His career as a *nagauta* chanter had been approved by Hakuryūsan, and so, when the right time came, would his bride.

Later I accompanied this party down to the fourth stage on the Kurosawa route. There under the Fudō waterfall, they said, Hakuryūsan would make his last appearance to them. They all changed into white loincloths or kimonos and made their way to the place where three jets of water fell from an embrasure hollowed out of the rock. The ancient *maeza*, clad only in a loincloth, was the first to stand here. The water splashed off his head with such force, as he stood with his white beard reciting spells, that it seemed as though a halo of white light shone all round him. The medium then took his place, standing under the jet of water looking wild and strange, her black hair streaming down over her wet kimono and her eyes open and staring. The old man stood in front of her murmuring and shouting, pointing his fingers at her in the stabbing mudras. When she was fully entranced, each member of the party came in turn to receive a final benediction from Hakuryūsan. This was bestowed by the medium in the form of thumps on the back and rubs with her rosary.

The whole party thus blessed, the medium was restored to herself, the party changed into dry white clothes and set off in taxis, previously bespoken, to catch the night train from Fukushima back to Tokyo.

I understood afterwards that the Ontake cult is popular among those whose profession is the stage. A dancer of incredible elegance, Takehara Han, told me that she used until she was over fifty to make the climb every summer. She showed me photographs of herself taken in the course of the pilgrimage, and I marvelled, remembering my own dirty and dishevelled appearance, to see how she had made her white attire seem like an elegant mode designed specially for herself, and how, on the most exhaustingly steep and cindery slopes near the summit, she never lost her dancer's immaculate grace and poise.

In the small hours of the morning of August 8th a magic bonfire known as *Shinkasai* is lit on the barren neck of land near the summit. It is one of the principal annual rituals of the Ontake cult, and in 1963 we were warned that the hut was likely to be so crowded that night with pilgrims that there would be no space to lie down. We would have to doze back-to-back in a sitting position. In fact the crowds proved less than on an ordinary night, since the news of a typhoon threatened off the coast of Kyūshū had discouraged people from making the climb. Sleep was nevertheless out of the question, for all night long the sounds of flapping wands, jingling bells and bursts of chanting never ceased. New parties arrived in the darkness and paid their respects with bells and mantras to the image on the edge of the lake. The party ensconced in the room above possessed an indefatigable medium, whose gutteral grunts and swishing wand continued uninterrupted until past midnight.

At 1.30 a.m. a small party set out from the hut to walk to the place of the fire. The moon had risen high in the sky, almost perfectly round, and so bright that we could follow the rocky path round the mountain without needing any other light. I saw our shadows fall, in single file, fantastically long and black down the rocky slope into the ravine, while far below the peak of Mikasayama, a symmetrical cone like one of the straw hats of the faithful, rose like an island out of a sea of white mist.

When we reached the place where the fire was to be lit,

already a great crowd of people were waiting, dressed entirely in white. Three curious wooden circles, like an intricate latticed woodhenge, rose a little higher than a man and about ten feet across. I had examined them a few hours earlier, in daylight, and had seen that they were constructed entirely from the small slips of pine wood called *gomagi*, just big enough to accommodate a man's name, age and heart's desire, written with a brush. Most of the wishes were stereo-typed and impersonal: freedom from illness, harmony at home, prosperity in the family business. They had all, many thousands of them, been carried up the mountainside on the previous day, and had been built into the circles by a team of believers a few hours before.

Flaring torches lit up the three wooden rings and the white crowd of believers stretching up the hill behind, while before us reared a craggy hill crowned with a great block of lava, like a fortress against the moonlit sky. Further along the skyline rose the black and antlered silhouette of the shrine.

At two o'clock the patriarch of the sect, Mr Watanabe, appeared in front of the central circle. In a resounding voice he read an invocation to the *kami*, making meanwhile lunges and sweeps with a long sword. The crowd of believers on the hillside broke into a chorus of chanting, ringing their bells to the rhythm of the chant.

Two figures in white with long flaring torches then set light to the middle ring. The delicate latticework burst into flames, and soon the whole intricate structure was marvel-lously visible, every tiny slip of wood showing red and distinct against the black. The two other wooden circles then caught fire, and soon the flames leapt high into the sky, illuminating red and yellow the chanting crowd of people behind. For some ten minutes the flames burnt fiercely, then died down into red flickering rings.

Several figures in white appeared and began to run, indeed scamper, round and round the dying circles. One of them I recognised to be Mr Ōmomo. From my position on the hillside I could see the figures still running as the flames died down to a glow, and the craggy landscape returned to its former lunar whiteness.

By way of postscript, I append some notes from my last

ascent of the mountain, in August 1967. In four years the mountain had suffered a devastating change. A large 'driveway' or motor road had been carved out of the mountainside as far as the seventh stage, Tanohara. You need not walk at all, we were told, before Tanohara, and there you will find a comfortable hotel. What about the *old* road, we enquired. It is still there of course, they said, but no one uses it now.

We set out to find the old road, and I saw at once that what they had said was true. Up the hairpin bends of the new road there roared a stream of traffic, taxis, cars, buses hired by *kō*, with straw hats and wooden poles projecting from the windows. A cloud of white dust hung like a pall over the track, obscuring the view of the mountain, thickly coating the trees and plants on either side. Along this road no one at all was actually walking.

Nor was a single white figure to be seen on the old road, when at length after some difficulty we found it. It led straight up the mountainside, out of the forest and over some high rolling hills covered with long grass and wild lilies. An ancient and deserted trackway it now seemed, green underfoot and flanked on either side with flowers and clusters of inscribed stones. It was utterly quiet. No one seemed to have trodden there for years, and the call of the *hokekyō* bird was the only sound to be heard. The pilgrims were a mile or so away, whirled upwards in dust and noise.

At Tanohara, in place of the sprawling wooden hut in the forest that I remembered from four years before, stood a streamlined concrete structure, in the midst of a concrete car park full of taxis and buses. Above this point everyone had to walk. But even here were significant signs of change. We had not been going long before we encountered an enormous *kō* from Kyoto, 400 strong and led by a huge man reminiscent of a Kabuki actor or *sumō* wrestler. He stood on a rock at the side of the path, bellowing the *rokkon shōjō* chant in a voice which seemed supernaturally resonant until I saw that he was in fact shouting through a microphone attached to a powerful loudspeaker. His huge flock moved slowly and ponderously upwards. They had no medium, we were told. Their leader always told them what to do.

That night we saw him again at the Shinkasai, itself also significantly changed. Gone was the red and white scene of four years before, the unaided human voices rising in the moonlit air, the rings of fire fiercely burning, the patriarch brandishing his sword before the latticed flames. Instead, dominating the scene, was the microphone, the blue flash of cameras, the nerveless beam of the television searchlight. Hugely amplified, the voice of the actor-wrestler from Kyoto ceaselessly chattered, warning, admonishing, introducing, *explaining* every step of the rite to the crowd surrounding him, as a radio commentator explains a baseball match or an unfamiliar ceremony. Ruthlessly he had destroyed the magic of the rite. Before his magnified voice, its enchantment withered into 'information', its power and beauty shrivelled into commonplace movements and sounds.

Very soon, I was confidently told, there would be a téléférique 'ropeway' to the top of the mountain. No one would then have to climb at all, and the craters would be filled with teahouses, from which cheerful amplified music would banish loneliness. Eventually the trances would disappear and Ontake would join the company of those other erstwhile holy mountains where only the odd name or the odd inscribed stone survives to remind the lay climber that in the past the ground beneath his feet was considered so holy that only the duly purified might tread there.

Exorcism

We have now arrived at the last stage of our investigation, the rituals whereby the powers of both the ascetic and the medium are used to deal with the lower spiritual entities which cause the symptoms of demoniacal possession. Already we have observed two or three examples of the manner in which a professional ascetic healer, alone and unaided, casts out the foxes and ghosts which cause possession. We now examine those older methods of exorcism whereby the exorcist does not confront the sufferer directly, but forces the spirit to transfer itself into the body of a medium, through whose mouth it must name itself and hold dialogue with him. Once more, therefore, we are concerned with the ritual of *yorigitō*, but it is directed now not towards prayer and petition to a superior spiritual being, but to the banishment and restitution of an inferior one.

We mentioned in a previous chapter that the use of a medium as a mere passive vehicle, a virtual zombie through whose mouth the spirit may speak, can be traced back to the ninth century when the doctrines and spells of esoteric Buddhism were first brought to Japan from China. We have seen too that the Abisha ritual prescribed the use of unblemished children for this purpose; bathed, dressed, anointed, purified and censed, they would tell one everything one wished to know of hidden and future things.

The use of children, untrained girls and even the elegant ladies of the court for this extraordinary purpose is recorded in many places in the literature of the Heian period. More often than as organs of prophesy, however, such people are found serving as mediums for the ascetic healers of the time; as vessels into whom the malignant spirit could be transferred from the body of the patient, and through whom it could be brought to subjection.

The ascetic exorcist at this time was usually either a priest of the Tendai or Shingon sect, or one of the *yamabushi* or *genja* who had accomplished noteworthy penances and austerities in the hills. Such people were often described as wild, uncouth and fierce—'yamabushi of the most repulsive and ferocious aspect' are recorded as summoned to the bedside of Kashiwagi in the 36th chapter of the *Genji Monogatari*.[1] The elegant priest described by Sei Shōnagon in her *Pillow Book*, compiled at the end of the tenth century, is exceptional. This vivid vignette of an exorcism shows us exactly what use was made of the medium at this time.

We see a house surrounded by trees and opening on to a garden. Inside, invisible in an inner room, lies someone sorely afflicted by an evil possession. A Buddhist priest in an extremely elegant dark brown robe, a clove-dyed fan in his hand, sits intoning the *Senju Darani* or Spell of the Thousand-handed Kannon. The medium is 'a rather heavily built girl with a good head of hair'. Eventually the power of the spell forces the spirit to leave the patient and enter into the girl, who accordingly wails, screams and falls prostrate on the floor in such a manner that her clothing is embarrassingly disordered. The patient is soon pronounced to be better, the medium regains consciousness, and the priest, before whom the household prostrates itself in awe, takes an urbane leave promising to come again soon.[2]

Another description of an exorcism occurs in the diary of Murasaki Shikibu, the celebrated writer of the *Genji Monogatari*. The Empress Akiko lies in labour so difficult and painful that a case of possession is suspected. Not one but many exorcists, Buddhist abbots and clerics, wild mountain ascetics specially brought down from their retreats in the hills, were shouting spells at the tops of their voices. Several court ladies had offered their services as mediums, and each one lay behind a screen with an exorcist allotted to her. The night having passed in a frightful hubbub of chanting, eventually towards morning the Empress was safely delivered of a son. The screams of the spirits were most uncanny to hear, wrote Murasaki, and one was so strong that it actually threw one of the exorcising priests to the ground. Yet none of the ladies acting as medium were molested in any way, and all were lamenting that their services had not proved more effective.[3]

Murasaki's account, in the second *Wakana* chapter of

Genji, of the treatment given to the sick lady Murasaki by a child medium is probably as authentic as the description in her diary. After a long struggle the spirit molesting the lady was transferred by the spells and fire rituals of the priests into the body of a small boy. The boy raved and raged, the hair on his head stood upright, great tears trickled down his cheeks, but through his mouth there was eventually spoken a terrifyingly comprehensible message which enabled them at once to identify the spirit who was causing the trouble.[4]

Before we proceed to describe how this method of exorcism has still survived to the present day in the practice of the Nichiren sect of Buddhism, let us first review a little more consistently than we have so far done the varied symptoms subsumed under the term 'possession'. Four different kinds seem to me to be usefully distinguished in Japan.

First, we have those symptoms where the body alone is affected. Aches, mysterious pains, lumbago, hacking coughs, fainting fits, loss of appetite, inexplicable fevers, all these are even now commonly laid at the door of spiritual agencies. Most of the cases recorded in Heian literature, moreover, seem to have been of this type. Depression, the enfeebled and morbid condition which apparently overtook so many of the elegant inhabitants of the capital, the discomforts of pregnancy and the difficulties of childbirth, were frequently attributed to the work of some angry or resentful spirit.

Secondly, there are symptoms which appear to signify mental imbalance but which do not bring about any trance or dissociation. Hallucinations, both visual and auditory, are a case in point. The patient complains of voices speaking in her ear, but remains nevertheless rooted in her own personality.

Thirdly, we have symptoms of altered personality, of mental states which could be described as trance, but in which no intruding entity speaks through the patient's mouth. A distressing report in the journal *Minzoku to Rekishi* of 1922 describes a case of multiple possession on just these lines. First the trusty servant, then the wife, then the eldest daughter of the family fell victim to the malady, which was unhesitatingly attributed to a fox. In each case the facial expression changed, with eyes upturned and mouth pouting into a snout. All three victims ate enormously, grabbing the food with their hands and stuffing it into their mouths. All three lost all memory, all sense of personal cleanliness and all power of speech. All exorcism was in vain and the family was utterly ruined.[5]

Lastly, we have the symptoms which are more generally recognised as those of possession, in which another entity, with a different voice and a different personality, speaks through the patient's mouth. Such cases are in fact comparatively rare, far less frequently encountered than those in the other three categories. Still among the best-described examples are those which Dr Baelz treated in his hospital in Tokyo in the 1890s. Over the years he admitted several women suffering from fox possession, through whose mouths the fox spoke in a dry cracked voice, and in uncouth and brutal terms. He describes one case in which a violent altercation took place between the fox and its unfortunate hostess. The fox, speaking with far more wit and cleverness than could be expected from the simple-minded woman he was possessing, continued a stream of rude invective for several minutes. Now and then the woman in her own voice besought him to be quiet and to treat the doctors with more respect. But her admonitions were unavailing, and it was only when after ten minutes the fox became bored that the woman was able to come to herself and beg with tears for forgiveness for the outrageous conduct of the fox.[6]

We may note in passing that the Catholic Church now recognises as cases of possession only those corresponding to those in our fourth category.[7] In the past it frequently attributed cases in the other three categories to the work of demons, but these are now considered to be explicable in terms of modern science. In Japan, however, the full range of symptoms may still be found classed as possession, and to the cure of such afflictions in Nichiren Buddhist temples today we now turn.

The Nichiren sect has long boasted a tradition of exorcist practices based on the sect's holy scripture, the Lotus Sutra.[8] The practices are carried out principally by priests of the Nakayama branch of the sect, which has its head temple at Hokekyōji in Chiba prefecture. Here, however, the *yorigitō* method making use of a *dairi* or medium has largely been abandoned in favour of a direct confrontation between exorcist and patient. In the temple of Hōkōji in Kanazawa, however, the older method still survives.

Like other ascetics in Japan, the Nichiren priests have to undergo a preliminary period of austerities before they are believed to be endued with the necessary power to deal with inferior spirits. For them, however, the regime is a particularly excruciating one. Known as the hundred days *aragyō* or rough austerities, it is carried out every winter either on the summit of Mt Minobu, the mountain not far from Fuji to which Nichiren retired in his old age, or in a secluded temple in the precincts of the Hokekyōji in Chiba prefecture.

As related to me by Hotta Ryūshō Shōnin, the incumbent of the Kanazawa temple, the hundred days *aragyō* start on November 1st and continue throughout the coldest days of the winter until well into the following February. The regime is as follows. The days starts at 3 a.m. with a bout of cold water *mizugori*. The exercitant priests, wearing only a loincloth, tip over their heads tub after tub of cold water. This exercise is repeated every three hours until 9 p.m., making in all seven times a day. Only two meals a day are allowed, and those consist only of thin rice gruel. The rest of the time is entirely taken up with the chanting of the Lotus Sutra and with practice in the use of the *bokken* or magic castanets. This peculiar instrument, a flat piece of wood with a ball attached, makes a sharp resonant click held to have a powerful effect on spiritual beings.

The last spell of Lotus chanting ends at 11 p.m., so that four hours sleep a night is all that is allowed to the exercising priests. Shaving and cutting the hair are prohibited throughout the hundred days, so that those who endure the course emerge on the last day with long hair and straggling beards. From the commemorative photograph which the Shōnin showed me I could see that his hair had gone prematurely white with the strain of the penances. And indeed, what with the appalling cold, the reduced diet, the lack of sleep and the extreme pain caused by the correct straight-armed manipulation of the *bokken*, the Nichiren regime is one of the most taxing and exhausting still to be found in Japan.

The Shōnin had undergone the treatment no less than five times on the summit of Mt Minobu, and was hence revered throughout the district for his powers. In his temple in Kanazawa a service of exorcism was held every morning throughout the year, which on average a dozen patients would attend, suffering from a variety of symptoms which they had reason to lay at the door of some spiritual agency.

When I visited the temple in the summer of 1967 the medium, who had served every day in this capacity for a number of years, was the Shōnin's mother. During the exorcism which I witnessed she did heavy duty, for in that one morning a total of one fox, three snakes, one jealous woman, one frantic man and one cat were 'called up' to speak through her mouth.

The ritual started at 9.30 in the morning with a dozen patients, mostly women, sitting at the back of the hall banging on drums until the Shōnin, clad in immaculate white, entered and took up his seat in front of the altar. For some minutes he recited passages from the Lotus Sutra in a nasal voice, rapping sharply meanwhile on the shelf in front of him with a wooden mallet.

Next there entered the medium, who knelt at the foot of the dais on which he was sitting. He then turned to face the room with a rosary in his hand.

In the procedure which followed the cases fell into three different and distinct kinds.

First, the Shōnin turned to a pile of papers lying next to him, on which were written problems submitted by patients and petitioners in the congregation. These, one by one, the Shōnin read aloud, and at once, in a firm and unhesitating voice, the medium provided an answer.

Most of the questions concerned sickness. My mother is suffering from a terrible pain in her back; what is causing it? My old father has awful stomach cramps in the middle of the night; what is causing them? I have a persistent voice talking in my ear and saying dreadful things; what is it?

A reply came immediately from the medium. Your mother simply has an attack of lumbago caused by sitting in a draught; her pain is not due to possession of any kind and she will soon recover if you keep her warm and quiet. Your father's cramps are caused by an unhappy ancestral ghost; he should come into the temple and receive the proper treatment. The voice speaking in your ear is that of a fox; you must come into the temple in order to get rid of it.

Other questions concerned missing persons and things. Here is an example. A few days ago my husband went to climb a certain mountain and has not yet come back. What has become of him? The answer came: you are afraid that he has met with an accident. There has been no accident. Your husband climbed the mountain in order to commit suicide. You will find his body about 500 metres from the summit on the east side.

The being who was giving those authoritative answers through the medium, I was afterwards informed, was Kumaō Daimyōjin, the guardian deity of the temple. It was he who determined the first step of every exorcism, the identification of the molesting spirit. It was he who pronounced whether the patient's trouble was spiritual in origin or not, and hence whether she needed to come into the temple to be cured, or was simply overtired and needed a rest. It was he too who distinguished the nature of the possessing spirit, and pronounced it to be a fox, snake or neglected ghost.

In this procedure, therefore, no need arose to force the spirit to name itself and state the reasons for its conduct, preliminaries which we shall find to be essential in the other, more direct method of Nichiren exorcism.

These written questions once disposed of, the Shōnin moved on to the second and most difficult stage of the proceedings. These were the cases of possession called and questioned for the first time. At this early stage the spirit required the full treatment known in the Nichiren sect as *zaishō-shōmetsu*, or the annihilation of sin-hindrances.

The Shōnin started by reading out the name and age of the patient. Then he recited in nasal tones a succession of passages from the Lotus Sutra and a good many repetitions of the *daimoku* or sacred formula, at the same time striking sparks from a flint and making rapid passes and sharp clicks on the *bokken*. These were all devices, I was told, calculated to force the spirit to leave the body of the patient at the back of the hall and to enter that of the medium, through whose mouth alone it could speak and be brought to submission.

The first case to come up was a male fox. It spoke through the medium's mouth in strong uncouth tones. As she gave utterance to these words the old lady crouched down on the floor with her hands clenched together in front of her, a position which I gathered was a common one for foxes to adopt, the clenched hands representing paws. A short dialogue took place between the Shōnin and the fox, in which the latter seemed chiefly to be begging for forgiveness, uttering over and over again the words, '*Kannin shite hoshii*!' The Shōnin then resumed his recitation of the sacred formula, the fox joining in in a singsong voice.

The next case to come up was the spirit of a dead man. The medium as she transmitted his utterances manifested extraordinary and exhausting emotion. She sobbed and wept, leaning forward so that long streams of saliva and mucus dangled from her nose and mouth. It was impossible for me to understand the low, choking gasps in which she spoke, and even the Shōnin had to bend forward several times in order to hear properly. But afterwards I was told that the patient, one of the women sitting at the back of the hall, was possessed by the spirit of her dead husband. Tormented with anxiety about the welfare of his family, whom he had left without adequate provision and who were suffering from poverty and neglect, he had possessed his widow in order to draw attention to his feelings.

Throughout the dialogue the Shōnin adopted a sympathetic and reassuring attitude. Poised on his dais above the medium, he nodded and smiled compassionately, now and then repeating the medium's words as though to make sure he had understood them properly. At the end of the colloquy the spirit's anxiety's seemed allayed, for it too began to sob for forgiveness. The usual sparks, magic passes of the *bokken* and recitations of the sacred formula ended the calling.

Next there was a jealous woman worrying about the welfare of her children. She had possessed a short dumpy woman who had apparently been charged to look after them. Again the medium flopped forward, sobbing out broken words in praise of the sutra and begging for forgiveness.

In this case the patient came forward from the back of the hall to ask questions of the spirit. This was permitted provided she asked the questions through the Shōnin, who alone could phrase them to the spirit in the right way.

With these three cases the second and most exhausting stage of the morning's proceedings were concluded. The third stage, comprising cases called for the second, third or fourth time, was much less taxing. Three snakes and one cat appeared in this category, one after the other in rapid succession. All four were brief and simple. There was no dialogue, no sobbing for forgiveness. The medium scarcely opened her mouth while the Shōnin performed his recitations. After the cathartic emotion of the first calling, I was told, the spirit needed to be called several more times in order to listen to the holy reading of the Lotus Sutra before it could be properly laid to rest.

The morning's session ended at about eleven o'clock with more drumming and rapping and reciting, the medium quietly and without ceremony leaving the hall after wiping her face.

Later in the morning this remarkable and courteous lady told me her story. Soon after her marriage she had fallen ill with tuberculosis of the spine. For four months she lay in hospital and all hope of her recovery had been abandoned. Someone then advised her as a last resort to visit the temple. She was conveyed there, and the cause of her trouble quickly discovered to be possession by a remote ancestor who had been a riding master in the service of a certain feudal lord. He had been drowned while trying to ford a flooded river on his horse, and had since been unable to achieve rest. At once the correct treatment of exorcism was started, and within a week she was well again.

Her marriage, however, was not a happy one. Her husband kept in the house no less than three concubines, who between them produced several children. She herself bore six children, but when it came to dividing the property the concubine's children were treated on a par with her own. When she protested she was driven out of the house. Taking with her her six children and her mother she took refuge in the temple. The Shōnin who was the incumbent of the temple at the time had just lost his wife, so before very long she married him. The present incumbent, Ryūshō Shōnin, was her son by this second husband.

Many mediums, she knew, remembered nothing of what they said in their trance state, but she remembered everything. She remembered the rude and uncouth words the fox had uttered through her mouth that morning. She remembered the tears running down her chin and the streams of saliva dripping from her mouth. Sometimes she 'received' the spirit too strongly and fell ill. But on the whole, as her long service in the temple attested, her health was remarkably good.

The ancient method of exorcism just described stands in interesting contrast with the techniques now employed by the Nakayama branch of the Nichiren sect, and which I witnessed on several occasions in 1963 in the temple of Barakisan Myōgyōji in Chiba prefecture.

In this temple they abandoned the use of the medium about a century ago, on the score that the spirit often refused to be transferred from the body of the patient so that no communication with it could take place. Their present more reliable method, whereby the exorcising priest directly confronts the patient, had been originally devised by Nichijun Shōnin, a priest celebrated during the last century for his remarkable powers.

The Myōgyōji temple differs from the one in Kanazawa in so far as the patients if they so wish are able to board in the temple for days or even weeks until they are completely cured. A large dormitory wing in the precincts is capable of accommodating several dozen people, and includes a large room for the daily recitation practice.

An important feature of the Myōgyōji method is that the patient herself must make strenuous efforts to cooperate with the exorcist. This she does by reciting, virtually all day long with only short intervals for rest, meals and the twice-daily services, the powerful formula *Nammyōhō rengekyō*, known as the *daimoku* and particularly venerated by the Nichiren sect. Indeed, no sooner had I walked through the gate of the temple than I could hear, from a distant wing, the sounds of a big drum beating and a chorus of voices repeating over and over again the mystic syllables. The power of the formula, it was later explained to me, worked on the evil entity inside the patient in such a way as to transform its nature and cause it to wish to leave its wrong abode. Eventually the patient's condition would become ripe for *o-shirabe*, the investigation or dialogue by which its final submission was achieved.

At eleven o'clock there was a loud blast on a siren and all the resident patients trooped into a long narrow room with an altar at one end and open on one side to the garden. A notice hung from the ceiling with instructions that everyone should at all times during the service keep their eyes shut and their hands clasped together. These orders were obediently followed by the quiet rows of patients, who numbered about twenty and who appeared to be mostly housewives in their thirties.

Presently the Abbot, Nichiyū Shōnin, swept into the room, resplendent in voluminous white muslin and a cope of red brocade embroidered with a pattern of white wheels. For ten minutes, in stern and resounding tones, he recited passages from the Lotus Sutra. Then suddenly he wheeled round to face the rows of patients, his right hand with the wooden *bokken* upraised in an impressive and menacing gesture. His arm, held stiff and straight in front of him, then began to flash to and fro in magical passes, while piercingly sharp wooden clacks came from the *bokken*.

At once several members of the congregation began to make convulsive movements. Some began to shake their clasped hands to and fro. One woman in the front row began to make writhing movements with her body, her clasped hands held above her head, while another began violently to jig up and down on her heels.

In a stern and threatening manner the Abbot addressed the latter woman:

'You, Fukuhara Michiko, aged thirty-five . . .'

At once the jigging movements became more frantic while her hands jerked up and down like flails. Pointing the *bokken* menacingly at her, the Abbot struck several sharp clacks, at the same time saying fiercely, '*Aratamemasu*'. By this word, which means change for the better, turn over a new leaf, he adjured the entity inside the woman. After a few seconds a choking sound came from her mouth and she repeated in a strangled voice the syllables *a-ra-ta-me-masu*.

The Abbot's next question, uttered in the same stern voice, was:

'How many years ago did you come into this woman?'

He had to repeat it several times—'*nannen mae kara . . . nannen mae kara . . .*'—with more fierce clacks on the *bokken* and fierce interpolations such as, 'Come on, I can't stand here waiting all day for the likes of *you*.' Eventually the choking voice gasped out, '*Sannen*', three years.

The Abbot made a business-like note with a brush and asked,

'Are you possessing anyone else besides this woman? Any of her relatives? Well?' A loud sharp clack and at last a strangled 'no' came from the woman's mouth.

The next question was, '*Where* did you first possess her?'

To this came the vague reply, 'Tokyo', which did not satisfy the Abbot at all. '*Ku wa nani ka?*'—what ward, he peremptorily demanded.

'Se-ta-ga-ya-ku', came the halting reply.

'What street?'

'Fu-ne-ga-o-ka'.

Next, '*Why* did you possess her? You ought to know that a human being is no place for the likes of you. Did you do it out of spite, or because you had nowhere else to go, or because you wanted something?'

The answer to this important question took a long time to come, but at last the syllables *u-ra-mi*, spite, were sobbed out.

The Abbot then for several minutes gave it a good scolding. 'Very, very bad and wrong of you', he repeated several times. Eventually he said,

'Well now, you're going to leave her, aren't you? When? In a month? In a week?'

There was another long pause while the *bokken* clacked threateningly. At length the strangled voice said, 'I'll go now'.

'Now. Right. You'll go away and let her get healthy and

309

fat again, will you? Look how thin and ill she has been since you have been troubling her. Promise? Promise?'

'*Ma-mo-ri-masu*', yes I promise. This was repeated three times, the woman's voice rising to a shriek. Then she collapsed and lay inert on the floor.

The Abbot made another brisk note or two with a brush, and turned to the woman sitting next to her in the front row. A similar dialogue began, but the woman's answers became more and more incoherent, the pauses longer, the sobbing moans louder. At length the Abbot decided that she was not yet ripe for the full treatment, and with a few stern words dismissed her until the following day. Turning once more to the altar, he recited more Lotus Sutra passages before sweeping impressively out of the room.

The exorcised woman sat limp and dazed on the floor while the rest of the company came up and solemnly congratulated her, their heads bowed down to the floor. They all then filed back to their own quarters to resume their recitation discipline.

For about a quarter of an hour they recited the *Nammyōhō* formula, loudly and with fierce concentration to the accompaniment of a rhythmic banging on two large drums. They then rested for a few minutes, after politely thanking the drummers. During one of these intervals several of them came over to the corner where I was watching and talked to me. One woman had lost her voice with so much loud chanting, but told me in a cracked whisper that she had come into the temple because she had been quarrelling with her husband, in a manner so uncontrollable as to make her suspect a possession. Another told me that her visit to the temple that day was a thank offering. Three years ago she had had a bad breakdown and fit of possession after her husband had died. She had come into the temple where her cure had been so complete that she had made a regular pilgrimage of gratitude once a month ever since. Another old lady discoursed on the wonderful powers of the Abbot. He never ate meat or fish, he had never married, he had done six winters of the *aragyō* at Hokekyōji. There were very few cases which proved beyond his powers. Nevertheless, everyone always had to play their own part in reciting the formula with might and main. Unless one made truly desperate efforts oneself, there was little that the Abbot could do to help. With that they all went back to the next bout of chanting.

Later in the day the Abbot received me in a beautiful room opening on to a garden with a pool full of carp, and explained the order of questions by which he conducted his investigation.

The first question was always 'Aratamemasu?'—are you going to turn over a new leaf? Usually by that stage the possessing entity answered Yes. Occasionally it answered No, in which case he would have to continue his *settoku*, persuasion, for half an hour or even an hour before it finally capitulated.

Then he needed to know how long it had been molesting the patient. Sometimes extraordinary answers such as fifteen years were given to this question. Next he needed to know what form its attack was taking. Was it causing illness to its host's mind or body, or was it causing general family misfortune? It often happened that one member of a family might be possessed for the misdemeanours of another. There was the celebrated case during the Meiji period, for example, in which the manager of the Noda Shōyu factory found that for no apparent reason all his soy beans were going bad. He had come into the temple to see whether the cause could be a spiritual one, where they soon discovered that his household *kami* had been offended by the way in which his son, intoxicated with the western knowledge so fashionable at the time, had insulted its shrine. The correct steps were at once taken to remedy the situation, after which the factory prospered.

The next question in the catechism was, where had the entity first possessed the patient. For this he required as nearly as possible the precise address.

Next he required the important information as to why it had possessed the patient. Was it *urami*, spite, or *tatari*, a curse wrought in revenge for an insult? Foxes offended by being woken from an afternoon nap, *kami* displeased by cavalier treatment of their shrine, were examples of *tatari* possession. Or was it *tanomi*, a request? An example of the latter might be a dead ancestor who felt that his descendants were neglecting his due obsequies, and who possessed some member of the family in order to draw attention to this dereliction of duty.

This answer to this last question determined the course of what followed. *Urami*, spite, required a good scolding. *Tatari* required both a scolding and a promise that the cause of the offence would be removed. A *tanomi* likewise required an undertaking that the request would be fulfilled. Here, however, further bargaining was sometimes necessary. A fox might demand, for example, five slices of fried bean curd before it would agree to leave its host.

What was always necessary, whether the being demanded it or not, was that a small shrine should be set up to the being and worship paid to it every day. Neglect the shrine only a little, and the entity would soon revert to its former evil ways.

This brief account of the Nichiren methods of exorcism may be concluded with one or two random reflections. In all districts of Japan where cases of malignant possession occur, the large majority of the patients are always women. In both the temples where I witnessed the ritual of exorcism there was an overwhelming preponderance of women among the sufferers. And of these, a large proportion were young housewives between the ages of twenty-five and thirty-five. The same phenomenon appears to obtain elsewhere. The private ascetic healers to whom I talked, Mrs Matsuyama and Mrs Nakano, for example, assured me that the great majority of their patients were women.

May we see in Japan, therefore, another example of the theory put forward by Professor Lewis, that symptoms of malevolent spirit possession are an unconscious attempt by women to protest against neglect and oppression in a society largely dominated by men? By exhibiting symptoms of spirit possession, Somali women, for example, can force their neglectful and stingy husbands to take notice of them, to spend large sums of money on the expensive treatment required, public performances of special music and dancing which must be paid for handsomely, or even to buy the expensive objects which the possessing spirit demands through the woman's mouth. These objects are often exactly

what the woman has long wished to possess with her conscious mind, a new sewing machine or a cake of soap. For
a short time, therefore, the woman becomes the centre of
attention in a manner which her husband cannot refuse or
gainsay.[9]

It is tempting to see parallels with these African cases in
Japan, but the analogy is not altogether appropriate.

In the first place, the possessed woman does not in a
public and flamboyant manner make a spectacle of herself
before her male relatives. The Nichiren rituals in temples
are unobtrusive and quiet. The private exorcists such as
Mrs Matsuyama who operate in their own houses are
likewise unobtrusive. None of the patients there could derive
any satisfaction from becoming the unwonted centre of
attention among usually neglectful men.

Nor are the rewards demanded by the spirit comparable
with the sewing machines or soap demanded by the Somali
women. Slices of fried bean curd are delicacies of which
foxes, not women, are passionately fond. And the little
shrine—what good will that be to the woman after her
recovery?

If we follow Professor Oesterreich's large book on possession we will realise that it is possible for the psyche to split
into multiple autonomous parts, each with its own personality. When one of these parts is too much repressed by the
conventions of family and society—and let us not forget that
young married housewives are among the most oppressed
people in Japanese society—it is apt to force its way to the
surface of the mind, upsetting the normal balance of the
personality and behaving in exactly the manner most
calculated to offend accepted convention. But once this
suppressed and neglected side is accepted and acknowledged,
the mind may once more return to its former balance.

Do we not see in the little shrine, and in the act of daily
worship performed there, exactly the attentions that might
be needed to restore order? The fox, snake or ghost, seen as
neglected, amoral but autonomous parts of the mind, can be
transformed by such means from a state of rebellion, uttering
rude, shocking and obscene invective, to a power for protection and good. It is interesting to note, in support of this

theory, that cases of fox possession only rarely find their way into mental hospitals in Japan. The patients still prefer the drama of the therapy to be conducted in religious terms, the malady caused by a being from another plane and the cure effected by a priest initiated into the sacred life.

16
Conclusion

The shamanic practices we have investigated are rightly seen as an archaic mysticism. On the basis of the world view uncovered by the shaman's faculties, with its vision of another and miraculous plane which could interact causally with our own, the more advanced mystical intuitions of esoteric Buddhism were able to develop.

Today, however, this world view is fast disappearing. The vision of another plane utterly different from our own, ambivalent, perilous and beyond our control, has faded. Instead the universe has become one-dimensional; there is no barrier to be crossed, no mysteriously other kind of being to be met and placated. The storms, droughts, sicknesses, fires which used to be laid at the door of *kami*, ancestors, foxes and ghosts, are now believed to lie within the competence and control of man. Even those forces that are not yet directly within his control are believed to be potentially so; their causes are discoverable by ordinary human faculties ungifted with sacred power. The mystery and ambivalent peril which surrounded the holy has gone, and with it the barrier which divided sacred from profane.

When the view of the other world fades, and its inhabitants dwindle to the predictable regularities called the laws of nature, the shaman and his powers are no longer needed. The beings whom the *miko* summoned vanish, and her capacity for receiving them atrophies from disuse. One by one the village oracles disappear for want of a suitable medium. Inexorably, as roads are cut through ancient holy mountains, their summits, which used to represent another mysterious world, are reduced by crowds and machines to the noisy playgrounds known perhaps ironically as 'Dreamland'. The sacred enclosure, cordoned off with its tasselled straw rope, which used to symbolise the qualitatively different kind of space into which *kami* could be summoned and persuaded to speak, is now shrilly lit with television searchlights and freely invaded by the man who, with tape recorder and

315

bored manner, thrusts his microphone in the direction of the sacred utterance. Time and again I have seen a rite made meaningless, its direction altered, its timing falsified, to suit the convenience of the television cameras. Gone therefore is the truth and beauty of the ritual, that which enabled it to make contact with another plane of existence.

In future we can expect to find only scattered vestiges of this ancient cult, only sparse reminders of the other world to which the shaman's faculties gave access. In conclusion I offer one more.

In the Nō play *Shakkyō*, the priest Jakushō, in the course of his travels through India and China in search of Buddhist holy places, arrives one spring at the foot of Mt Ch'ing-liang. Before him he sees a great stone bridge. He is just about to set foot on it when a boy appears.

This bridge may not easily be traversed, the boy cries. So deep are you now in the mountains that any moment you might see the immortals playing chess, and find like Wang-Chih that as you watched your axe had crumbled away with the years. Look how the waterfall above you plunges out of the clouds, and how the valley below lies as deep as Hell, so deep that your hair stands upright to think of it. See how narrow the bridge is, no more than a foot, and covered with slippery moss. No man ever built this bridge. It has been here since the beginning of the world, appearing stone on stone of its own accord. See how its arch leaps like a drawn bow, or like the rainbow which appears in the evening sun after rain. Who could dream of crossing it without a divine gift? Not even the eminent monks of old could traverse it until they had accomplished severe penances.

But beyond the bridge lies the paradise of Manjusri, where flowers fall from the sky, and the music of pipes, flute and zither breaks through the clouds. Wait here a while and you may see a miracle, the apparition of the bodhisattva himself.

And presently, as the priest watches, there comes forth from between the red and white peonies the figure of a lion, with long red hair and a golden face. He dances among the flowers to the old Chinese tune called Toraden.[1]

Abbreviations

Notes

Chapter 1

1   The play is translated by Arthur Waley in his *Nō Plays of Japan*;
    text in *Yōkyoku Taikan*, vol. 1, p. 155. The spell is a celebrated one,
    which Yanagita believes to have been in widespread use in ancient
    times as a summoner of spirits: see 'Yorimasa no haka', *YKS*, vol. 9,
    p. 280.

2   To take a random example, the religious group called Gedatsukai,
    whose premises in Kyoto I visited in 1969, are convinced that the
    cause of all human misfortune lies in the spiritual world, sickness
    and disaster of every kind being laid at the door of discontented
    ancestral spirits and Shinto numina. According to an investigation
    carried out by the Japanese Ministry of Education in 1956 into
    'superstitions in daily life', 15.52% of the sample believed divine
    chastisements to be 'definitely true', and 31.73% to be 'possibly
    true'. See *Japanese Religion*, published 1972 by the Agency for
    Cultural Affairs, p. 142.

3   To designate the shaman's altered state of consciousness I prefer to
    use the word 'trance' to the 'ecstasy' favoured by so many author-
    ities, simply because it is less easily confused with states of emotional
    rapture, exaltation or even madness. Memories of Drydon's 'mad
    prophet in an ecstasy', Milton's dim religious light and pealing
    organ which 'dissolve me in ecstasies', George Crabbe's 'muddy
    ecstasies of beer', and the vision of Ophelia 'blasted with ecstasy'
    all tend to obscure the fact that the shaman's state of conscious-
    ness is neither emotional nor insane.

4   Concerning the derivation of the word 'shaman', Professor Sir
    Harold Bailey has kindly furnished me with the following in-
    formation. From the Vedic *śram*, meaning to heat oneself or
    practise austerities, we get *śramanā*, one who practises austerities, an

ascetic. The word made its way into central Asia from India through the north-west Prakrit used in the Shan-shan Kingdom about 300 A.D. as an administrative language, as *ṣamaṇa*. Thence it may be traced through the Khotanese Saka *ssamana*, the Tokharian dialect—A *ṣāmam*, the Sogdian *šmny*, and other forms in Uigur Turkish, Asokan Greek and New Persian, until it reached China as *sha-men*. Thence it made its way to Japan as *shamon*.

See also Eliade's *Shamanism*, pp. 495–500, and N. D. Mironov and S. M. Shirokogoroff, 'Sramaná-shaman: etymology of the word 'shaman''. Shirokogoroff argues that the word is foreign to the Tungusic language, and that the appearance of shamanism in north Asia coincided with the dissemination of Buddhism in its Tantric or Lamaist form.

The first occurrence of the term to be traced in Chinese literature is in the *Hou Han Chi* of Yüan Hung (328–376 A.D.), *SPTK* ed. 10.5a, cited in Li Hsien's notes to *Hou Han-shu* 42 (biog. 32), Wang Hsien-ch'ien ed. 5a.

5   For this brief description I have relied on the following works: Mircea Eliade's *Shamanism: Archaic Techniques of Ecstasy*, an exhaustive and fascinating treatment of the phenomena of shamanism all over the world; also his 'Recent works on shamanism', *HR*, vol. 1, no. 1 (1961); M. A. Czaplicka, *Aboriginal Siberia: a Study in Social Anthropology*; L. Vajda, 'Zur phaseologischen Stellung des Schamanismus', *Ural-altaische Jahrbücher* 31 (1959); Leo Sternberg, 'Divine election in primitive religion', *Congrès International des Americanistes*, Compterendu de la XXIe Session, pt 2, 1924; Vilmos Diosózegi, *Tracing Shamans in Siberia;* Uno Harva, *Finno-Ugric and Siberian Mythology;* and Caroline Humphrey, 'Shamans and the trance', *Theoria to Theory*, vol. 5, no. 4 (1971) and vol. 6, no. 1 (1972).

6   See Hori Ichirō, *Nihon no Shamanizumu*, pp. 16–38, and *Folk Religion in Japan*, pp. 183–7. The account of Pimiko may be read in Ryūsaku Tsunoda and L. Carrington Goodrich, *Japan in the Chinese Dynastic Histories*, pp. 8–16. For the Korean shaman see Akiba Takashi, *Chōsen fuzoku no genchi kenkyū*, and for the Ryūkyū shaman see William P. Lebra, *Okinawan Religion* and Kamata Hisako, 'Daughters of the gods: shaman priestesses in Japan and Okinawa', in *Folk Cultures of Japan and East Asia*, ed. Joseph Pittau S.J., pp. 56–73. For the Ainu shaman see Neil Gordon Munro, *Ainu Creed and Cult*.

It is possible that in some parts of Japan hermaphrodite boys may also have served as *miko*. A skeleton excavated from a prehistoric site on Tanegashima island, 1957–9, is thought to be of such a person. The bones are those of a man, but the extraordinary profusion of shell ornaments—necklace, abundant bracelets, square brooches decorated with an endless knot pattern at the waist and loins—suggest only a woman. A flat depression on the forehead of the skull suggest that from a very early age the 'boy' had a hard round plaque tightly bound to his forehead. The body is thought to be that of a hermaphrodite *miko*, such androgynous persons being venerated as sacred in the Ryūkyū. See Kaneseki Takeo, 'Tanegashima Hirota iseki no bunka', *Fukuoka Unesco*, no. 3 (1966), p. 39–52.

7　Roy Miller, *The Japanese Language*, pp. 28–9; Charles Haguenauer, *Origines de la civilisation japonaise, Introduction à l'étude de la préhistoire du Japon*, pp. 168, 267.

8　Oka Masao et al., *Nihon Minzoku no Kigen*, pp. 59–68; Joseph Kitagawa, 'The prehistoric background of Japanese religion', *HR*, vol. 2, no. 2 (1963); Haguenauer, p. 173.

9　Hori Ichirō, *Folk Religion in Japan*, pp. 6–7.

10　William P. Fairchild's article, 'Shamanism in Japan', *FS*, vol. 21 (1962), is unfortunately marred by elementary misreadings of Chinese characters, wrongly cited references, statements unsupported by any known evidence and an English style so awkward as to be at times incomprehensible.

Chapter 2

1　The *kami* have been analysed and subdivided into a bewildering number of types and kinds. Here I attempt no such analysis. I concentrate only on the characteristics common to those *kami* who can be invoked, questioned and petitioned by the shaman.

Motoori's much-quoted passage is to be found in *Motoori Norinaga Zenshū*, vol. 1, pp. 150–2. D. C. Holtom has translated the passage at length in his *National Faith of Japan*, pp. 23–4. Some indication of the inscrutability of the *kami* may be inferred from Motoori's statement, 'I do not yet understand the meaning of the word *kami*.'

2　*Heike Monogatari*, book 8, 'Usa gyōkō no koto', Utsumi's edition, p. 444.

3　The Kiyomori story is in *Heike Monogatari*, book 3, 'Daitō konryū no koto', ibid., p. 155, and Yukitaka appears in book 6, 'Sunomata kassen no koto', p. 361.

The apparitions of *kami* in the *Heike Monogatari* are discussed by Hori in his 'Heike Monogatari ni arawareta shūkyōshiteki yōso', in *Shūkyō shūzoku no seikatsu kisei*.

4　Honda Yasuji, *Kagura*, pp. 6–7. Discussions of the different types of *yorishiro* may also be found in Ikegami Hiromasa, 'Rei to kami no shurui', and in Takeda Chōshū's 'Kami no hyōjō to saijō', both in *Nihon Minzokugaku Taikei*, vol. 8. Miwasan is the most celebrated example of a mountain which is in itself the vessel of the *kami*, and Itsukushima of an island.

5　*Kojiki*, book 1, chap. 17, verse 11, Donald Philippi's translation, p. 83.

6 Yanagita believes that the notion of the *kami* congregating in Izumo in the tenth month to be a later development of the idea that in that very month their seasonal work in the village is finished and they return to their mountain for the winter: 'Takusen to matsuri', *YKS*, vol. 9.

7 Examples of the oldest and most complex of such offerings may be found in the *Engishiki*, where the correct oblation for each shrine and each festival is prescribed: see F. G. Bock, *Engi-Shiki* book 1. Blood sacrifices, it may be noted, are not acceptable to the *kami*, who detest both death and blood.

8 The Ōharai ritual has been translated with ample commentary by Dr Karl Florenz, 'Ancient Japanese rituals, part IV', *TASJ*, First Series, vol. 27, reprinted with Sir Ernest Satow's previous three parts, December 1927; also by Donald Philippi, *Norito*, pp. 45–9.

On *imi* or the avoidance of pollution, see Yanagita, *Minzokugaku Jiten*, pp. 247 and 262.

9 An interesting account of the restrictions placed on menstruating women up to the end of the nineteenth century, including enforced seclusion in a special hut, is given in Segawa Kiyoko's 'Menstrual taboos imposed on women', in *Studies in Japanese Folklore*, ed. Richard Dorson.

10 On the rites of pacifying and shaking the *tama*, see Matsumura Takeo, *Nihon shinwa no kenkyū*, vol. 4, pp. 278–80. Also *Kojiki*, chap. 12, and the discussion in Honda Yasuji's *Kagura*, p. 10.

11 The belief that the *tama* did not separate from the body immediately upon physical death, but only after an interval of several days, is attested by the ancient institution of mortuary huts, *araki no miya* or *moya*. In these huts the corpse was kept during the intermediary period before it was considered to be irrevocably dead, in the course of which songs and dances were performed in the attempt magically to call back the spirit. Thus the *Kojiki* tells us that the corpse of Amenowakahiko, killed by an arrow, was put into a mortuary palace where for eight days and nights mourners dressed as birds danced and sang: *Kojiki*, chap. 34, verses 1–4.

Jōbutsu means literally 'becoming a Buddha', deriving from the usage whereby the dead are known as *hotoke* or Buddhas.

12 Evidence may be found in the *Kojiki* pointing to the belief that the *tama* could take the form of a white bird. Chapter 88 relates how the soul of Yamato Takeru no Mikoto was transformed into a giant white bird, and how his wife and children rushed after it weeping and singing songs, presumably in the attempt to catch it and bring it back: Philippi, p. 250. The bird disguises worn by the mourners at the funeral of Amenowakahiko have also been interpreted as ritual means of luring the bird-soul back into the body: ibid. p. 126.

13 Oka Masao, *Nihon Minzoku no kigen*, pp. 59–63. Yanagita's *Senzo no hanashi* contains a full discussion of his views on *kami* and *tama*; English translation by Fanny Hagin Mayer and Ishiwara Yasuyo, *About our Ancestors: the Japanese Family System.*

Origuchi discussed the problem in his 'Reikon no hanashi', in 'Kodai Kenkyū', *Origuchi Shinobu Zenshū*, vol. 3, pp. 260–76. See also the dialogue on the subject of the *tama* between Yanagita and Origuchi, 'Nihonjin no kami to reikon no kannen sono hoka', in *Minzokugaku Kenkyū*, vol. 14, no. 2 (1949).

Yet another view is advanced by Matsudaira Narimitsu in his 'The concept of Tamashii in Japan', in *Studies in Japanese Folklore*. He maintains that the *tama* is a spiritual entity in the process of becoming a *kami*, which is enabled to accomplish this transformation by means of offerings of consecrated, 'clean' food and drink. Thus the ritual food consumed at a festival will confer spiritual growth.

All these various theories as to the relation between *kami* and *tama* have been lucidly summed up and discussed by Matsumura Takeo, *Nihon shinwa no kenkyū*, vol. 4, pp. 241–308.

Ōkuninushi's meeting with his counterpartal soul is in Aston's *Nihongi*, pt 1, p. 61, and his *Shinto*, pp. 27–30.

14 Yanagita, *Senzo no hanashi*, chap. 29, *About our Ancestors*, pp. 71–3; also Takeda Chōshū, *Senzo Sūhai*, pp. 107–8.

15 Yanagita, *Senzo no hanashi*, pp. 138–9, 162–3.

16 Ibid., pp. 65, 93–4, 114–17.

17 The story of Sawara Shinnō may be read in Richard Ponsonby-Fane's *The Vicissitudes of Shinto*, pp. 83–6. His angry ghost has also been held responsible for the abandonment of Nagaoka as the capital in 794 and the subsequent move to the city which is now Kyoto.

18 Ponsonby-Fane also recounts the story of Michizane's ghost, ibid., pp. 87–92.

19 Yanagita, *Senzo no hanashi*, p. 123. Another similar example may be found in the case of Sakura Sōgorō near Narita, whose angry ghost proved so powerfully destructive that it was apotheosised and afterwards assumed to be equally powerful in blessing. The story of Sakura Sōgorō, crucified and his family butchered before his eyes for his attempts to lighten the burden of taxation levied from his village, may be read in Mitford's *Tales of Old Japan*.

An interesting recent work which sets out to prove that the fear of *onryō* or angry ghosts played a far more powerful part in the lives of the early Japanese than has been generally credited, is Umehara Takeshi's *Kakusareta Jūjika*. Mr Umehara believes that the Hōryūji temple, after its destruction by fire in 669, was rebuilt with the specific intention of 'sealing in' and pacifying the angry ghosts of Shōtoku Taishi and of his twenty-five descendants foully murdered by Soga no Iruka in 643. With this explanation, he believes, all the enigmas about the temple which have hitherto baffled historians are immediately soluble.

20 Koike Nagahiro, *Hito no shigo no hanashi*, pp. 41–52. In the *Kitano Tenjin Engi* scroll, the ghost of Michizane first appears as a youthful and immaculately dressed courtier, with nothing whatever about him to suggest that he is a ghost. His long trousers trailing over the edge of the veranda, he visits the temple of the Tendai Abbot Son-e. A turn of the scroll and we see a curious scene. Apparently a priest is entertaining a court noble to view his garden and to refresh himself from a plate of pomegranates. In fact we are looking at the instant before the start of a magical battle. The ghost has just announced its intention of wreaking revenge on the imperial family for the wrongs it has suffered, and has requested Son-e not to hamper this design with his magic powers. Son-e has just firmly refused. In a moment, the ghost will spit a pomegranate seed from its mouth, which will burst into raging flames as it hits the door. Son-e will calmly perform the water-sprinkling mudra, whereupon water will gush from his hand and extinguish the flames. Later the ghost appears in the likeness of a dark-red thunder god with horns and a ring of drums, filling the Seiryōden palace with black billowing smoke. *Nihon Emakimono Zenshū*, vol. 8, plates 24, 65, 66, 67 and colour plate 5.

The story of Raigō Ajari may be found in the *Heike Monogatari*, book 3, Utsumi's edition p. 155, but it is in the *Taiheiki* version that we find his ghost taking the form of 84,000 large rats with iron claws and stone bodies: *NBT* edition, vol. 17, pp. 435–7.

Chapter 3

1 Yanagita Kunio, 'Hebigami inugami no tagui', *YKS*, vol. 9, p. 261. The distribution of witch animals over the Japanese islands may be found clearly set out, with illuminating maps, in Ishizuka Takatoshi's *Nihon no tsukimono*, pp. 20–74.

2 Yanagita, 'Hebigami inugami no tagui', p. 261.

3 The distinction drawn by Professor Evans-Pritchard in his *Witchcraft Oracles and Magic among the Azande* may be useful here. A witch is someone who possesses innately harmful powers, such as overlooking, evil-eyeing. A sorcerer has to perform a ritual of some kind in order to achieve his ends.

4 'Kitsunegami oyobi kitsunetsuki jikkendan' by Yazu Shūsei, *Minzoku to Rekishi*, vol. 8, no. 1 (1922), pp. 218–22.

5 Quoted in Ishizuka, p. 192. Further information about the relation between the Izuna rite and foxes is given in Tsubosaka Yutaka, 'Izuna-hō', *Minzoku to Rekishi*, vol. 8, no. 1 (1922), pp. 187–90.

6   M. W. de Visser, 'The fox and badger in Japanese Folklore', *TASJ*, vol. 36 (1908–9), pp. 105–29. The Taira Kiyomori story is in *Gempei Seisuiki*, *NET* edition, vol. 15, pp. 36–8. The story of Fujiwara Tadazane, otherwise known as Chisokuin-dono, is in *Kokonchomonjū*, same edition vol. 10, p. 495. The priest Myōkitsu-jisha appears in the *Taiheiki*, same edition vol. 18, pp. 105–12.

7   The Dakini figure in Indian or Tibetan iconography bears no relation to a fox. In Tibetan Buddhism the *dakini* usually appear in the form of beautiful women, who bestow secret knowledge on the neophyte and render him aid in certain kinds of meditation. Elsewhere the *dakini* may appear as a group of three red demons, as illustrated in Mochizuki's *Bukkyō Daijiten*.

8   Miura Shuyu writes that in the Okayama district there still persists the belief that to live in the house of a former fox-owner will infect your own family with the stigma. The same suspicion attaches to the rice fields of former fox-owners. In the Izumo district few people will not hesitate to buy such land, however cheap the price. *San-in Minzoku*, no. 3, quoted by Ishizuka, pp. 131–2.

9   Yanagita, 'Hebigami inugami no tagui', p. 262. An abundance of information on cases of fox, dog and snake possession, albeit collected with a view to disproving it on rational grounds, may be found in Inoue Enryō's *Yōkaigaku Kōgi*, vol. 4, pp. 215–45.

10 Motoori Norinaga, 'Senshakō', *Motoori Norinaga Zenshū*, vol. 12, p. 172.

11 Ishizuka, pp. 86–116.

12 Hayami Yasutaka, *Tsukimono-mochi meishin no rekishiteki kōsatsu*, p. 46.

13 Miyake Hitoshi, 'Shugendō no tsukimono-otoshi', in *Yoneyama Keizō Hakase kanreki kinen rombunshū*, p. 292.

14 Anonymous report from the newspaper *Oita Shimbun*, 'Bungo no inugami-sawagi jitsuwa', quoted in *Minzoku to Rekishi*, vol. 8, no. 1, pp. 302–3.

15 Hayami, pp. 28–30.

16 Ishizuka, pp. 168–9.

17 Quoted in H. Y. Feng and J. K. Shryock, 'The black magic in China known as ku', *Journal of the American Oriental Society*, vol. 55, no. 1 (1935), p. 8. A full account of the dynastic feuds, in which numerous members of the imperial family were murdered, which the alleged practice of *ku* provoked in the early Han period, may be found in Michael Loewe's *Crisis and Conflict in Han China, 104 B.C. to A.D. 9*, chap. 2.

18 Feng and Shryock, p. 8.

19 Ibid. p. 27.

20 Ibid. p. 7.

21 *Sui shu* 31 (*chih* 26), 14a, b (*Po-na* ed.); Feng and Shryock, p.13.

22 Yanagita, 'Hebigami inugami no tagni', p. 262.

23 Feng and Shryock, p. 7.

24 Ishizuka, pp. 230–44.

25 Ishizuka writes that in some districts, notably Shimane and Oita' the *tsukimono* is prepared to accompany a bridegroom as well as a bride. Elsewhere the creature only goes with a girl. *Gedō* are said to multiply at the birth of a girl, but not of a boy. Ishizuka, p. 272.

26 I am grateful to Miss Theo Brown for valuable information on the black dog as a family ghost. See Edith Olivier, *Four Victorian Ladies' of Wiltshire*, pp. 33–4, for Miss Annie Moberley's vision of the Bishop of Salisbury's birds. Further examples of such visionary animals may be found in Professor Sidgwick's 'Report on the Census of Hallucinations', *Proceedings of the Society for Psychical Research*, vol. 10 (1894).

Chapter 4

1 Saigō Nobutsuna, *Kojiki no Sekai*, pp. 26–9. Saigō dismisses the euhemerist attempts of scholars since the Meiji period to associate Takamagahara with a particular geographical place—Manchuria or Tibet, or, nearer home, Yamato or Hitachi. The structure and function of the myths require Takamagahara to be an *other* world in the sky.

References to the topography of Takamaghara may be found in the *Kojiki*, Donald Philippi's translation, chapters 14, 16 and 21; also Aston's *Nihongi*, pt 1, p. 31, and the Ōharai liturgy, Donald Philippi's *Norito*, p. 47.

2 *Kojiki*, chapters 9 and 10; Saigō Nobutsuna, *Kojiki no Sekai*, pp. 48–61.

3 Matsumura Takeo, *Nihon shinwa no kenkyū*, vol. 2, pp. 394–407, gives a lucid account of the various theories propounded, notably by Gotō Shuichi and Tsugita Uruu, which relate the topography of Yomi with the structure of a tomb. Saigō prefers to associate it with the *araki* or mortuary hut, in which the corpse was placed for a period prior to burial in a tomb. During this period the soul was thought to be in an intermediate state, not irrevocably dead, but susceptible to recall by special songs and dances: *Kojiki no Sekai*, pp. 49–50.

4 It is not feasible here to embark on the vexed problem of who the Yamato people were and whence they came. Those wishing to

delve further may be referred to Joseph Kitagawa's lucid summing up of the arguments in his 'The prehistoric background of Japanese religion', *HR*, vol. 2, no. 2 (1963), p. 2.

5   Origuchi's theory of the *marebito* is developed in his 'Kokubungaku no hassei', pt 3, *Origuchi Shinobu Zenshū*, vol. 1, pp. 3–62; also in his 'Tokoyo oyobi marebito', *Minzoku*, vol. 4, no. 2 (1929), pp. 1–62.

Matsumoto Nobuhiro, *Nihon no shinwa*, pp. 90–6, believes the idea of *kami* coming from a land across the sea to visit the human world to be older than that of the *kami* descending from the sky. Oka Masao, *Nihon Minzokugaku Taikei*, vol. 2, pp. 7–9, holds the *marebito* to be of Melanesian origin, part of a culture transplanted to Japan in the middle Jōmon period—as early, that is to say, as the third millennium B.C.—from somewhere in the south Pacific.

On the outcast strolling players, see Hori Ichirō, *WK*, pp. 554–84. Hori describes the outcast groups of players, minstrels and mimes—the *sekizo*, the *monoyoshi*, the *maimai*, the *kotobure* and many others—who made their appearance during the dead period between the harvest and the New Year. See also his 'Mysterious visitors from the harvest to the New Year', in *Studies in Japanese Folklore*, ed Richard Dorson, pp. 76–103.

6   The multiple ambiguities of Tokoyo are too complex for detailed treatment here. Its underworld aspect is known also as Nenokuni. This is the mysterious land to which Susanoo, in the thirteenth chapter of the *Kojiki*, desired with howls and wails to go, and where his son Ōkuninushi, chapter 23, is immured in chambers of snakes, centipedes and bees, and is later compelled, in a great hall, to pick lice and centipedes from the head of his father. Yanagita, Origuchi and Matsumoto Nobuhiro—see his *Nihon no shinwa*, p. 94—all identify Tokoyo with Nenokuni. Yanagita contends that Nenokuni is not merely a dark underworld; it also carried the connotations of a 'Motherland', in the sense of a dimly remembered original home of the Japanese race. *Ne*, he says, anciently indicated not the 'root', growing underground, of its modern meaning, but a centre or starting-point, hence an original homeland. It is this word too which phonetically connects the whole complex with the Ryūkyū Nirai. 'Nenokuni no hanashi', *YKS*, vol. 1, pp. 85–8.

That Tokoyo is also an early name for what later came to be known as Ryūgū, the underwater palace, is clear from the story of Urashimanoko in the *Nihon Shoki*, and from the *Manyōshū nagauta* version of the story, in which the submarine palace is called Tokoyo. In the *Nihon Shoki* story the name is rendered by the characters for the Chinese paradisal island Hōraizan, but glossed with interlinear *kana* as Tokoyo.

The bewildering proliferations of meaning attached to the idea of Tokoyo, each with its own separate name, has been helpfully analysed by Ouwehand, *Namazu-e and their Themes*, p. 85. He distinguishes three principal meanings: (i) a paradise of everlasting life; (ii) an underworld of darkness; (iii) a land far distant from Japan. All three have a structural continuity, and examples of all three occur in the *Kojiki* and *Nihon Shoki*.

7 Yanagita Kunio, 'Kaijin shōdō', *YKS*, vol. 8, p. 37. These tales also convey the tension or polarity between the worlds of mountain and sea. The sticks or flowers from the mountain, things of no particular value there, become precious treasures at the bottom of the sea. In several of these tales the old man, when he reaches the underwater mansion, sees his bundles of firewood neatly stacked by the gate.

Evidence of a world beneath the earth, we might add, is scanty in Japanese myth and legend. We must not forget, however, the celebrated legend from Suwa in Nagano prefecture of Kōga Saburō, who was lowered down the shaft of a deep cave in a basket to an underground world where he married and had a son. But the fact that he later appears to have become a snake and to have made his abode in a lake, where he was worshipped as a water deity, gives us an immediate connection with the underwater world we have already noticed. See Yanagita, 'Kōga Saburō no Monogatari', *YKS*, vol. 7, p. 36, and *Minzokugaku Jiten*, article Kōga Saburō. An English version of the legend is given in Richard Dorson's *Folk Legends of Japan*, pp. 158–9. In Hiroko Ikeda's extremely useful *Type and Motif Index of Japanese Folk Literature*, the Kōga Saburō story is Type 301A. Another underworld motif is the *Nezumi-jōdo* or paradise of mice, to be reached by finding one's way down a hole. The hospitable mice usually regale the hero with magic presents, suggesting that this type, Dr Ikeda's 480C, is a 'dry' variant of the underwater paradise.

See also Seki Keigo's *Nihon Mukashibanashi Shūsei*, vol. 3, pp. 997–1034, for the folktale types and motifs which deal with the communication between the water world and the world of men. Of these the type known as *Ryūgū-dōji*, or dragon-palace child, is the most widespread, with variants ranging from Aomori, Iwate and Niigata prefectures in the north of the main island, right down through Shikoku and Kyūshū as far as the Ryūkyū archipelago. Always there is the structural connection between the hideous but miraculous child and water, a woman and a snake. Occasionally this 'small hero' appears of his own accord without the intervention of the lady at the bottom of the sea, but always the connection with water persists. The tiny child, still a bringer of wealth and joy, is washed up from the sea, or the fruit out of which he steps comes bobbing down a river at the feet of the old couple who adopt him. The Kumamoto version of the *Ryūgū-dōji* story, in which the ugly child is called Hanatarekozō and has a perpetually running nose and dribbling mouth, is given in full in Yanagita's *Nihon no Mukashibanashi*, p. 43. In Hiroko Ikeda's classification the *Ryūgū-dōji* stories are Type 470A.

8 Yanagita, 'Kakurezato', *YKS*, vol. 5, pp. 230–50. The Etchū legend is given at greater length in 'Zenwankashi no Nawaike' in *Nihon Minzoku Densetsu Zenshū*, vol. 6, p. 251. Oka Masao gives further examples of such legends in 'Ijin sono hoka' in *Minzoku*, vol. 3, pp. 89–91. Finally, Kitami Toshio has analysed nearly 150 surviving bowl-lending legends in central and south-west Japan. He found the highest proportion of them in Nagano prefecture in regions by rivers, lakes and deep pools. The guardian of the place who lent the vessels was usually a snake, a beautiful woman or the dragon god Ryūjin, though occasionally a kappa was credited with the power. In the dry entrances the guardian was a fox, badger or mujina. 'Nihonjin no ikyō-kannen no ichi dammen: wankashi densetsu wo megutte', in *Nihon Minzokugaku*, no. 4 (1954), pp. 111–18. The bowl-lending stories are Hiroko Ikeda's Type 730.

The motif of a cup or bowl borrowed from the other world is, as that immensely learned and insufficiently recognised authority Minakata Kumakusu pointed out in 1924 (*Kyōdo Kenkyū*, vol. 1, p. 297), remarkably widespread throughout the world.

In England several notable examples occur. Aubrey in his *Natural History of Surrey* tells us of a huge cauldron in the vestry of Frensham church, believed to have been originally lent by the fairies of Borough Hill nearby. Gervase of Tilbury tells of a forest in Gloucestershire full of boar and deer, with a green clearing in the middle and a hillock as high as a man. If anyone went alone to this hill and said 'I thirst', at once there would appear an elegant cup-bearer, holding in his outstretched hand a drinking horn adorned with gold and gems. It was full of delicious nectar which when drunk banished all heat and weariness. The custom continued until one day a knight, having drunk the nectar, stole the horn. The Earl of Gloucester, when he heard of the matter, condemned the robber to death and presented the horn to Henry I. See Keightley's *Fairy Mythology*, pp. 255–6 and 284–5.

The motif of a cup from fairyland not merely borrowed and kept, but deliberately snatched away, is likewise common. Hartland in his *The Science of Fairy Tales*, p. 145, tells us that of all the articles stolen from fairyland in European legend, by far the most frequent is the cup or drinking horn. Many such articles are still preserved in parts of northern Europe, of which the Luck of Edenhall and the Oldenburg horn are the most celebrated. He gives a good many examples from Scandinavia, adding that the motif of the stolen cup is exclusively a Teutonic, not a Celtic, possession.

On Sado island, Yanagita tells us, the guardian of the dry entrance to the fairy underworld was a *mujina* or badger called Danzaburō. A tribe of badgers, of which Danzaburō was the king, lived down a hole among some rocks, and were very obliging in lending cups and trays until people failed to return them. Occasionally a man made his way down the hole, to find himself in a magnificent royal palace, with the badger family attired in gorgeous robes eating delicious food. Tales of the supernatural lapse of time there were also current, three days in Danzaburō's palace being the equivalent of three years in the human world ('Kakurezato', *YKS*, vol. 5, pp. 243–4).

9   Those humans who come back from the water world are often bewildered, if not destroyed, by the supernatural lapse of time which has occurred there. The story of Urashimanoko is the most familiar example, but Yanagita gives some interesting parallel cases from the Ryūkyū islands. A young woman, for example, returned from the underwater world of Niruya after thirty-two years, looking not a day older than when she disappeared. Another woman returned after seven years, dressed in rich damask and brocade under a covering of seaweed. 'Kaijingū-kō', *YKS*, vol. 1, pp. 38–41. These tales, Yanagita was convinced, proved the identification of the Ryūkyū Nirai with the Japanese Ryūgū.

10   Hori Ichirō, *WK*, p. 239. For the transfer of this entire complex from sea to mountain, see also Origuchi, 'Kokubungaku no hassei, pt 3, *Origuchi Shinobi Zenshū*, vol. 1, p. 62, and Ouwehand, p. 95.

11   Ōba Iwao, 'Nihon ni okeru sangaku shinkō no kōkogakuteki kōsatsu', *Sangaku Shinkō Sōsho*.

12   Hori Ichirō, 'Manyōshū ni arawareta sōsei to takaikan reikonkan ni tsuite', in *Shūkyō shūzoku no seikatsu kisei*.

13   Hori in his *WK*, pp. 228–48, refers to the *Kumano Nendaiki* or records of priests who undertook the penance known as *Fudaraku-tokai* or voyage to Potalaka, the paradise of the Bodhisattva Kannon. These records, which begin in the year 818 and end in 1722, show that the men who embarked on this strange journey usually set out in the eleventh month, with provisions for several days and sometimes as many as thirteen companions. Though some may have embarked with the genuine intention of discovering, like Sudhana in the Avatamsaka Sutra, the paradise of Kannon, in most cases the practice seems to have functioned as a method of ritual suicide calculated to win a joyous rebirth in paradise. In the *Kumano Nachi Mandara* we have a picture of one of the boats about to set sail. It has a covered roof with a *torii* on each of the four sides, a feature which Gorai Shigeru believes points without question to a tomb.

It is possible that we have here a survival of the ancient horizontal other world beyond the sea, to be reached by boat in the same way as the *marebito* arrive in boats.

See also Gorai Shigeru, *Kumano-mōde*, pp. 154–68.

14   See for example *Konjaku Monogatari*, books 14 and 17.

15   Ōbayashi Taryō, *Sōsei no Kigen*, pp. 118–20. The author gives on pp. 116–17 an interesting map illustrating the areas of the globe

where a belief is held in a world of the dead in mountains. These include, besides Japan, Korea and Taiwan, parts of Java and Borneo, some Polynesian islands and two enclaves of North American Indians in the centre of the continent.

Chapter 5

1 For the Three Worms, or corpse-worms, see Henri Maspero, *Le Taoisme*, pp. 99–107; also N. Sivin, 'Folk medicine and classical medicine in traditional China', unpublished, 1972. These three worms, *san shih*, are treated fully in the therapeutic compendium *Ishimpō*, completed in 982 and drawn from Chinese sources. They are stated to cause disease in the parts of the body where they dwell, and to stimulate the gluttony and sensuality which shorten life. The superior worm, which is black, about three inches long and dwells in the head, stimulates love of horses, carriages and luxurious clothes. The green middle worm, situated in the back, promotes love of food, while the third one, white and in the stomach, stimulates sexual licence.

On the 57th day of each sexagenary cycle, the Kō-monkey or Kōshin day, they were believed to ascend to heaven and report to the Director of Destinies their host's transgressions during the previous period.

See also Kubo Noritada, *Kōshin shinkō no kenkyū*, pp. 39–103, for a list of the various names and functions assigned to the Three Worms by different authorities.

2 *Konjaku Monogatari*, book 12, *NBT*, vol. 8, p. 820.

3 Ibid. p. 829.

4 See the essays on Mokujiki Shōnin collected in vol. 9 of *Yanagi Sōetsu Senshū*, especially 'Mokujiki Shōnin hakken no engi' and 'Mokujiki Shōnin ryakuden'; also Hino Kazuyoshi, *Henreki hōrō no sekai*, pp. 165–76. Mokujiki's work was first discovered in 1923 when Yanagi Sōetsu went to a house in Kōfu to look at Korean ceramics and found there two wooden images. The following year he discovered the manuscript of Mokujiki's autobiography.

5 For the cult of mummies in Japan, see Hori Ichirō's 'Self-mummified Buddhas in Japan', *HR*, vol. 1, no. 2 (1961); also his 'Yudonosan-kei no sokushimbutsu (miira) to sono haikei', in *Tōhoku bunka*, March 1961. Also Andō Kōsei's *Miira* and the work compiled by the Nihon Miira Kenkyū Gurūpu or Group for Research into Japanese Mummies, *Nihon Miira no Kenkyū*.

On the corresponding Chinese cult of mummifying holy men, see Percival Yetts, 'Disposal of Buddhist dead in China', *Journal of the Royal Asiatic Society*, July 1911, pp. 699–725. The bodies of these priests, in the posture of meditation, were placed in earthenware boxes, hermetically sealed and buried for three years. If when the box was then opened the body was undecayed, a subscription was raised for gilding and enshrining the relic. Charcoal and salt were added, and sometimes the body was smoked. One particular temple in Anhui used to contain four or five of these 'dried priests', including that of the holy ninth-century monk Ti-tsang whose face, when the box was opened, was said to be exactly the same as it was when he was alive, though his bones rattled like a golden chain. The gilding process, unknown in Japan, was evidently an attempt to make the saint's skin conform with the golden lustre which is one of the thirty-two marks of Buddha-hood.

See also M. W. de Visser, *The Bodhisattva Ti-tsang (Jizō) in China and Japan*, p. 49-50.

6   A personal description of this fast may be read from the pen of a former Ajari, Hagami Shōchō, in his book *Dōshin*, pp. 108-14.

7   *Heike Monogatari*, book 5, Utsumi's edition, pp. 286-9.

8   Eliade discusses interior heat or *tapas* in his *Shamanism*, pp. 412-4, and in his *Yoga*, pp. 100-11, 330-34. The much-quoted story of Tibetan lamas drying wet sheets appeared to derive solely from Alexandra David-Neel's *Mystics and Magicians in Tibet*, p. 227. I raised the question with His Holiness the Dalai Lama during his visit to Cambridge on 9 October 1973. He confirmed that though he had never himself undergone such a test, it nonetheless used to be an accepted practice in Tibet. He had undergone other disciplines for stimulating interior heat, which he had eventually had to abandon because of their deleterious effect on his eyes.

Professor Nathan Sivin has kindly drawn my attention to an early Chinese instance of cold water rousing interior heat. In the *Hou Han-shu*, or *History of the Later Han*, the following anecdote is related of the celebrated physician Hua T'o, who practised at the beginning of the third century A.D. and whose longevity and sustained youth excited the curious admiration of his contemporaries.

Confronted with a case of a woman suffering from a chronic disease of the 'cold and hot possession type', Hua T'o prescribed that she should sit in a stone trough and be soused with a hundred buckets of cold water. The season being midwinter, after seven or eight dousings she looked as though she would die of shivering. Those who were doing the pouring were frightened and wanted to stop, but Hua ordered them to complete the full quota. By the eightieth dousing, clouds of hot *ch'i* came steaming out of her to a height of two or three feet. When the full hundred pourings had been performed, Hua lit a fire, warmed her bed and heaped covers over her. Sweat poured out of her and she thereupon recovered.

The anecdote is recorded in the notes to the text of the *Hou Han-shu* 82 (72), 6a, and ascribed to the *Hua T'o pieh chuan*.

The Manchu feat of diving in and out of holes in the ice is described by Shirokogoroff, *Psychomental Complex of the Tungus*, p. 352.

9 The Lotus Sutra is translated by H. Kern, *Saddharma Pundarīka or the Lotus of the True Law, Sacred Books of the East*, vol. 21. The *Fumombon* in chapter 24 is on pp. 413–18.

10 The Heart Sutra has been translated by Edward Conze, *Buddhist Wisdom Books*, pp. 76–107.

11 On En-no-Gyōja and the Peacock Dhāranī, see Tsuda Sōkichi, 'En-no-Gyōja densetsukō', *Tsuda Sōkichi Zenshū*, vol. 9. The story of Nichizō Shōnin is in *Konjaku Monogatari*, book 14, *NBT* edition, vol. 8, p. 686.

Hori mentions the interesting documents *Ubasoku Kōshinge* preserved in the Shōsōin Treasury at Nara. These are the written applications of ascetics for admission to the entrance examination of the Buddhist priesthood, and contain lists of all the sutras, dharani and mantras which the candidates had learnt by heart. Among the dharani in the lists were the *Senju Kannonju* or the Spell of the Thousand-handed Kannon; the *Juichimen Kannonju* or the Spell of the Eleven-faced Kannon; the *Sonshō Darani*, the *Kokūzō Darani*, etc. 'On the concept of the *hijiri* (holy man)', *Numen*, vol. 5, fasc. 2 (1958), p. 145. See L. A. Waddell, 'The 'Dharani' cult in Buddhism, its origin, deified literature and images', *Ostasiatische Zeitschrift*, 1912.

12 Tsuda Sōkichi, p. 362. The converse is also true. Ascesis is not truly powerful unless combined with a holy text. It is only because they are practised within a holy context, because the mind is throughout fiercely concentrated on the words of power, that the starvation and the waterfall are endurable.

13 *Nihon Ryōiki, Nihon Koten Zensho* edition, edited by Takeda Yūkichi, pp. 162–4.

14 Origuchi Shinobu, 'Reikon no hanashi', *Origuchi Shinobu Zenshū* vol. 3, pp. 260–74. See also Ouwehand's helpful analysis of the *utsubo* principle in *Namazu-e*, p. 122.

15 See below, chapter 10, p. 191.

16 *Hokke Genki*, in *Zoku Gunsho Ruijū*, vol. 8. The two types of ascetic are discussed by Hori, *WK*, pp. 99–104. The holy traveller is one of the principal themes of this important book.

17 *Makura no Sōshi*, section 5, Kaneko's edition, pp. 15–16.

18 For Enkū, see Ebara Jun and Gotō Hideo, *Enkū*; also Hino, *Henreki hōrō no sekai*, pp. 157–65.

Bashō's *Oku no Hosomichi* is translated in the Penguin Classics series by Nobuyuki Yuasa, *The Narrow Road to the Deep North*.

Chapter 6

1 The first two figures are in the Tokyo National Museum at Ueno, the third in the archaeology department of Kyoto University. All

three are beautifully illustrated in Miki Fumio's *Haniwa*, translated by Roy Miller, plates 2, 4 and 27. Torii Ryūzō gives an illustration of another *haniwa miko* from Gumma prefecture who carries the mirror with bells at her waist and wears the flat board on her head with jewels on her neck and arms, in his *Jinruigakujō yori mitaru waga jōdai no bunka*, p. 176.

Another figure in Miko Fumio's book, plate 34, which it is tempting to designate as a female shaman, wears the flat board on her head, and holds in her outstretched hand a cylindrical musical instrument, perhaps a clapper or rattle, made of a segment of bamboo sawn off at the internode. The expression on her face is utterly entranced and apparently singing. The only difficulty is that she wears no jewels at all, and indeed appears to be completely naked.

2   Saigō Nobutsuna, *Kojiki no Sekai*, pp. 31–2.

3   Torii devotes a whole chapter to the mystery and inherent power of mirrors, pp. 151–78, adducing examples of mirrors with six or even seven bells on the rim found in tumuli in Nagano prefecture, and of a *haniwa* figure from the Hōki district which wears a mirror on its chest in true shamanic style.

For the mirror in the costume of the Tungusic shaman see Eliade, *Shamanism*, p. 154.

4   The earliest *magatama* of the Jōmon period are simply claws and teeth perforated at one end, but by the end of the Jōmon period they are found carved from stone. Scarce in sites of the Yayoi period, they appear in vast profusion in the tombs of the Kofun period. Made of various kinds of stone and of glass, they are found in a number of shapes and sizes, including the peculiar frilly form known as *komochi* or mother-and-child. See J. E. Kidder, *Japan before Buddhism*, pp. 69, 180–1.

For *magatama* found not in tombs but as a ritual tool in sites at the foot of sacred mountains, see Ōba Iwao, *Shintō Kōkogaku Ronkō*, p. 540. In the Tamayorihime shrine in Nagano prefecture, for example, no less than 490 *magatama* were discovered, made of jade, jasper, agate, crystal and steatite.

The Ryūkyū *nuru* also wears on ceremonial occasions a necklace of one or three large claw-like beads, usually coloured, and at least two *nuru* were found who possessed a bronze mirror among their paraphernalia: Lebra, *Okinawan Religion*, p. 76.

5   For the *torimono* held in the *miko's* hand see Ōtō Tokihiko, 'Shintō yōgōshū', in *Nihon Bunka Kenkyūjo Kiyō*, no. 18 (1966), p. 24; also *Minzokugaku Jiten*, article 'Torimono'.

6   Eliade, *Shamanism*, p. 156. The quincuncial disposition of this ritual recalls the mandala so important to esoteric Buddhist symbolism.

7 The *Kojiki* accounts are in chapters 92 and 93, Donald Philippi's translation, pp. 257–61. The *Nihon Shoki* accounts are in Aston's *Nihongi*, pp. 224–6.
   Donald Philippi, p. 258, gives the possible date of 362 A.D. for these events.

8 Nakayama Tarō, *Nihon Fujoshi*, p. 278.

9 See below, chapter 13.

10 Yanagita, 'Takusen to matsuri', *YKS*, vol. 9, pp. 235–6.

11 The term *koto-age*, 'to raise up words', is defined by Donald Philippi, following Tsugita, as 'proclaiming one's own will in opposition to a god's will' in a particular manner against which there was a taboo. Compare the example in chapter 86 of the *Kojiki*, whereby Yamato Takeru-no-Mikoto 'raises words' against the mountain god, and is struck unconscious by a violent hailstorm.

12 *Kojiki*, chapters 92 and 93. According to the *Nihon Shoki* account, the Emperor did not immediately die by the deity's curse, but later through a mysterious illness.

13 Aston's *Nihongi*, pp. 225–6.

14 See below, chapter 13.

15 Nakayama Tarō, pp. 293–4, considers the *miko's* trance utterances to have been the 'womb of literature'. The *miko* thus receives the characteristically shamanistic gift of poetic inspiration. Nakayama also considers the *norito* or Shinto prayers to be examples of divine poetic deliverance through a *miko*: ibid., pp. 154–5.

16 Yanagita's long essay *Imōto no chikara*, the power of the sister, is largely devoted to this theme.

17 See William P. Lebra, *Okinawan Religion*, pp. 74–85, 101–3, 134–5; Kamata Hisako, 'Daughters of the gods; shaman priestesses in Japan and Okinawa', in *Folk Cultures of Japan and East Asia*, pp. 56–62; Nakahara Zenshū, 'Omoro no kenkyū', *Minzokugaku Kenkyū*, vol. 15, Sakurai Tokutarō, *Okinawa no shamanizumu* (1972).

18 Oka Masao, *Nihon Minzoku no Kigen*, p. 63; Yanagita, *Imōto no chikara*, *YKS*, vol. 9; Hori, 'Anshi ni kakariyasui Nihon no josei', in *Minkan shinkōshi no shomondai*, pp. 179–96.

19 See *Minzokugaku Jiten*, p. 292, for *shinkontan*.

20 *Kojiki*, chapter 53, Donald Philippi's translation, pp. 178–9.

21 Ouwehand, *Namazu-e*, pp. 153–4. The legend is vividly recalled in the Nō play *Kamo*, where a large white feathered arrow stands erect in the middle of the stage. A woman come to draw

water tells a passing priest that long ago just such an arrow was
picked up by a woman from the river. She took it home and
miraculously conceived a child, who was born as the god
Wakeikazuchi-no-kami. The woman, her son and the arrow are
now the three Kamo deities. The scene then shifts and the woman
and her supernatural son come forth to dance and confer blessings
on the land.

22 *Kojiki*, chapter 66.

23 Seki Keigo, *Nihon Mukashibanashi Shūsei*, vol. 2, pp. 16–34. I should
like to thank Professor Daniels for his kindness in lending me his
huge collection of cards, as yet unpublished, of snake lore throughout
Japan, classified according to the degree of longitude and latitude
where the story or ritual was collected.

24 *Heike Monogatari*, book 8, Utsumi's edition pp. 446–7. Seki Keigo
divides the *odamaki* tales into three basic types, the *Heike* version
being an example of type A. In type Ba the girl's parents follow
the thread to a pool, where they find the serpent killed or wounded
by the iron needle. The local villagers thereupon build a shrine to
appease the dead snake's spirit. In type Bb, the girl herself follows
the thread to the pool, plunges into the water and turns into a
snake. The villagers thereafter avoid the pool for fear of offending
the denizen by dropping an iron object into it. In type C the girl
or her parents follow the thread to a cave, and overhear the snake
say to its mother, 'She may have killed me with that iron needle
of hers, but at any rate I've got her with child.' 'Rubbish', its
mother replies, 'human beings are quite clever enough to know
that all they have to do in a case like this is to have a bath of sweet
flags.' The girl without more ado goes home and gets into a bath
of sweet flags, whereupon several small snakes come streaming out
of her body.

Seki believes the tale to have been brought to Japan from China
in an unknown form before the seventh century, and already by
the beginning of the eighth to have developed into type A, recorded
in the *Kojiki*, and type B, recorded in the *Fūdoki* and the *Nihon
Shoki*. Type A was quickly adopted by certain families to account
for their divine ancestry, while type Ba developed into the founding
legend of various shrines. Seki also sees the tale as reflecting the
ancient form of marriage known as *tsumadoi-kon*, and the custom
in certain families of worshipping white snakes as tutelary deities.
See 'The spool of thread: a subtype of the Japanese serpent-
bridegroom tale', in *Studies in Japanese Folklore*, pp. 267–88. In
Hiroko Ikeda's classification the Snake Paramour stories are type
411C.

25 Yanagita, 'Tamayorihime-kō', *YKS*, vol. 9, p. 54. We are here
confronted with the problem of *hahako-gami* or mother–son deities,

on which Ishida Eiichiro has written extensively. See his 'Mother-son deities', *HR*, vol. 4, no. 1 (1964). Also *Momotaro no Haha*, 1956. The child in these myths and rituals, Yanagita's celebrated 'small hero', is sometimes identified with the miraculous water boy, *Ryūgū-dōji* or *kaijin-shōdō*, and sometimes with the thunder child, *raijin-dōji*. Ouwehand analyses the Miwa myth type—thunder-serpent–child–woman—extremely helpfully in his *Namazue-e*, pp. 146–61.

26 *Kojiki*, chapter 45.

27 Leo Sternberg, 'Divine election in primitive religion', *Congrès International des Americanistes*, Compte-rendu de la XXIe session, pt 2, pp. 476–9; Eliade, *Shamanism*, pp. 71–81.

28 Matsumura Takeo, *Nihon shinwa no kenkyū*, vol. 3. pp. 761–88.

29 Nakayama Tarō, pp. 248–9.

30 *Minzokugaku Jiten*, pp. 490–1; Yanagita, *Imōto no chikara*, *YKS*, vol. 9, pp. 108–9.

31 *Kojiki*, chapter 19. These tales are Hiroko Ikeda's type 948.

32 Matsumura, vol. 3, pp. 196–218.

33 Origuchi's views on the *miko* as a one-night wife are to be found in his 'Nenchū-gyōji', *Minzokugaku*, vol. 3, no. 8, p. 5; Higo Kazuo, *Nihon shinwa*, pp. 122–42.

34 Torii Ryūzō, pp. 102–10.

35 See chapter 5 of De Visser's interesting article 'The snake in Japanese superstition'. The stories here mentioned may be found in *Kii zōdanshū*, *Shokoku kojidan* and *Kokonchomonjū*.

Chapter 7

1 Hori, *WK*, pp. 655–8; Miyake Hitoshi, *Shugendo girei no kenkyū*, p. 318; Kaempfer, *The History of Japan*, vol. 2, pp. 340–1.

2 Nakayama Tarō, *Nihon Fujoshi*, pp. 738–40.

3 Kamata Hisako, 'Daughters of the gods: shaman priestesses in Japan and Okinawa', in *Folk Cultures of Japan and East Asia*, pp. 69–73; Sakaguchi Kazuo, 'Niijima no yakamishū', *Nihon Minzokugaku*, vol. 5, no. 1 (1957).

4 General studies of these new religious groups may be found in Neill McFarland, *The Rush Hour of the Gods*; C. B. Offner and H. van Straelen, *Modern Japanese Religions* (1963); also the last chapter of Professor Joseph Kitagawa's *Religion in Japanese History*. I have

treated the specifically messianic aspects of the new religions in my 'Millenarian aspects of the new religions in Japan', in *Tradition and Modernization in Japanese Culture*, ed Donald Shively.

5 These thirteen groups were Kurozumikyō, Shuseikyō, Izumo Taishakyō, Fusōkyō, Jikkōkyō, Taiseikyō, Shinshukyō, Mitakeyō, Shinrikyō, Misogikyō, Konkōkyō, Tenrikyō, Taishakyō. Most of these developed from the religious clubs known as *kō*, many of which were founded by a shamanic person.

6 The *Japan Christian Yearbook* of 1937 reports, p. 31, that more than two hundred new religious sects had come to the notice of the authorities in the last few years, but that such 'superstitious mushroom cults' were already declining owing either to government pressure or to internal disorders.

7 General MacArthur's *Shūkyō Hōjinrei* or Religious Bodies Law of 1945 stipulated that a 'religious body' could enjoy the privilege of exemption from taxation on the income from its 'religious activities'. But it failed to specify any conditions by which a 'body' should call itself a religious one. A good many enterprises were not slow to take advantage of this loophole. Most notorious of these bogus cults was the Kōdōjikyō, which sheltered a number of smaller concerns under its wing, and whose activities were exposed in 1947. A subsequent investigation by the Mombushō revealed a shocking state of affairs. One registered 'church' proved to be a hot-spring hotel which claimed as its 'religious activity' the promotion of happiness in the lives of men and women. A hairdressing establishment claimed to be a religious body with the religious activity of making life more beautiful. Many diverse concerns—restaurants, old clothes shops—claimed to be religious bodies putting into practice the precept *seikatsu soku shūkyō*, life is religion. Such manifestly fraudulent groups were abolished by the new legislation, the *Shūkyō Hōjinhō* of 1951. Thereafter the number of registered groups fell steeply from 720 in 1951 to the comparatively modest figure of 171 in 1958. See *Sengo shūkyō kaisōroku*, published by the Shinshūren Chōsashitsu, 1961, pp. 170–3. This work is translated serially into English under the title of 'Reminiscences of religion in postwar Japan', in *Contemporary Religions in Japan*, from vol. 6, no. 2 (1965) until vol. 7, no. 3 (1966). The latest available figure, given in the *Shūkyō Nenkan* or Religions Yearbook of 1971, is 377 groups registered with the Ministry of Education, and 419 registered on the prefectural level.

Among the shortlived groups founded on strange and bizarre principles may be mentioned the Denshinkyō, founded by an electrician in Ōsaka, which worshipped electricity as its principal deity and Thomas Edison as one of its lesser deities, and the Dai Nippon Fusō Shinjinkai which worshipped the late Dr Frederick Starr of Chicago University.

8 For the remarkably uniform and distinctively shamanistic character of the life histories of the Founders, see Takagi Hiroo, *Shinkō Shūkyō*, pp. 144–64, and Hori Ichirō, 'Penetration of shamanic elements into the history of Japanese folk religion', in *Festschrift for Adolf Jenson*, ed E. Haberland.

9 Inui Tadashi, Saki Akio, Oguchi Iichi et al., *Kyōso*, pp. 12–54; Murakami Shigeyoshi, 'Bakumatsu ishinki ni okeru minshū shūkyō no sōshō', in *Nihon Shūkyōshi kōza*, vol. 2, pp. 208–36.

10 Inui et al., pp. 60–9.

11 Ibid., pp. 182–91; *Shūkyō Nenkan 1971*.

12 Personal communications from Ōgamisama, 1959 and 1961; also *The Prophet of Tabuse*, published by Tenshō Kōtai Jingukyō, 1954, passim but especially pp. 13–47.

13 Takagi, pp. 146–7; Hori, 'Penetration of shamanic elements', p. 254.

14 Hori, ibid. p. 257.

15 See Nakayama, chapter 6, note 13.

Chapter 8

1 Hori Ichirō, *WK*, pp. 664–5, and *Nihon no Shamanizumu*, pp. 185–7.

2 See three articles by Sakurai Tokutarō: (1) 'Minkan fuzoku no keitai to kinō', in *Rikuzen Hokubu no Minzoku*, ed. Wakamori Tarō; (2) 'Kuchiyose miko no seitai: Yamagata bonchi ni okeru o-nakama no seifu katei', *NMK*, no. 64 (1969); (3) 'Tsuguru itako no fuzoku', in *Tsugaru no Minzoku*, ed. Wakamori Tarō. Also two articles by Satō Shōjun: (1) 'Ojika hantō no miko', *NMK*, no. 7 (1959); (2) 'Miyagi-ken kita chihō no miko', *Shakai to Denshō*, vol. 2, no. 1 (1958).

3 The differences between the *itako* and the *gomiso* are discussed by Miyake, *Shugendō girei no kenkyū*, pp. 321–33; Also by Eda Yukiko, 'Tsugaru no gomiso', *NMK*, no. 40 (1965), and 'Aomori to Akita no gomiso', *Minzokugaku Hyōron*, no. 2, and 'Tsugaru no gomiso', in *Tsugaru no Minzoku*, ed. Wakamori Tarō.
   The *itako* are blind, the *gomiso* never. The *gomiso* are not mediums for spirit utterances; they use their inherent power to answer questions about hidden and future things. The *itako* experiences no supernatural call; the *gomiso* always does. The *itako* use an instrument, bow or rosary; the *gomiso* never do.

4 See above, chapter 1, note 7.

5 Sakurai (1), p. 302, and (2), p. 17.

6 Sakurai (3), p. 315.

7 Sakurai (2), pp. 11–12.

8 Ibid. pp. 13–14.

9 Sakurai (3), p. 321.

10 Ibid. p. 313.

11 Sakurai (1), p. 305.

12 Sakurai (3), pp. 313–14.

13 In Miyagi prefecture it was customary for the candidate to be seated on a sack of rice in front of the altar, from which she fell when properly entranced. She thus takes the place of the *gohei* wand. See Sakurai (1), p. 306. Hori in his account of the *itako's* initiation, *WK*, pp. 662–3, also describes the candidate as seated on a sack of rice.

14 For the archer's bow as the forebear of the zither see Henry Balfour, *The Natural History of the Musical Bow*. The bow is the 'parent form whence sprang a long line of descendants', the prototype of a large series of stringed instruments of music including harp and zither. The legend that the *wagon* or Japanese zither developed from six archer's long bows placed side by side, their strings made from the hanging moss *saru-no-ogase*, and music made by drawing grass and reeds across the strings, is given in E. Satow,' Shrines of Ise', *TASJ*, vol. 11 (1873), p. 130.

   Nakayama, *Nihon Fujoshi*, pp. 390–1, considers the *azusayumi* to be an importation from China. See also Hori, *Nihon no shamanizumu*, pp. 179–80.

15 Hori, ibid. pp. 176–7. Nakayama, p. 420, thinks the claws and teeth on the rosary may have originated in magical hunting talismans.

16 Literature on the *oshirasama* is fairly extensive. I have found the following titles useful: Konno Ensuke, *Bajō kon-intan*, discusses the various versions of the horse–girl marriage tale; Yanagita, 'Oshiragami', *YKS*, vol. 9, pp. 248–53; Ishizu Teruji, 'Tōhoku no oshira', *Tōhoku Bunka Kenkyūshitsu Kiyō*, no. 3 (1961). Nakayama gives the text of the story, pp. 651–8. In Miyagi prefecture the *gohei* wand which the girl holds in her hands at her initiation becomes the core of one of the figures: Sakurai (1), p. 309.

17 This flat drum belongs more to the Nichiren sect of Buddhism than to shamanic practices in Japan. The extremely important position assigned to the drum in Siberian shamanism finds no counterpart in Japan.

18 Nakayama, pp. 638–40. The box often contained a Buddhist image and the skull of a fox or cat. It is possible that the image may have functioned as a magic doll.

19 These taboo words, *imikotoba*, differ according to the district. They do not seem to convey any comprehensible meaning. *Tsugi no kara no kagami* appears to mean Next Chinese Mirror or Next Empty Mirror, and *Toshiyori kara no kagami*, Old Chinese Mirror or Old Empty Mirror. The *itako* themselves had no understanding of what the words might mean.

20 Sakurai (1), pp. 313–15.

21 Ibid. pp. 317–21.

22 Ibid. pp. 321–5.

23 Ibid. pp. 325–9; see also Satō Shojun (1).

24 Sakurai (2), pp. 17, 4, 9, 22.

25 The sight I describe, witnessed in 1959, may no longer be seen. The following year the event was discovered to be worth a few minutes' transmission, nation-wide, on television, with the result that the gathering of *itako* is now a tourist attraction, its atmosphere dominated by the media and their machinery. A huge car park has needless to say been added.

Chapter 9

1 The general characteristics of the *hijiri* are discussed by Hori in his major work *Waga kuni minkan shinkōshi no kenkyū*, and by Gorai Shigeru in the first two chapters of his *Kōya hijiri*. Hori has treated the subject in English in his 'On the concept of the *hijiri* (holy man)', *Numen*, vol. 5 (1958), fasc. 2, pp. 128–60 and fasc. 3, 199–232.

On the etymology of the various appellations of the ascetic, *ubasoku*, derived from the Sanscrit *upasaka*, and *shamon* derived from *śramana*, present no problems. *Hijiri*, however, as both Hori and Ochiai Naobumi in *Kotoban no Izumi* point out, originally indicated 'one who understood the movements of the sun', hence a wise man.

2 Hori, *WK*, p. 99–104.

3 The Shugendō is a complex subject almost completely neglected until recent years. Two notable studies appeared within the same improbable year, 1943, Wakamori Tarō's *Shugendōshi Kenkyū* and Murakami Toshio's *Shugendō no Hattatsu*. The most authoritative recent work is Miyake Hitoshi's *Shugendō girei no kenkyū*, which incorporates most of the author's distinguished earlier work in article form. Togawa Anshō's work on the Haguro branch of the order is also indispensable. See also Wakamori's small but extremely helpful recent book, *Yamabushi*.

The first work in a European language was G. Renondeau's *Le Shugendo: histoire, doctrines et rites des anachorites dits Yamabushi*. For a study based on accurate and painstaking fieldwork as well as on literary sources, see H. Byron Earhart, *A Religious Study of the Mount Haguro Sect of Shugendō*.

4   E. R. Dodds, *The Greeks and the Irrational*, pp. 102–21.

5   Descriptions of the correct iconographical details of Fudō's attributes and retinue may be found in Mochizuki's *Bukkyō Daijiten*, and in Sawa Ryūken's *Butsuzō Annai*.

6   Wakamori Tarō discusses Zaō Gongen in *Shugendōshi Kenkyū*, pp. 58–66. The story of his first appearance to En-no-Gyōja is cited in *Konjaku Monogatari*, *NBT*, and *Taiheiki*, book 26, *NBT*, vol. 18, p. 92.

7   One of these mirrors, now in the Nishiarai Sōjiji temple, Tokyo, has been designated a National Treasure. It depicts Zaō Gongen with a halo of flames encircling his head, hair standing stiffly on end, three glaring eyes, jutting tusks and a retinue of thirty-one attendants, some with markedly aquiline noses, others with animal faces and open mouths full of teeth. A date corresponding to the year 1001 A.D. is engraved on it. The mirror is thought to have been originally a cult object, displayed on a stand with legs. *Kokuhō*, vol. 2, plate 173, and supplementary volume, p. 114.

8   Two excellent examples of Fudō's sword and the Kurikara dragon may be seen in the talismanic charm issued by the Dainichibō temple, Senninzawa, Yamagata prefecture. Also in the superb lacquer sutra box dating from the Heian period, now a National Treasure in the custody of the Taimaderā near Nara.

9   Note that the name of the third of the Five Myōō, Gundariyasha, is derived from Kundalini. See Gopi Krishna's *Kundalini* for a vivid and horrifying description of the arising of the 'serpent power'; also Arthur Avalon's *The Serpent Power*. Though the images of Gundariyasha Myōō show no evidence of a snake, the Indian Buddhist representations of the deity depict him with snakes hanging from his arms and legs: Alicia Matsunaga, *The Buddhist Philosophy of Assimilation*, pp. 250–1.

10 Leo Sternberg, 'Divine election in primitive religion', *Congrès International des Américanistes*, Compte-rendu de la XXIe Session, pt 2, 1924, p. 479.

11 Butsuren's boys are in *Konjaku Monogatari*, book 13, *NBT*, vol. 8, pp. 861–2; Jōzō's are in *Kokonchomonjū*, ibid. vol. 10, p. 371, and Yuirembō, ibid. p. 728. The story of Mongaku is in *Heike Monogatari*, book 5, chap. 8, and the ascetic from Shinano appears in the *Uji Shūi Monogatari*, ibid. p. 32. The latter is illustrated in the late Heian handscroll *Shigisan Engi* (see Plates 11 and 12).

    These and other examples of supernatural boys are treated in my 'The divine boy in Japanese Buddhism', *AFS*, vol. 22 (1963).

12 *Konjaku Monogatari*, *NBT*, vol. 11, pp. 823–6.

13 De Visser, whose excellent article 'The tengu' contains a rich collection of *tengu* stories from the eighth to the nineteenth century, considers the creature to be older than Buddhism. 'In my opinion there existed, long before Buddhism came to Japan, an original Japanese demon of the mountains and woods, having the shape of a bird.' Later this 'demon' was identified by Buddhist priests with the Garuda, the Indian supernatural bird. *TASJ*, vol. 36, pp. 25–98.

14 *Taiheiki*, book 5, *NBT*, vol. 17, pp. 114–15.

15 *Zoku Teikoku bunko*, vol. 47, quoted by de Visser, 'The tengu', p. 77.

Chapter 10

1 *Mahāvastu, Sacred Books of the East*, vol. 16, p. 6.

2 J. J. Duyvendak, 'A Chinese Divina Commedia', T'oung Pao, vol. 41 (1952). This work, Professor Duyvendak writes, gives 'a general effect of almost uncanny similarity' with the *Divina Commedia*. In Hiroko Ikeda's classification, these *jigoku-meguri* or journey to hell stories are type 470.

3 The broom as a life-giving symbol occurs also in the *Hsi Yang Chi*. When Wang Ming arrives at the eighth and last of the hells, he sees demons sawing the bodies of sinners into small pieces. They then brush the pieces with a broom, and the sinners come to life again. Duyvendak, p. 31.

4 *Nihon Ryōiki*, book 2, story 7. Nakamura Kyōko in her interesting study of the *Nihon Ryōiki*, *Rei-i no Sekai*, writes that out of the 116 tales in the work, fourteen can be classified as other-world journeys. Of these, only one was to an upper heaven, two were to King Emma's palace, while eleven were journeys to hell (pp. 66–7).

5 Mu-lien is the Chinese name for Maudgalyāyana, whose cosmic journey in the *Mahavastu* we noted earlier. In China he became a well-known figure in popular Buddhism, dramas featuring his journey to hell being frequently performed at funerals. His mother's life of sin began, according to one version of the story, when she tied up a goat next to a large vat of sauce. She then lit a fire round the poor beast so that it was grilled alive. In its agony it fell into the vat of sauce, where she ate it with relish. She then killed and ate her own dog, and afterwards indulged in meat of all kinds. For these crimes she was thrown into the lowest hell.

Mu-lien sought her in many sectors of hell, and after several attempts to save her, eventually with the Buddha's help succeeded in having her conveyed, purged of her karma, to the Trayatrimsa Heaven. See Arthur Waley's translation of the Tun-huang version of the story in *Ballads and Stories of Tun-huang*, pp. 216–35. Another version is given in Henri Dore's *Recherches sur les superstitions en Chine*, vol. 6, pp. 159–61.

For the dissemination of the Mu-lien legend in Japan, see Iwamoto Yutaka, *Mokuren Densetsu to Urabon*. It is illustrated in the *Gaki Zōshi*, a twelfth-century scroll depicting the activities of the *gaki* or hungry ghosts. Section 3 of the scroll differs completely from the disgusting scenes depicted in the first two sections, in which the *gaki* are shown on burial grounds clutching skulls and femurs, or in public privy grounds lapping up excrement. Here we are shown Mu-lien searching for his mother in the Gakidō or Realm of Ghosts, and succeeding eventually in bringing her food.

6 *Nihon Ryōiki*, book 3, story 9.

7 *Jikkinshō*, book 5, story 17.

8 *Taiheiki, NBT* edition, pp. 673–7.

9 *Konjaku Monogatari*, book 17, story 18. For a general description of the Bodhisattva Jizō see M. W. de Visser, *The Bodhisattva Ti-tsang (Jizō) in China and Japan*. For Jizō as a psychopomp and saviour from hell see pp. 109–15.

10 *Fusō Ryakki*, book 25, *Kokushi taikei*, vol. 12, pp. 219–22. The story of Nichizō's journey to heaven and hell can be found in several other books, notably the *Genkō Shakusho* and the *Kitano Tenjin Engi* scroll.

11 *Nihon Ryōiki*, book 1, story 5.

12 *En-no-Gyōja Hongi, Nihon Daizōkyō*, vol. 38, pp. 245–56. The date of this work appears uncertain. Some authorities place it as early as the eighth century, others, notably the *Bussho Kaisetsu Jiten*, vol. 1, p. 265, as late as the Muromachi period.

13 The elements so commonly found in the Siberian shaman's initiatory drama of dismemberment, reduction to a skeleton and remaking by a smith or other magical craftsman, are rarely indicated in the Japanese stories. Here is the difference, Hori suggests, between a hunting culture and an agricultural one. The dismemberment and skeleton motifs suggest a hunting, pastoral people. The contrasting elements found in the Japanese tales of the cave, the passage through a hole down to a subterranean world, betoken a return to the womb of the earth mother goddess characteristic of an agricultural people. Hori is nevertheless impressed with the elements which the Japanese stories have in common with the Siberian tales, which thus transcend differences of culture, climate and race. *Nihon no shamanizumu*, p. 110.

14 For oral examples of the legend, see Yanagita Kunio, *Yama no jinsei, YKS*, vol. 4, pp. 77–8. Also *Minzokugaku*, vol. 2, no. 9, p. 558. For a general discussion of the phenomenon see my 'Supernatural abductions in Japanese folklore', *AFS*, vol. 26 (1967).

15 *Shasekishū*, book 8, story 11.

16 *Senkyō ibun, Hirata Atsutane zenshū*, vol. 3, pp. 167–9. I have translated this story in greater detail in my 'Supernatural abductions', pp. 135–7. In Hiroko Ikeda's classification, this 'origin of the silkworm' story is type 411E.

17 'Kokon Yōmikō', *Hirata Atsutane zenshū*, vol. 3, pp. 25–8.

18 *Senkyō ibun*, passim. I have discussed Torakichi's story in my 'Supernatural abductions', pp. 124–47.

19 Yanagita Kunio, *Yama no jinsei, YKS*, vol. 4, pp. 102, 109. These stories have been collected into a book to which I have unfortunately not had access, *Yūmeikai kenkyū shiryō*, published in 1921 and quoted by Yanagita, *Yama no jinsei*, pp. 84–5.

20 Yanagita Kunio, ibid., pp. 102, 109.

21 A useful short biography of Deguchi, treated in a context of other founders of religious cults during the last hundred years, may be found in *Kyōso*, by Oguchi Iichi et al., pp. 69–96.

22 The following perforce abbreviated account is taken from the first volume of the latest edition of *Reikai Monogatari*, 1969, with which Mr Kakehi of the Ōmoto headquarters at Kameoka kindly furnished me.

Chapter 11

1 *Kokonchomonjū*, book 2, *NBT*, vol. 10, pp. 382–4. The *jikkai-shugyō* or Discipline of the Ten Realms is also discussed in Murakami Toshio's *Shugendō no Hattatsu*, pp. 304–18, in Wakamori Tarō's *Shugendōshi Kenkyū*, pp. 138–46, and in his *Yamabushi*, pp. 82–7.

2 Kaempfer devotes a whole chapter to 'The jammabos or mountain priests, and other religious orders' in vol. 2 of his *The History of Japan*, pp. 43–56, and describes encounters with them in the course of his journey with the Dutch Embassy from Nagasaki to Edo in 1692, ibid. p. 342.

3 The Jesuits' encounter with the *yamabushi* has been described by Ebisawa Arimichi, *Kirishitanshi no kenkyū*, pp. 96–113, and by G. Schurhammer S.J. in his 'Die Yamabushis'.

4 Philip Rawson, *The Art of South East Asia*, pp. 227–39.

5 Miyake in his 'Shugendō no shisō' quotes extensively from the works of Sokuden, particularly the *Shugen Shuyō Hikesshū* and *Sambu Sōjō Hossoku Mikki*. Both of these are in *Nihon Daizōkyō Shugendō Shōso*, vol. 2. In his 'Shugendo no Nyūbu shugyo ni okeru shimborizumu' he cites Gakuhō's *Buchū Hiden*. All these explain the identification of the mountains with the mandalas of esoteric Buddhism.

6   The six lower realms are broadly classified as *meikai*, worlds of delusion, the four upper as *gokai*, enlightened worlds. The *śrāvakas shōmon* in Japanese are those who are enlightened through listening to the teachings of the Buddha, and whose goal is to become an *arhant*. The *pratyeka-buddha*, *engaku* in Japanese, is a self-enlightened Buddha.

7   The *Shugen Hiōshō* is in *Nihon Daizōkyō Shugendō Shōso*, vol. 1, p. 395. A useful note on the contents and provenance of this work will be found by Hattori Nyojitsu in *Bussho Kaisetsu Jiten*. I have discussed the *jikkai-shugyō* and the other early works in which the ten stages are mentioned in my 'Initiation in the Shugendō', in *Initiation*, ed C. J. Bleeker. Further discussions of the discipline may be found in Wakamori Tarō, *Shugendōshi Kenkyū*, pp. 139–46, and Murakami Toshio, *Shugendō no Hattatsu*, pp. 304–29.

8   Motoori Norinaga, 'Zaikyō Nikki', in *Koji Ruien*, vol. 33, p. 1105.

9   Gorai Shigeru's account of his ascent of Mt Ōmine is in his *Yama no Shūkyō*, pp. 153–221; Miyake's account is in his *Shugendō girei no kenkyū*, pp. 65–86.

10 The curious method of ritual execution known as *ishikozume* is relevant here. The guilty person was battered, crushed or pressed to death by *stones*, usually having first been lowered into a pit which was later to act as a grave. In the Shugendō, those *yamabushi* who had violated the rules of the order were executed by this brutal method, and there is evidence to suggest that in a number of feudal clans this extreme penalty was the lot of those found guilty of such crimes as adultery, rape, blasphemy or association with the *eta* or outcaste class. Origuchi identifies *ishikozume* with the *tanikō* penalty, the *yamabushi* who fell sick during his ascent of the holy Mt Ōmine being not only thrown into the valley but also pelted with stones. From this Origuchi draws the curious conclusion that pelting a man with stones was originally a ritual for bringing a man to life rather than killing him. The stone, as we saw earlier, is an *utsubo* vessel, a container of sacred power. Contact with this power is life-giving, hence covering a man with stones becomes a means of bringing him back to life after death.

   For an interesting treatment in English, citing some of the celebrated cases of ritual stoning, see H. Byron Earhart, '*Ishikozume*: ritual execution in Japanese religion', *Numen*, vol. 13, fasc. 2 (1966).

11 The most authoritative account of the *akimine* is undoubtedly Shimazu Dendō's *Haguro-ha Shugendō Teiyō*, in which the prescriptions for the ritual and symbolism are given in minute detail. Togawa Anshō's writings on the Haguro sect are also based on a lifetime of research and experience. H. Byron Earhart's *A Religious Study of the Mount Haguro Sect of Shugendō*, already mentioned, is the first study in English to base itself not only on written sources but on

personal experience of participation in the ritual as well. It thus gives a more balanced and exact account of the whole exercise than any previous study in a European language.

12 The quincuncial symbolism with the *daisendatsu* representing Dainichi at the centre is taken from the Taizōkai or womb-world mandala of esoteric Buddhism. It thus forms a link with the rest of the gestation and embryo symbolism enacted during the week.

13 So great a stress is laid on the ritual attire of the *yamabushi* and the symbolism inherent in each of the sixteen items that it may usefully be compared with the shaman's ritual costume, without which he cannot exercise his power. True, there is no one instrument in the *yamabushi's* panoply comparable with the shaman's drum, but the whole attire qualifies as the 'special costume' which Vajda designates as one of the distinctive characteristics of the shaman.

Other items still commonly seen are the straw hat, the rosary, the portable altar, the fur strip hanging from the waist behind, the rope, the straw sandals, the ringed staff. The items are listed and discussed by Earhart, *A Religious Study*, pp. 26–7, and Murakami, *Shugendō no Hattatsu*, pp. 232–60.

14 I must express my grateful thanks once more to Professor Hori and Mr Togawa for their kind and generous assistance. Also to the three other students in the party whose guidance and companionship were an indispensable encouragement: Miyake Hitoshi of Keiō University, H. Byron Earhart, now of Western Michigan University, and Miss Tsuyuki of Kokugakuin University.

15 These names were changed halfway through the week to ones ending in *-in*. I was surprised to find that the name assigned to me was Myōgakubō, later Myōgakuin, wondrous knowledge.

16 Shimazu says that it should happen six times, at the end of each item in the *rokkondan* or Six Roots Section. In 1963 three times was evidently considered enough.

Chapter 12

1 Plays of this type, in which a travelling priest is able to bring comfort or salvation to an unhappy ghost, are legion. Those by Zeami alone include *Akogi, Funabashi, Genji Kuyō, Higaki, Hotoke-no-hara, Izutsu, Ebira, Eguchi, Yūgao, Yorimasa, Yashima, Utō, Uneme, Tsunemasa, Tomonaga, Tomoe* etc.

2 *Konjaku Monogatari*, book 12, *NBT*, vol. 8, p. 820.

3 *Kasuga Gongen Genkie*, in *Nihon Emakimono Zenshū*, vol. 15, plate 39.

4 *Ishiyamadera Engie*, in *Nihon Emakimono Zenshū*, vol. 22, plate 47.

5 *Uji Shūi Monogatari, NBT*, vol. 10, p. 77; *Kokonchomonjū*, ibid. pp. 371–2; Kaempfer, vol. 2, pp. 47–8. Kaempfer was sceptical

of the *yamabushi's* vaunted power. Their claims to be able to handle burning coals and red-hot iron, to extinguish fires, to make cold water boiling hot or hot water ice cold in an instant, to keep people's swords so fast in the sheath that no force could draw them out, all these uncommon and surprising things would if closely examined be found to be no more than 'Juggler's tricks and effects of natural causes.' Ibid. p. 49.

6   Here the authoritative study is Miyake's chapter 2, section 3 of *Shugendō girei no kenkyū*, based on his earlier article 'Shugendō no genjutsu'. He takes examples of all five of the aforementioned feats from rituals in the *Nihon Daizōkyō* and *Shugendō Seiten*, and analyses their structure with the object of revealing their 'world view'.

7   Percival Lowell, *Occult Japan*, pp. 62–88. De Groot in his *The Religious System of China*, vol. 6, pp. 1290–1, describes this feat as performed in China by the 'divining youths' *ki tong*, in a state of possession.

8   Honda Yasuji, *Kagura*, pp. 126–7.

9   Miyake points out that although the fire-walking now customarily follows the *saitō-goma* ritual, enough instances are left of the feat performed before the rite to suggest that its original intention was to provide a 'heating' of the body preliminary to the trance communication with the deity. Later the 'show' element of the feat became stronger, resulting in its shift to the end of the rite.

   De Groot describes the feat as performed in China in vol. 6, pp. 1292–4.

Chapter 13

1   Suzuki Shōei, 'Hayama shinkō to Shugendō', *NMK*, no. 32 (1964), p. 17.

2   The main text describing this rite is Taishō Tripitaka no. 1277, *Sokushitsu ryūken Makeishuraten setsu Abishahō*. The *Hōbōgirin*, that excellent French dictionary of Japanese Buddhist terms which regrettably has as yet advanced no further than the letter D, contains a full description of the Abisha rite and translation of the text, with parallels in China and Annam.

   Compare also the passage in Taishō Tripitaka no. 1202, *Fudō shisha darani himitsuhō*: 'The spell should be performed in a purified place such as an empty room in a temple. It need not contain an image or a picture. Burn Parthian incense and take a clear mirror and concentrate your mind on it as you recite the formulae. Then cause a young boy or girl to gaze into the mirror. Ask him what he sees there and he will tell you all you wish to know.'

   The Sōō story is in the biography of Sōō Oshō, in *Shūi Ōjōden*, *Zoku Gunsho Ruijū*, biography section, p. 262.

3　Yanagita, 'Ebisu-oroshi Inari-oroshi', *YKS*, vol. 9, pp. 243-4. These boys are sometimes called *hitotsumono*, 'one thing', and sometimes *shidō*, 'corpse boy'. This peculiar term apparently comes from China, where strict Confucian usage demanded that at a funeral feast the grandson of the deceased man should 'represent' him. This boy was known as the *shih* or corpse.

For these boy mediums see also Yoshimura Shukuho, 'Yorimashi dōji; Tosa ni okeru kamigakari no gishiki', *Matsuri*, no. 12 (1967).

4　See, for example, 'Inukaiyama no kamioroshi', vol. 2, no. 1, pp. 45-7.

5　Iwasaki' principal work on the Hayama Matsuri is published in his, *Hompō shōshi no kenkyū*. See also Suzuki Shōei, 'Hayama shinkō to Shugendō, for a useful discussion of the Hayama cult.

6　Yanagita discusses the deities alternating between mountain and village, of which the principal example is the mountain god Yamanokami who becomes the rice field god Tanokami during his descent into the village, in *Senzo no hanashi*, section 30. See about out Ancestors, p. 74-5.

7　The following account is taken from Iwasaki, p. 53-65.

8　Familiar Buddhist words and names appear here in rustic disguise. The Hachidai Kongō dōji or Eight Great Vajra Boys may be discerned, also Yakushirurikō-nyorai or the Buddha in his aspect of the great Physician. The meaning of the invocation as a whole was not understood.

9　Five *bu* were said to be the yield for the average year: Iwasaki, p. 60.

10　Hori Ichirō, 'Isse gyōnin to toshi-uranai no kamizuke', in *Shūkyō shūzoku no seikatsu kitei*, pp. 236-44.

11　Yanagita, 'Hitokotonushi-kō', *YKS*, vol. 9, pp. 309-17. 'I think the true origin of Hitokonushi's name lies in the tradition that the god's oracular utterance to man on the things of the future was always transmitted in one very simple word'. (p. 317).

12　Quoted in Yanagita, 'Gohō-dōji', *YKS*, vol. 9, pp. 407-416, and by Nakayama Tarō, *Nihon Fujoshi*, pp. 437-8.

13　Miura Shuyu, 'Gohō Matsuri', in *Mimasaka no Minzoku*, ed. Wakamori Tarō; Suzuki Shōei, 'Shugendō to kamigakari', in *Matsuri*, no. 12 (1967), pp. 16-20, and 'Sangaku shinkō: Shugendō to shamanizumu to no kankei', *Otani Shigaku*, no. 8 (1961); Yasutomi Nobuko, 'Gohōtobi kembunki', *Okayama Minzoku*, no. 24 (1956).

14　I should like to thank Dr Tanaka for allowing me to join the party and for his generous help and guidance throughout the visit.

15 Ushio Michio, 'Kagura ni okeru takusen no hōshiki ni tsuite', *NMK*, no. 2 (1958).

16 Hagiwara Tatsuo, 'Ōmoto Kagura kengakki', *Matsuri*, no. 12 (1967), pp. 21–4, and 'Matsurikata', *NMT*, vol. 8.

17 On the 'snake rope', see F. J. Daniels, 'Straw snakes', *TASJ*, Third Series, vol. 7 (1959).

18 Iwasaki Toshio, pp. 66–7.

19 Ibid. pp. 68–71.

20 Miura Shuyu, 'Kōjin kagura no takusen', *NMK*, no. 31 (1963), contains a description of the Kōjin Kagura.

21 Iwasaki, p. 71.

Chapter 14

1 Percival Lowell, 'Esoteric Shinto, Part I, *TASJ*, vol. 21 (1893), pp. 109–15.

2 Described in subsequent sections of 'Esoteric Shinto' in vols 21 and 22 of the *TASJ*. Mr Lowell's account is regrettably marred by his tone of patronising facetiousness, which proves increasingly irritating as the work proceeds.

3 Useful information on the history and formation of *kō* groups can be found in Sakurai Tokutarō, 'Kō-shudan no soshiki to kinō', in his *Minkan Shinkō*, pp. 127–9; Hori Ichirō, *Folk Religion in Japan*, pp. 38–40; and Percival Lowell, *Occult Japan*, chapter 'Pilgrimages'.

4 See Ikegami Hiromasa's report on his survey of *kō* in fourteen villages in the neighbourhood of Mt Ontake, 'Nagano-ken Kiso no Ontake-kō', *Shakai to Denshō*, vol. 2, no. 1 (1958).

5 Yanagita offers evidence suggesting that in the past several other mountains may have been the scene of such séances. On Mt Tateyama the porters used to be known by the peculiar name of *chūgo*, 'between words', a name which Yanagita believes to be a survival of the days when porters acted also as intermediaries transmitting the words of the god. 'Tateyama chūgo-kō', *YKS*, vol. 9, p. 306.

6 In his useful article 'Kinsei Ontake shinkō no jittai', *Shakai to Denshō*, vol. 5, no. 2 (1961), Miyata Noboru has made use of documents in the Odaki shrine on Mt Ontake dating back to the eighteenth century.

7 For a discussion of *reijin* and their powers, see Miyata Noboru 'Ikigami shinkō no hatsugen', *NMK*, no. 28 (1963).

8 I should like to thank those friends who so staunchly accompanied me on those occasions, Oka Akira in 1961, David Huish in 1963, Joan Martin in 1967.

9 *Nihon Meisan Zue*, written and illustrated by Tani Bunchō. See Pl. 1.

10 The *kuji* is a spell of Taoist, not Buddhist origin, which at some time was adopted by the Shugendō and assigned its nine mudras. *Mikkyō Daijiten*, vol. 1, p. 331.

Chapter 15

1 I quote from Arthur Waley's translation, *Kashiwagi* chapter of *The Tale of Genji*, Houghton Mifflin edition p. 680.

2 *Makura no Sōshi*, section 297, Kaneko's edition pp. 575–8; English translations by Arthur Waley, *The Pillow Book of Sei Shōnagon*, pp. 135–8, and Ivan Morris, *The Pillow Book of Sei Shōnagon*, Vol. 1, p. 264–6.

3 *Murasaki Shikibu Nikki*, *NKBT*, vol. 19, pp. 447–51.

4 *The Tale of Genji*, Waley's translation p. 663. Many similar descriptions of malign possession by dead spirits, 'living spirits', or enraged *kami* are to be found in Heian literature.

5 *Minzoku to Rekishi*, vol. 8, no. 1 (1922), pp. 211–13.

6 Dr E. Baelz, who was Professor of Medicine in the University of Tokyo during the 1890s, and had many opportunities for personal observation of cases of fox possession in the hospital under his charge, has left several interesting descriptions. His 'Uber Besessenheit', in *Verhandlung der Gesellschaft deutscher Naturforscher und Aerzte* (Leipzig, 1907), was kindly procured for me by Professor Peter Baelz of Christ Church, Oxford. Extracts in English may be found in Oesterreich's *Possession, Demoniacal and Other*, pp. 224–8, and in B. H. Chamberlain's *Things Japanese*, p. 131.

7 I am grateful to my uncle Canon Ronald Pilkington for drawing my attention to the three specific signs of demoniacal possession indicated in the *Roman Ritual*. In its chapter 'De Exorcizandis Obsessis a daemonio', the Ritual warns that the presence of a demon should not be suspected unless the following signs are present:
(1) *Ignota lingua loqui pluribus verbis vel loquentem intelligere.*
(2) *Distantia et occulta patefacere.*
(3) *Vires super aetatis seu conditionis naturam ostendere.*

8 Ishizuka includes a short description of the Nichiren methods in his *Nihon no tsukimono*, pp. 179–80.

9 I. M. Lewis, *Ecstatic Religion*.

Chapter 16

1 I am grateful to Dr Lawrence Picken for information on the Toraden tune. According to Martin Gimm, *Das Yueh-fu tsa-lu des tuan An-chieh* (Wiesbaden, 1966), p. 270, the piece is attested for the time of the Emperor Jui-tsung, 710–712. The *Wamyōruijusho*, completed before the end of the tenth century adds the fact that it was a *taikyoku* or 'large tune' in the *ichikotsu* mode. In the *Shakkyō* play the tune was chosen for the play on its name, *tora* meaning also a tiger.

Select Bibliography

A *Works in Western Languages*

ASTON, W. G., *Nihongi*, London, 1956.
Shinto, the Way of the Gods, London, 1905.

AVALON, ARTHUR (Sir John Woodroffe), *The Serpent Power*, Madras, 1931.

BAELZ, E., *Verhandlung der Gesellschaft Deutscher Naturforscher und Aerzte*, Leipzig, 1907.

BALFOUR, HENRY, *The Natural History of the Musical Bow*, Oxford, 1899.

BLACKER, CARMEN, 'Animal Witchcraft in Japan' in *The Witch Figure. Folklore essays by a group of scholars in England honouring the 75th birthday of Katherine M. Briggs*, ed. Venetia Newall, London, 1973.

'The Divine Boy in Japanese Buddhism', *Asian Folklore Studies*, vol. 22, 1963.

'Initiation in the Shugendo: the Passage through the Ten States of Existence', in *Initiation: Contributions to the theme of the Study-Conference of the International Association for the History of Religions*, ed. C. J. Bleeker, Leiden, 1965.

'Millenarian Aspects of the New Religions in Japan', in *Tradition and Modernisation in Japanese Culture*, ed. Donald Shively, Princeton, 1971.

'Supernatural Abductions in Japanese Folklore, *Asian Folklore Studies*, vol. 26, 1967.

BOCK, F. G. (tr.), *Engi-Shiki; Procedures of the Engi Era*, 2 vols, Tokyo, 1970 and 1972.

BOYLE, JOHN ANDREW, 'Turkish and Mongol Shamanism in the Middle Ages', *Folklore*, vol. 83, 1972.

BUCHOLZ, PETER, 'Shamanism—the Testimony of the Icelandic Literary Tradition', *Medieval Scandinavia*, vol. 4, 1971.

CASAL, U. A., 'The Yamabushi', *Mitteilungen der Deutschens Gesellschaft für Natur—und Völkerkunde Ostasiens*, vol. 46, Tokyo, 1965.

CHADWICK, NORA, *Poetry and Prophesy*, Cambridge, 1942.

'Shamanism among the Tatars of Central Asia', *Journal of the Royal Anthropological Society*, vol. 66, 1936.

CHAMBERLAIN, B. H., *Things Japanese*, Tokyo, 1890.

CHAVANNES, EDOUARD, *Le T'ai Chan. Essai de monographie d'un culte chinois*, Paris, 1910.

CONZE, EDWARD, *Buddhist Wisdom Books*, London, 1958.

COOMARASWAMY, DONA LUISA, 'The Perilous Bridge of Welfare', *Harvard Journal of Asiatic Studies*, vol. 8, 1944.

CZAPILICKA, M. A., *Aboriginal Siberia: a Study in Social Anthropology*, Oxford, 1914.

DANIELS, F. J., 'Snake and Dragon Lore of Japan', *Folklore*, vol. 71, September 1960.

'Straw Snakes', *Transactions of the Asiatic Society of Japan*, Third Series, vol. 7, November 1959.

DAVID-NEEL, ALEXANDRA, *With Mystics and Magicians in Tibet*, London, 1931.

DIOSZEGI, VILMOS, *Tracing Shamans in Siberia*, Ousterhout, Holland, 1968.

DODDS, E. R., *The Greeks and the Irrational*, Berkeley and Los Angeles, 1963.

DORÉ, HENRI, *Recherches sur les superstitions en Chine*, 6 vols, Shanghai, 1914.

DORSON, R. M., *Folk Legends of Japan*, Tokyo, 1962.

DORSON, R. M. (ed), *Studies in Japanese Folklore*, Bloomington, Indiana, 1963.

DUYVENDAK, J. J., 'A Chinese Divina Commedia', *T'oung Pao*, vol. 41, 1952.

EARHART, H. BYRON, '*Ishikozume*: Ritual Execution in Japanese Religion, especially in *Shugendō*', *Numen*, vol. 13, fasc. 2, August 1966.

A Religious Study of the Mount Haguro Sect of Shugendō, Tokyo, 1970.

'Shugendō, the traditions of En no Gyōja, and Mikkyō influence', *Studies of Esoteric Buddhism and Tantrism*, Kōyasan, 1965.

EDER, MATTHIAS, 'Schamanismus in Japan', *Paideuma*, vol. 7, no. 7, 1958.

ELIADE, MIRCEA, *Birth and Rebirth: the Religious Meanings of Initiation in Human Culture*, tr. Willard R. Trask, New York, 1958.

Images and Symbols: Studies in Religious Symbolism, London, 1961.

The Myth of the Eternal Return, London, 1954.

Myths, Dreams and Mysteries: the Encounter between Contemporary Faiths and Archaic Realities, London, 1960.

Patterns in Comparative Religion, tr. Rosemary Sheed, London, 1958.

'Recent works on shamanism; a review article', *History of Religions*, vol. 1, no. 1, 1961.

Shamanism: Archaic Techniques of Ecstasy, London, 1964.

Yoga: Immortality and Freedom, London, 1958.

EVANS-PRITCHARD, E., *Witchcraft, Oracles and Magic among the Azande*, Oxford, 1937.

FAIRCHILD, WILLIAM P., 'Shamanism in Japan', *Folklore Studies*, vol. 21, 1952

FENG, H. Y. and SHRYOCK, J. K., 'The Black Magic in China known as Ku', *Journal of the American Oriental Society*, vol. 55, no. 1, 1935.

FLORENZ, KARL, 'Ancient Japanese rituals, part IV, the Oho-harahe', *Transactions of the Asiatic Society of Japan*, First Series, vol. 27, pt 1., reprinted December 1927.

FRAZER, SIR JAMES, *The Fear of the Dead in Primitive Religion*, 3 vols, London, 1935-6.

GOODRICH, L. CARRINGTON and TSUNODA RYUSAKU, *Japan in the Chinese Dynastic Histories*, South Pasadena, 1951.

GROOT, J. J. M. DE, *The Religious System of China*, 6 vols, Taipei, 1964.

HAGUENAUER, CHARLES, *Origines de la civilisation japonaise, Introduction à l'étude de la préhistoire du Japon*, Paris, 1956.

HARTLAND, SIDNEY, *The Science of Fairy Tales*, London, 1925.

HARVA, UNO (HOLMBERG), *Finno-Ugric and Siberian Mythology*, London 1927.

HATTO, A. T., 'Shamanism and Epic Poetry in Northern Asia', Foundation Day Lecture, School of Oriental and African Studies, University of London, 1970.

HOLTOM, D. C., *The Japanese Enthronement Ceremony*, Tokyo, 1972.
'The Meaning of Kami', *Monumenta Nipponica*, vol. 3, nos. 1 and 2, 1940, and vol. 4, no. 2, 1941.
The National Faith of Japan. A Study in Modern Shinto, New York, 1938.

HORI ICHIRO, *Folk Religion in Japan*, Chicago, 1958.
'Mountains and their importance for the idea of the other world in Japanese folk religion', *History of Religions*, vol. 1, no. 1, 1961.
'Mysterious Visitors from the Harvest to the New Year', in *Studies in Japanese Folklore*, ed. R. M. Dorson.
'On the concept of the *Hijiri* (holy man)', *Numen*, vol. 5, fasc. 2 and 3, April 1958.
'Penetration of shamanic elements into the history of Japanese folk religion', in *Festschrift for Adolf Jensen*, ed. E. Haberland, Munich, 1964.
'Self-mummified Buddhas in Japan', *History of Religions*, vol. 1, no. 2, 1961.
'Three Types of Redemption in Japanese Folk Religion', in *Types of Redemption*, ed. R. J. Zwi Werblowsky and C. J. Bleeker, Leiden, 1970.

HUMPHREY, CAROLINE, 'Shamans and the trance', *Theoria to Theory*, vol. 5, no. 4, October 1971 and vol. 6, no. 1, January 1972.

IKEDA, HIROKO, *A Type and Motif Index of Japanese Folk Literature*, FF Communications no. 209, Helsinki 1971.

ISHIDA EIICHIRŌ, 'Mother-son deities', *History of Religions*, vol. 4, no. 1, 1964.
'Unfinished but enduring: Yanagita Kunio's Folklore Studies', *Japan Quarterly*, vol. 10, no. 1. 1963.

KAEMPFER, ENGELBERT, *The History of Japan. Together with a Description of the Kingdom of Siam*, 1690–1692, 3 vols, Glasgow, 1906.

KAMATA HISAKO, 'Daughters of the Gods: shaman priestesses in Japan and Okinawa', in *Folk Cultures of Japan and East Asia*, ed. Joseph Pittau, *Monumenta Nipponica Monographs* no. 25, Tokyo, 1966.

KEIGHTLEY, THOMAS, *Fairy Mythology*, London, 1850.

KERN, H., *Saddharma Puṇḍarīka or the Lotus of the True Law*, Sacred Books of the East, vol. 21, Oxford, 1884, reprinted New York, 1963.

KIDDER, J. E., *Japan before Buddhism*, London, 1959.

KISHIMOTO HIDEO, 'The role of mountains in the religious life of the Japanese people', *Proceedings of the Ninth International Congress for the History of Religions*, Tokyo, 1958.

KITAGAWA, JOSEPH, 'Ainu Bear Festival (Iyomante)', *History of Religions*, vol. 1, no. 1, 1961.
'The prehistoric background of Japanese religion', *History of Religions*, vol. 2, no. 2, 1963.
Religion in Japanese History, New York, 1966.

KRISHNA, GOPI, *Kundalini*, London, 1971.

LEBRA, WILLIAM P., *Okinawan Religion*, Honolulu, 1966.

LEWIS, I. M., *Ecstatic Religion*, London, 1971.

LINDGREN, E. J., 'Notes on the Reindeer Tungus of Manchuria', Unpublished Ph.D. thesis, Cambridge 1936.

LOEWE, MICHAEL, *Crisis and Conflict in Han China*, 104 B.C. to A.D. 9, London, 1974.

LOWELL, PERCIVAL, 'Esoteric Shinto', parts I and II, *Transactions of the Asiatic Society of Japan*, vol. 21, 1893, pt III, vol. 22.

Occult Japan, or the Way of the Gods; an Esoteric Study of Japanese Personality and Possession, Boston, 1895.

MABUCHI TŌICHI, 'Spiritual predominance of the sister', *Ryukyuan Culture and Society*, Honolulu, 1964.

MACFARLAND, H. NEILL, *The Rush Hour of the Gods*, London, 1967.

MASPERO, HENRI, 'Les Procédés de "nourrir le principe vital" dans la religion taoiste ancienne', *Journal Asiatique*, vol. 229, April–June 1937.

Le Taoisme, mélanges posthumes sur les religions et l'histoire de la Chine, vol. 2, Paris, 1950.

MATSUDAIRA NARIMITSU, 'The concept of Tamashii in Japan', in *Studies in Japanese Folklore*, ed. R. M. Dorson.

MATSUMOTO NOBUHIRO, *Essai sur la mythologie japonaise*, Paris, 1928.

MATSUNAGA, ALICIA, *The Buddhist Philosophy of Assimilation*, Tokyo, 1969.

MAYER, FANNY HAGIN (tr.) with Ishiwara Yasuyo, *About our Ancestors: the Japanese Family System* (translation of Yanagita Kunio's *Senzo no Hanashi*), Tokyo, 1970.

MIKI FUMIO, *Haniwa*, tr. Roy Miller, Tokyo, 1960.

MILLER, ROY, *The Japanese Language*, Chicago, 1967.

MILLS, D. E., *A Collection of Tales from Uji: a Study and Translation of the Uji Shūi Monogatari*, Cambridge, 1970.

MIRONOV, N. D. and SHIROKOGOROFF, S. M., 'Śramana-Shaman: etymology of the word "Shaman" ', JRAS, North-China Branch, vol. 55, 1924.

MITFORD, A. B., *Tales of Old Japan*, London, 1871.

MORRIS, IVAN, *The Pillow Book of Sei Shōnagon*, 2 vols, Oxford, 1967.

MUNRO, NEIL GORDON, *Ainu Creed and Cult*, London, 1962.

NAUMANN, NELLY, '*Yama no kami*—die japanische Berggottheit', *Asian Folklore Studies*, vol. 22, 1963.

'Das Pferd in Sage und Brauchtum Japans,' *Asian Folklore Studies*, vol. 18, 1959.

OESTERREICH, T. K., *Possession, Demoniacal and Other among Primitive Races in Antiquity, the Middle Ages and Modern Times*, London, 1930.

OFFNER, C. B. and VAN STRAELEN, H., *Modern Japanese Religions*, Tokyo, 1963.

OLIVIER, EDITH, *Four Victorian Ladies of Wiltshire*, London, 1945.

OTTO, RUDOLPH, *The Idea of the Holy*, tr. J. W. Harvey, Oxford, 1950.

OUWEHAND, CORNELIUS, *Namazu-e and their Themes*, Leiden, 1964.

'Some notes on the god Susano-o', *Monumenta Nipponica*, vol. 14, 1958.

PHILIPPI, DONALD, *Kojiki*, Princeton, 1969.

Norito: A New Translation of the Ancient Japanese Ritual Prayers, Tokyo, 1969.

PITTAU, JOSEPH (ed), *Folk Cultures of Japan and East Asia*, Tokyo, 1966.

PONSONBY-FANE, RICHARD, *The Vicissitudes of Shinto*, vol. 5 of the Richard Ponsonby-Fane Series, Kyoto, 1963.

RAWSON, PHILIP, *The Art of South East Asia*, London, 1967.

REDFIELD, ROBERT, *Peasant Society and Culture*, Chicago, 1956.

RENONDEAU, G., *Le Shugendo: Histoire, doctrines et rites des anachorètes dits Yamabushi*, Paris, 1965.

ROTERMUND, HARTMUT O., *Die Yamabushi. Aspekte ihres Glaubens, Lebens und ihrer sozialen Funktion im japanischen Mittelalter*, Hamburg, 1968.

SARGANT, WILLIAM, *The Mind Possessed*, London, 1973.

SCHURHAMMER, GEORG, *Shin-to. The Way of the Gods in Japan. According to the Printed and Unprinted Reports of the Japanese Jesuit Missionaries in the Sixteenth and Seventeenth Centuries*, Bonn, 1923.

'Die Yamabushis', *Zeitschrift für Missionswissenschaft und Religionswissenschaft*, vol. 12, 1922, pp. 206–28. Reprinted in *Mitteilungen der Deutschen Gesellschaft für Natur- und Völkerkunde Ostasiens*, Tokyo, 1965.

SEGAWA KIYOKO, 'Menstrual taboos imposed on women', in *Studies in Japanese Folklore*, ed. R. M. Dorson.

SEKI KEIGO, 'The spool of thread: a subtype of the Japanese serpent-bridegroom tale', in *Studies in Japanese Folklore*, ed. R. M. Dorson.

'Types of Japanese Folktales', *Asian Folklore Studies*, vol. 25, 1966.

SHIROKOGOROFF, SERGEI M., *Psychomental Complex of the Tungus*, London, 1935.

SIDGWICK, HENRY, 'Report on the census of hallucinations', *Proceedings of the Society for Psychical Research*, vol. 10, 1894.

SIEFFERT, RENÉ, 'De quelques representations du jugement des morts chez les japonais', *Sources Orientales*, vol. 4, *Le Jugement des morts*, Paris, 1961.

'Le monde du sorcier au Japon', *Sources Orientales*, vol. 7, *Le Monde du sorcier*, Paris, 1966.

'Les songes et leur interpretation au Japon', *Sources Orientales*, vol. 2, *Les Songes et leur interpretation*, Paris, 1959.

SIVIN, NATHAN, '*Folk medicine and classical medicine in traditional China. A contribution to the definition of "Taoist"* ', unpublished, 1972.

STERNBERG, LEO, 'Divine election in primitive religion', *Congrès International des Américanistes*, compte-rendu de la XXIe session, pt 2, 1924.

TAJIMA RYUJUN, *Les Deux Grands Mandalas et la doctrine de l'ésoterisme Shingon*, Tokyo, 1959.

TENSHŌ KŌTAI JINGUKYŌ, pub. *The Prophet of Tabuse*, Tabuse, 1954.

TSUNODA, RYUSAKU and GOODRICH, L. C., *Japan in the Chinese Dynastic Histories*, South Pasadena, California, 1951.

VAJDA, L., 'Zur phaseologischen Stellung des Schamanismus', *Ural-altaische Jahrbücher* 31, 1959.

VISSER, M. W. DE, *The Bodhisattva Ti-tsang (Jizō) in China and Japan*, Berlin, 1914.

VISSER, M. W. DE—*continued*

The Dragon in China and Japan, Amsterdam, 1913.

'The Fox and Badger in Japanese Superstition', *Transactions of the Asiatic Society of Japan* , vol. 36, 1908–9.

'The snake in Japanese Folklore', *Mitteilungen des Seminars für Orientalische Sprachen*, vol. 14, 1911.

'The tengu', *Transactions of the Asiatic Society of Japan*, vol. 36, 1908.

WADDELL, L. A., 'The "Dhāraṇi" cult in Buddhism, its origin, deified literature and images', *Ostasiatische Zeitschrift*, 1912.

WALEY, ARTHUR, *Ballads and Stories of Tun-huang*, London, 1960.

The Nine Songs. A Study of Shamanism in Ancient China, London, 1955.

Nō Plays of Japan, London, 1921.

The Pillow Book of Sei Shōnagon, London, 1928.

The Tale of Genji, London, 1925.

YANAGITA KUNIO, *About our Ancestors: the Japanese Family System*, tr. Fanny Hagin Mayer and Ishiwara Yasuyo, Tokyo, 1970.

YETTS, PERCIVAL, 'Disposal of the Buddhist dead in China', *Journal of the Royal Asiatic Society*, July 1911.

B *Works in Japanese*

AKIBA TAKASHI, *Chōsen fuzoku no genchi kenkyū*, Tokyo, 1950.

ANDŌ KŌSEI, *Nihon no miira*, Tokyo, 1961.

DEGUCHI ONISABURŌ, *Reikai Monogatari*, Kameoka, 1969.

EBARA JUN, *Enkū*, Tokyo, 1961.

EBISAWA ARIMICHI, *Kirishitanshi no kenkyū*, Tokyo, 1942.

EDA YUKIKO, 'Aomori to Akita no gomiso', *Minzokugaku Hyōron*, no. 2.

'Tsugaru no gomiso', *Nihon Minzokugaku Kaihō*, no. 40, July 1965.

'Tsugaru no gomiso', in *Tsugaru no Minzoku*, ed. Wakamori Tarō, Tokyo, 1970.

Gempei Seisuiki, *Nihon Bungaku Taikei*, vol. 15.

GORAI SHIGERU, *Kōya hijiri*, Tokyo, 1965.

Kumano-mōde, Kyoto, 1967.

Yama no shūkyō, Kyoto, 1970.

HAGAMI SHŌCHŌ, *Dōshin*, Tokyo, 1971.

HAGIWARA TATSUO, 'Ōmoto Kagura kengakki', *Matsuri*, no. 12, 1967.

HATTORI NYOJITSU, *Shugendō Yōten*, Kyoto, 1972.

HAYAMI YASUTAKA, *Tsukimono-mochi meishin no rekishiteki kōsatsu*, Tokyo, 1953.

Heike Monogatari, ed. Utsumi Kōzō, Tokyo, 1952.

HIGO KAZUO, *Nihon shinwa*, Tokyo, 1942.

HINO KAZUYOSHI, *Henreki hōrō no sekai*, Tokyo, 1967.

HIRATA ATSUTANE, *Senkyō Ibun*, Hirata Atsutane zenshū, vol. 3.

HONDA YASUJI, *Kagura*, Tokyo, 1966.

HORI ICHIRŌ, 'Heike Monogatari ni arawareta shūkyōshiteki yōso', in *Shūkyōshūzoku no seikatsu kisei*, Tokyo, 1963.

'Isse gyōnin to toshiuranai no kamizuke', in *Shūkyō shūzoku no seikatsu kisei*, Tokyo, 1963.

HORI ICHIRŌ—*continued*
'Manyōshū ni arawareta sōsei to takaikan reikonkan ni tsuite', in
Shūkyō shūzoku no seikatsu kisei, Tokyo, 1963.
Minkan shinkō, Tokyo, 1951.
Minkan shinkōshi no shomondai, Tokyo, 1971.
Nihon no shamanizumu, Tokyo, 1971.
Nihon shūkyō no shakaiteki yakuwari, Tokyo, 1962.
Shūkyō shūzoku no seikatsu kisei, Tokyo, 1963.
Waga kuni minkan shinkōshi no kenkyū, 2 vols, Tokyo, 1960.
'Yudono-san-kei no sokushimbutsu (miira) to sono haikei', *Tōhoku
bunka*, March 1961.
IKEGAMI HIROMASA, 'Nagano-ken Kiso no Ontake-kō', *Shakai to Denshō*,
vol. 2, no. 1, 1958.
'Rei to kami no shurui', *Nihon Minzokugaku Taikei*, vol. 8, Tokyo, 1962.
'Tama to kami no shurui to arawarekata', *Nihon Minzokugaku Taikei*,
vol. 8, Tokyo, 1962.
INOUE ENRYŌ, *Yōkaigaku Kōgi*, 6 vols, Tokyo, 1897.
INUI TADASHI, SAKI AKIO, OGUCHI IICHI et al., *Kyōso*, Tokyo, 1955.
ISHIDA EIICHIRŌ, *Momotaro no haha*, Tokyo, 1956.
Ishiyamadera Engie, *Nihon Emakimono Zenshū*, vol. 22.
ISHIZU TERUJI, 'Tōhoku no oshira', *Tōhoku Bunka Kenkyūshitsu Kiyō*, no. 3,
March 1961.
ISHIZUKA TAKATOSHI, *Nihon no tsukimono*, Tokyo, 1959.
IWAMOTO YUTAKA, *Mokuren Densetsu to Urabon*, Kyoto, 1968.
IWASAKI TOSHIO, *Hompō shōshi no kenkyū*, Tokyo, 1963.
KANASEKI TAKEO, 'Tanegashima Hirota iseki no bunka', *Fukuoka Unesco*,
no. 3, 1966.
Kasuga Gongen Genkie, *Nihon Emakimono Zenshū*, vol. 22.
KITAMI TOSHIO, 'Nihonjin no ikyō-kannen no ichi dammen: wankashi
densetsu wo megutte', *Nihon Minzokugaku*, no. 4, March 1954.
Kitano Tenjin Engi, *Nihon Emakimono Zenshū*, vol. 8.
KOIKE NAGAHIRO, *Hito no shigo no hanashi*, Tokyo, 1960.
Kokonchomonjū, *Nihon Bungaku Taikei*, vol. 10.
Konjaku Monogatari, *Nihon Bungaku Taikei*, vols 8 and 9.
KONNO ENSUKE, *Bajo kon-intan*, Tokyo, 1956.
KUBO NORITADA, 'Dōkyō to Shugendō', *Shūkyō Kenkyū*, no. 173, December
1962.
Kōshin shinkō no kenkyū, Tokyo, 1961.
Makura no Sōshi, ed. Kaneko Genshin, Tokyo, 1929.
MATSUMOTO NOBUHIRO, *Nihon no shinwa*, Tokyo, 1956.
MATSUMURA TAKEO, *Nihon shinwa no kenkyū*, 4 vols, Tokyo, 1971.
MINAKATA KUMAKUSU, 'Minakata Zuihitsu', *Kyōdo Kenkyū*, vol. 1, p. 297.
MIURA SHUYU, 'Gohō-matsuri', in *Mimasaka no Minzoku*, ed. Wakamori
Tarō, Tokyo, 1963.
'Kōjin kagura no takusen', *Nihon Minzokugaku Kaihō*, no. 31, December
1963.

MIYAKE HITOSHI, *'Shugendō girei no kenkyū*, Tokyo, 1971.
'Shugendō no genjutsu', *Tetsugaku*, no. 48, March 1966.
'Shugendō no Nyūbu shingyō ni okeru shimborizumu', *Tetsugaku*, no. 46, February 1965.
'Shugendō no shisō; shugenja no shisō to kōdō', *Tetsugaku*, no. 43, January 1963.
'Shugendō no tsukimono-otoshi', *Yoneyama Keizō Hakase kanreki kinen rombunshū.*
'Shugendō no yorigitō', *Tetsugaku*, no. 50, March 1967.
MIYATA NOBORU, *Ikigami Shinkō*, Tokyo, 1970.
'Ikigami shinkō no hatsugen', *Nihon Minzokugaku Kaihō*, no. 28, May 1963.
'Kinsei Ontake shinkō no jittai', *Shakai to Denshō*, vol. 5, no. 2, 1961.
MORITA YASUJI, 'Ebise no wankashi densetsu', *Minkan Denshō*, vol. 8, no. 11, 1944.
MOTOORI NORINAGA, 'Senshakō', *Motoori Norinaga Zenshū*, vol. 12, Tokyo, 'Zaikyō Nikki', *Koji Ruien*, vol. 33.
MURAKAMI SHIGEYOSHI, 'Bakumatsu ishinki ni okeru minshū shūkyō no sōshō', *Nihon Shūkyōshi kōza*, vol. 2, Tokyo, 1959.
MURAKAMI TOSHIO, *Shugendō no Hattatsu*, Tokyo, 1943.
Murasaki Shikibu Nikki, Nihon Koten Bungaku Taikei, no. 19.
MURATAKE SEIICHI et al., 'Izu Niijima wakagō no shakai soshiki', *Minzokugaku Kenkyū*, vol. 22, no. 3–4, 1959.
NAKAHARA ZENSHŪ, 'Omoro no kenkyū', *Minzokugaku Kenkyū*, vol. 15, 1950.
NAKAMURA KYŌKO, *Rei-i no Sekai*, Tokyo, 1967.
NAKAYAMA TARŌ, *Nihon Fujoshi*, Tokyo, reprinted 1969.
NIHON MIIRA KENKYŪ GURŪPU, *Nihon Miira no Kenkyū*, Tokyo, 1969.
Nihon Ryōiki, Nihon Koten Zensho edition, ed. by Takeda Yukichi, Tokyo, 1950.
ŌBA IWAO, 'Nihon ni okeru sangaku shinkō no kōkogakuteki kōsatsu', *Sangaku Shinkō Sōsho*, no. 1, Tokyo, 1948.
Shintō Kōkogaku Ronkō, Tokyo, 1971.
ŌBAYASHI TARYŌ, *Sōsei no Kigen*, Tokyo, 1965.
OGUCHI IICHI et al., *Kyōso*, Tokyo, 1955.
OKA MASAO, 'Ijin sono hoka', *Minzoku*, vol. 3, no. 6, 1928.
Nihon Minzoku no Kigen. A discussion with Ishida Eiichirō, Egami Namio and Yawata Ichirō, Tokyo, 1958.
ORIGUCHI SHINOBU, 'Kagura no torimono', *Nihon Geinōshi Nōto*, Tokyo, 1955.
'Kokubungaku no hassei', *Origuchi Shinobu Zenshū*, vol. 1, Tokyo, 1966.
'Reikon no hanashi', *Origuchi Shinobu Zenshū*, vol. 3, Tokyo, 1966.
'Tokoyo oyobi marebito', *Minzoku*, vol. 4, no. 2, January 1929.
ŌTŌ TOKIHIKO, 'Shintō yōgōshū', *Nihon Bunka Kenkyūjo Kiyō*, no. 18, March 1966.
SAIGŌ NOBUTSUNA, *Kodaijin to Yume*, Tokyo, 1972.
Kojiki no Sekai, Tokyo, 1967.

SAKAGUCHI KAZUO, 'Niijima no yakami shū', *Nihon Minzokugaku*, vol. 5, no. 1, 1957.

SAKURAI TOKUTARŌ, 'Kuchiyose miko no seitai: Yamagata bonchi ni okeru o-nakama no seifu katei', *Nihon Minzokugaku Kaihō*, no. 64, August 1969.

'Miko to Shaman', *Nihon Minzokugaku Kaihō*, no. 43, January 1966.

'Minkan fuzoku no keitai to kinō', in *Rikuzen Hokubu no Minzoku*, ed. Wakamori Tarō, Tokyo, 1969.

Okinawa no shamanizumu, Tokyo, 1973.

'Tsugaru itako no fuzoku', in *Tsugaru no Minzoku*, ed. Wakamori Tarō, Tokyo, 1970.

SATŌ SHŌJUN, 'Iwate-ken no oshirasama no ruikei', *Shūkyō Kenkyū*, no. 162, 1960.

'Miyagi-ken kita chihō no miko', *Shakai to Denshō*, vol. 2, no. 1, 1958.

'Ojika hantō no miko', *Nihon Minzokugaku Kaihō*, no. 7, June 1959.

SAWA RYUKEN, *Butsuzō Annai*, Tokyo, 1967.

SEKI KEIGO, *Nihon Mukashibanashi Shūsei*, 3 vols, Tokyo, 1953.

Sengo Shūkyō Kaisōroku, published by Shinshūren Chōsashitsu, Tokyo, 1961.

Shigisan Engi, *Nihon Emakimono Zenshū*, vol. 2, Tokyo, 1958.

SHIMAZU DENDŌ, *Haguro-ha Shugendō Teiyō*, Tokyo, 1937.

Shugen Seiten, published by the Daigoji Sambōin, Kyoto, second ed. 1968.

SUZUKI SHŌEI, 'Genja to gohō-dōji', pamphlet published by the Bukkyō bungaku kenkyūkai of Ōtani Daigaku, Kyoto, 1962.

'Hayama shinkō to Shugendō', *Nihon Minzokugaku Kaihō*, no. 32, February 1964.

'Sangaku shinkō: Shugendō to shamanizumu to no kankei', *Otani Shigaku*, no. 8, November 1961.

'Shugendō to kamigakari', *Matsuri*, no. 12, 1967.

Taiheiki, *Nihon Bungaku Taikei*, vols 17 and 18.

TAKAGI HIROO, *Shinkō Shukyō*, Tokyo, 1958.

TAKEDA CHŌSHŪ, 'Kami no hyōjō to saijō, *Nihon Minzokugaku Taikei*, vol. 8, Tokyo, 1962.

Senzo Sūhai, Kyoto, 1957.

TANI BUNCHŌ, *Nihon Meisan Zue*, Edo, 1807.

TOGAWA ANSHŌ, 'Shugendō Haguro-ha goi ryakkai', *Kokugakuin Zasshi*, vol. 46, no. 11, November 1940.

Shugendō to Minzoku, Tokyo, 1972.

TORII RYŪZŌ, *Jinruigakujō yori mitaru waga jōdai no bunka*, Tokyo, 1925.

TSUBOSAKA YUTAKA, 'Izuna-hō', *Minzoku to Rekishi*, vol. 8, no. 1, August 1922.

TSUDA SŌKICHI, 'En-no-Gyōja densetsukō', *Tsuda Sōkichi Zenshū*, vol. 9.

Uji Shūi Monogatari, *Nihon Bungaku Taikei*, vol. 10.

UMEHARA TAKESHI, *Kakusareta Jūjika*, Tokyo, 1972.

USHIO MICHIO, 'Kagura ni okeru takusen no hōshiki ni tsuite', *Nihon Minzokugaku Kaihō*, no. 2, August 1958.

'Omoto Kagura', in *Nishi Iwami no Minzoku*, ed. Wakamori Tarō, Tokyo, 1962.

WAKAMORI TARŌ, *Shugendōshi Kenkyu*, Tokyo, 1943.

Yamabushi, Tokyo, 1964.

SELECT BIBLIOGRAPHY

WAKAMORI TARŌ (ed.), *Mimasaka no Minzoku*, Tokyo, 1963.
Nishi Iwami no Minzoku, Tokyo, 1962.
Rikuzen Hokubu no Minzoku, Tokyo, 1969.
Tsugaru no Minzoku, Tokyo, 1970.
WATANABE SHŌKŌ, *Shamon Kūkai*, Tokyo, 1967.
YANAGI SŌETSU, 'Mokujiki Shōnin hakken no engi', *Yanagi Sōetsu Senshū*, vol. 9, 1954.
'Mokujiki Shōnin ryakuden', *Yanagi Sōetsu Senshū*, vol. 9, 1954.
YANAGITA KUNIO, 'Ebisuoroshi Inarioroshi', in *Miko-kō, YKS*, vol. 9.
'Gohō-dōji', in *Kebōzu-kō, YKS*, vol. 9.
'Hebigami inugami no tagui', in *Miko-kō, YKS*, vol. 9.
'Hitobashira to Matsuura Sayohime', in *Imōto no Chikara, YKS*, vol. 9.
'Hitokotonushi-kō', *YKS*, vol. 9.
Hitotsume kozō sono ta, YKS, vol. 5.
Imōto no chikara, YKS, vol. 9.
'Kaijin shōdō', in *Momotarō no tanjō, YKS*, vol. 8.
'Kaijingū-kō', in *Kaijō no michi, YKS*, vol. 1.
Kaijō no michi, YKS, vol. 1.
'Kakurezato', in *Hitotsume kozō sono ta, YKS*, vol. 5.
'Kami no kuchiyose wo gyō to suru mono', in *Miko-kō, YKS*, vol. 9.
Kebōzu-kō, YKS, vol. 9.
'Kōga Saburō no monogatari', in *Monogatari to Katarimono, YKS*, vol. 7.
Miko-kō, YKS, vol. 9.
'Miroku no fune', in *Kaijō no michi, YKS*, vol. 1.
Momotarō no tanjō, YKS, vol. 8.
Monogatari to Katarimono, YKS, vol. 7.
'Ne no kuni no hanashi', in *Kaijō no michi, YKS*, vol. 1.
'Nezumi no jōdo', in *Kaijō no michi, YKS*, vol. 1.
Nihon no Mukashibanashi, YKS, vol. 26.
'Oshiragami', in *Miko-kō, YKS*, vol. 9.
Senzo no hanashi, YKS, vol. 10.
'Takusen to matsuri', in *Miko-kō, YKS*, vol. 9.
'Tamayorihiko no mondai', in *Imōto no chikara, YKS*, vol. 9.
'Tamayorihime-kō', in *Imōto no chikara, YKS*, vol. 9.
'Tateyama chūgo-kō', *YKS*, vol. 9.
Tōno monogatari, YKS, vol. 4.
Yama no jinsei, YKS, vol. 4.
'Yorimasa no haka', in *Miko-kō, YKS*, vol. 9.
YANAGITA KUNIO (ed), *Minzokugaku Jiten*, Tokyo, 1962.
YANAGITA KUNIO and ORIGUCHI SHINOBU, 'Nihonjin no kami to reikon no kannen sono ta', *Minzokugaku Kenkyū*, vol. 14, no. 2, 1949.
YASUTOMI NOBUKO, 'Gohōtobi kembunki', *Okayama Minzoku*, no. 24, December 1956.
YAZU SHŪSEI, 'Kitsunegami oyobi kitsunetsuki jikkendan', *Minzoku to Rekishi*, vol. 8, no. 1, August 1922.
YOSHIMURA SHUKUHO, 'Yorimashi dōji; Tosa ni okeru kamigakari no gishiki', *Matsuri*, no. 12, 1967.

Glossary

This list comprises all Japanese terms used more than once.

aka—Buddhist Libatory water, from the Sanscrit *argha*; one of the five officers in the Haguro autumn retreat.

akimine—the 'autumn peak' or autumn retreat; the most important of the four seasonal rituals of the Haguro sect of Shugendō.

aragyō—rough or severe austerities; especially those practised for a hundred days of the winter by the Nichiren sect on Mt Minobu and in the Hokekyōji temple in Chiba prefecture.

ayaigasa—a large straw hat, one of the items of the *yamabushi's* ritual costume; in the Haguro sect of Shugendō it is decorated with discs of white paper and represents the placenta which encases the embryo in the womb.

bikuni—a Buddhist nun; often, as with the Kumano *bikuni*, claiming powers of prophesy and divination.

bokken—a wooden instrument consisting of a small ball and board, which when correctly manipulated makes a sharp sound like castanets which is held by the Nichiren sect to be powerful in the process of exorcism.

bonden—a wand decorated with white paper streamers, often used as the vessel of the *kami* or the conductor through which the *kami* may enter the body of the medium. An especially large variety is used by the Haguro sect of Shugendō in their autumn retreat.

daimoku—the name given by the Nichiren sect to their sacred formula *Namu myōhō rengekyō*, hail to the Lotus of the Wonderful Law.

daimyōjin—a superior rank of *kami*.

dairi—the name given to the medium in the Nichiren method of exorcism.

daisendatsu—a superior rank in the Shugendō order, often indicating that nine periods of autumn retreat have been undergone; the leader of the five *sendatsu* in the Haguro autumn retreat.

dakini—in Tibetan Buddhism, the spirit woman who bestows secret knowledge on the neophyte and assists him in meditation; in Japan, a spiritual being identified with a fox.

dōshi—one of the five *sendatsu* officiating at the Haguro autumn retreat.

gaki—hungry ghosts or pretas, who inhabit the Gakidō or Realm of Hungry Ghosts, one of the Three Evil Realms on the Buddhist wheel of life.

gantsū—clairvoyant vision; one of the six miraculous powers which the ascetic acquires as a result of austerities.

gohei—a wand decorated with streamers of cut white paper, often used as a vessel for the *kami*, or a conductor through which a *kami* can enter a medium's body.

gohō-dōji—the guardian boy who appears in medieval Buddhism as an assistant spirit to a holy man.

gohōzane—local appellation for the medium at the Gohōtobi oracle.

goma—the esoteric Buddhist fire ritual; the term deriving from the Sanscrit *homa*.

gomiso—local appellation for the shamanic ascetic in Aomori and Akita prefectures.

goshintai—the vessel in which the *kami* dwells within a shrine.

gyō—ascetic practices designed to build up sacred power.

gyōja or *gyōnin*—one who practises *gyō;* an ascetic.

haniwa—clay pottery figures found in the tumuli of the fifth and sixth centuries.

hebi no mukoiri—the folktale type of the snake bridegroom, in which a supernatural snake in human disguise seduces or weds a human girl.

hi-watari—the fire-walking ritual performed by the Shugendō order, usually as a conclusion to their *saitō-goma* or magic bonfire rite.

hichiriki—a cylindrical double-reed pipe.

hijiri—one of the names of the shamanic ascetic current during the Heian period, ninth to twelfth century.

hito-bashira—a human pillar; a human sacrifice, usually of a woman, to a water-serpent deity.

hitsurugi—lit. fire-sword; the name given to the fire-walking ritual which precedes the descent of the god at the Hayama oracle.

hōin—a Buddhist priest, often associated with the Shugendō order and able to assume the role of shamanic ascetic.

hotoke—a word meaning both a Buddha and a dead ancestor.

hotokeoroshi—the rite whereby a dead ancestor is caused to descend into the body of a medium and speak through her mouth.

ichigenkin—a one-string lute, similar to a bow; when the string is tapped by a shamanic medium the sound is held to summon spirits.

ichiko—a shamanic medium.

ikigami—a living god or goddess; a term often applied to shamanic persons such as the Founders of new religions.

inugami—the spirit dog responsible for malignant possession in Shikoku and the Chūgoku district of the main island.

irataka-juzu—the long rosary used by the *yamabushi* as one of the items of his ritual costume; also by some *itako* in Aomori prefecture; the sound of the beads rubbed together will summon ancestral spirits and cow malignant ones.

ishikozume—ritual execution by stoning.

itako—local appellation for the shamanic medium in Aomori and Akita prefectures.

iwakura—the rock seat or large boulder to which a *kami* may be ritually summoned.

jōbutsu—literally, becoming a Buddha; the term denoting the final rest and salvation attained by the individual soul on merging with the corporate Ancestor.

kagura—ritual dances performed to petition or placate a *kami*.

kaihōgyō—the ascetic circumambulation of Mt Hiei, performed by certain monks of the Tendai sect for a hundred consecutive nights.

kami—the numina or spiritual beings who are the principal objects of worship in Shinto.

kamigakari—divine possession; the entry of a spiritual being into a human body.

kamigakushi—the abduction of a boy or a young man by a supernatural being.

kamioroshi—the rite whereby a *kami* is caused to descend into the body of a medium and speak through her mouth.

kari—one of the five *sendatsu* officiating at the Haguro autumn retreat.

katana-watari—the feat whereby the ascetic climbs barefoot up a ladder of swords.

kiai—a loud yell practised by ascetics in the course of the exorcising ritual; also sometimes used in the supplication of *kami* for favours.

kō—religious societies directed to the worship of certain holy mountains which organise an annual pilgrimage climb of members to the summit.

kogi—firewood, especially the wood used for the *goma* fire ritual; also the name of one of the five officers in the Haguro autumn retreat.

kokudachi—ascetic abstention from the five cereals.

komori—ritual seclusion in a cave or shrine for ascetic and purificatory purposes.

komorinin—the group of secluded, ritually clean boys who receive the deity at the Hayama oracle.

koshitori—waist-claspers; those entrusted with the task of restraining the medium from undue violence in his possessed state.

kotodama—lit. the soul of words; the magic power inherent in certain sounds.

ku—the Chinese system of magic whereby venomous reptiles and insects are put together in a pot, and the single survivor used for evil sorcery.

kuchiyose—the delivery of messages from a departed spirit in a state of trance.

kuyō—a requiem observance for the rest and comfort of a dead spirit.

kyōso—the Founder of a new religious sect; often a shaman.

maeza—in the ritual to obtain an oracle, the officer who summons and interrogates the *kami*, and sends him away at the conclusion of the rite.

magatama—the claw or comma-shaped jewel found in prehistoric tombs and ritual sites.

makura-kotoba—a 'pillow word' or fixed epithet, used in poetry.

marebito—supernatural guests; ancestral spirits believed to return at stated seasons in boats to bless and fertilise the land.

matsuri—the festival at which the *kami* is invited to descend among his worshippers, and is feasted, entertained and petitioned in a variety of ways.

miko—the shamanic medium who acts as mouthpiece for the *kami* or ancestor; also used today to designate women in large shrines who without the mantic gift assist in ritual.

mimitsū—clairaudient hearing; one of the six miraculous powers which the ascetic acquires as a result of austerities.

mizugori—the water austerity; performed either by standing under a waterfall or by pouring buckets of cold water over the head and back.

mokujiki—the ascetic practice of eating only the products of trees.

muenbotoke—dead spirits with no affinity, i.e. no family to accord them the worship they require for salvation.

nakaza—the medium in the ritual to obtain an oracle.

namban-ibushi—the smoke penance, associated with the realm of hell, practised in the course of the Haguro autumn retreat.

nikudachi—the ascetic abstention from meat.

norito—Shinto ritual prayers and invocations.

noriwara—local appellation for the medium at the Hayama oracle.

noro or *nuru*—the sacral woman or village priestess of the Ryūkyū islands.

nyūbu—the ritual 'entry into the mountains' for ascetic purposes formerly observed by the Shugendō at each of the four seasons.

nyūjō—the state of cataleptic trance in which the soul is believed to part company with the body, or in which the body is believed to exist in suspended animation.

odamaki—the 'spool' or hemp-thread variant of the Miwa legend, in which a girl is visited by a mysterious lover who turns out to be a serpent.

ofudesaki—the revelations of the founders of new religions, often recorded in automatic writing.

ogamin—local appellation for a shamanic medium in Miyagi prefecture.

ogamisan—local appellation for a shamanic medium in the Rikuzen district.

ogamiyasan—local appellation for a shamanic ascetic in the Kyoto district.

oi—a box or portable altar carried on the back; one of the items of the *yamabushi's* costume, which in the Haguro sect represents the mother's womb.

okina—the beaming old man who dispenses blessings and probably represents the Ancestor; he appears in the Nō play of that name at New Year and other times of special celebration.

onakama—local appellation for a shamanic medium in Yamagata prefecture.

onryō—angry departed spirits who require special requiem measures for their appeasement.

oshirasama—a pair of puppets, carved to represent a horse and a woman and clothed in layers of cotton; manipulated by the shamanic medium in north-eastern districts to aid the summoning of spirits.

reijin—a person possessing sacred power; appellation given to the officers of the Ontake *kō* after their death.

rokudō-meguri—the round of the Six Realms; the journey through the six transmigratory realms of the Buddhist cosmos.

ryūgū-iri—the folktale type distinguished by Yanagita Kunio, in which a human being visits the magical palace under the sea.

saitō-goma—a magic bonfire ritual; an enlarged and outdoor version of the esoteric Buddhist *goma* or fire ritual, and considered to originate in pre-Buddhist outdoor fire rituals.

sakaki—the small evergreen tree *Cleyera japonica*, used in Shinto for various sacred purposes including demarcating the four corners of a sacred temenos.

saniwa—literally a sand-garden; the temenos or space purified and cordoned off for a ritual; also the officer in the ritual who interrogates the deity.

segaki—ritual offerings of food or sutras to the *gaki* or hungry ghosts.

sendatsu—a leader or captain in the Shugendō order, a rank usually conferred on those who have performed a required number of ritual climbs and retreats; also the leader and guide of a *kō* party on its annual pilgrimage.

shamon—one of the early names for the Buddhist shamanic ascetic, derived from the Sanscrit *śramaná* and hence cognate with shaman.

shingyaku—the neophytes taking part in the Shugendō ritual climb.

shinkō-shūkyō—newly arisen religions; the new religious cults which arose often at the inspiration of a shaman, during the last hundred years and particularly since the end of the last war.

shō—a free-reed mouth-organ.

shōtai—the 'true form' of a *kami* as distinct from his other transformations.

takusen matsuri—a festival in which a *kami* is called down into the body of a medium and cajoled to deliver a *takusen* or oracle.

tama—a round ball, a jewel, a 'soul' which imparts vitality to the body in which it dwells.

tanikō—the penalty of 'throwing into the valley', meted out to any *yamabushi* so unfortunate as to fall sick in the course of the ritual climb into the holy mountain.

tatari—a curse inflicted by an enraged *kami* or ghost on a human being.

tengu—a supernatural creature usually represented as half-man and half-hawk, with wings, beak and glittering eyes; a variant form has a long red nose; closely associated with *yamabushi*.

torii—the ceremonial gate, often red, which marks the entrance to a Shinto shrine.

torimono—a wand or branch, sometimes a sword or spear, held in the medium's hand to induce divine possession.

tsumi—the pollutions or ritual contaminations which make a man unclean in the sight of the *kami* and unfit to approach a sacred place.

ubasoku—one of the early names for the Buddhist shamanic ascetic, derived from the Sanscrit *upasaka*.

urami—malice or spite; one of the emotions which attaches a ghost to this world and impedes its progress towards salvation.

utsubo—the quality of 'emptiness' which enables certain vessels such as gourds and stones to contain a supernatural principle.

yamabushi—one who 'lies' in the mountains; a member of the Shugendō order of mountain ascetics.

yorigitō—spells of prayers which cajole a *kami* to enter the body of a medium and speak through her mouth.

yorishiro—a vessel into which a *kami* is summoned in order to manifest himself.

vudate—the feat whereby the ascetic souses himself in boiling water and remains unscalded.

yuta—the female shaman of the Ryukyu islands.

zaishō—hindrances in the path of enlightenment; sin and delusion; sometimes personified in the form of a possessing spirit.

Index